CHICAGO
NEIGHBORHOODS
AND
SUBURBS

Ann Durkin Keating

CHICAGO NEIGHBORHOODS

AND SUBURBS

A HISTORICAL GUIDE

THE UNIVERSITY OF CHICAGO PRESS · Chicago and London

ANN DURKIN KEATING is
professor of history at North Central College in Naperville, Illinois.
She is the author of *Building Chicago:
Suburban Developers and the Creation
of a Divided Metropolis* (1988), *Invisible Networks: Exploring the History of
Local Utilities and Public Works* (1992),
and *Chicagoland: City and Suburbs in
the Railroad Age* (2005).

The University of Chicago Press, Chicago 60637
The University of Chicago Press, Ltd., London
© 2008 by The Newberry Library
All rights reserved. Published 2008
Printed in the United States of America

17 16 15 14 13 12 11 10 09 08   1 2 3 4 5

ISBN-13: 978-0-226-42883-3 (paper)
ISBN-10: 0-226-42883-4 (paper)

Library of Congress Cataloging-in-Publication Data

Keating, Ann Durkin.
    Chicago neighborhoods and suburbs : a historical guide
/ Ann Durkin Keating.
       p.   cm.
    Derived from: The encyclopedia of Chicago. Chicago :
University of Chicago Press, © 2004
    Includes bibliographical references and index.
    ISBN-13: 978-0-226-42883-3 (paper : alk. paper)
    ISBN-10: 0-226-42883-4 (paper : alk. paper)
    1. Chicago (Ill.)—Guidebooks. 2. Chicago Region
(Ill.)—Guidebooks. 3. Neighborhood—Illinois—Chicago—
Guidebooks. 4. Suburbs—Illinois—Chicago Region—
Guidebooks. 5. Chicago (Ill.)—History. 6. Chicago
Region (Ill.)—History, Local. 7. Neighborhood—
Illinois—Chicago—History. 8. Suburbs—Illinois—
Chicago Region—History. I. Encyclopedia of Chicago.
II. Title.
F548.18.K43 2008
917.73'11—dc22

                              2008028502

♾ The paper used in this publication meets the minimum requirements
of the American National Standard for Information Sciences—Perma-
nence of Paper for Printed Library Materials, ANSI Z39.48-1992.

CONTENTS

PREFACE AND ACKNOWLEDGMENTS

At the core of this volume—rooted in the work done for *The Encyclopedia of Chicago* on geographic location as a means of organizing the region and its history—are entries on the 77 community areas that Chicago city government and social scientists employ as units of analysis. Every part of the city rests within a community area, so every part of Chicago is represented here. Some of these areas comprise several neighborhoods, many of which are explored in separate entries. A selection of suburban entries rounds out the survey. Because it would not be possible to consider each of the many suburban communities in the metropolitan area in a book of this size, I have concentrated on suburbs that figure in the longer interpretive essays at the front of this volume, suburbs that are typical of settlement patterns in Chicagoland, and suburbs that exemplify the region's wide range of rich and interesting histories.

Each of these communities is, of course, tied to others. In the *Encyclopedia of Chicago*, and in this volume, those links are represented by cross-references to other entries (set in SMALL CAPITALS). The book opens with a set of essays examining neighborhoods, suburbs, and the interactions of their residents, businesses, and other institutions over the course of Chicago's history. The community area, neighborhood, and suburban entries follow, in alphabetical order. Maps that grew out of the encyclopedia project, under the direction of cartographic editor Michael P. Conzen, further illuminate themes developed in the essays and community entries.

This volume rests on work done in concert with my coeditors on the *Encyclopedia of Chicago*, James R. Grossman and Janice L. Reiff. A collaboration that began 15 years ago continues to yield new insights and questions. Neither the encyclopedia nor this volume could have been completed without the careful, thoughtful work of Douglas Knox. My thanks to Carol Saller and Joel Score for their expert editing of many of these pieces. I am grateful for the continuing support of North Central College. I thank Michael Ebner, Henry Binford, Jan Reiff, Susan Hirsch, and Bob Bruegmann for their willingness to include their interpretive essays here. Finally, dozens more historians have written the histories of neighborhoods and suburbs found in this volume. This book is dedicated to their work.

CONTRIBUTORS

JOSEPH L. ARNOLD

GABRIELA F. ARREDONDO

THOMAS A. AUGER

DAVID A. BADILLO

JAMES R. BARRETT

DAVE BARTLETT

DAVID BENSMAN

IRA BERKOW

WALLACE BEST

JOSEPH C. BIGOTT

HENRY BINFORD

JOHN BODNAR

CATHERINE BRUCK

ROBERT BRUEGMANN

DAVID BUISSERET

DOMINIC CANDELORO

ADRIAN CAPEHART

HEIDI PAWLOWSKI CAREY

EMILY CLARK

MICHAEL P. CONZEN

GERALD A. DANZER

MARK DONOVAN

MARGARET D. DOYLE

MICHAEL H. EBNER

STEVEN ESSIG

FRANKLIN FORTS

ELIZABETH S. FRATERRIGO

ERIK GELLMAN

MAX GRINNELL

JEAN LOUISE GUARINO

BETSY GURLACZ

MARK S. HARMON

RICHARD HARRIS

AARON HARWIG

SUSAN E. HIRSCH

ELIZABETH M. HOLLAND

THOMAS O. KAY

ANN DURKIN KEATING

JONATHAN J. KEYES

YING-CHENG (HARRY) KIANG

DOUGLAS KNOX

JOHN LAMB

JOHN H. LONG

MARK HOWARD LONG

DAVID MACLAREN

SARAH S. MARCUS

JUDITH A. MARTIN

LARRY A. MCCLELLAN

DENNIS MCCLENDON

IAN MCGIVER

EILEEN M. MCMAHON

STEPHEN G. MCSHANE

SHERRY MEYER

LAURA MILSK

RAYMOND A. MOHL

PATRICIA MOONEY-MELVIN

JAN OLIVE NASH

TIMOTHY B. NEARY

DOMINIC A. PACYGA

ELIZABETH A. PATTERSON

MYRIAM PAUILLAC

MARILYN ELIZABETH PERRY

CRAIG L. PFANNKUCHE

MARGARET FRANSON PRUTER

PATRICK M. QUINN

CHRISTOPHER R. REED

JANICE L. REIFF

TINA REITHMAIER

JOHN R. SCHMIDT

JOHN D. SCHROEDER

AMANDA SELIGMAN

ELLEN SKERRETT

DAVID M. SOLZMAN

JOHN W. STAMPER

ROBERT E. STERLING

TOM STERLING

ADAM H. STEWART

CLINTON E. STOCKWELL

JANE S. TEAGUE

CLAUDETTE TOLSON

LANCE TRUSTY

TODD J. TUBUTIS

MARTIN TUOHY

DEREK VAILLANT

RONALD S. VASILE

ANDREW WIESE

CAMILLE HENDERSON ZORICH

INTRODUCTION

Chicago Neighborhoods: Building Blocks of the Region

My neighborhood begins as I step from my house to a concrete sidewalk, then to a narrow parkway dotted with trees, and finally to a street. Both sides of the street are lined with houses: cottages, bungalows, Dutch colonials, ranches, and recently a few tear-downs. From here, I can walk to the bus stop or the Metra railroad station. Close by are schools, parks, places of worship, grocery stores, cleaners, restaurants, and other businesses. These places make up the basic building block of urban regions like Chicago: the neighborhood.

Most of us know only a handful of neighborhoods: where we live, where we work, where we gather with family and friends. Some neighborhoods contain most of what a household needs on a regular day, while others require residents to travel beyond their boundaries for basic services. While transportation advances and economic transformations have made it possible—indeed, necessary—for many of us to work outside our neighborhood, most of us still think in its parochial terms. I work in the historic east side neighborhood of NAPERVILLE, but I live in EDISON PARK, a neighborhood on the Northwest Side of Chicago, and where I live determines my identity. I am a Chicagoan because I live in the city, even if I spend more waking moments in Naperville. But my experience of city living is very different from that of someone who lives in a high-density neighborhood like the GOLD COAST. Like the suburbs that surround it, Chicago's neighborhoods vary dramatically.

Looking at the region as a collection of neighborhoods calls into question the too-simple opposition between suburb and city. City and suburb alike comprise different kinds of neighborhoods, each with its own particular character and each changing over time. My idea of what constitutes the near Northwest Side neighborhood of BUCKTOWN is certainly different from that of an area resident a century ago. Indeed, it may differ from a current resident's perspective. In the 1920s sociologists at the University of Chicago divided the city of Chicago into 75 "natural areas"—many delineated by barriers like railroads, parks, or bodies of water. These "community areas" have been used by the U.S. Census since the 1930s, with only a few modifications (notably two additions) over the years. Census material, summarized every ten years in a *Local Community Factbook*, makes them a

Bird's-eye view from the west, 1874, showing industrial and commuter suburbs. Artist: Unknown. Source: The Newberry Library.

useful designation for anyone interested in the history of Chicago neighborhoods. Some of these community areas closely resemble current neighborhoods; my neighborhood of Edison Park is also a community area. But other neighborhoods have more complicated connections to the community area into which they fall. Few people in PILSEN, for example, would identify themselves as residents of the LOWER WEST SIDE Community Area, while Edgebrook residents might not even know that their neighborhood sits within the FOREST GLEN Community Area.

While community areas do not constitute official government units, their size makes them comparable to individual suburban municipalities. Like community areas, many suburbs contain multiple neighborhoods, whose boundaries often shift over time. EVANSTON, for example, divides into a number of neighborhoods, including South Evanston and North Evanston. And Naperville's neighborhoods include many of its largest subdivisions, like the Highlands and Cress Creek.

Residents of city neighborhoods share much with their suburban counterparts. But whereas suburban residents rely on their own municipal resources and facilities, Chicagoans must look not to their community areas but downtown to the mayor, city council, and various departments to maintain basic infrastructure. Streets and streetlights, sidewalks, water and sewers—all are overseen by large-scale systems that entail high levels of expertise and often the latest in technological innovation. Chicagoans' public schools are part of the largest school district in the state. Their neighborhood park is part of the Chicago Park District, and the local library too is part of a citywide system. But resources are seldom divided equally across city neighborhoods; residents must necessarily negotiate, compete, and compromise with people living miles away, in other parts of the city, as Jan Reiff explains in her essay CONTESTED SPACES.

While residents of urban neighborhoods compete with each other for resources, suburban residents turn to smaller, more local governments to meet their basic needs. Housing and demographics are typically less disparate within suburban jurisdictions than in the city. Anthony Orum identifies three major differences that had been established between the city of Chicago and its surrounding ring of suburbs by the mid-1960s: suburban governments generally enjoy higher per capita tax revenues; a higher proportion of African Americans live in the city; and Democrats are predominant in the city and Republicans in the suburbs. As Michael Ebner argues in SUBURBS AND CITIES AS DUAL METROPOLIS, elite suburban residents have used suburban government to perpetuate "disparities between the neighborhoods" across the Chicago region.

Despite these significant differences, all Chicagoans live in neighborhoods. Differences in privilege, wealth, and access to power shape a given neighborhood. Characteristics such as housing type vary. Residents interact in particular ways with those in the neighborhoods that surround them—in some cases sharing schools or other services, in other instances creating physical or social barriers to limit interaction. The basic function remains the same: each neighborhood is composed of housing, local schools, churches, stores, and services (or some subset of these), a pattern replicated hundreds of times across the region. However large and complex it may be, the Chicago region is essentially made up of hundreds of these basic building blocks and the interactions between them.

The North, West, and South Side Neighborhoods

People create neighborhoods in response both to the natural landscape and to man-made features. Lake Michigan provides a monumental eastern boundary to the Chicago region (and as one crosses into Indiana, a northern boundary as well). The Chicago River provides a center, dividing the region into three parts: north and south of the main stem and west of its branches. Jean Baptiste Point de Sable built his house and outbuildings on the north side of the main stem, not far Lake Michigan, in the 1780s. Fort Dearborn was sited just to the south of the Chicago River in 1803. In the late 1820s the settlement (especially taverns) concentrated to the west around Wolf Point. Even in these early years, the river and the lake defined location.

The three sides of Chicago were reinforced in the 1830s, when the U.S. government first surveyed and platted the region. The Northwest Ordinance guided this survey, breaking the region into townships (generally of 36 square miles each). Surveyors used the Chicago River to delineate the three townships that initially comprised Chicago: the North Division, the South Division, and the West Division. The north boundary of the city of Chicago was initially set at North Avenue, the western boundary at Wood Street, and the southern boundary at 22nd Street. The West Division was easily twice as large as either of the other two townships. For much of the nineteenth and into the twentieth century, this real-estate (and sometimes political) division corresponded to distinctive patterns of city services, assessments, and parks.

As Chicago grew through annexation over the course of the nineteenth century, the size of the three sides became far more uneven. During the 1860s the West Division grew even more, dwarfing especially the North Division, which did not expand much until 1889, when Lake View and Jefferson Townships to the north, Hyde Park and Lake Townships to the south, and part of Cicero Township to the west were added to the city. With this merger, the geographic balance shifted significantly. The once-dominant West Side gained only a small amount of territory in 1889, while the South Side grew by a factor of at least six; Hyde Park Township, which included the largest harbor in the region, at Lake Calumet, had itself been bigger than the entire city of Chicago. The North Side grew, but not nearly as much, especially after Evanston repeatedly turned down annexation overtures in the 1890s. The South Side also had more room to expand because the Lake Michigan shoreline curves eastward.

The basic geography of the region favored transportation development toward the south and southwest during the nineteenth and early twentieth centuries. Chicago grew in part because it sat on a dividing line between the Great Lakes and the Mississippi River Basin. The Illinois & Michigan Canal, completed in 1848, linked the South Branch of the Chicago River with the Illinois River. Early settlements at BRIDGEPORT, SUMMIT, LEMONT, and JOLIET drew trade and then industry to the south. Between 1848 and 1855 the first rail lines were constructed in Chicago. Two ran north from the city center, one went west, and six took routes through the South Side. The South Side predominated in part because it controlled links to both the South and the East Coast, where most of the population in the United States was located. In addition, only Lake Calumet offered the potential of a major harbor development.

These early differential transportation patterns in turn affected—and were affected by—the geography of Chicago's economic development. The first large labor forces in the region were employed building the Illinois & Michigan Canal. Railroad construction likewise brought many laborers into the region. Both ventures were concentrated on the South Side and, once completed, these transportation lines drew industries and other businesses. The Union Stock Yard, founded in 1865, was soon one of the largest employers in the region, fostering the growth of the neighboring residential community, known as BACK OF THE YARDS. While the first rolling mill (for iron and later steel) was located on the North Branch of the Chicago River in WEST TOWN, most of the large iron and steel operations selected South Side locations such as SOUTH CHICAGO, HAMMOND, GARY, and CHICAGO HEIGHTS. Factories located along the Chicago River and along rail lines on the North Side, but none matched the scale of massive South Side enterprises like the stockyards or steel mills. Smaller factories, often set into residential streets, characterized worker neighborhoods adjacent to the North Branch of the Chicago River in West Town, LOGAN SQUARE, and AVONDALE. Residents in these neighborhoods had a range of employers and working conditions, which led to more variety in housing types and services. In the early twentieth century, large employers like the Western Electric's Hawthorne Works, just beyond the western boundary of NORTH LAWNDALE in CICERO, and the headquarters of Sears, Roebuck & Co., in North Lawndale, led to an industrial boom on the West Side.

Railroad Neighborhoods Build a Region

Most neighborhoods and suburbs in the Chicago region trace their history back to these years of phenomenal growth as an industrial and rail center. Perhaps the most obvious physical markers of this era are the hundreds of rail stations that dot (or once dotted) the Chicago landscape. Around these rail stations, farmers, industrial workers, commuters, and investors built settlements that would evolve into distinct neighborhoods and suburbs. While the economic basis for most of these railroad settlements has changed, the built environment and institutions that took shape generations ago continue to determine how and where current residents live.

The first railroad arrived in the area in 1848. Chicago soon established itself as a national railroad center, and railroad stops spurred growth in virtually every direction. Farmers, industrialists, commuters, and residents seeking leisure-time activities all took advantage of the speed and ease of rail travel. Daily "milk runs" brought dairy products and farm produce into the city from across the metropolitan area. ARLINGTON HEIGHTS, JEFFERSON PARK, and HARVARD were centers for dairying and truck farming into the twentieth century. Bricks from NORTH CENTER, PARK RIDGE, WEST LAWN, Dolton, and WEST RIDGE, as well as limestone from Naperville and ELMHURST, were shipped into Chicago along the railroad, especially after the fire of 1871. Ice harvesting relied on railroads to carry ice to Chicago from McHenry County communities including CRYSTAL LAKE and ANTIOCH.

Stockyards also developed along the rail lines. The Union Stock Yard in 1865 consolidated facilities that had been located to the south and southwest of Chicago, although outlying facilities continued to operate throughout the nineteenth century, in such places as Naperville, WEST CHICAGO, and Hammond, Indiana. Agricultural processing industries also located near the rails: Argo established the largest corn-milling plant in the world in Summit; Gail Borden developed a condensed milk factory in ELGIN; and the Ovaltine Company established a factory in Villa Park.

Heavy industry too located along the railroad lines. Rolling mills on the Near North and Southwest Sides gave way to larger plants built at some distance from the city center, in areas like HEGEWISCH, HARVEY, and SOUTH DEERING that had access to multiple rail lines. WAUKEGAN, Elgin, AURORA, Joliet, and Gary were labeled "satellite cities" by the turn of the nineteenth century and grew as industrial centers. The massive Pullman Company operations in PULLMAN, along the Illinois Central Railroad; the Hawthorne Works of Western Electric, located in Cicero; and the South Works of U.S. Steel on the EAST SIDE all took advantage of easy rail and water transportation to obtain raw materials and ship finished products.

As Susan Hirsch notes in ECONOMIC GEOGRAPHY, "although the combination of space and transportation drew some industries to the edge of the city, many still found the resources of the old central city more useful." Chicago's industrial landscape evolved in the form of a dense ring around downtown, with radial development outward along rail lines.

At the same time, railroads served the pursuit of leisure, carrying workers from the suburbs or neighborhoods where they lived and worked on Sunday excursions to ballparks, cemeteries, picnic groves, and music halls. In WEST GARFIELD PARK, picnic groves, a bicycle track, a horse racing track, and greenhouses drew visitors from across the metropolitan area. Some Chicagoans ventured further from the city center; during warm weather, dancing pavilions, picnicking, and camping attracted thousands to stops like DES PLAINES, 17 miles northwest of the Loop on the Des Plaines River. The development of Crystal Lake, Antioch, and other communities established McHenry County as a resort area at the turn of the twentieth century, as railroads and interurban lines opened metropolitan access to its lakes and the Fox River. An older German picnic grove along the Chicago River in North Center was transformed into an amusement park called Riverview in 1904 (it remained in operation until 1967). The Sans Souci Amusement Park in WOODLAWN opened around the same time. Robert Ilg built a recreational park along a streetcar line in NILES for his workers that included two outdoor swimming pools and a replica of the Leaning Tower of Pisa. Chicagoans of varying means found recreational sites far from home along the rail lines of the region.

In the years after the Civil War, commuters who worked in professional and managerial positions in the LOOP found new and existing railroad settlements attractive as home sites. Unlike their working-class counterparts, these upper-middle-class Chicagoans had the money and time to commute to work. Developers in railroad towns subdivided property and usually graded streets and paved sidewalks. Sometimes they began the process of providing other services (water, sewer, gas, and electricity) to attract their affluent clientele. Such suburban subdivisions developed both within and beyond the current Chicago city limits: RIVERSIDE, MORGAN PARK, KENILWORTH, Elmhurst, IRVING PARK, AUSTIN, Park Ridge, BEVERLY, NORWOOD PARK, ROGERS PARK, WILMETTE, LA GRANGE, HOMEWOOD. All catered to railroad commuters and their families.

The pattern that developed during the railroad age remains visible to this day. The regional landscape came to have two parts: strings of settlements that hugged the rail lines and the areas between them. Places near rail stations were often closer in commuting time to the city center than inner-city neighborhoods. Some of these localities developed as commuter suburbs; at the beginning of the twentieth century, residents of Evanston, Morgan Park, or Riverside could commute downtown in little more than half an hour. Others became farm centers, industrial towns, or recreational/institutional centers. Farmers in CHESTERTON and Harvard could get their milk and garden produce to Chicago's market on a daily basis. Furniture from Naperville, wallpaper from Joliet, and watches from Elgin could be shipped into and out of Chicago (and beyond) as easily as products manufactured in the city center.

This scheme of regional development—with neighborhoods forming first around rail stations and later between stops and the rail lines themselves—runs counter to the concentric model of urban growth developed by University of Chicago sociologist Ernest Burgess in the 1920s. In the Burgess model, development moved out from the city center in waves in a contiguous fashion. Not until the twentieth century, however, would in-filling—notably the construction of the bungalow neighborhoods that are now such a familiar part of Chicago's landscape—result in a contiguous built-up region spreading out from the city center. In areas beyond easy reach of rail stations, intensive development languished: farmers were less able to serve the urban market, the distance from raw materials and consumers precluded factories, idyllic spots were not worth developing as recreational sites, and commuters had no hope of reaching downtown workplaces in a timely manner.

Neighborhoods after the Railroad Age

By the turn of the twentieth century, streetcars and elevated train lines were beginning to complicate the radial pattern established by the rail lines. The automobile further transformed the place of the old railroad settlements in the logic of regional economic growth. Older railroad settlements evolved in response to these changes, while developers founded new neighborhoods and suburbs in response to the new conditions.

Developments aimed at the middle and working classes began to emerge around streetcar and elevated lines (as well as other transportation improvements) in the late nineteenth and early twentieth centuries. PORTAGE PARK, HERMOSA, CHATHAM, WEST ELSDON, GAGE PARK, West Ridge, and other Chicago communities grew after World War I, as builders constructed bungalows in the large, newly accessible tracts of land between railroad lines. Bungalows also formed an important part of new neighborhoods in suburbs like Evanston, OAK PARK, and Elmhurst. Whereas railroad development had left large pockets of farmland across the region, mass transportation and the increasing use of automobiles made these undeveloped tracts attractive to developers by the 1910s and 1920s. As Robert Bruegmann notes in BUILT ENVIRONMENT OF THE CHICAGO REGION, bungalows soon "encircled the city center and extended outward to suburbs like BERWYN."

Starting in the 1950s, the interstate highway system once again reworked the patterns of regional growth. Places that had remained rural, or very small, were now drawn into the metropolitan web and grew in new ways. BOLINGBROOK, SCHAUMBURG, and ELK GROVE VILLAGE are among the suburban settlements born in the interstate highway era. Arlington Heights, a small farming and industrial settlement in the nineteenth century, grew dramatically in the twentieth as businesses and homes took advantage of road improvements. While interstate construction in outlying areas displaced farmland, within the city it required the demolition of built-up areas, cutting wide swaths through city neighborhoods in every direction from downtown. West Garfield Park, Jefferson Park, DOUGLAS, and GRAND BOULEVARD all lost considerable housing stock and many local businesses as the expressway system expanded in the late 1950s and early 1960s.

In contrast to the private development of railroads and streetcars, funding for the interstate system came from the federal government and was administered by the state highway department. Federal influence extended beyond the interstates. Federal insurance for home building had by the 1950s also helped to promote suburban growth. Such programs, coupled with increasing affluence, allowed many Chicagoans to purchase a home rather than rent, and GARFIELD RIDGE, FLOSSMOOR, LOMBARD, Oak Lawn, Des Plaines, Park Ridge, PARK FOREST, and other areas grew dramatically. Federal funds also underwrote urban renewal and public housing projects that reconfigured many inner-city neighborhoods. Whole sections of the NEAR NORTH SIDE, the NEAR SOUTH SIDE, the NEAR WEST SIDE, the Loop, Douglas, Grand Boulevard, and EAST GARFIELD PARK were razed and redeveloped using over $150 billion in federal urban renewal funds during the 1950s and 1960s. While it would have been cheaper to build public housing on less expensive land in outlying areas and suburbs, the politically expedient decision was made to build most such projects in the metropolitan area in a ring around downtown Chicago.

Interstate construction, suburbanization, and urban renewal accompanied major changes in Chicago's economy. Industry had long propelled the region's growth, but it declined precipitously in the second half of the twentieth century. The closing of factories affected many neighborhoods both inside and outside Chicago: NEW CITY, LAKE VIEW, and South Chicago, as well as MAYWOOD, West Chicago, Elgin, and Gary. In Gary, Indiana, steel industry employment dropped from over 30,000 jobs in the late 1960s to fewer than 6,000 in 1987.

These economic changes had a less detrimental effect on areas that were able to develop in new directions. When the Kroehler Furniture Factory, which had been Naperville's largest employer for nearly a century, closed in the mid-1970s, it did not trigger the decline of the community. Positioned to take advantage of new metropolitan growth along interstate highway corridors, Naperville moved successfully into service and light industry. At the same time, the closure of factories around the Near South Side's PRAIRIE AVENUE spurred renewed residential development and dramatically increasing property values.

Metropolitan growth in the closing decades of the twentieth century was also bolstered by developments in high-technology industries and in the service sector. New urban centers emerged around suburban shopping and commercial centers like OAK BROOK and Schaumburg. Corporate headquarters, professional offices, hotels, theaters, and restaurants joined retail outlets to create what Joel Garreau has described as an "edge city." Suburbs like TINLEY PARK and ORLAND PARK grew in response to these new trends. Often located at the junction of interstate routes, these new centers have further filled the gaps left by radial development in the railroad era.

These new suburban developments have drawn white-collar workers out from the Loop. Unlike their counterparts in the nineteenth century, who commuted from suburban homes into the central city, white-collar workers in the twenty-first century often commute from suburb to suburb. The dispersal of work locations has made them increasingly reliant on automobile rather than rail travel. Working-class Chicagoans, who in the nineteenth and early twentieth centuries lived near their industrial jobs, have also joined the ranks of commuters. High commuting costs, in both time and money, are especially challenging for low-paid workers. At the same time, more white-collar workers are making the Loop their home as well as their place of work, as the downtown area turns increasingly residential.

As Jane Jacobs insightfully observed in the early 1990s, there are now "foot people" and "car people." Nonetheless, neighborhoods remain the basic unit of organization in city and suburbs. Some neighborhoods are friendlier to car people, others to foot people. And here again, the legacy of the region's early development is apparent: foot-friendly neighborhoods, in Chicago and in its suburbs, tend to be those that grew around rail stations, while those that filled in the pockets between rail lines in the mid- to late twentieth century are generally more car-friendly.

Changing Neighborhood Residents

Neighborhoods, whether foot- or car-friendly, have also been reshaped by population growth and changing demographics. Regional population continues to grow, but new residents do not necessarily build new neighborhoods on the outskirts of the region. Instead, new immigrants and migrants jostle with established residents for jobs, housing, and other necessities. In nearly every generation, a significant proportion of a neighborhood's or suburb's population moves to new quarters. Census statistics chart this population change, but the history is best seen in the stories of individual communities and families. As Henry Binford describes in MULTICENTERED CHICAGO, Chicago's ethnic neighborhoods "were more centered than bounded ... spreading, shrinking, hiving off pieces, changing with generations."

Each of the neighborhood and suburban histories contained in this volume provides particular examples of population change. For instance, German and Irish immigrants were the earliest residents of Pilsen, a neighborhood on Chicago's near Southwest Side. By the 1870s Bohemians were drawn to factory jobs in the area; it was these immigrants who named the neighborhood Pilsen, after the second largest city in Bohemia. By the 1920s Mexican immigrants had begun to move into the neighborhood. While the neighborhood shifted from Eastern European to Mexican, it remained working-class until the late twentieth century, when gentrification began to threaten class as well as ethnic change. As local factories closed their doors, real-estate developers transformed these large spaces first into artists' lofts and then into upscale housing.

On the West Side, North Lawndale offers a different narrative. It initially developed after the Great Fire of 1871 when the McCormick Reaper Works opened just to the east. By the 1920s Russian Jews dominated the neighborhood, which burgeoned with the opening nearby of Western Electric and the headquarters of Sears, Roebuck & Co. These Russian Jews developed a host of institutions and businesses but abandoned the neighborhood as African American migrants from the American South moved into the area. The closure of the Sears headquarters in 1974 helped trigger a population decline that continued to the end of the twentieth century.

The developments in these neighborhoods (and in other communities) reflected wider ethnic and racial changes across the region (and across the United States more generally). During the nineteenth century, the region's population grew dramatically as industrialization created thousands of new jobs. Immigrants from Western and then Southern and Eastern Europe poured into the region to take these jobs (and ultimately to develop neighborhoods and suburbs). By 1890, 79 percent of Chicagoans were either immigrants or the children of immigrants.

The promise of industrial jobs drew new residents into the Chicago metropolitan area. Until after World War II, most industrial workers lived near work, or near a streetcar line that would quickly take them there. In the early industrial era, just before and after the Civil War, immigrants from Germany and Ireland worked alongside native-born migrants. By the turn of the century, Eastern and Southern Europeans joined their ranks, and in the 1910s and 1920s Mexican Americans and African Americans came to work in industrial areas as wide-ranging as the Lower West Side, Gary, and Waukegan.

Between 1924 and 1965 the U.S. government halted most European immigration, but African American migrants and Mexican immigrants continued to fuel Chicago's population growth. The African American population, which comprised no more than 2 percent of the region's population in 1910, grew to 7 percent by 1930 and 38 percent by 1975. This outgrowth of the "Great Migration" of black southerners has profoundly affected Chicago's neighborhoods and suburbs. In the last three decades, a new wave of immigration has also affected neighborhoods within and outside the city of Chicago. Both highly educated professionals and low-skilled workers are part of this new immigration from Asia, Africa, and Latin America.

As each new immigrant and racial group arrives in Chicago—following jobs, family, and other opportunities—it must wrestle for a place in existing neighborhoods and suburbs. All have confronted financial limitations and persistent discrimination, yet African Americans have faced particular impediments. Over time, ethnic and racial patterns emerged, as different groups gravitated toward specific job opportunities and institutions in neighborhoods and suburbs across the region. Boundaries created by racial restrictive covenants, zoning, and violence, however, kept African Americans from moving freely across the region. Current population patterns in the region reflect not only recent policy and events, but also historical decisions and processes. Even after the fall of most legal and extralegal constraints on African American residential choices, black Chicagoans remain the predominant group in much of the South and West Sides; those who have moved to outlying areas have settled largely to the west and south suburbs.

Neighborhoods Make a Region

The migration of residents, as well as the geography of transportation and industry, has differentially shaped the history of Chicago's North, West, and South Sides. Allegiances and rivalries between these sides are a central part of Chicagoans' self-identification and the city's public life, enmeshed with histories of employment opportunity, race relations, and public policy. The cultural salience of Chicago's sides extends even to discussions of literature and authors: the writing of James T. Farrell and Richard Wright relates specifically to the South Side, that of Jane Addams to the West Side, that of Harriet Monroe to the North Side.

Because these allegiances and rivalries are so colorful, it is easy to stick to superficial descriptions of Chicago's sides. But the differences reach far beyond the rivalry between the North Side Cubs and the South Side White Sox. Geography and wider patterns of economic, transportation, and population change all have affected the distribution of neighborhood types across the region. Over time, different kinds of neighborhoods have filled an evolving regional shell. This shell is relatively flat, but is not featureless, having been shaped by natural and artifically constructed waterways, by patterns of railroad and expressway development, and by waves of migrants and immigrants who have made the Chicago region home.

Ann Durkin Keating

FURTHER READING: Bigott, Joseph C. *From Cottage to Bungalow: Houses and the Working Class in Metropolitan Chicago, 1869–1929.* 2001. ∎ Ebner, Michael. *Creating Chicago's North Shore.* 1988. ∎ Jacobs, Jane. *The Life and Death of Great American Cities.* 2002. ∎ Keating, Ann Durkin. *Chicagoland: City and Suburbs in the Railroad Age.* 2005. ∎ Grossman, James R. *Land of Hope: Chicago, Black Southerners, and the Great Migration.* 1989. ∎ Holt, Glen E., and Dominic A. Pacyga. *Chicago: A Historical Guide to the Neighborhoods: The Loop and South Side.* 1979. ∎ Chicago Fact Book Consortium, ed. *Local Community Fact Book: Chicago Metropolitan Area, 1990.* 1995. ∎ Mayer, Harold C., and Richard M. Wade. *Chicago: Growth of a Metropolis.* 1969. ∎ Pacyga, Dominic A., and Ellen Skerrett. *Chicago, City of Neighborhoods: Histories and Tours.* 1986. ∎ Seligman, Amanda I. *Block by Block: Neighborhoods and Public Policy on Chicago's West Side.* 2005. ∎ Solzman, David, *The Chicago River: An Illustrated History and Guide to the River and Its Waterways.* 1998, 2006.

NOTE ON FURTHER READINGS

The authors hope that the essays in this book will encourage readers to investigate further the history of Chicago's neighborhoods and suburbs. Research on local history can start with the large collections at the Newberry Library, the Chicago Public Library, and the Chicago History Museum. However, the most important resources are often found in local public libraries and historical societies. Many Chicago Public Library branches and suburban libraries have local history sections, and almost all have accumulated material not readily available elsewhere, such as files of clippings that predate Internet archives. Some local historical societies also offer small libraries of primary and secondary materials about their communities; the local public library may be the best source regarding access to these collections, although an increasing number of historical societies support Web sites.

Catalogs for the Newberry Library and Chicago Public Library are accessible online, and the following groups have shared electronic catalog systems: North Suburban Library System, DuPage Library System, and the Suburban Library System (southern suburbs).

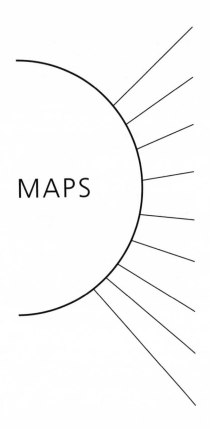

MAPS

Chicago's Community Areas

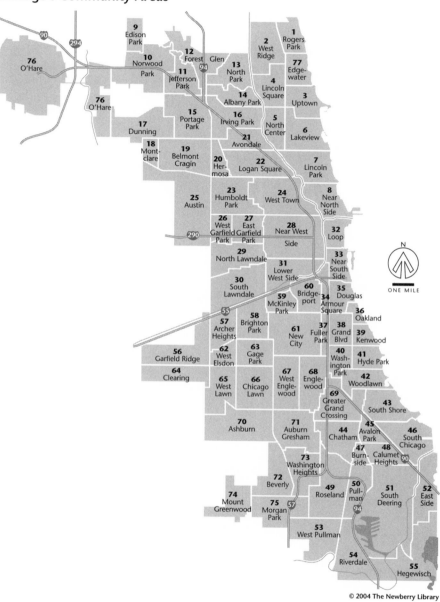

9 Edison Park
76 O'Hare
10 Norwood Park
12 Forest Glen
11 Jefferson Park
13 North Park
2 West Ridge
1 Rogers Park
77 Edge-water
76 O'Hare
14 Albany Park
4 Lincoln Square
3 Uptown
17 Dunning
15 Portage Park
16 Irving Park
5 North Center
6 Lakeview
18 Mont-clare
19 Belmont Cragin
21 Avondale
20 Her-mosa
22 Logan Square
7 Lincoln Park
25 Austin
23 Humboldt Park
24 West Town
8 Near North Side
26 West Garfield Park
27 East Garfield Park
28 Near West Side
32 Loop
29 North Lawndale
31 Lower West Side
33 Near South Side
30 South Lawndale
59 McKinley Park
60 Bridge-port
34 Armour Square
35 Douglas
36 Oakland
57 Archer Heights
58 Brighton Park
61 New City
37 Fuller Park
38 Grand Blvd
39 Kenwood
56 Garfield Ridge
62 West Elsdon
63 Gage Park
40 Wash-ington Park
41 Hyde Park
64 Clearing
65 West Lawn
66 Chicago Lawn
67 West Engle-wood
68 Engle-wood
42 Woodlawn
69 Greater Grand Crossing
43 South Shore
70 Ashburn
71 Auburn Gresham
44 Chatham
45 Avalon Park
46 South Chicago
47 Burn-side
48 Calumet Heights
73 Washington Heights
72 Beverly
49 Roseland
50 Pull-man
51 South Deering
52 East Side
74 Mount Greenwood
75 Morgan Park
53 West Pullman
54 Riverdale
55 Hegewisch

N
ONE MILE

© 2004 The Newberry Library

Economic Origins of Metropolitan Chicago's Communities

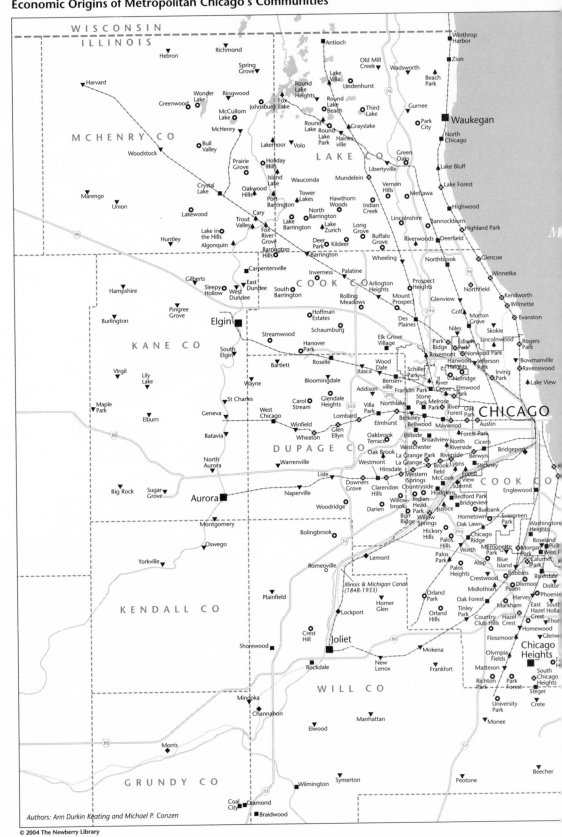

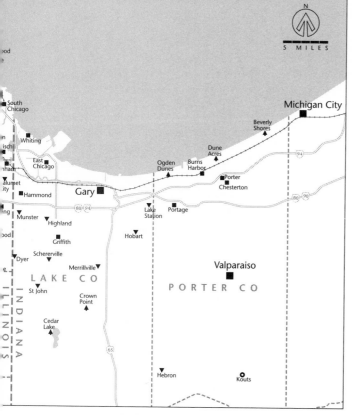

INITIAL IMPETUS FOR SETTLEMENT

- ■ Satellite cities
- ■ Industrial suburbs
- ◆ Canal towns
- ⊗ Railroad commuter suburbs
- ○ Automobile commuter suburbs
- ▲ Recreational towns
- ▼ Agricultural trade centers

————— Commuter railroad lines in 2001
········ Expressways in 2001

N

5 MILES

LAKE
MICHIGAN

South
Chicago

Michigan City

Beverly
Shores

Whiting

Dune
Acres

94

East
Chicago

Ogden
Dunes

Burns
Harbor

Porter

Chesterton

Gary

Hammond

80 94

Lake
Station

Portage

80 90

Munster

Highland

Hobart

Dyer

Griffith

Schererville

Merrillville

LAKE CO

Valparaiso

PORTER CO

St John

ILLINOIS

INDIANA

Crown
Point

Cedar
Lake

65

Hebron

Kouts

Land Subdivision and Urbanization on Chicago's Northwest Side

1851

Parcels shown are the original government sales units, 1840–48

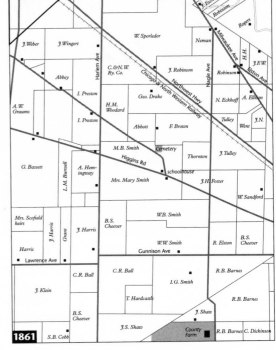

1861

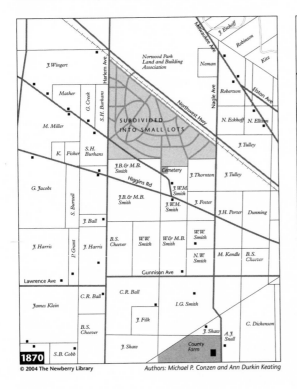

1870

© 2004 The Newberry Library

1901

Authors: Michael P. Conzen and Ann Durkin Keating

Land Subdivision and Urbanization on Chicago's Northwest Side

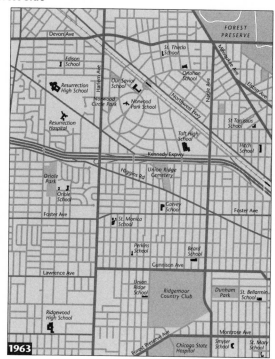

Chicago-Area Expressways in 2003

Neighborhood Change: Prairie Avenue, 1853–2003

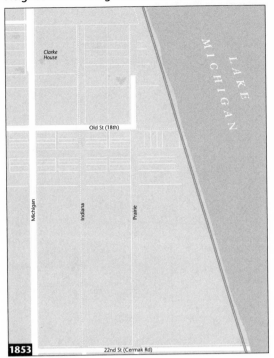

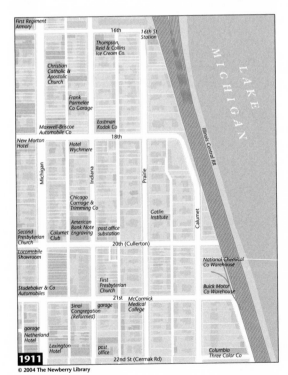

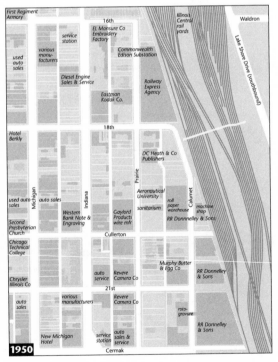

Neighborhood Change: Prairie Avenue, 1853–2003

Residential buildings ▪ Industrial/Commercial buildings ▪ Institutional buildings ▪ Park

Authors: Michael P. Conzen and Douglas Knox

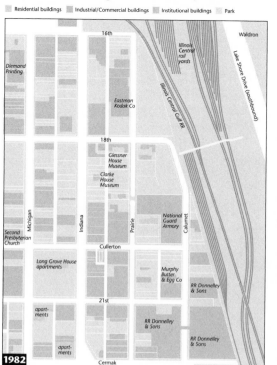

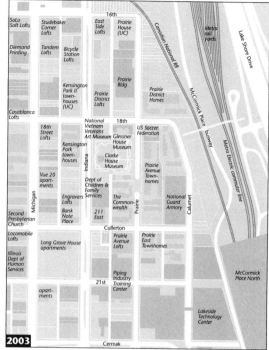

Chicago's Evolving Economic Geography

Mercantile Chicago, 1854

Galena & Chicago Union RR
Railroad shops
Passenger station
Kinzie
Freight depot
Chicago River
Hospital
South Water
Market
Des Plaines
Jefferson
Clinton
Canal
West Water
Market
Franklin
Wells
LaSalle
Clark
Court House
Randolph
Dearborn
Lake
Market
State
Wabash
Michigan
Washington
Madison
Passenger station
Illinois Central RR

- ■ Banks
- ▫ Exchange offices and brokers
- ● Forwarding and commission merchants
- ■ Lumber dealers
- ▫ Coal merchants
- ▽ Provision dealers
- ▲ Grocery dealers
- ⊛ Ship chandlers
- ⊙ Expresses
- ▨ Area beyond original townsite

N
500 FEET

LAKE MICHIGAN

Industrial Chicago, 1925

■ Industrial areas
— Railroads

Des Plaines
Morton Grove
Evanston
Park Ridge
LAKE MICHIGAN
Franklin Park
Elmhurst
Melrose Park
Oak Park
Loop
Cicero
Berwyn
La Grange
Hinsdale
Clearing
Summit
Sanitary & Ship Canal
Des Plaines River
CHICAGO
Oak Lawn
Cal-Sag Channel
South Chicago
Pullman
Lake Calumet
Whiting
Orland Park
Blue Island
Dolton
Calumet City
East Chicago
Gary
Porter
Harvey
South Holland
Hammond
Homewood
Thornton
Highland
Hobart
New Lenox
Chicago Heights
Griffith

Authors: Michael P. Conzen and Mark Donovan

N
5 MILES

Information-Age Chicago, 1990

Commercial office buildings
- · under 10,000 sq ft
- · 10,000–100,000 sq ft
- ● 100,000–1 million sq ft
- ⬤ over 1 million sq ft
- ▨ Parks and forest preserves
- — Rail transit lines
- ═ Expressways

Waukegan
Barrington
Arlington Heights
Northbrook
Elgin
Schaumburg
Des Plaines
Skokie
Evanston
LAKE MICHIGAN
St. Charles
Wheaton
CHICAGO
Oak Park
Cicero
Oak Brook
Aurora
Naperville
Oak Lawn
Orland Park
Lansing
Joliet
Matteson

N
5 MILES

Changing Origins of Metropolitan Chicago's Foreign-Born Population

FOREIGN-BORN RESIDENTS

(census designations)
- 100 people
- 900 people

China

Japan

India

Turkey

United Kingdom

Norway

Finland

Sweden

Russia

Canada

Ireland

Belgium

France · Holland

Denmark

Switzerland

Chicago

Mexico · Cuba

Other Central and South American

Germany

Hungary

Bosnia/ Serbia/ Montenegro

Romania

Austria

Spain

Other European · Greece

Italy

Eight-county metropolitan area population 2,805,869

1910 34% foreign-born

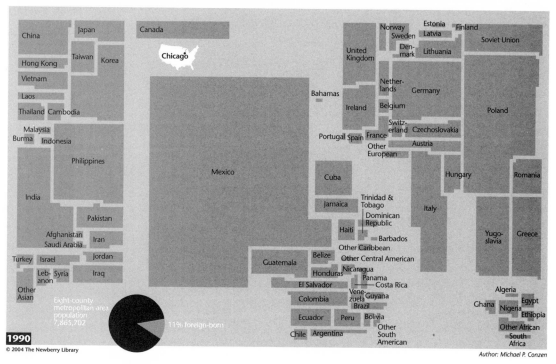

China

Japan

Canada

Hong Kong

Taiwan · Korea

Chicago

Vietnam

Norway · Estonia · Finland

Sweden · Latvia

Soviet Union

Laos

United Kingdom

Den-mark · Lithuania

Thailand · Cambodia

Malaysia

Burma · Indonesia

Nether-lands

Germany

Philippines

Bahamas

Ireland · Belgium

Poland

India

Portugal · Spain · France

Switz-erland · Czechoslovakia

Other European · Austria

Pakistan

Mexico

Cuba

Hungary

Romania

Afghanistan

Saudi Arabia · Iran

Jamaica

Trinidad & Tobago

Italy

Dominican Republic

Turkey · Israel

Jordan

Haiti

Barbados

Yugo-slavia · Greece

Leb-anon · Syria · Iraq

Other Caribbean

Guatemala

Belize

Other Central American

Other Asian

Honduras · Nicaragua

Panama

Costa Rica

Algeria

El Salvador

Vene-zuela · Guyana

Egypt

Colombia

Brazil

Ghana · Nigeria

Ethiopia

Ecuador

Peru · Bolivia

Other African

Chile · Argentina

Other South American

South Africa

Eight-county metropolitan area population 7,865,702

1990 11% foreign-born

© 2004 The Newberry Library

Author: Michael P. Conzen

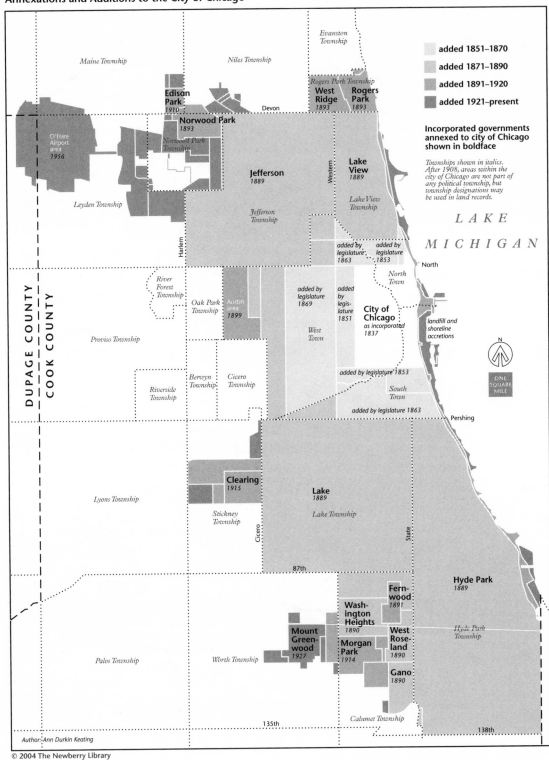

added 1851–1870
added 1871–1890
added 1891–1920
added 1921–present

Incorporated governments annexed to city of Chicago shown in boldface

Townships shown in italics. After 1908, areas within the city of Chicago are not part of any political township, but township designations may be used in land records.

Evanston Township

Maine Township

Niles Township

Devon

Rogers Park Township

West Ridge *1893*

Rogers Park *1893*

Edison Park *1910*

Norwood Park *1893*

Norwood Park Township

O'Hare Airport area *1956*

Leyden Township

Jefferson *1889*

Western

Lake View *1889*

Lake View Township

Jefferson Township

LAKE
MICHIGAN

added by legislature 1863

added by legislature 1853

North

River Forest Township

Oak Park Township

Austin area *1899*

added by legislature 1869

added by legislature 1851

North Town

City of Chicago *as incorporated 1837*

landfill and shoreline accretions

DUPAGE COUNTY
COOK COUNTY

Harlem

Proviso Township

West Town

Berwyn Township

Cicero Township

added by legislature 1853

South Town

N

ONE SQUARE MILE

Riverside Township

added by legislature 1863

Pershing

Lyons Township

Clearing *1915*

Lake *1889*

Lake Township

Stickney Township

Cicero

State

87th

Palos Township

Worth Township

Mount Greenwood *1927*

Washington Heights *1890*

Morgan Park *1914*

Fernwood *1891*

West Roseland *1890*

Gano *1890*

Hyde Park *1889*

Hyde Park Township

135th

Calumet Township

138th

Author: Ann Durkin Keating

© 2004 The Newberry Library

Chicago's Railroad Pattern in 1950

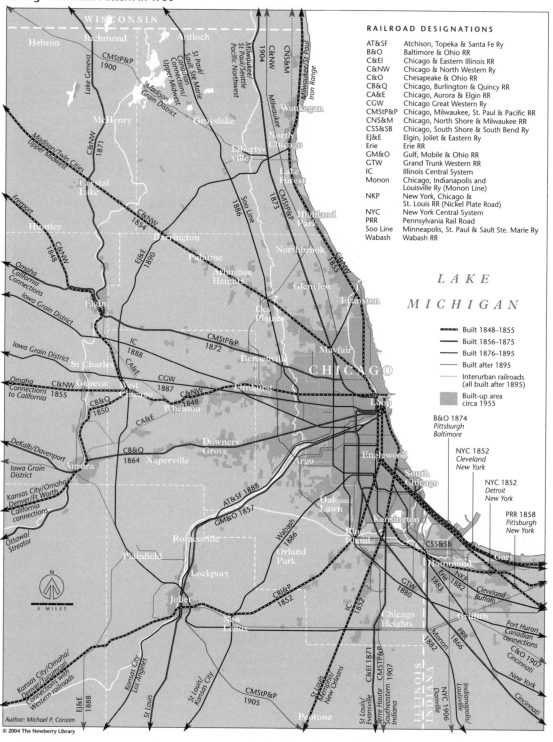

RAILROAD DESIGNATIONS

AT&SF	Atchison, Topeka & Santa Fe Ry
B&O	Baltimore & Ohio RR
C&EI	Chicago & Eastern Illinois RR
C&NW	Chicago & North Western Ry
C&O	Chesapeake & Ohio RR
CB&Q	Chicago, Burlington & Quincy RR
CA&E	Chicago, Aurora & Elgin RR
CGW	Chicago Great Western Ry
CMStP&P	Chicago, Milwaukee, St. Paul & Pacific RR
CNS&M	Chicago, North Shore & Milwaukee RR
CSS&SB	Chicago, South Shore & South Bend Ry
EJ&E	Elgin, Joliet & Eastern Ry
Erie	Erie RR
GM&O	Gulf, Mobile & Ohio RR
GTW	Grand Trunk Western RR
IC	Illinois Central System
Monon	Chicago, Indianapolis and Louisville Ry (Monon Line)
NKP	New York, Chicago & St. Louis RR (Nickel Plate Road)
NYC	New York Central System
PRR	Pennsylvania Rail Road
Soo Line	Minneapolis, St. Paul & Sault Ste. Marie Ry
Wabash	Wabash RR

LAKE MICHIGAN

- Built 1848–1855
- Built 1856–1875
- Built 1876–1895
- Built after 1895
- Interurban railroads (all built after 1895)
- Built-up area circa 1955

Author: Michael P. Conzen

© 2004 The Newberry Library

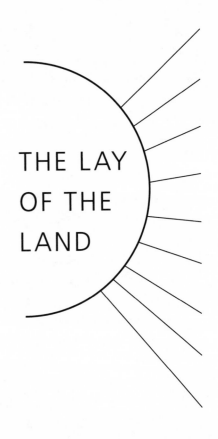

THE LAY
OF THE
LAND

SUBURBS AND CITIES AS DUAL METROPOLIS

MICHAEL H. EBNER

Chicagoans inhabit a dual metropolis, experiencing daily reminders of decay and glitter, despair and aspiration. As of 2000, the region encompassed 293 municipalities (263 in Illinois) spread over 4,401 square miles in Cook, DuPage, Kane, Lake, McHenry, and Will Counties, plus the northwestern Indiana counties of Lake and Porter. What sociologists refer to as spatial mismatch is among the region's dominant and most entrenched characteristics: technologically oriented job opportunities requiring high skill levels, mostly concentrated along suburban corridors; poorly educated, underemployed labor pools, more often than not in the most socially isolated locales within central cities; and disparities in transportation networks, inhibiting opportunities for links between residence and work. The poorest residents of inner cities, contentiously labeled an "underclass," suffer disproportionately from the compound effects of their environs as one affliction builds upon another.

The contemporary metropolis—for all its stark residential and occupational contrasts—reflects national political structures and an economic system that too often proves disdainful of the inner city, its depleted resources, and its most beleaguered inhabitants. A quandary with deep historical roots, the mismatch intensified during the 1980s. Historian Richard C. Wade foresaw as early as 1982 that the Reagan administration's policy—an artifice with the positivist label "new federalism"—would deepen imbalances between tax-rich municipalities and their poorest neighbors.

> ## Medgar Evers in Chicago
>
> One of Medgar's greatest pleasures during those summers in Chicago was the chance to explore the suburbs. Whenever he could, he would borrow a car and drive out of the city to wander up one street and down another looking at houses. He had a dream of the sort of house he hoped someday to live in, the kind of street and neighborhood and town where he might raise a family, and the white suburbs of Chicago seemed to him right out of that dream. He would spend whole days just driving slowly through the suburbs of Chicago's North Shore, looking at the beautiful houses and wishing. Years later, when we were in Chicago together, he took me on these drives and by that time he had picked out specific houses that came closest to his dream.
>
> Myrlie B. Evers with William Peters,
> *For Us, the Living.* 1967.

Between 1980 and 1990 federal spending on cities diminished from 15 to 6 percent of the national budget; in 1991 the nation's central cities were home to 43 percent of Americans below the poverty line, up from 27 percent in 1959. In 1989 the ratio of median family incomes between metropolitan Chicago's richest and poorest communities was nine to one; in 1960 it had been roughly five to one. The United States Conference of Mayors itemized the accumulating urban afflictions in 1986: population loss, impoverishment, racial concentration, deindustrialization, unemployment, homelessness, crime, poor schooling, and high taxes. European urban experts visiting American cities expressed puzzlement upon encountering conditions comparable to those in the third world.

Historian Kenneth T. Jackson has argued that a single process—population deconcentration—has shaped American metropolitan areas during the twentieth century. (The category of suburban is avoided, wherever possible, because it confuses as much as it explains.) While this process was already evident in the nineteenth century, when American demographic patterns were established, it accelerated in the final third of the twentieth century.

Two fateful statistical benchmarks reached in 1990—both widely reported and assessed—underscored the consequences of sustained deconcentration. First, Chicago's total population fell below 3 million for the first time since 1920; between 1970 and 1990, the city lost 17 percent of its population as its collar-county suburbs advanced 24 percent. Second, the percentage of Chicago workers employed in the private sector dropped to slightly under 40 percent for the first time; it had been 56 percent in 1972. In 1992 Sears, Roebuck attracted attention when it moved its corporate headquarters, and five thousand employees, from the downtown Sears Tower to a newly constructed, horizontally organized 1.9-million-square-foot facility (as of 2002 expanded to 2.4 million square feet) in the northwestern suburb of Hoffman Estates.

Embodying the bleakest circumstances of the dual metropolis is Census Tract #3805 on Chicago's South Side. Lying four miles south of the Loop, the area included the Chicago Housing Authority's Robert Taylor Homes. Constructed between 1960 and 1962, this complex comprised 28 identical high-rise buildings, each 16 stories, with a total of 4,415 apartment units. Demolition of the Taylor Homes, and Stateway Gardens to the north, commenced in 1997, part of the CHA's self-proclaimed Plan for Transformation ("a blueprint for positive change . . . that will reinvent public housing"). Their construction too had been part of a wider public policy. The second wave of the Great Migration increased Chicago's black population from 277,731 to 1,102,620 between 1940 and 1970. Only 8 percent of the city's population in 1940, black Chicago constituted one-third of the city by 1970. The public housing high-rises were intended to contain this increasing black popula-

Cabrini high-rises, 1959. The Chicago Housing Authority completed this "Cabrini Extension" in 1958, alongside the Frances Cabrini Homes, which had been built in 1941–42. With the construction of the William Green Homes in 1962, the complex became known as simply "Cabrini-Green." Photographer: Betty Hulett. Source: Chicago History Museum.

tion within existing ghettos. The physical isolation of this CHA site was exacerbated by the completion in 1962 of the Dan Ryan Expressway immediately to its west; residents were effectively sealed off from jobs, facilities, and the white residents on the other side of the 10-lane highway. The census of 1990 documented the grim statistics of hyperpauperization: 100 percent of the census tract's 2,169 residents were African American; 89 percent lived below the poverty line, as contrasted with 64 percent of the population of the surrounding area; 89 percent of the families were headed by a female; 58 percent of the civilian labor force was unemployed (versus 11 percent citywide); 44 percent were under the age of 13; and only 6 percent of all adults had graduated from high school.

KENILWORTH, in contrast, exemplifies the glitter and aspirations of the dual metropolis. In 1990 it ranked as the wealthiest place in the metropolis, with a per capita income of $69,814. It was the nation's ninth richest community and had one of the highest proportions (163 per 10,000 adults) of listings in *Who's Who in America*; 83 percent of its adult population held at least a bachelor's degree and 98 percent had graduated from high school. Situated in the northeastern corner of Cook County, Kenilworth is one of the eight suburban municipalities known collectively as the North Shore, all linked to Chicago by a railroad operating since 1855. The rush-hour commute by rail covers 16 miles in 32 minutes. Such places—whether on Philadelphia's Main Line or north of New York City in Westchester County—amount to classic suburbs. Cultural homogeneity, reinforced by restrictive covenants—white Protestants only—defined the vision of Kenilworth's founder. Contrived as a sociological island, it was purposefully designed to resist the sweeping social and cultural changes unleashed by the economic transformation of the nineteenth century. By 1990 only 60 of Kenilworth's 2,562 residents were nonwhite. The median housing price exceeded $500,000.

FORD HEIGHTS, while also a suburb, represents a textbook case study of decay and despair. Twenty-five miles from Chicago in southern Cook County, it was identified in 1990 as the nation's poorest suburb. Known until 1987 as East Chicago Heights, it changed its name when attempting (unsuccessfully) to annex an adjacent unincorporated site upon which the Ford Motor Company operated a factory. Between 1980 and 2000, the population of Ford Heights declined from 5,437 to 3,456; 96 percent of its residents were African American. Per capita income (adjusted for inflation) declined 22 percent between 1979 and 1989, to $4,660, compared to Chicago's $12,889 and Kenilworth's $69,814. Unemployment in Ford Heights approached 40 percent, and only 30 percent of its housing stock was privately owned. In 2000, it registered the nation's highest percentage of single-mother households (34 percent).

As recently as 1950, NAPERVILLE, 30 miles west of Chicago, looked like a typical commuter suburb and stood 91st among Illinois municipalities in total population. Today it exemplifies an outcome of deconcentration that defies traditional assumptions about urban and suburban. Some 200 similar communities—variously called boomburbs, edge cities, technoburbs, and totalized suburbs—are now scattered across the United States (Bellevue, Washington; Gwinnett County, Georgia; Overland Park, Kansas; and Tysons Corner, Virginia are other examples). Each is situated 30 to 40 miles from their original urban center, along interstate highways, with easy access to major airports; other characteristics include reliance upon automobiles, excellent public schools, proximity to university research centers, and rapid economic development led by assorted technology-related and retail enterprises. Naperville's corporate roster includes BP Amoco Research Center, Dow Jones & Co., Lucent Technologies, Nalco Chemical Company, and Nicor. Nearby are Argonne National Laboratory and Fermi National Laboratory.

In the 1990s Naperville experienced the second biggest population surge among the 20 largest municipalities within the collar counties, growing by 43,007, or 50 percent, to 128,358. When it surpassed 100,000 in 1994, it was the 10th-fastest-growing city in the nation. In 2000 it ranked fourth in population statewide (ahead of Peoria and behind AURORA). In new-home construction it ranked first among the collar counties as of 1982. Naperville is the largest city in DuPage County (and its oldest, founded in 1831), and has spilled over into Will County, where 29 percent of its inhabitants live. In physical size, it expanded from 5.8 square miles in 1960 to 38 square miles as of 2000, the result of nearly 400 separate annexations. And in its demographic attributes, Naperville changed notably. Among its 5,272 residents in 1940, 99.9 percent were white. In 2000 nonwhites accounted for 15 percent of its total population (Asians made up 9.6 percent of the total, African Americans 3 percent). In the six-county region, Naperville ranked eighth—in the company of traditional immigrant centers such as Aurora (#3), WAUKEGAN (#4), and SKOKIE (#5)—in foreign-born population (14,963). Yet despite greater diversity than is commonly associated with suburbs, in 1992 Naperville was singled out as having the lowest poverty rate (1.5 percent) among U.S. cities nationwide with populations of at least 50,000.

Metropolitan Chicago's deconcentration is hardly a contemporary phenomenon. From 1860 to 1910, the city's population increased by a factor of 20, to nearly 2.2 million; New York City's, in the same period, grew sixfold. By 1910 Chicago's population exceeded Berlin's (2 million) and was approaching that of Paris (2.9 million). Although Chicago's physical size had expanded significantly between 1880 and 1900, from 43 to 169 square miles, as a result of consolidation and annexation, thereafter its growth stagnated. Suburbs—among them EVANSTON and OAK PARK—began to reject annexation during the 1890s. Their residents demonstrated a determination to set their communities apart politically and culturally.

The Loop, since its completion in 1897, has symbolized Chicago's magnetism. Drawing on major advances in the of electrified rail technology realized in the late 1880s, the elevated line encircled the central business district and connected it to the South, West, and North Sides. The district pulsated. Each workday, according to a 1910 study, approximately 650,000 commuters journeyed to the Loop. During the evening rush, it was estimated in 1916, 100,000 passengers used the trains between 5 and 6 p.m. Street-level space was at a premium. The top cost per front foot at the corner of State and Madison—possibly the world's busiest intersection—was $10,000 in 1910. Ten years later it was almost $25,000. Correspondingly, rents for downtown office space soared, increasing 15 percent in 1902 and again in 1903. Between 1905 and 1911 the city, county, and federal governments each erected major downtown office structures. LaSalle Street was the financial center. The Loop was also close to a complex of newly opened edifices housing renowned cultural institutions, including the Auditorium (1889), the Art Institute (1893), the Chicago Public Library (1897), Orchestra Hall (1904), and the Field Museum of Natural History (1920).

Of the many forces acting in the Loop, none caused more chaos than the competition among drivers of motorized vehicles, horse-drawn wagons, and streetcars, a problem confounded by the proliferation of automobiles. A 1907 traffic survey reported 1,421 automobiles entering the district via the Rush Street bridge in a 12-hour period; eight years later the figure reached 10,158. By 1911 approximately 85 police officers were assigned to daily traffic duty; parking time was limited beginning that year to 60-minute intervals and in 1915 was reduced to 30 minutes. Traffic lights were introduced, with only limited success, in 1916. A survey in 1919 revealed 130,000 vehicles—motorized and horse-drawn—entering the Loop daily. Yet whenever Chicago's aldermen deliberated on the question of new restrictions on parking, proprietors of small businesses objected, fearing the loss of customers.

William A. Wieboldt realized the predicament caused by congestion in the Loop. In 1917 he established a major retail operation, the eight-story Wieboldt Department Store, at the intersection of Lincoln, Belmont, and Ashland Avenues—entirely outside the central business district. Sears first opened neighborhood branches in 1925, and Marshall Field's launched its suburban stores in 1929. Recognizing audience demands in outlying neighborhoods, local movie theaters—the Pastime on West Madison, the Tivoli at Cottage Grove and 63rd Street, Schumacher's in the BACK OF THE YARDS—likewise commenced operations during the 1920s. Wholesale and manufacturing enterprises also required less costly, more expansive sites away from the Loop. Notable relocations included Western Electric (1903), Sears, Roebuck (1904), Montgomery Ward (1906), and Edward Hines Lumber (1906). SOUTH CHICAGO emerged as a major center for heavy manufactured products, and by 1916 commerce along the Calumet River exceeded that on the Chicago River by a factor of five; 10 years before, the two had been equal. Another mark of the decentralization of economic activity was the founding of GARY, Indiana, in 1906 by the United States Steel Corporation. Just beyond the eastern boundary of Illinois at the southernmost tip of Lake Michigan, it was the nation's first instant industrial city, although its fortunes were linked to Chicago's transportation network and labor supply.

Daniel H. Burnham embodied the hopes inspired by Chicago's monumental progress since the Great Fire of 1871. He had risen to fame as chief of construction for the World's Columbian Exposition of 1893. In 1906, in the culminating assignment of his career, he was retained by the Merchants Club of Chicago to formulate a comprehensive design for future growth. The heralded *Plan of Chicago,* written in collaboration with Edward H. Bennett, appeared on July 4, 1909, and caused an international sensation. (The Merchants Club and the Commercial Club merged in 1908; hence the Commercial Club is credited with having sponsored the plan.) Burnham's Plan combined fanciful aspiration and practicality. Its focus was the metropolis, not the city alone. After Haussmann's plan for Paris of 1853–1859, Chicago's amounted to the next step in the progression toward a comprehensive urban design. Distinguishing the work of Burnham and Bennett was the attention to the city in the age of rapid, mechanized mobility. Some of their recommendations were fulfilled, notably the preservation of the lakefront as a central space for culture, recreation, and leisure. Also enduring, although in less dramatic terms, was the attention to traffic patterns on streets and waterways. Other objectives remained unfulfilled, none more regrettably than their call for a unified commuter-rail terminal facility.

But the deconcentration of Chicago's population, as the authors of the *Plan of Chicago* recognized, could not be denied. Between 1900 and 1910 the population of the city and the six-county region increased by nearly 30 percent. Lake County, Illinois, was the fastest-growing county in the metropolis, gaining 60 percent to Cook's 31 percent. During the following decade the population of Chicago increased 24 percent, but the average growth of the combined northern and western suburbs was 100 percent. Significant advances in population registered in WIN-NETKA (113 percent), Oak Park (105 percent), WILMETTE (58 percent), and Evanston (49 percent). Starting in the mid-1920s, major corporations offering well-paid employment departed Chicago in search of more space for their operations: Abbott Laboratories moved to NORTH CHICAGO, G. D. Searle to Skokie, Jewel Tea Company to BARRINGTON, Motorola to FRANKLIN PARK and later SCHAUMBURG.

A 1947 census bureau study of the redistribution of population within American metropolises identified multiple causal factors: improved mass transit, the cachet of a suburban address, the deconcentration of industry, and technological advances such as telephone and electrical services. But the primary cause—"a factor of great importance," wrote Warren S. Thompson—was the automobile. The marriage between suburb and automobile was consummated during the 1920s: vehicle registration nationwide reached 8 million in 1920 and 26 million by 1929.

This 1968 image shows the dividing line between suburban and agricultural areas in Buffalo Grove, where Levitt & Sons developed the subdivision in the foreground. Photographer: Hedrich-Blessing. Source: Chicago History Museum.

Following World War II, the suburban trend—in Chicago and across the nation—seemed a self-fulfilling prophecy. Families coveting security after 15 exhausting years of depression and war often realized their quest in suburban communities. A record 2.2 million marriages occurred during 1946, and 20 percent more babies were born that year than in 1945. The federal government also exercised an important influence. Many new homes were situated on the metropolitan periphery, constructed inexpensively and with federally subsidized mortgages. There were twice as many housing starts between 1946 and 1955 as in the preceding 15 years. Suburban life inspired two-car families, and many women remained in the postwar labor force; *Glamour* (1953) linked home ownership to two-income households. New car sales nationwide soared from 69,500 in 1945 to 2.1 million in 1946 and 5.1 million in 1949; Chicago's automobile count increased from 428,000 in 1945 to 765,000 in 1953. Highway construction burgeoned, reaching $2 billion in 1949 and $4 billion by 1955 across the United States.

As early as 1943, the federal government had urged metropolises nationwide—including the governments of Chicago and Cook County—to devise plans for a postwar system of modern highways. The culmination was the Interstate Highway

Act of 1956, which spurred a transcontinental network of superhighways stretching 42,500 miles and costing $60 billion. This included a complex of expressways in and around Chicago: the Bishop Ford Freeway (begun 1953, completed 1956), the Edens Expressway (1951–1958), the Tri-State Tollway (1953–1958), the Eisenhower Expressway (1954–1960), the East-West Tollway (1958–1972), the Kennedy Expressway (1958–1960), the Dan Ryan Expressway (1961–1962), and the Stevenson Expressway (1964–1966). Residents of Naperville, appreciating the benefits of improved access to Chicago, campaigned unabashedly to have the East-West Tollway routed just north of their city's boundary.

Postwar deconcentration of retailing underscored consumer proclivities first evident during the 1920s. The proliferation of suburban malls (42 were built in the 1950s around Chicago) affirmed the preference for living and shopping in automobile-dependent suburbs. To the consternation of businesses in the central business district, Chicago's segment of metropolitan revenue derived from retail sales—measured in the billions of dollars—dropped from 71 percent in 1949 to approximately 40 percent in 1972. Receipts in downtown movie palaces had dropped as early as 1947. Woodfield Mall opened in the northwestern suburb of Schaumburg in 1971. Its 2.3 million square feet featured four major department stores, 230 smaller retail establishments, and 11,000 parking spaces spread over nearly 200 acres. Malls became a new type of civic space, featuring artistic performances and civic meetings as well as consumer-oriented pursuits.

At the beginning of the twenty-first century, meaningful plans to ensure Chicago's metropolitan future centered on an abiding faith in our capacity as a democratic nation to foster renewal and change, with the suburban majority discovering compelling reasons to recast its sensibilities on a regional scale. One project, originally advanced by the mayor of Schaumburg in 1997 and endorsed by other municipalities along the northwest suburban corridor, anticipated shortages in the private-sector workforce and took aim at alleviating the spatial mismatch. This unprecedented plan—as yet unrealized—would expand the reach of Chicago Transit Authority rail lines into the northwest suburbs, with new stations strategically situated at Hoffman Estates and Woodfield Mall. The CTA outlined a more comprehensive design in 2002 to extend itself beyond the city in other directions as well.

During the 1990s several Chicago-based not-for-profit organizations—the Chicago Community Trust, the Civic Federation, the John D. and Catherine T. MacArthur Foundation, and the Metropolitan Planning Council—also worked to advance regional solutions. More often than not, their ally was the Northeastern Illinois Planning Commission. A public agency created by the state of Illinois in 1957, NIPC identifies salient regional issues but lacks legislative authority for implementation. ("We're like the United Nations except that we have no army—and more governments," a representative observed in 1993.) Because of the leverage resulting from its philanthropic resources and its sustained commitment to the future of Chicago, the MacArthur Foundation emerged as a champion of regional initiatives rooted in consensus. Favorites included enlarged transportation systems, metropolitan land-use planning, augmenting the stock and dispersing the locations of affordable housing, and consolidation of metropolitan government and tax structures.

But disagreement surfaced about how to implement policy objectives. Activists—urban and suburban—envisioned political action and welcomed the likelihood of needier communities contesting for the perquisites savored by their prosperous neighbors. Whether by means of consensus or contention, the desired end might culminate in a series of political and economic imperatives—involving the public and private sectors, diverse neighborhoods and communities, giant corporations, small enterprises, and labor unions—at the local, state, and even national levels.

Legal scholar Gerald E. Frug has raised the possibility of interlocal political institutions. The Puget Sound Regional Council, founded in 1991 to encompass four counties constituting metropolitan Seattle, is a singular example. Its constituencies, in addition to the 4 counties, include 70 municipalities, 3 public authorities, and 2 state agencies. The problems it contends with—in the areas of transportation, economics, and growth management—are caused mainly by population deconcentration. In other metropolises, initiatives have taken varied forms, among them Minnesota's Fiscal Disparities Act (1971), Oregon's Urban Growth Boundaries (1973), the South Coast Air Quality Management District in Southern California (1976), and the Georgia Regional Transportation Authority (1999). And widely acclaimed is a comprehensive planning and redevelopment initiative launched by New Jersey (1988), cited by Joel Garreau as "unquestionably the most sophisticated growth-management scheme ever attempted statewide in this country." Chicago's programmatic strategy, embodied in Metropolis 2020, is by contrast decidedly ad hoc.

"Metropolitan" is a contested word in the glossary of American urban history. How people conduct their lives—or, more precisely, how they configure their basic day-to-day assumptions about cities and suburbs—comprises a fundamental and perplexing contemporary question. Whether singly or in combination, heightened racial, ethnic, and class divisions exert themselves. The consequences influence, and even reorder, the many daily choices people make: where to purchase foodstuffs or household supplies, where to seek health care, where to enjoy a play or musical performance, where to attend a sports event, where to worship, where to educate their offspring, and ultimately where to reside. The lack of provision for cities in the federal system, reaching back to the very inception of the American nation-state, has rendered their status perpetually unresolved. Skeptics see "metropolitan" as pejorative, evoking images of people furtively escaping into their local suburban enclaves, seeking to elude the intricacies associated with their daily lives as citizens of the metropolis. Alternatively, this key word can point to a set of programmatic solutions directed toward diminishing rather than perpetuating the disparities between the neighborhoods and communities that separate the citizens who inhabit the dual metropolis.

FURTHER READING: Of great value, because it frames issues globally, is Sir Peter Hall, *Cities in Civilization* (1998). The American metropolis is provocatively reconceptualized in Peter Marcuse, "The Ghetto of Exclusion and the Fortified Enclave: New Patterns in the United States," *American Behavioral Scientist* 41:3 (November/December 1997): 311–26, and Kenneth T. Jackson, "Gentlemen's Agreement: Discrimination in Metropolitan America," in *Reflections on Regionalism*, ed. Bruce Katz (Washington, D.C.: Brookings Institution Press, 2000), 185–217 ; the authors update to the end of the twentieth century the specter of people striving to fashion metropolitan lives on sociological islands apart from everyday realities, a notion first explicated in the context of the Industrial Revolution in Robert H. Wiebe, *The Search for Order, 1877–1920* (1967). William Julius Wilson, *When Work Disappears: The World of the New Urban Poor* (1996), and Douglas S. Massey and Nancy A. Denton, *American Apartheid : Segregation and the Making of the Underclass* (1993), are paramount for comprehending the ramifications of the dual metropolis. Kenneth T. Jackson, *Crabgrass Frontier: The Suburbanization of theUnited States* (1985), is the sine qua non but must be read in tandem with Robert Fishman, *Bourgeois Utopias: The Rise and Fall of Suburbia* (1987), Margaret Marsh, *Suburban Lives* (1990), and Dolores Hayden, *Building Suburbia: Green Fields and Urban Growth, 1820–2000* (2003). Still indispensable is Warren S. Thompson, *Population: The Growth of Metropolitan Districts in the United States, 1900-1940* (1947). For an informative rhetorical analysis of the American metropolis, turn to Zane L. Miller, "Pluralizing America: Walter Prescott Webb, Chicago Sociology, and Cultural Regionalism," in *Essays on Sunbelt Cities and Recent Urban America*, ed. Robert B. Fairbanks and Kathleen Underwood (1990), 151–76. For a critical appreciation of how journalists and scholars assay the contemporary American metropolis consult William Sharpe and Leonard Wallock, "Bold New City or Built-Up 'Burb? Redefining Contemporary Suburbia," *American Quarterly* 46:1 (March 1994): 1–30. Joel Garreau, *Edge City: Life on the New Frontier* (1991), has exerted strong influence on how issues of growth and change affect the fringe of the metropolis but must be augmented by Robert Fishman, "The American Metropolis at Century's End: Past and Future Influences," *Housing Policy Debate* 11:2 (2000): 199–213, as well as Michael B. Katz and Mark J. Stern, *One Nation Divisible: What America Was and What It Is Becoming* (2006), and Claude S. Fischer and Michael Hout, *Century of Difference: How America Changed in the Last One Hundred Years* (2006). Framing cities and suburbs in a broad context are Elaine Tyler May, *Homeward Bound: American Families in the Cold War Era* (1988); James T. Patterson, *Grand Expectations: The United States, 1945–1974* (1996); Jon C. Teaford, *The Metropolitan Revolution: The Rise of Post-Urban America* (2006); and Derek Bok, *The State of the Nation: Government and the Quest for a Better Society* (1996). James T. Lemon, *Liberal Dreams and Nature's Limits: Great Cities of North America since 1600* (1996), devotes an expansive chapter to viewing Chicago circa 1910, but also essential is Ann Durkin Keating, *Chicagoland: City and Suburbs in the Railroad Age* (2005). Focused on metropolitan policy issues are Richard C. Wade, "The Suburban Roots of the New Federalism," *New York Times Magazine* (August 1, 1982), 20–21; Jon C. Teaford, *Post-Suburbia: Government and Politics in the Edge Cities* (1996); and Robert J. Waste, *Independent Cities: Rethinking U.S. Urban Policy* (1998). Four studies examine important dimensions of the altered metropolis: Lizabeth Cohen, *A Consumers' Repub-*

lic: The Politics of Mass Consumption in Postwar America (2003); Robert M. Fogelson, *Downtown: Its Rise and Fall, 1880–1950* (2001); Gerald E. Frug, "Beyond Regional Governance," *Harvard Law Review* 155:7 (May 2002): 1766–1836; and Peter O. Muller, "The Suburban Transformation of the Globalizing American City," *Annals of the American Academy of Political Science*, no. 551 (May 1997), 44–58. Also instructive is Neil Harris, *Cultural Excursions: Marketing Appetites and Cultural Tastes in Modern America* (1990). Furnishing a compelling contrarian interpretation of contemporary metropolitan America is Robert Bruegmann, *Sprawl: A Compact History* (2005). Harold Henderson contributed four informative articles to the *Chicago Reader*, an alternative weekly, probing the debates over regional strategies: "Cityscape: Who Planned This Mess" (March 12, 1993), "Up against Sprawl" (September 6, 1996), "The Great Divide" (January 31, 1997), and "The Future Is Theirs" (January 25, 2002). Deeply informing Chicago-area research is the *Local Community Fact Book*, published each decade by the Chicago Fact Book Consortium.

MULTICENTERED CHICAGO

HENRY BINFORD

Chicagoans like to think of their home as "multiethnic," or as "the city of neighborhoods." Indeed, the celebration of neighborhood is one of the binding rituals of Chicago culture. The shelves of local bookstores are crammed with neighborhood guides, and in the 1990s Mayor Richard M. Daley harnessed neighborhood consciousness to the marketing of tourism, officially defining certain well-known districts with banners, signs, and dramatic arches. When visitors come to the city one of the things they frequently ask to see is "Chicago's ethnic neighborhoods."

Yet every big city in America is a city of neighborhoods—forged by migration, employment patterns, race, religion, and other factors in addition to ethnic culture. Boston, San Francisco, and many other cities have their own rich patterns of colorful locales. What, if anything, makes Chicago's multicentered settlement pattern distinctive? Answering that question requires setting aside notions of neighborhood geography and diversity that became widespread in the mid-twentieth century but have been challenged by recent scholarship. It requires looking beyond the notion of "neighborhood," as that term has been commonly and vaguely used, and thinking about Chicago's many spatial subcommunities as changing manifestations of history and human initiative. It requires looking deeper into Chicago's past, recognizing how the city's growth fits into the long history of national urbanization, and defining certain features of Chicago's development that were unusual.

For many observers in the twentieth century, the most obvious factor shaping Chicago's social geography seemed to be its role as a magnet for newcomers, with each new group establishing a highly visible presence in some piece of the city and the city overall growing as a mosaic of cultural tiles, a collection of discrete and durable ethnic/racial cells, resistant to rapid change. Chicago was touted having more Poles than any other city except Warsaw or, in a darker view, as the most segregated city in America. Social scientists of the "Chicago School" promoted the idea that such well-defined subareas were "natural," the product of physical and ecological processes governing urban growth.

In the past two decades, students of the city's history have noted limits to this vision of neighborhood development. With the important exception of the African American ghetto, Chicago's ethnic communities were never so well-defined or homogeneous as common knowledge would have it. Even in Irish-dominated BRIDGEPORT or the West Side's LITTLE ITALY, there were always people from other backgrounds. The world of Jurgis Rudkus, in Upton Sinclair's *The Jungle*, was centered in Lithuanian Catholic culture, but his neighbors were diverse, and his neighborhood was shaped as much by economic forces as by ethnicity. What's more, sociological assumptions about "natural areas" masked the dynamic qualities of ethnic and other neighborhoods—the enormous effort that Chicagoans invested in actively shaping their own communities: promoting them, sometimes defending them, and often moving them. Immigration and migration do not by themselves account for the pattern that has so vividly impressed visitors for more than a century: a great sprawling metropolis, comprising dozens of far-flung and constantly changing clusters and scores of dispersed centers of employment and commerce. Chicago is more than an assembly of cultural chunks; its parts are ever changing, and its multicenteredness is rooted deep in the way it grew.

This is an essay about the variety of forces that have shaped not just the overall configuration of Chicago but the smaller spaces and communities in which Chicagoans have lived and worked. It is also about the variety of ways Chicagoans have imagined those subunits. Most residents, in the course of their daily lives, assume multiple roles and encounter the city as a complex and shifting array of focal points—places of work, worship, education, and amusement—rather than as a set of bounded cells. But there have been times and places where boundaries were important, and there has also been a history of "imagined communities" resulting from the needs of government or information management or even the simple psychological need to simplify a hugely complicated landscape. All of these kinds of subcommunities have a history in every big city and a distinctive history in Chicago.

The flow of people into Chicago and the local communities they created were conditioned by three characteristics particular to the city's history. First, Chicago grew in a setting that is relatively—but not entirely—flat, and one that has been shaped and reshaped by numerous natural and artificial waterways. On the one hand, flatness made outward growth easy; on the other, it made an endemic problem of managing water: supplying it, disposing of it, trying to make it go to some places and not to others. Second, Chicago's most spectacular growth spurt occurred when the national economy was driven by railroads, heavy industry, and European immigration. The city did not share in the long period of seaport growth that put East Coast cities and even inland ports like Cincinnati and St. Louis well on the way to big-city status, and its growth slowed when the centers of investment and production shifted westward in the second half of the twentieth century.

Third, rapid growth offered extraordinary opportunities for both planning and conflict, and Chicago's landscape bears the marks of some of the most noble and some of the most invidious attempts at community building in American history.

Today's social geography is a product of the interaction of these three Chicago-specific characteristics, and today's Chicago bears the imprint of five prior, and in some cases overlapping, phases of multicentered development. For convenience, they might be called periods of natural division, speculation and engineering, migrant clustering and industrial villages, cellular mapping, and elite community redevelopment. Each phase produced a new version of the multicentered city, occupying successively larger amounts of space.

Natural Division, 1780–1830

The natural environment was paramount in shaping Chicago's earliest communities. The Chicago River and its two branches divided the site of initial settlement into three parts, which by the early nineteenth century would be known as the North, West, and South Sides. Native Americans who passed through and the European-descended people who settled permanently in the early nineteenth century built little clusters of dwellings in all three sectors. A small group of civilians settled close to Fort Dearborn in what is now the northeast corner of the LOOP. Fur traders, tavern keepers, and mariners settled on the North and West Sides. Early Chicago contained several collections of huts, stores, shops, and warehouses strung out along the waterways. The British Kinzies on the North Side did not always get along with the mixed-blood LaFramboise clan down the South Branch, but they all built their houses close to the river that provided transportation for the community.

Yet water was a force for division as well as a focus of common activity. The river, sluggish and relatively narrow though it was, raised formidable obstacles to travel between the three segments of town. The first few decades of Chicago's history as a settlement are full of tales of ferries begun and abandoned, bridges erected and then washed away in spring floods. Even away from the river, the marshy, muddy quality of the site became a standing joke in early accounts of the town and a long-term problem for those trying to cultivate or build. In these circumstances, glacial ridges and other scraps of high ground, stretching away from the village near the river's mouth, became the basis for roads and then linear farming settlements starting in the early 1830s. The high ground underlying the future Clark Street, Archer Avenue, and Cottage Grove Avenue provided the foundation for the first subcommunities to be added to the early commercial center near the fort and the river's mouth. Partly through historical accident, this first stage of development also inscribed lasting social distinctions on the landscape. The DuSable-Kinzie house, the largest and most opulent of Chicago's early dwellings, established a long tradition of affluent residences on the NEAR NORTH SIDE, while the "Hardscrabble," a settlement of traders and fur company workers on the South Branch, represented the first in a long line of economically marginal but proud communities in that vicinity.

Speculation and Engineering, 1830–1880

The hallmark of the second stage, from the early 1830s to the period of postfire rebuilding in the 1870s, was an effort to reshape "natural" space, and the principal tools were political, economic, and technological. The initial events in this stage centered on the project to join the Mississippi River and Great Lakes watersheds by means of a canal. That project, first envisioned in the seventeenth century, moved from long-term dream to near-term likelihood between the early 1820s and 1836. A series of surveys by state-appointed canal commissioners culminated in the platting of Chicago by James Thompson in 1830, a preparatory step to development. The federal government contributed by surveying northeastern Illinois into townships and sections, and granting more than 280,000 acres within the proposed canal zone in subsidy of that project. Long before there was much substantive evidence of either the canal or the town, the precision of surveyed lines and grids imposed a matrix for the creation of speculative communities.

Speculation brought many new people to Chicago and created new roles for some old inhabitants. The most powerful actors in this new gridded landscape were of course those who had the means to deal in property, using either their own or other people's money. After the defeat of Black Hawk's rebellion in 1832, and especially after the opening of a federal land office in 1835, Chicago received a flood of investors, land dealers, and potential settlers. Old-timers like the Kinzies and newcomers like William B. Ogden scrambled to profit by platting "additions" to the original city or seizing control of potentially valuable "water lots" miles from the existing settlement—even in locations as far away as Calumet and SUMMIT. The formation of companies to build railroads expanded this pursuit, attracting attention to investment sites away from existing waterways. The timing of this speculative burst was full of implications for the city's future. When rail-based development came to older cities, even older interior cities such as Cincinnati or St. Louis, a large amount of capital and energy had already been invested in water-related facilities: levees, docks, shipyards, ropewalks, and the like. Remaking the fabric of the city to accommodate rail facilities involved either displacing or circumventing these established elements. Although Chicago also began life as a water-oriented town, the process of fitting the city around a railroad skeleton began almost immediately and with few obstacles, either man-made or natural. In this sense, the city was "born modern"—and also born to sprawl.

Even before canal construction started, the speculative process had created a development engine that radically accelerated Chicago's decentralization and shaped the building of neighborhoods for decades to come. Land speculation, of course, including speculation in urban land, was an old practice. Investors in many other American cities had grown rich buying undeveloped land and waiting for it to appreciate. But for individuals like John Jacob Astor in New York or Nicholas Longworth in Cincinnati, city land was a long-term investment, as development moved slowly outward from old mercantile cores. In Chicago, by contrast, both speculation and development went into hyperdrive and stayed there for several decades, with only a few short interruptions. Investors sought both short- and long-term gains, bought in many places at once, and did not wait for urban growth but pushed it in directions they wanted it to go. Profit depended on promotion, and thanks to elaborately embellished and colored maps, Chicago's imaginary landscape raced far in advance of reality. Yet the real city quickly caught up with the maps. Many successful promoters plowed their profits back into town building, constructing wharves and warehouses, and joining together to dredge the river and clear the large sandbar from its mouth. To finance such development in a capital-starved region, they created land companies as conduits for eastern investors. Outsiders, especially from New York, poured capital into Chicago as they never had into Cincinnati or St. Louis, and the urban development process was thus, from the beginning, tied into larger regional and national interests. Local entrepreneurs and builders spurred the growth process further through rapid adoption of innovations like the balloon frame method of quickly erecting houses and commercial structures. Chicago's relatively flat landscape encouraged not only intercity railroad but street railroad promoters; by 1880 the city was not only the midcontinental hub of the national rail system but also had local rail lines surpassed in mileage by only three of the older coastal metropolises. The whole process benefited, as older city growth had not, from federal largesse with land and federal policies of Indian removal.

The engine of city building was also an engine of subcommunity development. The result was that Chicago became not only the first of the nineteenth century's "instant cities" but also a city of instant neighborhoods. Despite local rivalries, such as the one that led North Sider William B. Ogden to complain that "all the business is going over to the other side," the overall effect was to create dozens of new and varied settlements in the 1830s through the 1860s. A few of these were residential promotions aimed at the prosperous elite—first near the city, as in the Near North Side island of gentility cultivated by the Ogdens, McCormicks, and Farwells; then farther out along the rail lines, as in Paul Cornell's development of HYDE PARK or Henry AUSTIN's investments in the suburb that bore his name. Other subcommunities were inadvertent creations near worksites along the river and the railways, such as the cluster near McCormick's Reaper Works or the dozens of later settlements around the stockyards. The process of sorting space according to its developmental potential—for residential, commercial, or industrial purposes—produced new geographic reference points and categories. Especially in promoting middle- and upper-income residential areas, entrepreneurs worked hard to attach their own labels to the collective mental landscape, as in Hyde Park, OAK PARK, and RAVENSWOOD. In other cases, new names arose from common usage, as in McCormickville, BACK OF THE YARDS, and the numerous "patches"—clumps of worker-immigrant settlement near major employment districts.

The arena of community-building activity was not coextensive with the built-up area or even the municipality. By the time of the 1871 fire, "Chicago" included not only the continuously developed area within about a mile of the river's mouth but also an array of residential suburbs, manufacturing communities, quarry villages, rail yard settlements, and market-gardening centers that merged gradually into the sprawling hinterland becoming linked by rail to the city. Historian William Cronon has shown how Chicago's metropolitan growth was symbiotic with a dramatic transformation of the environment for hundreds of miles around. In a more deliberate way, Chicagoans were also transforming the environment in and close to the city. Partly through necessity, partly through competitive zeal, Chicago's elite moved quickly to use new technology in refashioning the city, creating what Cronon calls "second nature" not only on the former prairies of Iowa but also in the former marshes of downtown. Beginning in the 1850s the city undertook a decades-long project of raising the grade of its streets to allow for the building of sewers. Under the guidance of engineer Ellis Chesbrough, Chicago became an internationally known experiment in water management. First in planning for drainage and then, in the 1860s, in the cutting-edge water supply system that drove a tunnel under Lake Michigan and set up the Water Tower and Pumping Station on the North Side, city authorities began a century-long process that would remake the hydrological profile of an area hundreds of square miles in extent.

All the features of Chicago's early development—sudden and massive investment in a flat landscape, the codevelopment of city and rail lines, entrepreneurial zeal for both community building and huge technological systems—encouraged a multicentered pattern of growth. Chicago did not just spread outward from its core, it grew as a region, with many scattered centers developing simultaneously and in connection. Peripheral centers that were eventually annexed, such as ANDERSONVILLE or Bridgeport, were initially developed in the speculative boom of the 1830s. Even outlying parts of the metropolitan complex—the North Shore suburbs, the canal towns to the southwest, the industrial centers near Calumet—are almost as old as the city itself.

Migrants and Community Building, 1840–1930

Developmental ventures attracted migrants who further diversified the city's geography. Alongside the highly visible engine of speculative development and engineering, there was another engine of ethnic and religious community formation. This second engine was less obvious than the first, but it would ultimately shape at least as much of the city's geography. And like the speculative engine it continued working well into the twentieth century, as the arena of city building and community making continued to expand. Canal, river, and railroad development gave birth to working-class and immigrant settlements, but the residents quickly became community builders in their own right. Near the old Hardscrabble area on the South Branch, the mostly Irish laborers who dug the canal created the community called Bridgeport, which would later attain legendary status in the city. Maritime workers on the canal, the river, and the lake fostered several raucous communities of boardinghouses and saloons on both sides of the South Branch near downtown, the most notorious of which was called Conley's Patch. Germans and Scandinavians who found work in the warehouses, shops, and breweries of the Near North Side established two zones of settlement, one between the North Branch and Wells Street, the other near the lake north of Chicago Avenue. In each of these cases, churches, taverns, clubs, and stores quickly followed, creating local cultures in which German, Norwegian, and Swedish mingled with English and compelling the city to hire interpreters for elections and at tax time. All of these developments were well under way by 1850, when the city was barely a decade old, and each of these communities in turn spawned more centers of ethnic life as these early immigrants sought work, land, and housing throughout the area. Other settlements—of French, Danish, Polish, German Jewish, and African American migrants—followed the same pattern in the 1840s and 1850s. By the time of the Civil War, Chicago was not only abloom with speculative additions, subdivisions, and suburbs but also displayed numerous overlapping ethnic clusters, each growing, each seeding its own centrifugal migration.

In the period between the fire of 1871 and the Great Depression, Chicago grew from a regional center to the second largest city in the country, the most important U.S. rail hub, the seat of many of the largest heavy industrial plants, and the destination for hundreds of thousands of European immigrants. The so-called new immigration of Southern, Eastern, and Central Europeans transformed the social geography of Chicago and most other great cities in the United States between 1880 and 1920, but it produced different effects in different places. Chicago was a prime

Maxwell Street, 1941. Photographer: Russell Lee. Source: Library of Congress.

destination for the new immigrants, receiving more of them than any other urban center except Manhattan and Brooklyn. Toward the end of this period some observers began circulating the idea that Chicago was home to more Poles than any city except Warsaw. This claim was not quite true: metropolitan New York City, whose two million immigrants nearly equaled the total population of Chicago by 1910, had more citizens of Polish birth, as it did members of most other immigrant groups. But Chicago did have more Poles than any one of New York's five boroughs, and it had larger communities of Czechs, Lithuanians, Swedes, Danes, and Luxembourgers than any city in the country. What's more, the still-powerful cultural and institutional legacy of earlier immigrants—Irish, Germans, Scandinavians—made Chicago's blend of old and new hyphenated communities distinctive. New York City was the mecca of new immigrants; Milwaukee, a stronghold of old; Chicago had huge numbers of both.

The expansion of heavy industry and the flood of newcomers introduced new varieties of community building that affected the entire metropolitan area. On the edges of the old city, the super rich of the 1870s and 1880s promoted three new concentrations of mansions. They followed the leadership of Marshall Field on Prairie Avenue, Potter Palmer on Lake Shore Drive, and Samuel J. Walker along Ashland Avenue on the West Side. Meanwhile, the prohibition of wood-frame buildings in the city's core, imposed after the 1871 fire, encouraged new construction at the outskirts to house the flood of working-class newcomers. The result was a wide belt of small dwellings stretching from the OLD TOWN area on the Near North Side through the NEAR WEST SIDE to the stockyards, Bridgeport, and the Black Belt south of the Loop. Within this belt were many clusters, old and new. Beyond, stretching out along the still-growing street rail lines on Lincoln, Milwaukee, Lake, Taylor, and Ogden, were more clusters of new settlement, housing slightly more prosperous immigrants and their descendants. On the far South Side, industrial satellites appeared at PULLMAN, in the steel complex at the mouth of the Calumet River, and eventually in the huge manufacturing district stretching southeast into Indiana.

In a pattern that echoed earlier themes, speculative developers like Samuel Gross fueled the engine of geographic mobility by tailoring clusters of new homes for various pocketbooks. Subsequently the engine of cultural creativity enriched the new spaces with churches, schools, and other institutions that made them special places for this or that kind of people. By the late nineteenth century, the skyline was dotted with steeples—still evident today in older areas of ethnic settlement—which served as markers of the complex, interpenetrating, multilingual array of devotional communities that Chicagoans created in this greatest surge of the city's growth. Especially for Roman Catholics (then and now a large segment of the population), but to some extent for Lutherans and others, the proliferation of parishes and congregations provided the most important framework of spatial orientation and loyalty in the city for a century after the fire.

The same great surge of growth between fire and Depression produced another kind of community whose influence on the history of the city has been even stronger and more lasting than that of the immigrant clusters: the enormous and geographically isolated African American ghetto on the South Side. Popular accounts often trace the "Black Belt" to the Great Migration of the World War I era, but its history is far longer and more complicated. The three major areas of African American residence in Chicago, one in each division of the city, all trace their origins to tiny prefire settlements that once resembled those of many other migrants. They were primarily communities of manual workers who lived near rail yards, industrial centers, or wealthy neighborhoods where they could find employment as "hands" or as domestic workers. The South Side community was always the biggest, and like other migrant settlements it had its institutions, most notably, in the early years, Quinn Chapel AME church. Even before the Great Migration, the explosive growth of the late nineteenth century brought many thousands of black newcomers to Chicago and boosted the population of the South Side community to well over 40,000 by 1910. In the following two decades, at least another 70,000 arrived from the South, swelling and crowding the South Side black community just as white resistance to African Americans as neighbors made it the most ethnically homogeneous and isolated district in the history of Chicago.

Cellular Mapping, 1880–1940

The growing complexity of Chicago's social geography was accompanied by a growing series of efforts at simplified description. Already in the 1850s newspaper articles occasionally exaggerated and caricatured the homogeneity and cultural isolation of Irish and German communities. In 1881 veteran reporter F. B. Wilkie, his tongue lodged firmly in his cheek, published an apocalyptic vision of Chicago in 1906. His city of the future was divided into two huge sections, "Teutonia" on the north and "Hibernia" to the south, separated by a 60-foot east-west wall down the middle of Madison Street. One very small section of English speakers, called "First Ward," occupied the area of the Loop. Other journalists, then and later, played up the activities of street gangs in defining and defending ethnic turf, and all of these writings worked to produce one of the lasting myths of Chicago's geography: the notion of stable, segregated, homogeneous, cellular ethnic neighborhoods.

Astute writers (including Wilkie) knew that the reality of Chicago's social geography was more complicated, and recent scholarship has emphasized that complexity. With the notable exception of the African American (and for a time the Italian) communities, Chicago's ethnic clusters were shaped more by internal affinities than by distinctions from other groups. They were more centered than bounded. Locales were mixed, and most communities were dynamic—spreading, shrinking, hiving off pieces, changing with generations. To describe this dynamism, Robert Park, Ernest Burgess, and other scholars of the "Chicago School" of sociology popularized the idea of "neighborhood succession," in which newer and poorer groups inherit neighborhoods left behind as more successful citizens seek better housing farther from the center.

Given all the evidence of complexity, the tendency toward cellular thinking becomes in itself a thing to be explained, and a piece of Chicago's distinctive version of multicenteredness. It was not just journalists who contributed to the vision of an urban mosaic. Beginning in the 1890s, philanthropists, scholars, and settlement house workers focused renewed public attention on certain "new immigrant" districts within the sprawling belt of worker housing. Between 1895 and 1936 Florence Kelley, Edith Abbott, and Sophonisba Breckinridge produced a series of publications, based on research that began at Hull House and continued using students from the University of Chicago's School of Social Service Administration, that graphically mapped conditions in many districts around the city. Although these researchers knew and appreciated the city's complexity, their color-coded maps and colorful descriptions of national cultures had the effect of attaching ethnic labels to the neatly delineated localities on their maps. The same sociologists who stressed "neighborhood succession" also helped to crystallize the notion of cells by promoting the idea that large cities are made up of "natural areas" separated by lasting physical boundaries. Robert Park, in what was probably a casual remark, produced a phrase that would take on a life of its own when he referred to a "mosaic of little worlds." In one of academia's most dramatic contributions to the imagined landscape of any city, these scholars established the "community areas" that have served as tools of both valuable analysis and misleading simplification since the 1920s.

For some ordinary Chicagoans, other kinds of cellular thinking gained importance in this period, sometimes with tragic results. By the Depression, the South Side Black Belt was already the anomalous extreme case among Chicago's subcommunities. When a still larger migration came after World War II, a similar community sprawled across the West Side, and by the late twentieth century Chicago's million-plus African Americans were probably the most segregated large urban population in the nation's history. These two black communities were at once the nearest approximation of the mythic mosaic cell *and* the geographic element against which many other communities defined themselves. The parallel institutions of the African American community—businesses, churches, entertainment centers—made it a vital matrix of innovation not only for black Chicagoans but for African Americans nationwide.

Yet the innovations fostered by the ghetto were double-edged. As it grew, whites honed new methods of confinement. Some of these were political. A governing system based on 50 independent wards encouraged the building of the legendary Democratic Party organization, assembled slowly starting in the time of Mayor Anton Cermak and perfected by Richard J. Daley. Thousands of political workers and city employees were bonded to precinct and ward organizations run by powerful aldermen, who spread largesse strategically within their wards and carefully monitored voter turnout at election time. Until the 1960s this was a system dominated by white males, with black participation limited to those few wards where African Americans were the majority. For the huge proportion of Chicago's white population that was Catholic, parish boundaries became defensive lines as the growing African American population sought housing in new areas. A parallel process occurred within school districts, which, like wards and parishes, became battlegrounds in the racial struggles that played a central role in Chicago's geographic evolution from the 1940s through the 1960s. When Martin Luther King Jr. declared, in 1966, that he had never encountered Chicago's kind of racism in the South, he was commenting indirectly on the passions engendered by battles over particular and multiple kinds of urban territory.

Elite Community Redevelopment, 1940–2000

Although Daniel Burnham, in the planning arena, and Anton Cermak, in the political, each had a broad vision of Chicago's future, it was the Great Depression, more
than any individual vision, that opened the way for those with money and power
to remake the city. From the mid-1930s through the 1960s, the availability of federal subsidies allowed public agencies to "modernize" Chicago through slum clearance, the construction of expressways, and the building of public housing projects, all of which had more extensive and dramatic (as well as controversial) consequences for Chicago than for most other large cities. From the start, private actors—neighborhood groups, hospitals, universities, and developers—played large
roles in shaping the redevelopment process. From the 1970s on, into the beginning
of the twenty-first century, private initiatives, especially those of developers, out-
stripped public ones in clearance and redevelopment. The combined effect of this
public and private activity was to erase whole areas of the older city and to create
a new armature for spatial thinking and investment. Elements of the city's geography that were once highly visible and widely known—Little Italy, GREEKTOWN,
MAXWELL STREET—were either vanished or vestigial by the end of the twentieth
century. Taking their place in the collective spatial consciousness are labels that
had no meaning before the Depression: CABRINI-GREEN, River North, the GAP.

Like the creation of Chicago in the early nineteenth century, the remaking of
Chicago in the late twentieth involved a particular combination of vigorous local initiatives with large trends beyond the city. Just as the city's greatest growth
spurt coincided with the rise of railroads and heavy industry, the post–World War
II transformation coincided with the rise of interstate highways and a decentralized manufacturing economy. A truck-based growth pattern and a mass hunger for
suburban housing led to a drain of both jobs and people from the city into an ever-
expanding belt of suburbs. Throughout the second half of the century the suburbs
grew at a faster rate than the city, which suffered net population declines in every
postwar decade except the 1990s.

The atrophy of Chicago's enormous rail facilities, steel mills, and meatpacking
plants and the relocation of many factories to the distant suburbs were at the same
time a stimulus to and a prerequisite for the redevelopment of space. Just as the greatest European exodus brought new residents to Chicago during its rise to Second City
status—when Chicago was the gateway to the West and at the cutting edge of rail- and
industry-based growth—the greatest migrations of African Americans, Latinos, and
Asians came during deindustrialization, when the leading edge of industrial growth
had moved out of the city and to some extent out of the Midwest.

Two huge demographic trends—the shift of white Chicagoans to the suburbs and the rise of what scholars call a "spatial mismatch" between job creation on the fringe and the growth of a job-needy population in the core—set the stage for community building after 1950. Led by Mayor Richard J. Daley, postwar civic and business figures focused on the drain of tax dollars and attacked the problem through large-scale planning: creating O'Hare Airport and annexing it to the city, and clearing "blighted" districts. They also began a tradition of encouraging high-end private developments, from Arthur Rubloff's SANDBURG VILLAGE to the condominium and town house complexes on old railroad land near the Loop. These measures, which preserved more vitality in central Chicago than in most old industrial cities, were intertwined with other, more damaging policies. Alarmed by the drain of white population, city officials and private organizations cooperated in reinforcing racial segregation into the 1960s, most notably by building the "second ghetto" of high-rise public housing.

In the last decade of the twentieth century, the second Mayor Daley led yet another wave of elite redevelopment, intended in part to correct the unfortunate consequences of many earlier activities. The hallmark of this effort has been the rapid destruction of most of the high-rise public housing and the promotion of mixed-income communities instead. Like so many previous community developments, this one has been shaped by the continuing pressures of speculation in land, by shifts in the currents of migration, by a tendency to think big, by the vigorous and vocal involvement of local populations, and by intense controversy. As in so many earlier steps, Chicago is distinctive—taking bigger actions than any other city, attracting national attention, and once again remaking its social landscape.

No single feature of Chicago's social geography is unique: not the flat setting, not the immigrants, not the industry, not the politics, not the racial conflict, not the urge to plan. It is in *how* and *when* the prominent features of Chicago's development came together, and how they interacted, that the city's distinctiveness lies. Between 1850 and 1930, in a city sprawling as no city ever had, Chicago produced hundreds of new communities, most of them tangled together physically but having clear and strong integrity in the minds of their residents. As the Irish and the Germans and the Italians and Jews moved outward—and, for so very long, the African Americans did not—both the real and the imagined localities exerted a powerful influence on the unfolding and changing meaning of "neighborhood" to the citizens. There has always been more than one Chicago in this location on the lake, and the metropolis that residents celebrate and visitors acclaim today is a product, a synthesis, not only of the many Chicagos of today but of all those that came before.

FURTHER READING: An exploration of Chicago's communities should begin with the development of Chicago's larger physical and economic setting. Two works by geographers are fundamental: Irving Cutler, *Chicago: Metropolis of the Mid-Continent*, 3rd ed. (1982); and Michael P.

Conzen, "The American Urban System in the Nineteenth Century," in *Geography and the Urban Environment*, ed. D. Herbert and R. J. Johnston (1981). On the way metropolitan Chicago's earliest communities grew in this setting, see Edward Ranney et al., *Prairie Passage: The Illinois and Michigan Canal Corridor* (1998), and *Studies on the Illinois and Michigan Canal Corridor* (1987–1994), a fine series of books on the canal towns edited by Michael Conzen et al. Chicago's evolving relationship with an extended hinterland is the subject of William Cronon, *Nature's Metropolis: Chicago and the Great West* (1991).

The best starting place for study of entrepreneurial development is still Homer Hoyt, *One Hundred Years of Land Values in Chicago: The Relationship of the Growth of Chicago to the Rise in Its Land Values, 1830–1933* (1933). Also essential are Ann Durkin Keating, *Building Chicago: Suburban Developers and the Creation of a Divided Metropolis* (1988), and Michael H. Ebner, *Creating Chicago's North Shore* (1988). Carl W. Condit provided a valuable if opinionated overview of twentieth-century growth in his two volumes *Chicago, 1910–29: Building, Planning, and Urban Technology* (1973) and *Chicago, 1930–70: Building, Planning, and Urban Technology* (1974).

The shaping of small areas by European immigrants and southern African Americans is a theme in many of the works already mentioned. Two useful gateways to more detailed information on settlement by particular groups are Melvin G. Holli and Peter d'A. Jones, *Ethnic Chicago: A Multicultural Portrait*, 4th ed. (1995), and Dominic A. Pacyga and Ellen Skerrett, *Chicago, City of Neighborhoods: Histories and Tours* (1986). Particularly valuable in showing how work patterns and class relations influenced communities are William Kornblum, *Blue Collar Community* (1974); and Lizabeth Cohen, *Making a New Deal: Industrial Workers in Chicago, 1919–1939* (1990). An old but excellent summary of the early growth of Chicago's African American community is to be found in St. Clair Drake and Horace R. Cayton, *Black Metropolis: A Study of Negro Life in a Northern City* (1945). Among many works on the twentieth-century sharpening of racial lines and the building of the African American communities are Thomas Lee Philpott, *The Slum and the Ghetto: Neighborhood Deterioration and Middle-Class Reform, Chicago, 1880–1930* (1978); James R. Grossman, *Land of Hope: Chicago, Black Southerners, and the Great Migration* (1989); John T. McGreevy, *Parish Boundaries: The Catholic Encounter with Race in the Twentieth-Century Urban North* (1996); Arnold R. Hirsch, *Making the Second Ghetto: Race and Housing in Chicago, 1940–1960* (1983); Adam P. Green, *Selling the Race: Culture, Community, and Black Chicago, 1940–1955* (2007); and Amanda I. Seligman, *Block by Block: Neighborhoods and Public Policy on Chicago's West Side* (2005).

Insights into the ways Chicagoans both created a cellular model for thinking about the city and transgressed the imagined "boxes" in their everyday lives may be obtained from Harvey Warren Zorbaugh, *The Gold Coast and the Slum: A Sociological Study of Chicago's Near North Side* (1929); Albert Hunter, *Symbolic Communities: The Persistence and Change of Chicago's Local Communities* (1974); Perry Duis, *Challenging Chicago: Coping with Everyday Life, 1837–1920* (1998); Carl Smith, *Urban Disorder and the Shape of Belief: The Great Chicago Fire, the Haymarket Bomb, and the Model Town of Pullman* (1995); and Robin F. Bachin, *Building the South Side: Urban Space and Civic Culture in Chicago, 1890–1919* (2004).

CONTESTED SPACES

JANICE L. REIFF

Sunday, July 27, 1919, dawned hot in Chicago. As the day wore on, city dwellers crowded onto the beaches lining Lake Michigan seeking relief from the heat. Late that afternoon, 17-year-old Eugene Williams dove off a raft that had wandered toward the 29th Street beach. The African American teenager was unaware of a confrontation that had occurred earlier that day when black Chicagoans had walked into a space conventionally limited to whites. Spotting him in the water, a group of bathers began throwing stones at Williams, who struggled, disappeared, and drowned. As news of his death spread, further violence erupted on the beach, then radiated out from it. Four days of rioting followed, engulfing large sections of the city. When the violence subsided, 38 persons were dead, 537 were injured, and over 1,000 were left homeless.

Sometime late on the night of Williams's death, *Chicago Tribune* cartoonist John T. McCutcheon sketched two groups of Lake Michigan bathers, one white and the other black, facing off across a rope. The divisions in Chicago between areas understood to be black and those seen as white were not as formally drawn as in the Jim Crow South. Nonetheless, informal segregation was common, reflecting the changing racial boundaries of the neighborhoods nearby. The beach near where Williams drowned, not officially maintained by the city, was widely used and hotly contested. Between the "white" beach and a "black" beach immediately to the north lay an invisible line in the sand and water, a line that Williams crossed and that McCutcheon gave graphic form in his powerful cartoon. In the aftermath of the riots, the Chicago City Council considered codifying that line through a proposed ordinance that read, in part,

> Resolved that a commission composed of members of both races be formed for the purpose of investigating the causes of the recent riots and to ascertain if it is possible to equitably fix a zone or zones which shall be created for the purpose of limiting within its borders the residences to only colored or white persons.

The ordinance did not pass, but much of white Chicago hardened its commitment to racial separation in daily life, especially as the city's black population swelled

The color line has reached the north.

Cartoon by John T. McCutcheon, *Chicago Tribune,* July 28, 1919. Artist: John T. McCutcheon. Source: Chicago Tribune.

with continued migration from the South. Ongoing demands by black Chicagoans for equality ensured that the city's racial boundaries would remain sites of negotiation and conflict.

Contests over space in the Chicago region both predated and long outlived Eugene Williams's fateful swim. In 1812, struggles between peoples—the United States, Great Britain, and various Indian nations—who viewed the western Great Lakes in starkly different ways led to the abandonment of a fort on the banks of the Chicago River and the loss of life on the site that has since become the PRAIRIE AVENUE Historic District. That contest, familiarly known as the Fort Dearborn Massacre, became the city's foundational event, memorialized by one of the four stars on the city's flag. Throughout Chicago's history, spatial contestation has encompassed a wide variety of issues, from race relations to divergent views on land use. Chicagoans, like residents of other cities, have divided over all aspects of urban space, from how it is planned, to how it is experienced in everyday life, to the less tangible question of how it is perceived.

Twenty-five years before Williams died, Pullman workers provided a vivid example of how conflict could grow out of vastly different understandings of a space. From its inception in 1880, the planned community of PULLMAN was carefully advertised and widely accepted as a solution for various ills that made many of Chicago's working-class neighborhoods unpleasant and even dangerous areas in which to live. With its attractive brick buildings and numerous amenities, Pullman seemed an ideal home for workers and their families. To many who lived there, however, it was less a well-designed ideal than a paternalistic nightmare. As one worker explained:

We are born in a Pullman house, cradled in a Pullman crib, paid from a Pullman store, taught in a Pullman school, confirmed in a Pullman church, exploited in a

Pullman shop, and when we die we'll be buried in a Pullman grave and go to a Pull-man hell. (*Chicago Evening Journal*, February 16, 1918)

These divergent understandings of Pullman not only helped to launch a strike in May 1894; they also served as critical elements in the progress of the strike and the subsequent fate of the town.

To those who perceived the town as the Pullman Company portrayed it, the workers' demands seemed inappropriate at best and ungrateful at worst. Strikers, on the other hand, sought support by articulating their vision of Pullman's space to visiting delegates from the American Railway Union and anyone else willing to listen, including state officials, who eventually forced the Pullman Company to sell the town.

These two perspectives on Pullman demonstrate how different the same space can look to various observers, and the implications of such differences. But Pull-man, like other working-class neighborhoods tied to nearby employment, also provides a stark contrast to a very different kind of community—bedroom sub-urbs like PARK FOREST, where William Hollingsworth Whyte profiled the world of the classic "Organization Man" in the 1950s. For residents of Pullman, work, home, and even leisure were located in a relatively small geographic area that included the company town and parts of nearby communities. Men and women spent their days in different workspaces but shared a social geography. In Park Forest, by con-trast, the everyday space of many male residents included offices in downtown Chi-cago and the commuter trains that brought them there, while their wives' everyday space was more likely to be limited to the suburb itself.

Though few have been as violent as that of 1919, contests over space have been a consistent part of Chicago's history. Some have been ongoing, created by legal requirements, social differences, environmental factors, or the real-estate market, with its pressure for ever more space and rising values. Others have been shorter lived, the product of a particular issue or climate. Some have been largely symbol-ic, with practical effects reaching far beyond the metropolitan region. Many have simmered for a long time before coming to the public's attention, sometimes qui-etly, sometimes dramatically. This essay provides one way of thinking about met-ropolitan space by contemplating spatial contests across a variety of arenas—polit-ical, economic, social, and environmental. To a much greater degree than physical places, spaces are not static: space changes as planned uses, actual uses, and the meanings associated with those uses compete and evolve.

Government at all levels is instrumental in both defining and planning space. Even after early contests about how states and counties would organize the place that became metropolitan Chicago were resolved, various governmental units

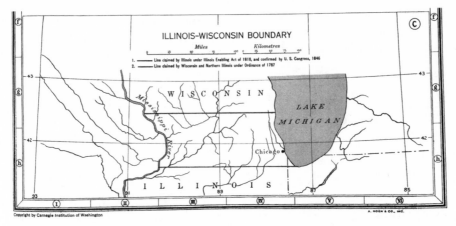

The changing Illinois-Wisconsin boundary line. Cartographer: Charles O. Paullin. Source: The Newberry Library.

continued to divide the physical space into sometimes competing entities. A property tax bill readily indicates the number of overlapping agencies (park districts, school districts, special districts, sanitation districts) that have evolved to govern metropolitan space. During the early years of the Great Depression, the taxes demanded by those different entities led to a short-lived tax strike that spread from the metropolitan region across the state and left the city of Chicago in even more desperate financial straits. Zoning is perhaps the classic twentieth-century example of governmental definition of urban space. Invoking eminent domain to redefine the uses of particular spaces for community needs like expressways and public institutions is another.

Congressional districts and city wards are two sets of political spaces that change according to law and custom. Seats in the U.S. House of Representatives are reapportioned every 10 years to reflect population changes, and when states gain or lose seats, congressional districts must be redrawn. Throughout most of the nineteenth century and the first decades of the twentieth, Illinois gained population and seats. Chicago was growing especially rapidly—its population accounting for almost a third of the total Illinois population—and downstate legislators feared the city's potential influence in state politics. One way to limit that power was to draw boundaries that created congressional districts of roughly equal space, albeit of very unequal population. Beginning with the redistricting following the 1870 census, and continuing for nearly a century, that strategy—and a similar strategy applied to state legislative districts—ensured that Chicago's political influence would not keep pace with its population.

Even as the state emphasized territory, city leaders fastened on a different formula for the organization of wards and representation in the city council. As class and ethnic pockets grew and shaped affiliations to political issues and parties, ward lines began to follow the perceived socioeconomic boundaries of the city's neighborhoods. As wards grew geographically smaller and came to be represented by one council member rather than two, and as patterns of residential clustering and segregation sharpened, individual wards came to be seen as the domain of particular groups and parties. In the first half of the twentieth century, wards provided ethnic and racial groups with access to political power and added to the importance of neighborhoods in the fight for resources.

In 1962 the U.S. Supreme Court ruled in *Baker v. Carr* that districting schemes allowing huge discrepancies in population were unconstitutional. New contests over redistricting soon erupted as different political players tried to maximize their "clout" through the old practice of gerrymandering—drawing political boundaries to enhance the voting strength of one group at the expense of others. Reapportionment has since become hotly contested; political parties have sought to manipulate legislative boundaries to improve their electoral chances, interest groups have worked to secure or preserve an electoral voice, and incumbents have placed a priority on retaining their seats.

If politicians have shaped and reshaped space to determine the distribution of power, others in government have shaped perceptions and realities of how people inhabit particular spaces—and how much those habitations are worth. Between 1935 and 1940, the Home Owners' Loan Corporation, a federal agency established in 1933, conducted a massive survey to determine current and future values of real estate to help lenders decide which neighborhoods would be good lending targets. Surveyors visited neighborhoods, consulted local institutions, and filed reports that assigned ratings of "A," "B," "C," or "D" to each community surveyed. An "A" or "B" rating encouraged lenders, a "C" discouraged them, and a "D" ensured that residential lending would virtually disappear, an outcome known as "redlining."

Although not applied uniformly across the country, these ratings were applied in Chicago and elsewhere in ways that reinforced existing prejudices and practices. Older neighborhoods, built before central heating and modern plumbing, were flagged as poor targets for the new long-term mortgages and for home improvement loans to be guaranteed by the federal government. So too were neighborhoods experiencing ethnic or racial change, "mixed" neighborhoods, and neighborhoods whose older industries had closed or moved to new suburban locations. Newer, more homogenous, and more well-to-do neighborhoods received high marks. By 1939 most residential space in the Chicago metropolitan area had been surveyed and rated, and after World War II the ratings helped to shape a new residential geography. Mortgage money flowed into new developments in the suburbs and, to a more limited extent, into the city's "A" and sometimes "B" communities.

"C" communities were deemed risky bets for lenders, neighborhoods that might be improved but might also fall into the category of "blighted." "D" communities were dismissed as already blighted. Such classifications shaped perceptions of, experiences in, and planning for those spaces for decades. They helped to stimulate the postwar boom in the suburbs and outlying areas of the city, and to shape the contours of urban renewal, encouraging white Chicagoans in the belief that the presence of African Americans lowered property values and providing tacit support for agencies to limit residential lending in mixed and African American neighborhoods.

By the 1960s Chicago had become a symbol of the problems associated with spatial segregation and the efforts to dismantle it, a status highlighted in 1966 by the Chicago Freedom Movement. Local civil rights leaders invited Martin Luther King Jr. to lead a fight for open housing in Chicago and to help dismantle the formal and informal practices that had made the city the most racially segregated in the nation: for Chicago to achieve some kind of neighborhood racial parity, 9 of 10 white Chicagoans or 9 of 10 black Chicagoans would have had to move within the city. From NORTH LAWNDALE (where King took an apartment) to Soldier Field and City Hall (where protesters demanded open housing), city spaces became sites of contests over space. The most infamous of these was surely the clash at the border of MARQUETTE PARK, where hostile whites screaming racial epithets at marchers protesting the practices of real-estate agents helped mold a new image of working-class ethnic whites. No image was stronger than that of King bleeding from the forehead after being struck by a brick thrown by a white demonstrator.

A different kind of contest over space, relating more to its use in the past, has taken place in metropolitan Chicago's industrial districts. From the unwelcome stench of Chicago's sewage in cities like LOCKPORT, downstream after the Chicago River changed direction, to the polluted air that contributed to the respiratory problems of all who lived downwind from a steel mill or a chemical plant, concerns over the environment have produced their own conflicts. For generations, many of the region's industries created toxic waste and pollutants along with their products and the jobs necessary to create them. The pages of Upton Sinclair's *The Jungle* are filled with vivid descriptions of such pollution in and around the stockyards, from the canning room floors to the banks of "Bubbly Creek." Over time, pollutants built up, devastating the land in and around the plants, tainting nearby water sources, and filling the air with particulate matter. Assumptions about the degraded nature of those spaces combined with zoning regulations to encourage the nearby placement of further environmental threats such as landfills. For much of the last half of the nineteenth century and first half of the twentieth, pollution was taken for granted as a fact of industrialization and a characteristic of working-class life, both on the job and at homes near the plants. A community newspaper described the drive down the Calumet Expressway in 1964, from 103rd to the city limits, as "a path only for the strong of stomach."

As these areas deteriorated, the surrounding neighborhoods changed as well. As industrial wages improved with unionization, many workers at the plants moved away from the worst of the pollution, leaving their former homes available for families that, because of discriminatory practices or limited incomes, had fewer housing choices. Business patterns also took their toll. As industries started to close, communities from WAUKEGAN to MICHIGAN CITY were economically devastated. Activists, union leaders, and politicians responded by launching local and national programs for environmental justice. Plans for transforming "brownfields," the Environmental Preservation Agency's designation for the most polluted of these spaces, involved both removing the most toxic pollutants and bringing in new activities that might help sustain the neighborhoods around them.

As the image of the active smokestack, once the sign of a productive space promising lucrative employment, has come to be associated with industrial pollution, Chicagoans have become accustomed to contested spaces on the ground generating equally fierce debates about the air above their homes. When, in 1947, Chicago planners decided that Municipal Airport (Midway) could not meet the future demands of air traffic (local residents had already begun to protest the noise), the city began developing O'Hare International Airport and, in 1956, annexed it to the city. In the decades since, developers and urban growth have transformed the former farmland to the city's northwest, little disturbed by the air traffic, into expensive residential suburbs greatly bothered by ceaseless jet noise. The political climate has also changed as suburbs have developed new clout and noise has become an issue for government regulation. Not-in-my-back-yard (or NIMBY) campaigns in the neighborhoods around O'HARE have become powerful enough to contest the will of the city of Chicago. As a result, further O'Hare expansion has been caught up in complicated negotiations between Chicago, O'Hare's nearby suburbs, and more distant locations like Peotone and Springfield, Illinois, GARY and Indianapolis, Indiana, and even Washington, D.C.

What constitutes "success" for a given space can thus mean something different to its residents, planners, and developers. This is clearest in the case of urban gentrification, but it can also be witnessed in rural areas. In Kane and McHenry Counties, efforts are under way to preserve farms and farmlands from the seemingly unrelenting spread of residential, commercial, and industrial development. Interested in maintaining a way of life and a historical identity, as well as managing the inevitable demands of growing populations, residents of those counties have

Richard Brummel harvesting soybeans on one of the last farms in the Naperville area, October 2000. Photographer: Mario Petitti. Source: Chicago Tribune.

come together to limit development. Standing in sharp opposition to this movement are developers and farm owners who know that homes and businesses make their acreage far more valuable than do soybeans or corn.

Although this contest on the outer edges of the metropolitan area may seem very different from other struggles over space, it is part of an ongoing contest that began with the settlement of Chicago itself. The contest between rural and urban space is as important a part of the city's experience as the struggles over race and ethnicity, which themselves often involve contested boundaries. All of these struggles have involved planned spaces, perceptions about kinds of spaces, and historical uses of space, and have had much to do with how people use their space.

FURTHER READING: Much has been written about urban space and about Chicago's specific contests over space. The most important sources for this essay were Henri Lefebvre, *The Production of Space* (1974; English translation by Donald Nicholson-Smith, 1991); Kevin Lynch, *The Image of the City* (1980); and the many works of David Harvey, especially *Social Justice and the City* (1973). These texts must, however, be considered in light of the rich scholarship produced by the Chicago School, which helped to introduce space as an important issue for understanding cities. See especially Louis Wirth, "Urbanism as a Way of Life," *American Journal of Sociology* 44.1 (1938): 1–24; Ernest W. Burgess, "The Growth of the City: An Introduction to a Research Project," in Robert E. Park and Ernest W. Burgess, eds., *The City* (1926); and more recent scholarship such as Albert Hunter, *Symbolic Communities: The Persistence and Change of Chicago's Local Communities* (1974), Gerald D. Suttles, *The Social Construction of Communities* (1972), and the many works of Brian J. L. Berry.

For more on particular topics in this essay, see Allen H. Spear, *Black Chicago: The Making of a Negro Ghetto, 1890–1920* (1967); William M. Tuttle, *Race Riot: Chicago in the Red Summer of 1919* (1972); Chicago Commission on Race Relations, *The Negro in Chicago: A Study of Race Relations and a Race Riot in 1919* (1922); Janice L. Reiff, "Rethinking Pullman: Urban Space and Working

Class Activism," *Social Science History* 24.1 (2000): 7–32; William H. Whyte, *The Organization Man* (1956); Edward C. Banfield, *Political Influence* (1961); Ross Miller, *Here's the Deal: The Buying and Selling of a Great American City* (1996); Anna J. Merritt, ed., *Redistricting: An Exercise in Prophecy* (1982); Gail Radford, *Modern Housing for America: Policy Struggles in the New Deal Era* (1996); Kenneth T. Jackson, *Crabgrass Frontier: The Suburbanization of the United States* (1985); Donald Alexander Downs, *Nazis in Skokie: Freedom, Community, and the First Amendment* (1985); James Ralph, *Northern Protest: Martin Luther King, Jr., Chicago, and the Civil Rights Movement* (1993); David J. Garrow, ed., *Chicago 1966* (1989); Felix M. Padilla, *Puerto Rican Chicago* (1987); Andrew Hurley, *Environmental Inequalities: Class, Race, and Industrial Pollution in Gary, Indiana, 1945–1980* (1995); David N. Pellow, *Garbage Wars: The Struggle for Environmental Justice in Chicago* (2002); Arnold R. Hirsch, *Making the Second Ghetto: Race and Housing in Chicago, 1940–1960* (1985); and the *Journal of Urban History* 29.3 (2003), a special issue devoted to Hirsch's book.

ECONOMIC GEOGRAPHY

SUSAN E. HIRSCH

American cities grow or decline because of their roles in the national economy. The village of Chicago became the country's second largest city in 1889 because it captured many of the fastest-growing sectors of that economy. Businessmen and politicians enhanced Chicago's geographical position at the eastern edge of the nation's agricultural heartland, making it the center of multiple transportation networks. These networks supported wholesale trade and manufacturing, which spurred the city's growth. Industry determined the physical development of the city itself, preempting space for zones of commerce and manufacturing and channeling the expansion of residential neighborhoods. During the twentieth century, new economic trends undermined Chicago's position; decentralization favored suburbs over cities, and the rise of the South and West created new centers of competition for the most dynamic sectors of the economy.

Chicago developed because its site was convenient for commerce. For hundreds of years, American Indians gathered each summer to trade where the Chicago River enters Lake Michigan. In 1673 the French explorer Louis Jolliet recognized Chicago's potential for wider trade: it sits on a low divide between the drainage areas of the Great Lakes and the Mississippi River, and only one large portage breaks an all-water route between Lake Michigan and the Gulf of Mexico via the Chicago, Des Plaines, Illinois, and Mississippi Rivers. During the rainy season, the "Chicago portage" between the Chicago and Des Plaines Rivers could be traversed by canoe. Jolliet suggested cutting a canal across this portage to link the Gulf and French Canada, but French officials ignored him.

Chicago's first permanent resident, Jean Baptiste Point de Sable, settled near the mouth of the Chicago River in the late 1780s to take advantage of this geography to trade with the Indians. In 1795 the new United States government also recognized the site's potential and acquired a piece of land, six miles square around the mouth of the river, by treaty with the Indians. Fort Dearborn, erected in 1803, secured the site for Americans. Trading eastern manufactured goods for furs established a base for Chicago's economy, consistent with de Sable's more limited enterprise. After 1819 the American Fur Company, headed by John Jacob Astor in New York, monopolized the fur trade of Chicago and the Great Lakes region. From this point, Chicago's economy was tied to national and international markets and financing. By the late 1820s overhunting had depleted the game of Illinois, and the American Fur Company left Chicago for points farther west. Rather than wither, however, the village of fewer than a hundred residents began a rapid expansion as others saw new opportunities in the site.

National business and political leaders created the conditions for the rise of Chicago. When New York's Erie Canal connected the Great Lakes to the Atlantic Ocean in 1825, they recognized the need for a port at the western end of the lakes to serve the potential trade with the new settlers who were developing the country's western territories. Eastern businessmen and Illinois politicians revived Jolliet's vision of connecting the lakes to the Mississippi through Chicago, and in 1829 state legislators began planning the Illinois & Michigan Canal. For easterners to settle northern Illinois, however, the Indians had to be dispossessed. In 1833 the federal government pressured the united Potawatomi, Chippewa, and Ottawa nations to cede all their lands east of the Mississippi River, opening the path for easterners to seek their fortunes in northern Illinois.

Chicago had no natural harbor, but the sandbar at the mouth of the Chicago River created a sheltered spot for boats. The river became a federal harbor in 1834, when government aid for cutting a channel across the bar, constructing piers, and dredging made the river into the port of Chicago. The state authorized construction of a canal in 1836, and bonds sold well to eastern capitalists. Starting in the mid-1830s, Chicago developed as a transfer point—shipping Midwestern agricultural products to New York and eastern manufactured goods to farmers on the plains.

Many people came to Chicago to engage in this trade. Others came because they believed a city would develop around the port. Real-estate speculation fueled town development in nineteenth-century America and was an important avenue to wealth. Speculation in Chicago real estate boomed in 1835 in anticipation of the construction of the canal. Several thousand people, including many New Yorkers, migrated to the city. William B. Ogden, Chicago's first mayor, came to oversee a relative's real-estate investments and bolstered their value by developing transportation facilities. He promoted the first swing bridge to span the Chicago River and link the North and South Sides of the city. In 1836 he helped found Chicago's first railroad, the Galena & Chicago Union, to connect the Great Lakes port to the lead mining center on the Mississippi.

Still other Chicagoans established factories to process the farm produce and natural resources that were shipped to the city. In 1829 Archibald Clybourne began meatpacking, and a lumber mill settled near his factory on the North Branch

Grain elevators and cargo ships on the Chicago River, before 1871. Photographer: J. Carbutt. Source: Chicago History Museum.

of the Chicago River. The city's first manufacturing district developed there, with the river providing transportation and waste disposal.

The national economic depression of 1837 halted work on the canal and the railroad. Trade atrophied, and Chicago land values plummeted. Still, in 1840 Chicago was a small city of some four thousand people, with the outline of the transportation network that would make it the center of wholesale trade in the west. Once the national economy revived in the mid-1840s, Chicago's potential came to fruition.

1848 was a key year for the city—the canal was completed, the first railroad opened, the telegraph reached town, and the Chicago Board of Trade was founded. The canal facilitated trade in bulky goods, not only farm produce but also coal from southern Illinois to fuel the city's homes and industries. Initial plans called for a deep-cut canal to allow boats to pass directly from the lake to the river system, but lack of funds led supporters to settle for a narrow, shallow one. This necessitated switching goods from lake boats to barges, which reinforced Chicago's position as a transfer point. Traffic on the canal peaked in 1882. In the long run, Chicago's development as a rail hub was more important for its dominance in wholesaling.

Private companies built railroads radiating out from Chicago in all directions to tap the farms of the Midwest. By 1856, 10 trunk railroads ended in Chicago, making the city a breakpoint for railroad traffic as well as waterborne trade. Tracks paralleled the river and canal to facilitate transfers of goods between railroad cars, canal barges, and lake ships. Wholesale traders set up along the river on South Water Street to direct this commerce. By 1854 Chicago claimed title as the greatest primary grain port in the world, and the grain elevators lining the river dominated the skyline. The grain trade grew rapidly as a national speculative futures market developed. The telegraph made such a market technologically feasible, but the Chicago Board of Trade made it a reality. It created standards and measures, such as grades for wheat, along with an elevator inspection system, giving eastern capitalists enough confidence to invest in grain sight unseen. The lumber trade also boomed, as lumber from the Midwestern woods was shipped by boat on the lake to be milled in the city. A huge lumber district, with sawmills and extensive storage yards, developed on the Chicago River's South Branch. After milling, the lumber was shipped by rail, mostly to the west to build farmhouses, barns, and fences.

Chicago merchants combined wholesale and retail operations; they sent dry goods to small stores throughout the Midwest and kept stores in the city center for travelers and residents alike. The large retailers congregated on Lake Street, and Chicago's department stores developed as these establishments enlarged and diversified. The downtown rose around the wholesalers and retailers, with hotels, restaurants, saloons, and less reputable businesses established to service traveling men and conventioneers.

Although wholesale trade was the most important element in Chicago's economy until the 1870s, industries for processing agricultural and raw materials also developed. Pork—salted, pickled, and otherwise preserved—was the primary product manufactured for easterners. At the same time, Chicago businessmen saw the potential of producing goods for farmers in Chicago rather than acting as middlemen for eastern manufacturers. In 1847 Cyrus H. McCormick opened his Reaper Works and initiated one of the city's most important industries—agricultural machinery.

The Civil War extended the advantages conferred by geography and human initiative. St. Louis, an older and larger city, was Chicago's rival for the western trade. Chicago's railroad network was already making the city more attractive to shippers, but Union forces delivered the decisive blow to St. Louis when they closed the Mississippi River during the war. Trade that shifted to Chicago did not return to St. Louis when the route was reopened.

Contracts for supplies for the Union forces also stimulated Chicago enterprise, especially among the meatpackers. The packing plants, scattered around the city, had always been a nuisance because they created pollution. Now huge numbers of animals driven through the streets caused intolerable congestion. Chicagoans wanted the plants moved, and the packers needed more space for pens and better access to railroads to minimize production delays. Chicago's first planned manufacturing district—the Union Stock Yard—opened in 1865 to solve these problems. The packers and the railroads chose a site just outside the city limits at 39th and Halsted Streets. With access to the canal and major railroads, it was the prototype of future industrial developments that would move to the edge of the city in search of space and better transportation.

This 1860s bird's-eye view of Union Stock Yard suggests the impact of industries on the residential geography of the city. Built on the unsettled prairie, the stockyards attracted hundreds of thousands of workers, whose homes transformed the empty land into residential neighborhoods that, in 1889, were annexed to the city of Chicago. Artist: James Washington Sheahan. Source: The Newberry Library.

By the end of the Civil War, Chicago was poised to build on its dominance in Midwestern trade and its manufacturing base. Growth came quickly, as the completion of the transcontinental railroad vastly expanded Chicago's potential market. Federal subsidies, in the form of land grants to railroads laying new track, underwrote this rapid development. Once again the joint efforts of politicians and businessmen secured Chicago's future. As the eastern terminus of important western railroads and the western terminus of eastern railroads, Chicago remained the central transfer point for people and freight. In the next decades, railroad building devoured more of Chicago's physical space, and rights-of-way guided the siting of industry and residences.

The Great Fire of 1871 decimated the center of the city, but it did not slow development. It spared most of the outlying areas, including the manufacturing district, the lumber district, the Union Stock Yard, the grain elevators, and the railroad freight terminals. This infrastructure supported the rapid rebuilding of the central business district and residential neighborhoods because it gave the eastern investors who financed reconstruction confidence that the city would recover and investors would profit.

From 1870 to 1920 Chicago was "the metropolis of the West," the hub of transcontinental trade and the most dynamic center of manufacturing for the new national market. In the 1870s Gustavus Swift financed the development of the railroad refrigerator car, which allowed meat butchered in Chicago to be shipped fresh to the East. He established sales offices and refrigerated warehouses in eastern cities and launched a national advertising campaign to overcome consumer fears about meat that was not butchered locally. Other newcomers to the city, like Philip D. Armour, followed his lead, and soon Chicago's "Big Five" packing companies controlled the nation's meatpacking industry. By 1900 these companies were expanding internationally, both exporting Chicago products and opening subsidiary plants abroad.

As production at the stockyards increased, the surrounding residential neighborhoods grew polluted and congested. The slums of Packingtown were peopled by poor workers, primarily immigrants from Central and Eastern Europe who struggled to support their families and sustain their cultural traditions. Large working-class neighborhoods characterized by industrial pollution, congestion, poverty, and cultural diversity developed wherever industry located.

By 1890 Chicago had a population of more than one million people and had surpassed Philadelphia to become the second-largest city in the nation and the second-largest manufacturing center. The diversity as well as the size of its industries spurred this development. Manufacturing based on the trade in agricultural commodities, like brewing and baking, flourished. The furniture industry, developed from the lumber trade, prospered even after the woods of the northern Midwest had been decimated and the lumber trade declined in 1880s. Established industries like agricultural machinery also expanded, as other manufacturers followed McCormick to Chicago. The merger of several of these companies to form International Harvester, in 1902, capped Chicago's leading position in this industry.

New industries such as iron and steel production also pushed Chicago ahead of other cities. The North Chicago Rolling Mill produced the city's first steel rails in 1865 but soon relocated to SOUTH CHICAGO. This move signaled not only the plant's need for more space but also a new factor in the city's economic geography. The transcontinental railroads skirted the bottom of Lake Michigan, and production costs were minimized for manufacturers who obtained access to both lake boats and railroads by locating there. The new steel plant, which later became the United States Steel South Works, anchored the north end of the vast iron-and-steel-producing district that developed along the lake from South Chicago to GARY, Indiana. Like the stockyards, this district attracted workers, especially immigrants from Eastern and Southern Europe, and created new neighborhoods on the fringes of the city.

Industries that used iron and steel, including those that manufactured machinery, machine tools, and railroad cars and equipment, also developed, mostly near the steelmaking district. George Pullman, who manufactured railcars, saw the potential of the area around Lake Calumet; major railroads ran nearby and the lake provided an inland harbor with access to Lake Michigan by way of the Calumet River. He built the town of PULLMAN on the western edge of the lake in 1881 to house his workers and a new factory. Unlike most of Chicago's manufacturing districts, Pullman's model town was neither polluted nor congested. It became a tourist attraction—a vision of what people wished the city would be. No other manufacturers followed Pullman's lead in building decent neighborhoods, although others followed him to the Calumet region. In 1889 and 1893 Chicago annexed all these suburban districts as well as extensive territory to the north, more than tripling its area.

Although the combination of space and transportation drew some industries to the edges of the city, many still found the resources of the old central city more useful. Garment manufacturing was one of Chicago's most important industries, and Chicago led the nation in the production of men's clothing thanks to firms such as Hart, Schaffner & Marx. Because the cheap labor of women and children was their most important requirement, garment makers settled in lofts west of the downtown near Chicago's poorest neighborhoods.

Perhaps the most important resource of the central city was the concentration of communication companies. Chicago's printing and publishing industry, second only to New York's, developed with companies such as R. R. Donnelley & Sons, which located near the downtown because of the demand for business information and the proliferation of commercial journals. Chicago businessmen who pioneered and came to dominate a new form of trade—mail-order sales—also utilized this concentration. Montgomery Ward was first in the field, but Sears, Roebuck & Co. would become even larger. This revolution in retailing used printed catalogs to reach out to individual customers in rural areas and created white-collar "factories" in the center city—office buildings full of clerical workers who processed orders that arrived by mail and filled them from huge warehouses situated on the river and the railroads.

The continuing vitality of the old core was most apparent in the central business district, known as the LOOP after 1882, when it was encircled by a cable car line. Chicago banks had expanded quickly after the Civil War; by the end of the century, the city ranked second nationally in banking and wholesaling, as well as manufacturing and population. Large banks now joined the Board of Trade and the Stock Exchange to make LaSalle Street Chicago's financial center. The concentration of public transportation on the Loop enhanced the area's retail potential too, affording middle- and upper-class shoppers easy access from outlying residential neighborhoods. The department stores moved from Lake Street to State Street in the late 1860s, when Potter Palmer developed the latter as a fashionable street. Stores

Midwest Stock Exchange, 1940. Photographer: Kaufmann & Fabry. Source: Chicago History Museum.

such as Marshall Field's and Carson Pirie Scott reached a new level of elegance, appealing to the prosperous clientele created by the city's expanding economy, as well as to the growing tourist trade. To serve the tourist trade, the Loop provided hospitality and entertainment for every taste and budget—from the elegant Palmer House to the cheapest transient hotels, and from the best theaters to the infamous Levee, Chicago's vice district. Tourism hit a peak in 1893, when Chicagoans hosted the World's Columbian Exposition.

Growing demand for office space in the Loop, combined with technological advances, led upward. Chicago's skyscrapers became the symbol of business success and set the architectural fashion for central business districts throughout the country. Clerical and managerial workers used public transportation to commute to the Loop from a variety of residential neighborhoods. Districts of boardinghouses and apartments for those without children and middle-class housing for families sprang up in a ring around the inner areas. Construction was the city's largest employer and real-estate speculation was still a major avenue to wealth. Some contractors, such as S. E. Gross, built large developments of single-family houses, comparable in scale to more recent subdivisions.

To maintain their economic prominence, Chicagoans sponsored more trans-

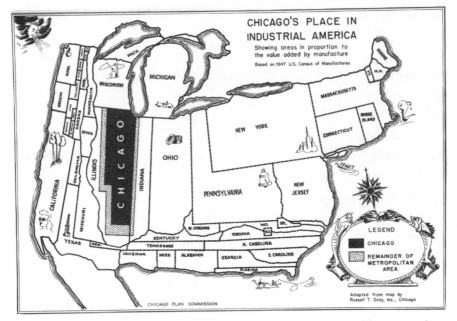

This cartogram captures Chicago's industrial dominance in the United States even as factories started moving to the suburbs and the sunbelt and the city's traditionally important industries, like railroads and farm equipment, began to decline. Creator: Chicago Plan Commission. Source: Chicago History Museum.

portation improvements, like the Chicago Sanitary and Ship Canal, built in the 1890s to replace the obsolete Illinois & Michigan Canal. Like comparable projects, it boosted industrial development outside the city limits. The Chicago Outer Belt Line Railroad, completed in 1887, facilitated freight traffic and spurred manufacturing in CHICAGO HEIGHTS, AURORA, JOLIET, and ELGIN. Although outlying areas had always attracted industry, the implications for Chicago changed in the twentieth century. When the city limits reached already established communities like OAK PARK and EVANSTON, Chicagoans found the path to expansion blocked. After 1900 outlying communities resisted annexation to Chicago, and the metropolitan area developed as an integral economic unit without political control or social unity. The limits on Chicago's development were set.

After 1920 the suburbs grew faster than the city. New transportation, the car and the truck, encouraged the suburbanization of people and industries and reversed the century-old pattern of increasing concentration. Railroads had spurred suburban development, but chiefly along their rights-of-way. Cars and trucks allowed industries and people to disperse throughout the area, providing access to the large tracts necessary for single-floor factories that utilized continuous-flow automated technologies.

As deconcentration increased, however, the metropolitan economy also experienced new competition. Detroit monopolized the most important new industry of the early twentieth century—automobiles. Even more significant were long-term shifts in regional development; the Midwest stagnated as the West and the South boomed. After 1920 cities in the Sunbelt enjoyed advantages in location and transportation similar to those that previously had stimulated Midwestern economic growth. Chicago businesses reeled during the Great Depression of the 1930s, then boomed because of World War II defense contracts, but the regional shift determined the long-term trend in economic growth and hence in population, and in 1990 Los Angeles surpassed Chicago as the second city in population and wholesaling.

Chicago's economy did not fall behind for lack of leadership or innovation. Businessmen and politicians fostered transportation improvements such as the Mississippi-Illinois Waterway to accommodate modern barge traffic. Chicago port facilities modernized, although, like many economic functions, they did so by moving out of the center of the city. After the Calumet Sag (or Cal-Sag) Channel between Calumet Harbor and the Illinois River opened in 1922, Calumet Harbor replaced the Chicago River as the city's port. Chicagoans also embraced new technologies and developed Midway Airport in the 1920s, making Chicago the breakpoint for cross-country air traffic as it was for water and rail. The country's largest airline, United, was based in Chicago. To keep pace with increased air traffic after World War II, Chicagoans developed the larger, more modern O'Hare.

The building of the interstate highway system in the 1950s and 1960s initially helped the area's economy, because the first expressways paralleled existing transportation routes and reinforced older metropolitan areas. Transcontinental bus lines routed through Chicago, and the largest company, Greyhound, established its headquarters in the city. The Chicago area also became the country's leading trucking center. The interstate system also intensified the appeal to industry of suburban locations, especially those south of the city, where the major east-west and north-south routes meet.

Between 1920 and 1970 the Chicago area retained most of its traditional industries. In 1954 it even surpassed Pittsburgh, the old leader, in iron and steel manufacturing, producing one-quarter of the nation's output. Production remained high in machinery, primary metals, printing and publishing, chemicals, food processing, and fabricated metals. The consumer electronics industry expanded greatly, as firms such as Motorola, Zenith, and Admiral captured a significant share of the market for radios and televisions. The first big loss, however, was meatpacking. The industry had been decentralizing since the turn of the century, as Chicago companies shifted to multiple plant locations in western cities, closer to the feedlots. The Chicago stockyards closed in the 1960s.

Although the area's industrial economy remained strong, the city's did not. Companies closed aging factories within the city in favor of new suburban plants. The McCormick Reaper Works was demolished in 1961, and production shifted to a new plant south of HINSDALE. Many new industries, such as Sara Lee's frozen foods, began in the suburbs. As jobs became more plentiful outside the city, people migrating to the Chicago area often settled in the suburbs, bypassing the city entirely. This was only true, however, of white migrants; because of discrimination, African Americans were largely restricted to the city. Out-migration accelerated after 1950, when the city's population peaked at 3.6 million people. White people followed the jobs, as Chicago's share of the area's manufacturing dropped from 71 percent to 54 percent between 1947 and 1961.

The history of the Loop during this period reflected both the struggle to remain competitive and the process of deconcentration. Financial institutions stayed on LaSalle Street, though not all retained their dynamism. The Chicago Board of Trade stayed on top of the national futures market by creating innovative contract markets in new fields such as financial instruments. Chicago banks, however, serviced the Midwest, and they grew slowly, in step with the sluggish regional economy. Beginning in the 1950s, many corporations moved their headquarters out of the skyscrapers to suburban "campuses." Headquarters thrive on quick access to air transport, and O'Hare drew them out of the Loop to the northwest suburbs. Most notable was Sears, which trumpeted its success by building the world's tallest skyscraper, then moved to Hoffman Estates. The Loop's tenuous economic situation has been reflected in a series of building booms and busts since World War II, which have often left some of the world's most innovative skyscrapers half empty.

The Loop's retail functions also ebbed. Marshall Field's and other Loop department stores opened their first branches in the suburbs in the 1920s. City officials replaced the cluttered and decaying South Water Street with Wacker Drive in the 1920s, but new building in the Loop virtually ceased for decades, while North Michigan Avenue became the MAGNIFICENT MILE. Suburban competition became intense in the 1950s with the opening of shopping malls. The Loop, however, continued to attract conventioneers thanks to the construction of the McCormick Place convention center, and Loop hotels, theaters, and museums drew tourists to the lakefront of the central city.

Since 1970 the character of Chicago's metropolitan economy has been transformed; manufacturing and wholesaling play lesser roles than in the past. Chicagoans hoped to gain international commerce with the opening of the St. Lawrence Seaway, but the oceangoing trade was not as successful as projected. Furthermore, foreign competition undercut many manufacturing companies. Older plants in

Chicago closed first; newer ones in the suburbs followed. Some corporations, even giants such as International Harvester, failed. Both central city and suburbs suffered, as the area lost almost all railcar and agricultural machinery production and most of its consumer electronics industry. The steel industry declined precipitously but has since rebounded; at the end of the century it employed, however, only one-third as many workers as it did in the 1970s. A high-tech corridor has developed in the western suburbs, but most of the new industries are centered elsewhere.

The service sector has been the source of most new growth in the metropolitan economy. The old central city is now almost totally dependent on business services and tourism for its vitality. Where the river empties into the lake, a Ferris wheel replaces the grain elevator as a symbol of what makes the city great. The diversity of the area's economy remains a strength, but its future, like its past, will depend on national and international economic trends. Chicago was geographically well situated to become the capital of the Midwest. It retains this position, but the old dream of dominating the continent has died.

FURTHER READING: Cronon, William. *Nature's Metropolis: Chicago and the Great West*. 1991. ■ Marsh, Barbara. *A Corporate Tragedy: The Agony of International Harvester Company*. 1985. ■ Mayer, Harold M., and Richard C. Wade. *Chicago: Growth of a Metropolis*. 1969.

BUILT ENVIRONMENT OF THE CHICAGO REGION

ROBERT BRUEGMANN

Architecture has always loomed large in accounts of Chicago. Architects like William Le Baron Jenney, Daniel Burnham, Louis Sullivan, Frank Lloyd Wright, and Mies van der Rohe and firms like Skidmore, Owings & Merrill are firmly embedded in local history and lore, as are the buildings they designed: the Monadnock, the Rookery, the Auditorium Building, Robie House, the Sears Tower. In Chicago, even the cab drivers seem to know the major architects and their buildings. Whereas in older European and American cities the major monuments are often palaces, government buildings, and cathedrals, Chicago's monuments have more often than not been business buildings, houses, schools, and churches. In emphasizing these landmarks of daily use, the city seems to celebrate its democratic, mercantile, and middle-class character. The creation of a comfortable built environment for a large portion of the population, more than any individual buildings, stands as the Chicago area's crowning architectural achievement.

From the Founding to the Fire

For the great city of Chicago to rise from its marshy site a number of important infrastructure works were necessary. In the years before the Great Fire of 1871 the most important were the Illinois & Michigan Canal, constructed between 1836 and 1848; the water system, designed by engineer Ellis Chesbrough in the 1860s; and the city's great railroad system. Yet despite these impressive achievements, most observers in the mid-nineteenth century would have seen little to distinguish Chicago from many other young and fast-growing Midwestern towns. Small, mostly wood, buildings straggled alongside unpaved roads that were alternately dusty and muddy. Even the most conspicuous structures in the city were relatively small and unimpressive by the standards of larger Midwestern cities like St. Louis, not to mention those of Eastern cities and the European capitals. It was only in the last years before the fire that great commercial emporia like Marshall Field's and hotels like the Palmer House rose on State Street, giving Chicago monuments to rival those in more established places.

From a small gridiron plat around the meeting of the south and north forks of the Chicago River, the city bounded outward by annexing adjacent development, virtually all of it laid out in conformity with the regular mile-square grid pattern of the American land survey specified by Congress in 1785. The relatively low density of Chicago's residential neighborhoods and the high percentage of single-family detached homes (in contrast to the tightly packed tenements and row houses of cities in the eastern United States and Europe) was in part the result of a new construction technique, the balloon frame, which, coupled with the new availability of lumber in standardized sizes and machine-cut nails, made possible rapid and inexpensive construction. The balloon frame has sometimes been claimed as a Chicago invention, but this claim is dubious; the technique, one step in a long process of substituting prefabrication for handwork, appears to predate the founding of Chicago. Whatever its origin, the balloon frame undoubtedly helped make possible, during the middle decades of the nineteenth century, a construction boom in Chicago unmatched by any city up to that date. By the time of the Great Fire a large part of the population, including many factory workers, could afford what was then the extraordinary luxury of a single-family detached home, often a small one-story or story-and-a-half frame or brick house known as a workman's cottage. Entire neighborhoods of these cottages were erected on all sides of the central business district. Many can still be seen today in close-in neighborhoods like BRIDGEPORT on the South Side or OLD TOWN on the North Side.

Another reason the city could expand so quickly and at densities so much lower than older cities was that Chicago was one of the first large cities in the world to grow up with public transportation. The advent of the steam railroad, starting in the late 1840s, permitted suburban settlements well beyond the continuously developed urban fabric, while the horse-drawn street railway and cable car allowed a vast expansion all along the edge of the settled area. By the time of the 1871 fire, railroad lines radiated outward from the central city along the railroad lines like the spokes of a wheel, each beaded with suburbs. Many of the railroad suburbs were upper-middle-class enclaves. RIVERSIDE, designed by Frederick Law Olmsted and Calvert Vaux with large lots, curving streets that followed the topography, and generous public open spaces, was the most famous early American suburb in the picturesque mode. Other outlying communities, like BLUE ISLAND, were industrial, accommodating factories and working-class housing.

From the Fire to the First World War

The Great Fire of 1871 wiped out a large portion of central Chicago. Because much of the infrastructure and industrial capacity of the city had already decentralized, however, this disaster did not destroy the city's production capacity. Moreover, with the aid of insurance money and investment funds, drawn primarily from Eastern cities, the city rebuilt rapidly. Despite new laws enacted to eliminate the worst fire hazards, the earliest postfire construction tended to reproduce prefire configurations.

In the years between the Great Fire and World War I, Chicago became a great industrial power and saw its greatest sustained growth. It also captured the popular imagination. People from around the world came to see the emerging metropolis of the future, the "shock city" of its day. This growth was made possible in part by sweeping improvements in basic infrastructure. Perhaps the most far-reaching program sought to protect public health: a monumental engineering project, directed by the newly formed Sanitary District of Chicago and completed at the turn of the century, reversed the flow of the Chicago and Calumet Rivers, which had previously carried untreated sewage into the lake, the source of the city's fresh water supply. Another major undertaking was the creation by the federal government of a major port at Lake Calumet, by means of dredging that started at the end of the 1860s. Finally, there was the extension of the transportation system; the electric streetcar made its appearance in the 1880s, followed in the early 1890s by the elevated rapid transit train.

The most striking physical manifestation of the city's modernity was seen in the LOOP, the central business district named originally for a circuit of cable car lines that was reinforced, after 1897, by a similar circuit of elevated rail lines. In the Loop, starting in the 1880s, a number of buildings burst through the four- to five-story plateau that until then had marked the upper limit of practical commercial construction. Promptly dubbed skyscrapers, these new buildings had become practical with the advent of the passenger elevator, new methods of constructing foundations and fireproofing, and other technological advances. Skyscrapers had appeared in New York in the 1870s, a decade earlier than in Chicago, but it was in Chicago's smaller business district, along broad, regular streets like Dearborn and LaSalle, that these buildings found their most striking and characteristic expression. As the pace of construction accelerated in the 1880s, they formed vast canyons of masonry walls, often almost devoid of ornament but punctuated by enormous plate-glass windows. This novel cityscape attracted worldwide attention and comment. Although Chicago's great buildings were a source of civic pride, their enormous scale and fears about their safety also inspired intense hostility. One result was the passage, in 1893, of a height limit. This limit would subsequently rise and fall until it was supplanted by provisions of a zoning ordinance in 1923.

The office buildings, lofts, and retail buildings of the Loop were the work of a large number of urban professionals, including developers like the Brooks brothers of Boston, agents like Owen Aldis, architects like William Le Baron Jenney, Burnham & Root, Holabird & Roche, and Adler & Sullivan, engineers like Charles Strobel, William Sooy Smith, and Corydon T. Purdy, and contractors like George

A. Fuller, who developed the first large-scale general contracting firm in the country. All of these men played major roles in the creation of the first buildings with complete metal skeletons and relatively thin exterior claddings, a system that came of age around 1890 and that was often called the "Chicago frame."

As land prices rose in the business district, activities that required large amounts of inexpensive space moved further afield. This led to the creation, among other industrial areas, of the Chicago Union Stock Yard starting in the 1860s, the company town of PULLMAN in the 1880s, and the Central Manufacturing District, perhaps the country's first planned industrial district, at the turn of the century.

Explosive growth also brought congestion, noise, and pollution. This led to a constant outward movement of families searching for greener, less congested living environments, which in turn promoted segregation within the city's residential areas. The contrast between rich and poor neighborhoods became starker. Slums and tenement areas lay close to the Loop, while the wealthy, concentrated in the area just south of the business district in the late nineteenth century, relocated starting around 1900 to what would come to be known as the GOLD COAST, the lakefront portion of the NEAR NORTH SIDE. Both poor and affluent areas were relatively small, though, compared to the large working- and middle-class subdivisions that pushed outward in all directions. During these years residential developers, led by Samuel E. Gross, perhaps the country's largest, transformed the housing industry by building large numbers of units and entire subdivisions at a time. Single-family houses were interspersed with the city's characteristic two-flat and three-flat apartment buildings as well as, in affluent areas, the newly fashionable "French flats," or apartment buildings for the affluent.

Complementing the new residences were neighborhood schools, churches, and other community buildings as well as miles of retail frontage along arterial streets, particularly the major diagonal roads and the large streets that delineated the mile-square grid. Also complementing the residential subdivisions was a major system of parks and boulevards, projected in the late 1860s but not finished for several decades, that encircled the built-up portion of the city from Jackson Park in the south to Lincoln Park in the north. This system was in part a sanitary effort, offering what citizens of the time thought of as reservoirs of light and air in a congested and polluted city, and in part a means to enhance the real-estate value of adjacent property.

The same diversity marked the railroad suburbs beyond the city limits. At the upper end of the scale were elegant places like EVANSTON and KENILWORTH on the North Shore. The most affordable included southern suburbs like Dolton and East Chicago in Indiana. The vast majority of suburban communities, on all sides of the city, fell in the middle range. Beyond the suburbs, satellite industrial cities like JOLIET, AURORA, WAUKEGAN, and GARY, Indiana, were also booming, each with a business center and outlying districts as well as a range of economic activities, income levels, and building types similar to those of Chicago itself but on a reduced scale.

This period also saw the first efforts at systematic city planning. The White City, site of the World's Columbian Exposition of 1893, featured coordinated planning and pristine white architecture, in marked contrast with the often chaotic gray city to the north. It became a model for subsequent planning efforts and a major inspiration for the famous 1909 *Plan of Chicago* by Daniel Burnham and Edward Bennett Although most of the ideas espoused in the Burnham Plan had been formulated previously by others, and although only a few of its provisions were actually executed, this plan quickly became the country's most famous urban planning document. It was widely emulated across the country in the decades after its appearance, and it continues to exert a strong hold on the imagination of Chicagoans.

Between the Wars

Between the world wars, particularly during the boom years of the 1920s, the trend toward more intensive land use in and around the Loop continued, as did the push of residential development, at ever lower densities, at the urban periphery. This pattern was possible because increased affluence had led to greater personal mobility; in particular, the 1920s saw a dramatic increase in car ownership and the construction of new and better roads. By the onset of World War II an expressway system had been planned for the entire metropolitan area, and a stretch of Lake Shore Drive with limited access and cloverleafs, one of the earliest such installations in the country, had already been constructed. Another key addition to the infrastructure was Municipal (later Midway) Airport, which opened in 1927 and soon became the nation's busiest.

Also during this period came major new efforts to exert governmental control over the development process, notably through the use of zoning. Chicago's first zoning ordinance, similar in conception to one adopted in New York City in 1916, was enacted in 1923 and controlled both the use of buildings and their height and bulk. Within the Loop a new generation of sleek high buildings, many with stepped-back towers permitted by provisions of the new ordinance, rose to dominate the skyline. The completion of a bridge over the Chicago River at the north end of Michigan Avenue extended the great commercial boulevard onto what had been Pine Street and made possible a new retail district north of the river that would eventually eclipse State Street as Chicago's most important center for upscale shopping.

The increasing affluence of the 1920s also allowed for a vast expansion in residential development, often in large subdivisions protected against industrial and commercial incursions by the new zoning regulations. A broad band of solid but modest structures known as "Chicago bungalows," really an updated version of the worker's cottage, encircled the city center and extended outward to suburbs like BERWYN, which had a particularly spectacular collection of these houses. Another important development was the growth of apartment districts in places like UPTOWN, ROGERS PARK, HYDE PARK, and SOUTH SHORE, where railroad and rapid transit lines provided easy access to downtown. With the rapid development of new residential districts and the increasing use of the automobile came the growth of regional shopping and business centers, the most notable located at the elevated stations at ENGLEWOOD on the Southwest Side and Uptown on the North Side. These became miniature versions of the Loop, each with its own department stores, specialty shops, movie theaters, and other urban services. Development further out grew even more quickly, with new subdivisions springing up around existing railroad suburbs and entirely new communities forming in areas opened up by the automobile. As in previous eras, these suburbs ranged from elegant upper-income enclaves to working-class towns and industrial satellites.

The Postwar Decades

After World War II most of the building patterns established in the 1920s resumed, but on a larger scale. The long postwar boom was fueled by tremendous investment in infrastructure, particularly for automobile and air travel. Construction of the regional expressway system, projected in the 1930s, started in earnest after the war with local funding but was greatly accelerated once the Interstate Highway Act of 1956 made federal funds available. Air travel too increased enormously, particularly with the development of commercial jet airliners and the creation of a new airport, O'Hare Field, which soon took over from Midway the title of the nation's busiest.At the same time, the area's public transportation system, temporarily buoyed by ridership increases during the war, continued a long decline. The Chicago Transit Authority, created in 1947 to take over private transit operations, first required a subsidy in 1970 and has, since then, seen round after round of subsidy hikes as ridership has declined.

Despite the apparent vigor of the region, there was considerable concern about the future. Chicago's industrial plant had not been updated sufficiently during the long years of the Depression and World War II to keep pace with developments in the Sun Belt and elsewhere. Much of the central business district was old and congested. Beyond the Loop were many square miles of industrial and residential land that were considered obsolete and blighted. Civic and government leaders hoped to counter these problems with new planning techniques and an aggressive program of urban renewal.

In the Loop itself, a building boom that began in the late 1950s, after a relatively short postwar lull, and continued through the 1960s rivaled those of the 1880s and

1920s. The new structures, mostly corporate headquarters and speculative office buildings, included some of the largest and tallest buildings in the world, notably Sears Tower and the John Hancock Building, both designed by Skidmore, Owings & Merrill, Chicago's most successful postwar corporate architecture firm. Other major undertakings in the central business district included Illinois Center, a large planned development on the former Illinois Central railroad yards along the lakefront between Randolph Street and the river; McCormick Place, an enormous lakeside convention center complex to the south of the Loop; and, to the north along Michigan Avenue, elaborate mixed-use complexes, starting with Water Tower Place in the early 1970s.

The prognosis for residential areas around the Loop, however, was less bright. Here postwar planners saw mostly older houses, decay, and blight. They initiated aggressive urban renewal programs that resulted in the demolition and rebuilding of large areas, including most of the NEAR SOUTH SIDE. There, in place of the demolished structures, rose new houses and apartment buildings such as Prairie Shores and Lake Meadows, institutional structures like a new Michael Reese Hospital, and a new campus for the Illinois Institute of Technology. The city's urban renewal efforts were highly controversial. In some cases, like the Hyde Park A & B project with its row houses and apartments on the South Side and the apartments of SANDBURG VILLAGE on the North Side, the planners' intentions of stabilizing neighborhoods and retaining middle-income residents in the city were at least partially realized. At the same time, the creation of massive public housing projects, particularly the high-rise apartment buildings of the ROBERT TAYLOR HOMES on the South Side and the CABRINI-GREEN complex on the North Side, proved to be highly problematic.

Many of the most successful developments seemed to have had nothing to do with planning. Many older, apparently decaying neighborhoods near the center that were spared demolition under urban renewal bounced back as middle- and upper-middle-class communities through a process of private restoration and gentrification. This change coincided, however, with the continuing loss of jobs and income in many neighborhoods further out. Large parts of the South and West Sides, in particular, were hard hit as high-paying industrial jobs disappeared and racial and ethnic change created instability.

While city population declined after World War II, suburban development boomed. At one end of the spectrum were places like Barrington Hills to the northwest and OAK BROOK to the west. Here substantial houses occupied lots that often exceeded an acre in size. At the other end of the scale was PARK FOREST, a planned community developed immediately after the war in the far south suburbs that contained a mix of small ranch houses (the postwar equivalent to the interwar bungalows) and garden apartments as well as a shopping center and a wide variety of community structures. This attempt to build a community around a comprehensive master plan, while widely hailed and intensively studied, never became typical. Instead most development proceeded as it had in the past, with a patchwork of residential subdivisions and industrial and retail development, separately planned by private interests, and schools, parks, and public buildings put in place by local governments. The vast majority of suburban development was based on subdivisions of middle-class ranch houses and split-levels with four to eight houses per acre; examples include Morton Grove and NILES to the north and FRANKLIN PARK and MELROSE PARK to the west.

With residential growth came major new business developments. Industrial concerns continued their push out from the center to the periphery, occupying complexes they themselves had created or quarters in planned industrial parks. The Centex Industrial Park, for example, located just west of O'Hare Airport, was the largest of its kind in the country. Along with the industrial parks came office parks and shopping districts, such as a trio of pioneering open-air centers constructed in the 1950s: River Oaks Center in the south suburbs, Oak Brook Center in the west suburbs, and Old Orchard Shopping Center in the north suburbs.

Since the 1970s

In recent decades renewal at the core has proceeded alongside continued outward growth. Despite all of the fears, particularly during the dark years of industrial decline and civil unrest in the late 1960s and early 1970s, Chicago's central area has not collapsed. An increase in the number of jobs in the Loop devoted to high-level corporate, financial, and legal business, as well as a growing economy based on tourism and culture, led to a massive office building boom starting in the 1980s. The central area also saw an increasing residential population, with the construction of large new apartment buildings such as Presidential Towers just west of the Loop, the conversion of loft and office buildings like those in the PRINTER'S ROW area just south of the Loop, and the development of entire new residential neighborhoods like DEARBORN PARK, just south of Printer's Row. Meanwhile, gentrification spread from a small nucleus in Old Town on the Near North Side to include substantial areas of the North, Northwest, Near West, and South Sides. One of the factors favoring this gentrification was an extensive program to demolish virtually all of the high-rise public housing projects operated by the Chicago Housing Authority and to renovate many of the low-rise ones. By 2000 new building and rehabilitation were evident even in some of the most depressed areas of the West and South Sides, giving reason for some optimism despite continuing high rates of poverty and crime in many Chicago neighborhoods and growing problems in some inner-ring suburbs and elsewhere in the area.

Despite the stabilization and revitalization of the core, the majority of growth in the metropolitan area has continued to take place at the periphery. In some key areas important new infrastructure has been constructed. Difficult problems of flooding and wastewater treatment were addressed by new wastewater treatment facilities and the massive Tunnel and Reservoir Project (TARP, more commonly known as the Deep Tunnel), which stores water after heavy rains until wastewater treatment plants have the capacity to treat it. The transportation infrastructure, on the other hand, has not kept up with demand. Although automobile ownership and use has continued to increase, relatively few new highways have been built, and public transit has not managed to maintain, let alone increase, its share of trips areawide. The result has been increasing congestion. Much the same problem plagues the city's airports. Even with massive rebuilding at O'Hare and Midway, the region's air traffic system has become increasingly inadequate, threatening the region's economic vitality and quality of life.

Despite well-intentioned regional plans produced by agencies like the Northeastern Illinois Planning Commission (NIPC) and Chicago Area Transportation Study (CATS), merged into the Chicago Metropolitan Agency for Planning in 2007, most development in the area has been due to private initiative rather than public planning, which is largely local and often piecemeal. By 2000 suburban residential development had pushed to the east along the south shore of Lake Michigan toward the Michigan border, to the south toward Kankakee, to the west well past the Fox River, and to the north deep into southern Wisconsin. House sizes have increased at all economic levels, although lot sizes have declined in the city and in the suburbs. Increasingly large numbers of rental apartments and row houses are now being built in the suburbs. Beyond the suburbs, vast areas of very low density exurban development, particularly to the north and west of existing suburbs, have lured families seeking large lots and a rural atmosphere.

Along with the residential developments have come new shopping centers, strip malls, discount centers, and other retail establishments. Office, business, and industrial parks, like the Meridian Business Park in Aurora, have grown in size and sophistication. The most spectacular phenomenon of the last several decades has been the rise of large outlying business centers. The most important is located at SCHAUMBURG, where Woodfield Mall was the largest enclosed shopping center in the country at the time of its completion in 1971. Around the mall has grown a collection of office, retail, and hotel buildings that at the opening of the twenty-first century constituted the largest business district in Illinois outside of Chicago's Loop. Together with other business centers, from the master-planned center at Oak Brook to the largely unplanned centers near O'HARE and Rosemont, these business districts have helped create what is effectively a multinucleated structure for the metropolitan area.

One of the most remarkable aspects of this outward expansion since the 1920s has been the large increase in occupied land that has accompanied relatively slow population growth. For an increasing number of critics this constitutes "sprawl," which they consider to be an undesirable, uncoordinated, and wasteful development pattern. The decline in density has actually slowed since World War II, however, and environmental problems, while significant and troubling, are almost certainly less worrisome, at least at the local level, than they were in the largely unregulated era of the late nineteenth and early twentieth centuries. It is perhaps more useful to consider recent developments, like the history of Chicago's development from the beginning, as an apparently hasty, unplanned, and chaotic process that, nevertheless, has actually been marked by a great deal of internal order and that can be seen as the logical result of a vast increase in wealth, mobility, and choice by a very large number of Chicagoans.

FURTHER READING: Harold M. Mayer and Richard C. Wade, *Chicago: Growth of a Metropolis* (1969), is unsurpassed as a treatment of the built environment of a large American city. Carl Condit created a valuable corpus of work on the architecture and infrastructure of the city; his most important books include *The Chicago School of Architecture* (1964); *Chicago, 1910–29: Building, Planning, and Urban Technology* (1973); and *Chicago, 1930–70: Building, Planning, and Urban Technology* (1974). These large compendia are complemented by important works on more specific topics. Frank A. Randall's *History of the Development of Building Construction in Chicago* (1949; 2nd ed., 1999) remains the best source for information about buildings in the central business district, and *Chicago Public Works: A History* (1973), published by the city's Department of Public Works, provides a good overview of public infrastructure development.

Since the 1970s a number of books have appeared that examine the building of the region from new perspectives. Among these are Ann Durkin Keating, *Building Chicago: Suburban Developers and the Creation of a Divided Metropolis* (1988) and *Chicagoland: City and Suburbs in the Railroad Age* (2005), both of which give excellent accounts of the relationship between city building, metropolitan services, and government structures; Daniel Bluestone, *Constructing Chicago* (1991), which has chapters on aspects of Chicago development that had been somewhat neglected earlier (notably the park system, public buildings, and religious, civic, and cultural facilities), as well as an excellent treatment of the history of the skyscraper; and Miles Berger, *They Built Chicago: Entrepreneurs Who Shaped a Great City's Architecture* (1992), a good account of the financial underpinnings of Chicago's famous buildings. The University of Chicago Press has made a considerable contribution with its series Chicago Architecture and Urbanism; for example, in *The Architects and the City: Holabird & Roche of Chicago, 1880–1918* (1997), Robert Bruegmann discusses a wide variety of building types in the urban fabric as manifested in the work of a single large firm. In *Chicago Architecture: Histories, Revisions, Alternatives*, edited by Charles Waldheim and Katerina Ruedi (2005) a number of authors provide new insights into the built environment of the region. *Chicago Architecture, 1872–1922: Birth of a Metropolis* (1987) and *Chicago Architecture and Design, 1923–1993: Reconfiguration of an American Metropolis* (1993), a pair of catalogs created for exhibitions held at the Art Institute of Chicago and edited by John Zukowsky, provide multiple perspectives on a wide variety of subjects connected with the built environment of the city. The *AIA Guide to Chicago* (2004), produced by the American Institute of Architects, Chicago Chapter, and edited by Alice Sinkevitch, provides a copious amount of information about famous and interesting buildings and their architects. Much of the research noted above was synthesized by the authors of the entries in the *Encyclopedia of Chicago* (2004).

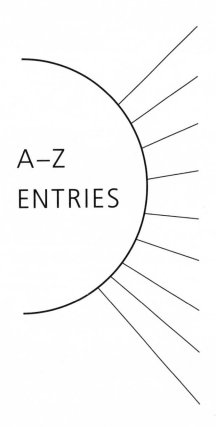

A–Z
ENTRIES

Airport Homes, neighborhood in the WEST LAWN Community Area, built by the Chicago Housing Authority in 1946 for returning veterans.

Albany Park, Community Area 14, 8 miles north-

14
Albany Park

west of the Loop. Albany Park grew from a sparsely settled farming community to a dynamic urban neighborhood in the course of one generation. In 1868 local entrepreneur Richard Rusk turned an initial 10-acre investment of land into a large farm that included a profitable brickyard along the North Branch of the Chicago River and the Rusk Race Track, where late-nineteenth-century Chicagoans often took day excursions to watch horse racing and enjoy the bucolic environs. As Chicago's population exploded in the 1870s and 1880s, the suburban community became increasingly popular. In 1889 Chicago annexed the area along with the rest of Jefferson Township.

In 1893 a group of investors purchased 640 acres of the nearby McAllister farm for development. The real-estate syndicate included four prominent Chicagoans: streetcar magnate DeLancy Louderback, John J. Mitchell of Illinois Trust and Savings Bank, Northwestern Elevated Railroad owner Clarence Buckingham, and Charles T. Yerkes, who developed both elevated interurban rail and streetcar lines. Louderback, a native of Albany, New York, named the development after

his hometown. These investors brought transportation lines to Albany Park, which proved essential to the area's early commercial and residential expansion. Electric streetcars ran along Lawrence Avenue between Broadway and Milwaukee Avenues as early as 1896, and the Kedzie Avenue streetcar line extended north to Lawrence Avenue by 1913. Most significant was the extension of the Ravenswood Elevated train to the intersection of Kimball and Lawrence Avenues by 1907. Beginning in 1904, the Chicago Sanitary District widened and straightened the meandering North Branch of the Chicago River between Belmont and Lawrence Avenues. The river relocation, completed in 1907, defined previously ambiguous property lines and improved sewage disposal in Albany Park.

The completion of the Ravenswood Elevated line set off a building boom clustered around the train terminal at Lawrence and Kimball. Commercial development included small shops, department stores, and theaters. Land valued at $52 per front foot in 1909 sold for $2,750 per front foot by 1929. Residential builders constructed bungalows and two-flats at a furious pace during the 1910s and 1920s, by the end of which Albany Park was almost completely developed. The 1910 census counted 7,000 inhabitants; that number nearly quadrupled by 1920, to 26,676, and doubled again by 1930, to more than 55,000. Albany Park's population peaked at 56,692 in 1940.

Throughout the twentieth century, Albany Park acted as a gateway community for aspiring middle-class ethnic groups. German and Swed-

What Are Community Areas?

In the nineteenth century, the United States Bureau of the Census used the ward system to break down data within cities. This approach, however, thwarted comparisons across time, because ward boundaries changed with each census cycle. The Federated Churches of New York pioneered the concept of the census tract in 1902; Chicago first used census tracts in 1910.

Members of the University of Chicago's Local Community Research Committee wanted the information gathered by the Census Bureau to reflect real, not arbitrary, divisions within the city. Sociologist Robert Park argued that physical barriers such as rivers, parks, and railroads created "natural areas" within cities. These natural areas had distinctive histories and consistent rates of various social ills, regardless of who lived there. Chicago's Department of Public Health also had an interest in tracking local variations in birth and death rates. The two institutions collaborated to produce a map with 75 community areas, into which 935 census tracts were distributed. The University of Chicago Press published editions of the 1920, 1930, and special 1934 census with information presented for each community area. The Local Community Fact Book series continued this tradition after each census except 1970.

With two exceptions, there have been only minor changes in the community area map.

Because the original map was designed after the great wave of annexations at the end of the nineteenth century, O'HARE (CA 76) has been the only addition to the city that needed a separate designation. In 1980 EDGEWATER wrested a symbolic secession from UPTOWN, and was recognized as a distinct entity (CA 77).

Despite the uses scholars and planners have found for the concept of community areas, they do not necessarily represent how Chicagoans think about their city. Scholars have challenged the validity of the idea of "natural areas" since its introduction. Prominent neighborhoods such as PILSEN and BACK OF THE YARDS are subsumed into the less familiar LOWER WEST SIDE and NEW CITY. Many Roman Catholics are as comfortable with the names of parishes as those of community areas. And the virtue of the community areas, their stability, means that they cannot accommodate transformations in the geography of Chicago, such as the mid-twentieth-century expressways that cut through once-coherent neighborhoods.

Amanda Seligman

Further reading: Burgess, Ernest W., and Charles Newcomb, eds. *Census Data of the City of Chicago, 1920.* 1931. ● Hunter, Albert. *Symbolic Communities: The Persistence and Change of Chicago's Local Communities.* 1974. ● Smith, T. V., and Leonard D. White, eds. *Chicago: An Experiment in Social Science Research.* 1929.

ish immigrants initially settled the area. After 1912 Albany Park became home to a large number of Russian Jews leaving the crowded neighborhoods of Chicago's NEAR WEST SIDE. The community remained predominantly Jewish through the 1950s. Between 1910 and 1940 several synagogues and churches, public schools, and public parks opened. After World War II, many Jewish families—like the generation before them—moved north, this time to suburban LINCOLNWOOD and SKOKIE.

The suburban exodus led Albany Park into economic and social decline. Population decreased, homes and stores lay vacant, and property values plummeted. In the 1970s, 70 percent of the commercial property along Lawrence Avenue stood va-

cant. Empty buildings attracted illegal drug trade, prostitution, and gangs. Relief came in 1978 when city government, the North River Commission, and the Lawrence Avenue Development Corporation cooperated to improve Albany Park's appearance. Albany Park's renewal included streetscape beautification, the Facade Rebate Program, low-interest loans, and other financing packages. Redevelopment efforts led to a decrease in commercial vacancies and an increase in residential property values in the 1980s and 1990s.

After the 1970s, Albany Park became a port of entry for immigrants from Asia and Latin America. In 1990 the community area claimed the largest numbers of Korean, Filipino, and Guatemalan immigrants in Chicago. The Korean community played important commercial and civic roles in the revitalization of the area. The number of homes sold annually increased 125 percent between 1980 and 1989. Albany Park's pattern of population shifts continued in the 1990s, as more prosperous Korean immigrants began moving to northern suburbs.

Timothy B. Neary

FURTHER READING: Ader, Inez C., ed. "Community History of Albany Park." 1944. Manuscript Collection, Sulzer Regional Public Library, Chicago. ■ Bjorklund, Richard C. "Ravenswood Manor: Indian Prairie to Urban Pride." 1964. Manuscript Collection, Sulzer Regional Public Library, Chicago. ■ Drury, John. "Old Chicago Neighborhoods: Albany Park." *Landlord's Guide* (August 1950): 6–8.

Altgeld Gardens, neighborhood in the RIVERDALE Community Area, built by the Chicago Housing Authority in 1945.

Andersonville, located in the southwest corner of the EDGEWATER Community Area, began as a Swedish community. In the late 1980s Andersonville became an attractive area of settlement for gays and lesbians who sought cheaper homes and apartments north of BOYS TOWN.

Erik Gellman

FURTHER READING: Pacyga, Dominic A., and Ellen Skerrett. *Chicago, City of Neighborhoods: Histories and Tours.* 1986. ■ Stuyvesant, Judith Erickson. "Recollections of Andersonville and Swedish Life in Chicago." 1997. Collections of the Swedish American Museum, Chicago.

Antioch, IL, Lake County, 47 miles NW of the Loop. The village of Antioch is located in Antioch Township in the northwest corner of Lake County, Illinois, a region known as the Chain of Lakes. Brothers Darius and Thomas Gage were among the earliest to file land claims and build houses along Sequoit Creek after the winter of 1837. Hiram Buttrick built a sawmill on the creek in 1839. Population reached 300 by 1852.

Some early residents were devout followers of the Protestant sect now known as the Disciples of Christ. The name Antioch (a reference to a city in early Christian history) was chosen as the result of an exchange between zealous Disciples and their ridiculing neighbors, who initiated the idea of a biblical name. The settlement was a local center of support for abolitionism.

Small shops were established in the village, and in 1856 John Elliott built a steam gristmill to accompany the sawmill. The new settlers were mostly of German, Irish, and English descent.

Tourism was a spur to Antioch's economy after it became a station on the Wisconsin Central rail line, between Chicago and Stevens Point, Wisconsin, in 1885. The recreational possibilities of hunting, fishing, and boating on dozens of small nearby lakes made Antioch a popular vacation spot for Chicagoans. Local farmers transformed their homes into tourist boardinghouses, while others built hotels and summer cottages. Antioch became the gateway to the Chain of Lakes, including the flowering lotus beds covering hundreds of acres on nearby Grass Lake.

Antioch incorporated as a village in 1892. After a series of fires, the village installed a public water system in 1905 and began to build more brick buildings.

Other industries slowly developed alongside tourism. The ice harvesting industry took advantage of the area's lakes and rail service to Chicago. Employers hired hobos from Chicago as seasonal laborers and put them up in boardinghouses built near the ice houses. The Pickard China Company moved to Antioch from Chicago in 1937 as it expanded its operation from hand-decorating imported china to full-scale domestic production. Thelen Sand and Gravel has been a prominent local enterprise since 1947.

The village maintained a small-town character with slow growth into the mid-1980s. After 1990 there was more rapid residential development, with developers building hundreds of homes in several new subdivisions. The village population

Wisconsin Central trains brought hundreds from Chicago on summer Saturdays to the Chain of Lakes region, ca. 1928. Photographer: Unknown. Source: Lakes Region Historical Society.

as of the 2000 census was 8,788, with 21,879 in Antioch Township.

Passenger rail service to Antioch, which had ended in 1965, returned in 1996 when Metra opened a new suburban passenger rail line, the North Central, with Antioch as its terminus. Ridership figures turned out to be higher than projected, leading to calls for expanded service.

Douglas Knox

FURTHER READING: *Antioch, Illinois: A Pictorial History, 1892–1992.* Antioch: Lakes Region Historical Society, 1992.

Archer Heights, Community Area 57, 7 miles SW of the Loop. The urban history of Archer Heights is largely a twentieth-century story. Indians had little use for its swamps and prairies except as part of the passage that connected the Chicago and Des Plaines Rivers. Most of the land in the area had been acquired by land speculators and

57
Archer
Heights

farmers by the 1850s, but it was not until the early twentieth century that it became the focus of real-estate developers and manufacturers. Its name reflects both sets of interests. "Archer" refers to Archer Road, named for Illinois & Michigan Canal commissioner and land speculator William B. Archer. For a while the area was known as the Archer Road district. "Heights" stems from the fanciful name of an early-twentieth-century subdivision; the topography is in fact as flat as any in the region.

The Illinois & Michigan Canal, which ran where the Stevenson Expressway does now; the Chicago & Alton Railroad, which paralleled the canal; and Archer Road were the first thoroughfares to Chicago, but they had little effect on the area's development in the nineteenth century. Not even the three railroads that encircled it in the 1880s (now known as the Belt, Santa Fe, and Indiana Harbor) or annexation to Chicago in 1889 (as part of Lake and Cicero Townships) changed much of the district's character or economic role.

After 1900 speculators developed the southern sections of Archer Heights for residential use, while railroads maintained control of most of the north-side real estate. Archer Avenue offered horsecars in the 1890s and electric streetcars by 1906, which helped attract immigrant laborers. Poles emigrated in the largest numbers, followed by Italians, Lithuanians, Czechs, and Russian Jews. The area saw its largest increase in population between 1920 and 1930. During this decade, modern urban infrastructure and two Catholic parishes, St. Bruno's (1925) and St. Richard's (1928), accommodated the population surge. Though the Great Depression halted most residential construction, the Archer Heights Civic Association (1938), the oldest neighborhood organization on the Southwest Side, looked after the interests of those already living there.

During the 1930s and 1940s industrial and commercial growth overtook residential growth. Industry, initially in the Crawford Industrial District (a project of the Central Manufacturing District), eventually covered approximately two-thirds of the area, including the Santa Fe Railroad piggyback yard and the Kenwood Manufacturing District. Manufacturing and commercial transport (including Midway Airport, which opened in 1927) employed many Archer Heights residents. Commercial strips formed along Pulaski Road, Archer Avenue, and 47th Street, the major thoroughfares.

Residential growth picked up again after World War II. Between 1930 and 1950 Archer Heights's population inched upward from 8,120 to 8,675; it grew to 10,584 by 1960 and peaked at 11,143 in 1970. Then, as O'Hare supplanted Midway as Chicago's main airport, it declined: to 9,708 in 1980 and 9,227 in 1990. Despite these fluctuations, the community's composition has stayed notably consistent. For more than 90 years, its residents have been predominantly white (96 percent in 1990), with a large proportion foreign-born (27 percent in 1990) and a strong Polish cohort. Only recently has any nonwhite group dented the percentages. In the 1990s Hispanics, primarily Mexicans, rose

to 8 percent of the population. African Americans remain less than 1 percent.

At the close of the twentieth century, approximately 60 percent of the area was devoted to manufacturing and bulk transportation facilities, 30 percent to residences, and 10 percent to commerce. There was no distinct downtown or distinguishing landmarks. The regularity of the modest, well-kept housing combined with the large manufacturing presence established the neighborhood's character.

Jonathan J. Keyes

FURTHER READING: Chicago Fact Book Consortium, ed. *Local Community Fact Book: Chicago Metropolitan Area, 1990.* 1995. ▪ Karlen, Harvey M. *Chicago's Crabgrass Communities: The History of the Independent Suburbs and Their Post Offices That Became Part of Chicago.* 1992.

Arlington Heights, IL, Cook and Lake Counties, 23 miles NW of the Loop. Arlington Heights lies in the southwest corner of Wheeling Township, in an area originally notable for the absence of groves and trees. When the General Land Office began selling land here in 1835, most of the buyers were Yankees. In 1853 William Dunton, originally from Oswego, New York, persuaded the Illinois & Wisconsin Railroad to make a stop here, and laid out a town called Dunton.

By then the area had largely changed its ethnic composition, as many German farmers from Saxony had arrived during the 1840s. John Klehm, for example, was at first a potato farmer, supplying the Chicago market; in 1856 he began a nursery for cherry, apple, and pear trees, later moving into spruce, maple, and elm and eventually flowers. By the late 1850s the area was noted for its truck farms, sending dairy products as well as vegetables to Chicago on the railroad.

The little depot town slowly grew, acquiring a blacksmith, a cheese factory, a hardware store, and a hotel. The first churches, reflecting the origins of the citizenry, were Presbyterian (1856)

and Methodist (1858), with a German Lutheran church following in 1860; Catholics had no
church here until 1905. The town incorporated
as Arlington Heights in 1887, when its population numbered about 1,000. Most were farmers, but they were joined by others who worked
in Chicago, for Arlington Heights was an early
commuter suburb.

By the turn of the century Arlington Heights
had about 1,400 inhabitants, and it continued to
grow slowly, with a good many farms and greenhouses, after World War II. By then Arlington
Heights was also known for its racetrack, founded
in 1927 by the California millionaire H. D. "Curly"
Brown on land that had formerly constituted 12
farms. Camp McDonald and two country clubs
were founded in the 1930s.

The great population explosion took place in
the 1950s and 1960s; the spread of automobile
ownership, together with growth of the Chicago-area economy, drove the number of people
in Arlington Heights—expanded by a series of
annexations—up to 64,884 by 1970. By then virtually all the available land had been developed,
and the formerly isolated depot stop found itself
part of a continuously built-up area stretching
from Lake Michigan to the Fox River.

David Buisseret

FURTHER READING: *Chronicle of a Prairie Town: Arlington Heights, Illinois, Its People and Progress.* 1997.

Armour Square, Community Area 34, 3 miles S

of the Loop. The Armour
Square Community Area il-
lustrates the difference between a neighborhood and a
community area. This long
thin area (an assemblage of
leftovers from adjacent com-
munity areas, 21 blocks long, 4–5 blocks wide) is
wedged between rail lines, expressways, and the
South Branch of the Chicago River. It contains
three distinct neighborhoods. African Americans
dominate the population to the south; the middle
section holds recently arrived Hispanics; and

34
Armour
Square

along with a few Italians and blacks, CHINATOWN
fills the northern section.

Armour Square has been, from the beginning,
principally a working-class area. Germans and
Irish arrived during the Civil War; later, Swedes
joined the population. These groups used the area
as a way station as they moved southward and
climbed in social and economic status. Armour
Square lay south of the burned area during the
Chicago Fire of 1871 but was nonetheless greatly
affected by the disaster. Laws enacted after the
fire required brick or stone construction in the
central city. The resulting increase in costs drove
many working families out to the edge of the
"brick area," and Armour Square received many
of them. Armour Square subsequently lost blocks
of housing as the tracks of bordering railroads
were elevated. These changes cut off the area from
neighborhoods to the east and west.

By 1899 Italian immigrants arrived and formed
the Roman Catholic parish of Santa Maria Incoro-
nata. Commercial operations began to displace
housing in the area. Some of the encroaching
businesses were extensions of the notorious Levee
district just to the east. In 1909 Charles Comiskey
built a new baseball park for the Chicago White
Sox between 34th and 35th Streets, and the old
Sox park became home to the American Giants of
the Negro League. In 1991 the White Sox moved
into another new stadium, just south of the old
Comiskey Park; the Negro Leagues had by then
long since vanished.

Around 1912 Chinese living in an enclave at the
south edge of the LOOP began a mass movement
southward. The Chinese encountered severe racial discrimination, however, and were forced to
do business through an intermediary. The H. O.
Stone Company acted on behalf of 50 Chinese
businessmen to secure 10-year leases on buildings
in the new area. Chinatown became a major tourist attraction boasting an impressive entrance gate
and many other distinguishing features.

As the city's "Black Belt" began to expand during World War I, African Americans moved into
Armour Square's southern section, numbering

about 4,000 by 1930. This figure remained stable through the Great Depression and World War II until, in 1947, the Chicago Housing Authority completed Wentworth Gardens at 37th and Princeton and the neighborhood reached an all-time high population of over 23,000, with blacks making up nearly half the total. In the early to mid-1960s, widespread demolition made way for construction of the Dan Ryan and Stevenson Expressways and their interconnecting ramps, which set off a continuing decline in population.

In 1999 Chinese constituted over half the area's population. A rejuvenated Chinatown continued as a major tourist attraction with many shops and famed restaurants, and Chinese were moving west into BRIDGEPORT. An outside investor from Hong Kong developed Appleville apartments, and a consortium of Chinese businessmen and local banks developed Chinatown Square and Jade City apartments. Ping Tom Memorial Park, a new park along the river at 18th Street, was constructed in 1998 at the site of an old rail yard. Adaptive reuse of old structures, nearby infill housing, and the recently enlarged McCormick Place to the east added energy to the area.

David M. Solzman

FURTHER READING: "The Chinese in Chicago: The First One Hundred Years." Chap 13 in *Ethnic Chicago: A Multicultural Portrait*, 4th ed., ed. Melvin G. Holli and Peter d'A. Jones. 1995. ■ Chicago Fact Book Consortium, ed. *Local Community Fact Book: Chicago Metropolitan Area, Based on the 1970 and 1980 Censuses*. 1984. ■ Holt, Glen E., and Dominic A. Pacyga. *Chicago: A Historical Guide to the Neighborhoods: The Loop and South Side*. 1979.

Ashburn, Community Area 70, 10 miles SW of the Loop. Improvement in greater Ashburn began with the coming of the railroads, just after the area was annexed to Chicago as part of the town of Lake. The original 1893 subdivision, Clarkdale (named after its developer), was platted near 83rd and Central Park along the new

70
Ashburn

Chicago & Grand Trunk Railway (Grand Trunk Western Railroad) in the hope that the area would flourish after the World's Columbian Exposition. By 1894 the early Dutch, Swedish, and Irish population had built only 30 homes; 11 years later just 18 more residences had been added.

Chicago's first airport, Ashburn Flying Field, opened in 1916, spurring Chicago's drive to be an aviation center. During World War I it became a training camp for the Signal Corps, and Ashburn's population rose to 1,363. Afterward it had U.S. Post Office airmail contracts but, being situated on marshy prairie land, quickly lost them due to the field's remoteness and the prohibitive drainage costs. In 1927 Municipal Airport (now Midway) opened, and further interest in Ashburn diminished. Ashburn Field remained open until 1939; in the 1950s the site became Scottsdale, a suburban-style mall and subdivision.

By the eve of World War II the population had shrunk to 731. The years during and after the war were marked by industrial expansion between Pulaski and Cicero in Ashburn and neighboring WEST LAWN. This included Chrysler's 1943 Dodge plant for the manufacture of bomber engines, Tucker's automobile manufacturing in 1946–1947, and Ford's Korean War production. In 1960 the boundary between the two community areas was redrawn, creating Ashburn's jagged northern perimeter and uniting the industrial areas within the boundaries of West Lawn.

The automobile and the post–World War II baby boom spurred the community to meteoric growth. For over two decades the prairie surrendered to new housing construction, and population peaked at 47,161 in 1970. The prairie plants on the site were replanted in MARQUETTE PARK. The new neighborhoods—Ashburn, Wrightwood, Scottsdale, and Parkview—were predominantly white, until a 1993 subdivision, Marycrest, emerged racially mixed.

In the 1960s Ashburn was the site of significant racial strife over school desegregation. In subsequent decades, schools, churches, and neighborhoods integrated with the Greater Ashburn Planning Association (GAPA), working to minimize racial conflict.

Though hardly ostentatious, Ashburn has maintained an extremely high home ownership rate. Many early residents have moved to the southwestern suburbs; Ashburn Baptist Church has a satellite parish in ORLAND PARK. Retirement housing is under development to help families age in place—if the old stay it is hoped the young also will. Racial steering is not tolerated: For Sale signs, a tool in blockbusting, have been cooperatively banned; lawsuits are filed against realtors who do not comply. In recent years the only signs that have appeared on Ashburn lawns—en masse—read: "We're sold on Ashburn." A 1990 home equity assurance program protects property values.

Economic and aesthetic greening are paramount concerns. Having suffered a significant loss of industry and commerce, GAPA actively courts a diverse range of employers; it was also instrumental in the city's designation of a tax increment financing district along Columbus Avenue. The 2000 census population was 39,584.

Sherry Meyer

FURTHER READING: Karlen, Harvey M. *Chicago's Crabgrass Communities: The History of the Independent Suburbs and Their Post Offices That Became Part of Chicago.* 1992. ■ Kitagawa, Evelyn M., and Karl E. Taeuber, eds. *Local Community Fact Book of Chicago.* 1963. ■ Young, David, and Neal Callahan. *Fill the Heavens with Commerce: Chicago Aviation, 1855–1926.* 1981.

Auburn Gresham, Community Area 71, 9 miles SW of the Loop. The low, flat, swampy land upon which Auburn Gresham was built was located in the southeast section of the town of Lake, which was annexed to Chicago in 1889. Early settlers were German and Dutch truck farmers. When railroad lines were laid in the mid-nineteenth century, Irish railroad workers came to the area. The World's Columbian Exposition in 1893

71
Auburn
Gresham

attracted prospective homesteaders to the South Side through the extension and improvement of city services to the area, including streetcar lines. Between 1913 and 1918 the city further extended the lines on Halsted to 119th Street and the cars on Racine and Ashland Avenues to 87th Street. The 79th Street line ran from Western Avenue to the Lake Michigan beaches.

Auburn Gresham's accessibility to transportation made the neighborhood an easy sell for developers looking to attract families who were trying to escape older and more congested sections of the city. Many Auburn Gresham residents migrated from the working-class neighborhoods of BRIDGEPORT, Canaryville, and BACK OF THE YARDS, as well as from ENGLEWOOD. Twenty-one percent of Auburn Gresham's population were of Irish stock in the 1930s. German Americans, Swedish Americans, and some Polish, Italian, and French Americans also took up residence in the area. Many stockyard workers commuted to work on the Halsted streetcar. City workers such as police and firefighters, as well as railroad and construction workers, found the neighborhood convenient. Between 1920 and 1930 the population of Auburn Gresham nearly tripled, from 19,558 to 57,381. Most of the housing built there were bungalows, two- and three-flats, and apartment buildings.

Approximately 44 percent of Auburn Gresham's population in the 1920s were Roman Catholics, concentrated into five large parishes. There were six Lutheran, three Methodist, and two Episcopal churches, as well as small Presbyterian, Baptist, and nonaffiliated congregations. Ethnic groups tended to live near their respective churches. Many Catholics were clustered near St. Leo's and St. Sabina's parishes. There was no overt Protestant-Catholic hostility here as in other Chicago neighborhoods, probably because few residents were nativists of Anglo-Protestant stock.

Auburn Gresham weathered the Great Depression and World War II and enjoyed the peaceful and prosperous 1950s. By the end of that decade, African Americans seeking housing beyond the overcrowded and decaying Black Belt began to move into neighborhoods adjacent to Auburn Gresham. While this provoked racist anxieties among many residents, in 1959 several churches and civic organizations formed the Organization of Southwest Communities (OSC). Modeled on Saul Alinsky's community organizing tactics, the OSC's goals were to maintain property values and appearances, stop blockbusting by real-estate agents, educate residents to dispel racist stereotypes, and prevent violence while allowing peaceful, stable integration.

In its first five years, OSC enjoyed wide and even enthusiastic support from residents who felt protected from property-value declines and racial violence. In the 1960s, however, crime in the Gresham police district rose at a faster rate than in the city as a whole; crimes ranged from purse snatchings and bicycle thefts to home break-ins. At the same time, Auburn Gresham's population, which for 20 years had remained relatively stable, increased dramatically, growing from 59,484 to 68,854 between 1960 and 1970. The swell of cars and noise made the area less appealing, and parking difficulties at night made crime-fearing residents more anxious.

City and national events also played a role in chilling race relations in Auburn Gresham. In 1966 violence greeted the civil rights march of Martin Luther King Jr. in nearby MARQUETTE PARK. King's death in Memphis on April 4, 1968, set off riots in Chicago and across the county. Many white residents in Auburn Gresham came to the conclusion that violence was an inevitable by-product of racial mixing.

By 1970 Auburn Gresham was 69 percent black, including many middle-class federal employees and Chicago Transit Authority workers. Most African Americans initially settled in the eastern portion of the neighborhood. While OSC could not maintain integration, it did make the transition from white to black more peace-

ful, less destructive to property values, and a less embittering experience for many.

Eileen M. McMahon

FURTHER READING: McMahon, Eileen M. *What Parish Are You From? A Chicago Irish Community and Race Relations.* 1995. ■ Pacyga, Dominic A., and Ellen Skerrett. *Chicago, City of Neighborhoods: Histories and Tours.* 1986.

Aurora, IL, DuPage and Kane Counties, 35 miles W of the Loop. The city of Aurora, the economic anchor of the Fox River Valley area, has a population of over 110,000. It began in 1834, when Joseph and Samuel McCarty came from New York looking for a river site to build a mill. A strategic bend in the Fox River at this location satisfied the McCarty brothers. The river served as a power source for mills and early factories even as periodic floods destroyed businesses, bridges, and dams.

The town incorporated in 1845. In 1854 a second town incorporated west of the river, and three years later, the separate municipalities united. To ease political tensions between the two, civic offices were located on an island in the river; ward boundaries ended at the river, and the mayor was elected from alternate sides until 1913. While the east side was initially much larger than the west, both physically and in population, the river now divides the town into roughly equal geographic areas.

Following the establishment of textile mills and gristmills, Aurora became a manufacturing center, primarily of heavy-machine building equipment. In 1856 the Chicago, Burlington & Quincy railroad located its railcar construction and repair shops in Aurora, and it remained the town's largest employer until the 1960s. These businesses were located primarily on the east side and provided employment for four generations of European immigrants. Aurora's professional and managerial workers came from Yankee stock and settled across the river, making the west side more afflu-

A celebration in 1940 marked the 90th anniversary of the first rail connection between Aurora and Chicago. The car shown is a Pullman sleeping car, introduced later in the nineteenth century. Photographer: Unknown. Source: The Newberry Library.

ent. The combination of these three factors—a highly industrialized town, a sizable river dividing it, and the Burlington shops—account for much of the dynamics of Aurora's political, economic, and social history.

Aurora's character formed early. Philosophically, the town was inclusive and tolerant, welcoming a variety of European immigrants and openly supporting abolitionist activity prior to the Civil War. Mexican migrants began arriving after 1910. In 2000 Aurora's population was 32 percent Hispanic and 11 percent black.

Socially, the town was progressive in its attitude toward education, religion, welfare, and women, establishing the first free public school district in Illinois in 1851 and a high school for girls in 1855, supporting 20 congregations (including two African American churches) representing nine denominations in 1887, and establishing a YWCA in 1893 that is still in operation today.

As late as the post–World War II boom, manufacturing companies continued to locate in Au-

rora to take advantage of the abundant workforce, good transportation, and favorable economy. Few labor problems affected Aurora.

With the closing of many factories in the 1980s, the town's unemployment rate reached 16 percent. In response, Aurora initiated downtown redevelopment and border annexations, welcoming riverboat casinos, mixed-use business parks, and residential communities to create 20,000 jobs.

Aurora is frequently referred to as a Chicago suburb, most often by the nonlocal media or for promotional purposes. The city remains a self-sufficient community, independent of Chicago for its identity, but connected to it through the economic patterns that link suburbs, edge cities, and central cities.

Catherine Bruck

FURTHER READING: Barclay, Robert. *Aurora, 1837–1987.* 1988. ■ Derry, Vernon. *The Aurora Story.* 1976. ■ Palmer, Susan L. "Building Ethnic Communities in a Small City: Romanians & Mexicans in Aurora, Illinois, 1900–1940." Ph.D. diss., Northern Illinois University. 1986.

Austin, Community Area 25, 7 miles W of the  Loop. Austin, on Chicago's western border, evolved from a country village to a dense urban neighborhood between 1870 and 1920. For the next 50 years it was a large community of solidly middle class residents, but since 1970 it has experienced a profound social and economic transformation. Austin had three important early influences: its founder, Henry Austin (also instrumental in the development of Oak Park); transit lines, notably the Chicago & North Western Railway and the Lake Street Elevated; and a rivalry with neighboring OAK PARK.

25
Austin

In 1865 developer Henry Austin purchased 470 acres for a temperance settlement named "Austinville" (Chicago Avenue to Madison Street, and Laramie to Austin Boulevard). Though Austin himself lived in Oak Park, he clearly intended the settlement to foster gracious living, with tree-lined parkways and other public amenities, and an emphasis on home ownership. By 1874 the village had nearly 1,000 residents, its growth owing largely to steadily improving suburban railroad service. With over 4,000 residents by the 1890s, Austin was the largest settlement in Cicero township. In 1899 Austin was voted out of the township and into Chicago by residents of other parts of the township. Austin's residents sought to maintain an independent identity after annexation. An ambitious illustration was the construction, in 1929, of Austin Town Hall, modeled on Philadelphia's Independence Hall.

By 1920 Austin was one of Chicago's best-served commuter areas, with street railways to downtown Chicago every half mile, the busiest being the Madison Street "Green Hornet." The area was also served by the Lake Street "L" rapid transit. Commerce in Austin followed transit lines, with significant business development along Madison Street, Chicago Avenue, and Lake Street. Despite its commercial range and volume, Austin lacked the intense concentration of retail and service-oriented businesses of WEST GARFIELD PARK (on Madison, between Pulaski and Cicero) or of Oak Park (at Lake and Harlem). By 1950 Austin was a predominantly residential community, with major industrial corridors to the east, north, and south.

Austin early attracted upwardly mobile Germans and Scandinavians, followed by Irish and Italian families. These groups built the community's mid-twentieth-century landmarks: a half-dozen sizable Roman Catholic parishes, which annually educated thousands of children and provided the social base for much of the community. By the 1930s Greek migrants had arrived in south Austin, building their own landmark, the Byzantine-style Assumption church. Austin had 130,000 residents by 1930.

Dense housing development almost completely supplanted the village landscape of large frame homes in the early twentieth century: north Austin sprouted brick two-flats, small frame houses, and the ubiquitous brick story-and-a-half bungalow; in south Austin, row houses, sizable corner apartment blocks, and a multitude of brick three-flats and courtyard apartment buildings flourished. Despite the massive scale change, the nineteenth-century village residential core is still visible in the Midway Park area north of Central and Lake, a designated National Register historic district in 1985. This neighborhood boasts stately neoclassical and Queen Anne–style homes, many designed by architect Frederick Schock, as well as several structures by Frank Lloyd Wright and his students.

Austin's crown jewel was Columbus Park (1920). Designed in a Prairie mode by renowned landscape architect Jens Jensen, the park featured a lagoon, a golf course, athletic fields and a swimming pool, as well as winding paths and an imposing refectory overlooking the lagoon. Assaulted by expressway construction in the 1960s, the park was extensively restored in 1992.

Austin's demographic profile shifted dramatically beginning in the late 1960s. By 1980 its population was predominantly African Ameri-

Trolley bus, Central Avenue at Lake Street, 1930s. Photographer: Unknown. Source: Chicago Public Library.

can, more than 96 percent in south Austin. Like other west-side communities, Austin experienced housing disinvestment, vacancy, and demolition, as well as loss of jobs and of commerce as its white population moved to the suburbs and to Chicago's Northwest Side. Neighborhood groups like the Organization for a Better Austin have worked to stabilize the community, as have nonprofit housing developers aided by South Shore Bank.

Judith A. Martin

FURTHER READING: Martin, Judith A. "The Influence of Values on an Urban Community: The Austin Area of Chicago, 1890–1920." M.A. thesis, University of Minnesota. 1973. ■ Pacyga, Dominic A., and Ellen Skerrett. *Chicago, City of Neighborhoods: Histories and Tours*. 1986. ■ Sinkevitch, Alice, ed. *AIA Guide to Chicago*. 1993.

Avalon Park, Community Area 45, 10 miles SE of the Loop. The area now known as Avalon Park was so swampy during most of the nineteenth

century that the few houses located there had to be perched on stilts to avoid flooding and infestation. The main natural features were Mud Lake and Stony Island. For a time, Avalon Park's isolation made it a site for waste disposal. The borders of the community are South Chicago Avenue and the Chicago Skyway to the northeast, 87th Street to the south, and the Illinois Central Railroad to the west. A 30-acre park of the same name is situated on the southwestern corner of Avalon Park.

45
Avalon Park

Although swampy conditions discouraged early attempts at permanent settlement, railroad workers of German and Irish descent began to reside in the northern section of the community by the late 1880s. In addition to railroad workers, skilled mechanics, many of them Germans employed in nearby PULLMAN or BURNSIDE, also made Avalon Park their home. Annexation to Chicago in 1889, the World's Columbian Exposition of 1893, and the installation of drainage in 1900 stimulated residential growth.

Like many communities, Avalon Park's history has been characterized by successive waves of home building and population growth, although its population began to decline after 1970. The most active period of single-family home building occurred between 1900 (just after drainage) and 1910. In 1910 the community, which had unofficially been called "Pennytown," was officially named Avalon Park. A second housing boom occurred in the 1920s and a third after World War II, when single-family brick bungalows and a few apartments were constructed. The postwar boom coincided with a rise in jobs in nearby steel mills and industrial plants.

By 1930 more than 10,000 people resided in Avalon Park, up from 2,911 a decade before. The community remains primarily residential, served by a shopping district at 79th Street and Stony Island, as well as several schools and churches. Owner-occupancy rates have consistently been over 70 percent in recent decades.

Transitions have occurred along both class and racial lines. By 1930 residents of Swedish origin, having joined the earlier, predominantly German and Irish residents, constituted 19 percent of Avalon Park's population. Most were railroad, steel mill, and factory workers. The African Americans who began to move into Avalon Park during the 1960s, like their neighbors in adjoining CHATHAM, were for the most part middle-class doctors, lawyers, businessmen, and other professionals. In 1970 Avalon Park reached a population high of 14,412, of whom 83 percent were African American. By 1980 African American residents made up 96 percent of a population of 13,792.

Avalon Park's population dropped significantly by the end of the century, falling to 11,147, just below the level of 1950. In the late 1990s, to counter this trend, real-estate developers planned several multiunit housing developments along 83rd Street.

Wallace Best

FURTHER READING: "South Side Camelot." *Chicago Tribune*, April 17, 1992. ■ "South Side Living." *Chicago Tribune*, January 31, 1998. ■ Chicago Fact Book Consortium, ed. *Local Community Fact Book: Chicago Metropolitan Area, 1990.* 1995.

Avondale, Community Area 21, 6 miles NW of the Loop. The Avondale Community Area lies west of the North Branch of the Chicago River between Addison on the north and Diversey on the south, and stretches west to the tracks

21
Avondale

of the Chicago, Milwaukee, St. Paul & Pacific. At the beginning of the nineteenth century, the prairie site was traversed by a meandering Indian trail. After 1848 the trail was straightened and planked as Milwaukee Avenue. Avondale developed along this road and the railroad lines that subsequently paralleled it west of the Chicago River. The Milwaukee road's planks, however, broke under heavy loads or warped in the sun. Worse, the road was interrupted by tollgates, which added the insult of expense to the already uncertain and uncomfortable ride. In 1889 some citizens of Avondale dressed as Indians rioted and burned down a tollgate, killed its owner, and stripped the planks from the stringers for firewood.

More farms appeared after the Chicago, Milwaukee, St. Paul & Pacific tracks were extended to Milwaukee in 1870, and in 1873 a post office was built at the corner of Belmont and Troy where the Chicago & North Western Railway made a stop. In the 1880s a small group of about 20 African American families settled east of Milwaukee Avenue and built the first church in Avondale, the Allen Church.

Rapid growth began in 1889 when the area was annexed to the city of Chicago. The city soon hard-surfaced Milwaukee Avenue. Further

Riverview Park, Western, Belmont and Clybourn Aves., View from River, Chicago.

Postcard of Riverview Park, ca. 1909. Photographer: Unknown. Source: Chicago History Museum.

transportation improvements including the electrification and extension of the street railway lines on Milwaukee and Elston Avenues. Construction of the Logan Square branch of the elevated line led to prodigious development between 1890 and 1920. The railroads and a horsecar line on Milwaukee Avenue provided relatively rapid transportation to jobs in the city.

By 1920 the population exceeded 38,000. More than one-quarter of these residents were foreign-born, mostly Germans along with some Swedes and Austrians. By 1930 Poles constituted 33 percent of the population of 48,000. As new waves of Poles entered the community from the tenements west of the city center, German, Scandinavian, and even some of the earlier Polish residents began to move further northwest. Poles remained the dominant ethnic group in 1980, but by 1990 Hispanics accounted for 37 percent of the total population.

Avondale developed as a working-class community, since the rail lines and the river served to attract industry. Numerous clay pits and brick

factories were concentrated near Belmont Avenue in an area that came to be known as Bricktown. This brick was much in demand after the 1871 fire demonstrated the usefulness of materials other than wood for city construction. After 1920 Grebe's Boatyard occupied the west bank of the Chicago River north of Belmont. Grebe's produced luxury powered yachts for wealthy patrons but also minesweepers and other small naval vessels during World War II. Across the river rose Riverview Amusement Park, with its storied roller coaster, "the Bobs." Riverview Park is gone now, and so is the boatyard. Today, along the river, luxury town houses, condominiums, and shopping malls are replacing the old industrial belt, causing the loss of many of the industrial jobs that have for so long supported this old working-class neighborhood.

David M. Solzman

FURTHER READING: Chicago Fact Book Consortium, ed. *Local Community Fact Book: Chicago Metropolitan Area, Based on the 1970 and 1980 Censuses.* 1984. ■ Schnedler, Jack. *Chicago.* 1996. ■ Solzman, David M. *The Chicago River: An Illustrated History and Guide to the River and Its Waterways.* 1998, 2006.

Back of the Yards. Situated in a heavily industrialized location, populated by successive generations of immigrants, and animated by some of the most dramatic social conflicts of modern times, Back of the Yards captured the attention of novelists, activists, and social scientists alike for most of the twentieth century. Located in the New City Community Area, the neighborhood extends from 39th to 55th Streets between Halsted and the railroad tracks along Leavitt Street, just south and west of the former Union Stock Yard and adjacent packing plants, a giant sprawl that was until the 1950s the largest livestock yards and meatpacking center in the country.

The concentration of railroads in the mid-nine-teenth century, the establishment of the Union Stock Yard in 1865, and the perfection of the refrigerated boxcar by 1880 led to a giant expansion of meatpacking in the neighborhood. Part of the town of Lake until annexation by Chicago in 1889, Back of the Yards was settled by skilled Irish and German butchers, joined in the 1870s and 1880s by Czechs. Here, in 1889, developer Samuel Gross built one of his earliest subdivisions of cheap workingmen's cottages. By the turn of the century the area was transformed into a series of Slavic enclaves dominated by Poles, Lithuanians, Slovaks, and Czechs, with most communities organized around ethnic parishes that serve as social and cultural as well as spiritual focal points for residents' lives. Small numbers of Mexican immigrants entered Back of the Yards and neighboring Bridgeport as early as World War I and the 1920s, but the community retained

This 1950 photo shows the then still-operating William Mavor bath, constructed in 1900 and named after a Chicago alderman. The third municipal bath opened by the city of Chicago, it was located at 4645 S. Gross (later McDowell) Avenue. Photographer: Mildred Mead. Source: Chicago History Museum.

its Slavic character until the 1970s, when it gradually became a largely Chicano community with a minority of African Americans.

Immortalized for its pollution, squalor, and poverty in Upton Sinclair's *The Jungle* (1906), government reports, and University of Chicago sociology studies, Back of the Yards was in fact home to particularly vibrant and cohesive working-class communities over time. The sprawling stockyards and adjacent plants with their unique combination of pollution, erratic work schedules, occupational diseases, and low wages exacted a heavy toll on the community in the years up to the Great Depression, but workers and their families organized a series of struggles in and outside the plants to improve and protect their communities.

In the Depression and World War II years residents created two key social movements: the Packinghouse Workers Organizing Committee (later the United Packinghouse Workers of America, or UPWA-CIO) and the Back of the Yards Neighborhood Council (BYNC). The UPWA-CIO, a particularly effective industrial union movement, became a progressive mainstay of the labor movement. The BYNC, a coalition of dozens of neighborhood and parish groups, became Saul Alinsky's model for community organizing throughout the country. While the UPWA-CIO raised wages, stabilized employment, and fought for civil rights in the plants, the BYNC galvanized a broader community identity among the diverse ethnic groups and addressed an array of community problems.

With the end of Chicago's meatpacking industry by the 1960s, Back of the Yards once again faced economic decline and physical deterioration. At the end of the twentieth century, as the city worked to develop a new manufacturing district on the site of the old Union Stock Yard, the newer residents resumed the old struggle to maintain a strong community.

James R. Barrett

FURTHER READING: Barrett, James R. *Work and Community in the Jungle: Chicago's Packinghouse Workers, 1894–1922.* 1987. ■ Jablonsky, Thomas J. *Pride in the Jungle: Community and Everyday Life in Back of the Yards Chicago.* 1993. ■ Slayton, Robert A. *Back of the Yards: The Making of a Local Democracy.* 1986.

Barrington, IL, Cook and Lake Counties, 32 miles NW of the Loop. While the oak grove and prairie land that lay between Chicago and the Fox River in the 1830s were both attractive and fertile, fear of Indian attack during the 1832 Black Hawk War and the lack of milling facilities kept Eastern farmers from entering the area. After the war, mills were erected along the Fox River at Dundee and Algonquin, and land-hungry Yankees flowed in.

William Butler Ogden became interested in connecting the developing northwest to Chicago's growing port facilities. He gained control of the Chicago, St. Paul & Fond du Lac Railroad (later the Chicago & North Western Railway) in 1854 and pushed its tracks to the northwest corner of Cook County, where a station named Deer Grove was built.

Although it meant improved profits, many area farmers feared the railroad would bring too many saloons and Irish Catholics to the area. In response to the opposition, Robert Campbell, a civil engineer working for the Fond du Lac line, purchased a farm two miles northwest of Deer Grove and platted a community there in 1854. At Campbell's request, the railroad moved the station building to his new community, which he called Barrington, after Barrington, Massachusetts, the original home of a number of area farmers.

The prosperity of the Civil War era increased Barrington's population to 300 in 1863. Because leaders believed the growing community needed tax-supported improvements, an election to incorporate Barrington was held on February 16, 1865. Homer Willmarth became the first village president. The village prospered as many Chicago grain merchants whose homes were destroyed in the Great Fire of 1871 constructed opulent Queen

Anne–style residences along Barrington's tree-shaded streets.

The Elgin, Joliet & Eastern Railway was built through Barrington in 1889, and the village continued to serve agriculturally based trading interests into the twentieth century. Dairy farming was the major activity on the meadows and woodlots surrounding the community. Fueled by post–World War I prosperity, however, a number of Chicago business leaders built their residences on large woodland tracts around the village, bringing an end to dairying.

The large estate acreage, which tended to remain in family hands decade after decade, protected Barrington from the densely packed residential developments that came to neighboring communities in the 1950s and 1960s. Barrington's population grew from 3,213 in 1930 to only 5,435 in 1960. But with the construction of the Northwest Tollway five miles to the south in the early 1960s, development did come to Barrington's south side. Population reached 10,168 in 2000.

Barrington's leaders continue their opposition to dense population developments when estate acreage comes up for sale. A proposal to turn the Elgin, Joliet & Eastern Railway into a suburb-to-suburb commuter line with Barrington as a major stop also met strong disapproval based on the fear that such a transportation development would clog the city with traffic and noise, as had happened in towns along the Northwest Tollway.

Craig L. Pfannkuche

FURTHER READING: Lines, Arnett C. *A History of Barrington, Illinois*. 1977. ■ Messenger, Janet. "Country Living." *Northshore Magazine*, December 1997, 73–94. ■ Sharp, Cynthia Baker. *Tales of Old Barrington*. 1976.

Belmont Cragin, Community Area 19, 8 miles NW of the Loop. Belmont Cragin is a community built on commerce and industry. The first business was a saloon opened by George Merrill sometime after 1835, when he settled with his family at

19
Belmont
Cragin

the intersection of Armitage and Grand Avenues. Operating the saloon out of his home, Merrill catered to truck farmers carrying produce over the plank road (Milwaukee Avenue) to the city. The corner, named Whiskey Point, prompted many colorful and romanticized legends but attracted few permanent residents.

In 1862 Michael Moran established a hotel at Whiskey Point, but the area remained rural until 20 years later, when Cragin Brothers & Company moved their tin plate and sheet iron processing plant nearby. The plant and warehouses covered 11 acres, and the Chicago, Milwaukee, St. Paul & Pacific Railroad built a station at Leclaire Avenue to accommodate all the employees. Cragin also purchased a rivet company and moved machinery and workers from Connecticut to the location. Job opportunities and rail service brought settlers and a new-housing boom to the town, now named Cragin. Within the first two years the population rose to 200, and the community boasted a general store, two schoolhouses, and a Congregational church.

Railroads drew more factories and workers to the area, which was annexed to Chicago as part of Jefferson Township in 1889. The Belt Railway Company extended its service in 1883, and plants developed in the new neighborhoods of Hanson Park and Galewood. In the same year the Washburn and Moen Manufacturing Company launched a branch for its wire products, and the Western Brick and Tile Company found Galewood's superior clay soil conducive to business. By 1891 Westinghouse, Church, Kerr & Company Iron Works, the Pitts Agricultural Works Warehouse, and the Rice and Bullen Malting Company brought more people into Cragin. In 1922 W. F. Hall Printing Company erected a plant on 17 acres adjacent to the Northwestern railroad line, which further spurred manufacturing development.

Swedish, German, and Irish workers were among the earliest to move near these factories. By 1920 jobs drew Poles and Italians as well, and the population of the area more than quadrupled in the next decade. By 1930 the population escalated to 60,221, one-third of whom were foreign-born. Slower growth ensued. In the 1930s the community area became known as Belmont Cragin. Builders inundated the area to fill the housing needs of area workers. Bungalows, Cape Cods, and two-flats offered a range of housing choices. Especially popular was the subdivided residential neighborhood on the eastern border named Belmont Park.

Shopping districts added to the commercial atmosphere. In the 1940s Belmont-Central was constructed with a dozen stores, a parking lot, and a children's playground. During the postwar years the Chicago Transit Authority extended its Belmont Street bus service beyond Central, transporting new patrons into the district. The March 1976 opening of the Brickyard Shopping Mall, on the former site of the Carey Brickyard property at Narragansett and Diversey, added new vitality to the community, drawing city shoppers away from suburban malls. The addition of a nearby parking garage in 1981 also contributed to business prosperity.

Belmont Cragin's overall population grew by more than 6 percent in the 1980s and 37 percent in the 1990s. The Hispanic population grew from 3,072 in 1980 to 16,846 in 1990; by the 2000 census the area was 65 percent Hispanic. Polish immigrants and businesses also came to the area during these years. A number of young middle-class professionals joined blue-collar laborers in the area. Residents formed an active coalition called the Northwest Neighborhood Federation to address increases in crime, gangs, and school overpopulation.

By 1995 Hall Printing and other plants had closed their doors. The area experienced a drop in manufacturing employment and a decline in retail activity during the 1980s. Concerns over unemployment and an increasing poverty level have led residents to organize a home reinvestment campaign and to study ways of reviving the commercial climate in the area.

Marilyn Elizabeth Perry

FURTHER READING: Clipping file. Chicago Public Library, Portage-Cragin branch. ■ Karlen, Harvey M. *Chicago's Crabgrass Communities: The History of the Independent Suburbs and Their Post Offices That Became Part of Chicago.* 1992. ■ Krob, Gregory James. "The Economic Impact of a Regional Shopping Center on the Central City: A Study of the Brickyard Shopping Center, Chicago, Illinois." M.A. thesis, University of Illinois at Chicago. 1982.

Belmont Terrace, neighborhood in the DUNNING Community Area.

Bensenville, IL, DuPage County, 17 miles W of the Loop. The village of Bensenville occupies the northeast corner of DuPage County near O'Hare Airport. Bensenville has evolved from rural farming community to railroad town to mature airport suburb, reflecting changes in the Chicago area.

As in other DuPage communities, the Potawatomi tribe represented the largest Indian presence before their removal after 1833. New Englanders Hezekiah Dunklee and Mason Smith established claims near Salt Creek soon after the Indian removal in a wooded grove west of present-day Bensenville in Addison Township. Political strife in Europe contributed to building the area's population, as many German immigrants settled in the area.

These farmers raised wheat and dairy products. A stage road connecting Chicago, ELGIN, and Galena and a plank road that paralleled Irving Park Road promoted travel, trade, and settlement in the region. The opening of the Galena & Chicago Union Railroad in 1849 to the south also contributed to growth and provided a glimpse into the role of transportation in the community's future.

In the early 1870s Dietrich Struckmann, T. R. Dobbins, and Roselle Hough purchased and subdivided the land that would become Bensenville. The Chicago, Milwaukee, St. Paul & Pacific Railroad began service between Chicago and Elgin with a stop in the area. Discussion of incorporation soon began, and on May 10, 1884, the measure passed handily.

Over the next 30 years Bensenville began to resemble a suburb. The first school opened in 1886, and storm sewers were constructed a year later. Other amenities, such as telephone service, concrete sidewalks, and electricity, followed in the early 1900s. Most significant, the Chicago, Milwaukee & St. Paul constructed a roundhouse and freight yard in Bensenville in 1916. The yard provided many jobs and attracted new residents, including many Mexicans. Bensenville soldiered quietly forward through the 1920s and 1930s, reaching a population of 1,869 by 1940.

In 1940 the federal government announced plans to construct an aircraft plant to manufacture cargo planes just outside Bensenville in Cook County. The plant operated from 1943 to 1945. Chicago purchased the complex in 1946 to develop a large airport. The proposed facility required additional land in unincorporated DuPage County, which Chicago planned to acquire. Nearby Bensenville challenged Chicago's right to annex this land in court, but lost. Many unincorporated Bensenville structures were moved or demolished to accommodate portions of O'Hare Airport, which began domestic commercial service in 1955.

Bensenville's population grew dramatically after World War II, doubling by 1950 and nearly tripling by 1960. O'Hare provided the catalyst for increased industrial development between the airport and residential areas, but it also created substantial noise pollution. Bensenville joined 16 other area suburbs in 1969 in forming the O'Hare Area Noise Abatement Council to address this issue.

Like its eastern DuPage neighbors, Bensenville has nearly reached its limits in terms of land development. The village still attracts residents from many ethnic backgrounds, including Indians, East Asians, and Eastern Europeans, and grew slightly, to a population of 20,703, in 2000.

Aaron Harwig

FURTHER READING: Jones, Martha Kirker. *Bensenville*. 1976. ■ *Knowing Our History, Learning Our Culture*. Videotape. 42 min. 1993. Bensenville Community Library.

■ Ritzert, Kenneth. "Bensenville." In *DuPage Roots*, ed. Richard Thompson. 1985.

Berwyn, IL, Cook County, 9 miles W of the Loop.

In June 1856, Thomas Baldwin bought 347 acres in the southern section of modern-day Berwyn from the Illinois & Michigan Canal Company, hoping to create an affluent community called LaVergne. Baldwin's property became part of Cicero Township in 1857. With the canal a mile to the south, LaVergne was initially accessible only via the Southwest Plank Road (Ogden Avenue). The Chicago, Burlington & Quincy Railroad ran through the area by 1864 but did not stop in LaVergne until a decade later.

By 1880 a real-estate syndicate that included Marshall Field had acquired Baldwin's land and platted a new LaVergne subdivision. Large numbers of Swedish immigrants settled north of the railroad tracks on a section of Baldwin's former property soon known as Upsala. The Mutual Life Insurance Company acquired the northernmost portion of the canal company land, surveying and subdividing it in 1887. More than a mile removed from LaVergne and Upsala, the area developed quite independently.

In 1890 the Field syndicate sold 106 acres to investors Charles E. Piper and Wilbur J. Andrews. The developers subdivided the land, constructing streets, sidewalks, and sewers, and named the new subdivision Berwyn, after a Philadelphia suburb listed on a Pennsylvania Railroad timetable. Middle-class Chicagoans were quickly drawn to the desirable new community, with its many amenities. In 1891 Piper and Andrews acquired additional land, nearly doubling the town's size.

By 1900 Chicago was hungrily annexing surrounding communities. To prevent its annexation, Berwyn voted in 1901 to separate from Cicero Township and become an independent village. Only seven years later Berwyn incorporated as a city. The community began to draw large numbers of Czechoslovakian families, along with Germans, Poles, and Italians. Population more than doubled between 1910 and 1920, with new building concentrated in south Berwyn. Because the city prohibited heavy industry within its borders, the community remained largely residential. Many Berwyn residents worked at the nearby Hawthorne Works of the Western Electric Company. Thus Berwyn suffered a great loss when in July 1915 the excursion boat *Eastland*, chartered for a Western Electric company outing to MICHIGAN CITY, Indiana, capsized in the Chicago River, drowning 812.

Berwyn experienced phenomenal growth during the 1920s, gaining a reputation as Chicago's fastest-growing suburb. The city's stringent building codes resulted in block upon block of well-built, two-story brick bungalows. To serve its expanding population, Berwyn established an independent park district and created Illinois' first municipal health district. The street improvements that sparked the boom also helped unify north and south.

Berwyn's growth slowed substantially during the Great Depression, but the community experienced a second building boom after World War II, pushing its population to 54,226 in 1960. Population began to fall thereafter, as longtime residents aged and their offspring moved away. By 1990 some of these children were returning to Berwyn to raise their own families. Often more affluent than their parents, they demanded new services and drove up real-estate prices, leaving old-timers "house poor." And while Berwyn's Czech heritage retained its importance, increasing ethnic diversity further tested the city. Despite these challenges, however, Berwyn remains a solidly middle-class bedroom community.

Elizabeth A. Patterson

FURTHER READING: *Berwyn Views*. Miscellaneous pamphlets. Undated. Chicago History Museum, Chicago. ∎ Chicago Fact Book Consortium, ed. *Local Community Fact Book: Chicago Metropolitan Area, 1990.* 1995. ∎ *Twenty-five Years of Progress with Berwyn, Cicero, and Stickney, November 1951: The Life Newspapers' Silver Anniversary Edition.* 1951.

Beverly, Community Area 72, 12 miles S of the

72
Beverly

Loop. Known for its spacious homes, tree-lined streets, and racially integrated population, Beverly has retained its reputation as one of Chicago's most stable middle-class residential districts. Originally part of the village of WASHINGTON HEIGHTS (1874), this area was annexed to Chicago by 1890 but remained sparsely settled for decades. Residents often identify their community as "Beverly Hills," a reference to the glacial ridge just west of Longwood Drive, the highest point in Chicago. Whether the community was named after Beverly, Massachusetts, or Beverly Hills, California, remains subject to debate, but in the 1890s the Rock Island Railroad (Chicago, Rock Island & Pacific Railroad) designated its 91st Street station Beverly Hills, and by World War I the telephone company had established a Beverly exchange.

In 1886 real-estate developer Robert Givins constructed a limestone castle at 103rd and Longwood Drive in the Tracy Subdivision of Washington Heights, but the surrounding neighborhood did not achieve residential maturity for decades. The situation was the same north of 95th Street, where Civil War general Edward Young and W. M. R. French, the first director of the Art Institute, built homes along Pleasant Avenue in the 1890s. Vast sections of Beverly, especially the area south of 99th Street and west of Western, remained prairie until the 1940s and 1950s.

From its earliest days, this community symbolized upward social mobility, first for white Anglo-Saxon Protestants, and later for Irish Roman Catholics and African Americans. Like MORGAN PARK to the south, Beverly has always been a dry area, prohibiting saloons and the sale of liquor in the area east of Western Avenue. The community's suburban setting was further enhanced by Ridge Park with its imposing field house (1912) designed by local architect John Todd Hetherington and by its close proximity to Beverly and Ridge Country Clubs and the Dan Ryan Forest

Preserve. Its housing stock remained predominantly single-family with only a few apartment buildings clustered along the Rock Island Railroad tracks that link Beverly to downtown Chicago. Although the 95th Street commercial district included a variety of shops and restaurants, it never rivaled ROSELAND's Michigan Avenue or 63rd and Halsted. Indeed, the Beverly Theater was built outside the community's boundaries at 95th and Ashland Avenue in the mid-1930s and residents did not have their own branch of the Chicago Public Library until 1981.

Beverly's churches and public schools reflected the community's growth from east to west. Bethany Union (1872) and Trinity Methodist (1896), originally located on Prospect Avenue, built architecturally significant houses of worship in the 1920s closer to Longwood Drive.

In the 1920s Beverly's ethnic composition expanded to include Irish Catholics and German Lutherans, who established St. Barnabas church and school (1924) and St. John the Divine Lutheran (1929). Anti-Catholic sentiment ran so high that residents had property at 100th and Longwood Drive condemned for a public park to prevent its use by the Catholic congregation. But St. Barnabas parish persisted, and in 1936 a second Catholic parish, Christ the King, was organized in north Beverly. By the time St. John Fisher was formed in 1948 in the newest section of the community, Catholics had become the largest denomination in Beverly.

Beyond the post–World War II baby boom, Beverly's increase in population between 1940 and 1960, from 15,910 to 24,814, was due in large measure to racial change in such neighborhoods as ENGLEWOOD, Normal Park, and SOUTH SHORE. The community's churches experienced new growth and many embarked on ambitious building campaigns. Beverly's Unitarians, who had purchased Givins's landmark castle in 1942, for example, welcomed families from the People's Liberal Church of Englewood. In 1949 members of Bethlehem Swedish Lutheran Church at 58th and Wells Street financed a new complex at 94th and Claremont Avenue. Among the new houses of worship constructed, some for established congregations, were St. Paul Union (1944), Society of Friends (1948), Ridge Lutheran (1948), Beverly Covenant (1952), Christ the King (1953), St. John the Divine (1953), the Episcopal Church of the Holy Nativity (1954), Salem Baptist (1955), St. John Fisher (1956), and St. Barnabas (1969). From the late 1950s until 1974, the community also included Beth Torah Synagogue.

In 1971 the Beverly Area Planning Association (founded in 1947) was reorganized to respond to residents' concerns about "blockbusting" by real-estate brokers interested in profiting from rapid racial change. BAPA's annual home tours brought thousands of visitors to the community, and the group promoted Beverly's and Morgan Park's inclusion on the National Register of Historic Places in 1975. In 1981 the city of Chicago granted landmark status to the Prairie-style bungalows designed between 1909 and 1914 by Walter Burley Griffin on the 1700 block of West 104th Place, as well as 12 blocks on Longwood Drive and three blocks along Seeley Avenue between 98th and 110th Streets. The Ridge Historical Society (1971) maintains a library and museum to aid residents and researchers in documenting the community's past.

Like Chicago's HYDE PARK and ROGERS PARK, Beverly is a racially integrated neighborhood, but the community has no large institutional anchor comparable to the University of Chicago or Loyola University. In 1995 Beverly became one of several city neighborhoods to adopt cul-de-sacs. The 11 concrete cul-de-sacs and diverters in the area north of 95th Street restrict automobile access to north Beverly to three points of entry: 91st and Western, 95th and Leavitt, and 95th and Damen. Critics charged that the traffic plan was racially motivated, but Alderman Virginia Rugai cited security concerns expressed by both black and white residents.

Ellen Skerrett

FURTHER READING: Commission on Chicago Landmarks and Chicago Department of Planning and Development.

Chicago Historic Resources Survey. 1997. ■ Pacyga, Dominic A., and Ellen Skerrett. *Chicago, City of Neighborhoods: Histories and Tours.* 1986.

Beverly Shores, IN, Porter County, 36 miles E

of the Loop. The resort community of Beverly Shores, Indiana, lies among the sand dunes of Lake Michigan's southern shore, surrounded by Indiana Dunes National Lakeshore. The history of Beverly Shores is linked to that of the electric interurban rail line initially known as the Chicago, Lake Shore & South Bend, which began to provide through-service from South Bend to Chicago shortly after 1900. Chicago utilities magnate Samuel Insull reorganized the railroad as the Chicago, South Shore & South Bend in 1925, investing millions in upgrades and advertising to encourage commuters and vacationers to ride the line. Among the improvements was a series of tile-roofed, Spanish revival depots, one of which appeared in the nascent community of Beverly Shores.

Beverly Shores was the brainchild of the Frederick H. Bartlett Company, Chicago's largest real-estate developer of the era. Encouraged by Insull's investments and the opening of the Dunes Highway several years before, the Bartlett Company purchased 3,600 acres of duneland west of MICHIGAN CITY in 1927. The company envisioned Beverly Shores, named for Frederick Bartlett's daughter, as only one portion of a much larger development that would rival Atlantic City. The crash of 1929 led the Bartlett Company to scale back its grand plans, but Beverly Shores nevertheless began to take shape soon thereafter.

To lure buyers, Robert Bartlett, who purchased the venture from his father's company in 1933, built roads, a school, a championship golf course, a botanical garden, a riding academy, and a Florentine revival hotel. He relocated six model houses

and a re-created colonial village from the Century of Progress World's Fair to Beverly Shores. He enticed a group of players from the Goodman Theatre of Chicago to present weekend performances at the Beverly Shores playhouse. His salesmen fanned out across Chicago's neighborhoods, recruiting potential buyers and transporting them to Indiana on special South Shore trains. Bartlett's promotional efforts met with success, and both vacation homes and year-round residences appeared amid the dunes during the 1930s and 1940s.

When Robert Bartlett withdrew from Beverly Shores in 1947, the community was forced to incorporate in order to provide services for its residents. By this time, activists in Indiana and Chicago, fearing further industrial intrusions into the dunes landscape, had begun to lobby for creation of a national lakeshore park. In response to the efforts of the Save the Dunes Council (founded in 1952), among others, Congress established the 8,330-acre Indiana Dunes National Lakeshore in 1966. In 1976 the park's boundaries were expanded to include part of Beverly Shores, leaving the remainder of the village an island surrounded by parkland.

Beverly Shores still struggles with its island status; a reduced tax base makes providing services a challenge. But the village increasingly looks to its past to strengthen its future. Just outside the village proper, the National Park Service has plans to rehabilitate the five remaining Century of Progress houses. More important for village residents, the shuttered South Shore depot has been renovated, and the remainder of the landmark station serves as a museum of the community's unusual history.

Elizabeth A. Patterson

FURTHER READING: Cohen, Ronald D., and Stephen G. McShane, eds. *Moonlight in Duneland: The Illustrated Story of the Chicago South Shore and South Bend Railroad.* 1998. ■ Engel, J. Ronald. *Sacred Sands: The Struggle for Community in the Indiana Dunes.* 1983. ■ Miscellaneous newspaper clippings and pamphlets on the Chicago, South Shore & South Bend Railroad; House of Tomorrow; Indiana Dunes; and Save the Dunes Council. Chicago History Museum, Chicago.

Opera houses such as the Blue Island Opera House, featured in this 1908 postcard, provided venues for performances of all kinds and served as symbols of status and culture for the communities in which they were located. Photographer: Curt Teich & Co. Source: Curt Teich Archives, Lake County Discovery Museum.

Blue Island, IL, Cook County, 16 miles S of the Loop. Blue Island stands on the southern end of an ancient glacial ridge five miles long, extending northward along Western Avenue and Vincennes Road from 131st Street to 87th Street. The ridge stood as an island in glacial Lake Chicago, the predecessor of Lake Michigan. Bands of Ottawas, Ojibwas, and Potawatomi lived along the Little Calumet River and Stony Creek until 1835.

To a springtime traveler on the Vincennes Trail, the glacial bluff that rose out of the prairie south of Chicago took on a bluish hue from haze or blue wildflowers. In 1836 the first inn opened along the Vincennes Trail at Blue Island. Excavation of a Calumet–Blue Island feeder canal in the 1840s diverted water from the Little Calumet River to the Illinois & Michigan Canal near LEMONT. Transplanted Yankees established the village as an agricultural market center. German agricultural laborers began arriving in the 1850s, and by the 1890s they had usurped political and economic power from the Yankees.

Small-scale factories, brickyards, breweries, and cigar shops arose after 1880. Between 1886 and 1889 workers affiliated with Knights of Labor Local Assembly 6581, and in 1893 they organized Local 3 of what became the United Brick and Clay Workers Union.

Railroads bolstered employment until the 1950s. The Chicago, Rock Island & Pacific Railroad arrived in 1852; its 1868 brick depot at Vermont Street remains in use today. Between 1888 and 1893 several belt railroads crossed the southern and western parts of town, while the Rock Island line constructed an expansive freight yard, shops, and roundhouse. Engineers and craftsmen lived in the respectable center of town, laborers across the tracks on the east side. During the 1894 Pullman Strike, American Railway Union president Eugene V. Debs exhorted railroad workers to stop Rock Island traffic. Two Rock Island trainmen blocked the line on June 30 by derailing a slow-moving train just south of the Vermont Street station. Although local railroaders remained disciplined, riotous brick makers toppled cars and jeered strikebreakers, prompting a federal injunction and suppression of the strike nationwide. Early on the morning of July 4, 1894, the 15th U.S. Infantry arrived in Blue Island and imposed martial law. While protests and violence raged elsewhere after July 4, Blue Island quickly succumbed under the occupying army.

In 1901 Blue Island incorporated as a city to avoid annexation by Chicago. In 1915 residents rejected annexation while nearby MORGAN PARK joined Chicago. Italians, Poles, and Slovaks settled in Blue Island between 1900 and 1920, and African Americans who were excluded from the town incorporated ROBBINS in 1917. Population plateaued at 16,000 to 21,000 between 1930 and 1990. Despite chain stores and Western Avenue's designation as the Dixie Highway in the 1920s, the central business district declined. Political and fiscal conservatism blocked annexation of the future Alsip industrial district, and landlocked industries left the city. During the 1990s, however, the city appeared to revive slowly. Old industries such as Modern Drop Forge and Clark Oil Refineries thrived, while antique stores, theaters, and Mexican restaurants lined Western Avenue.

Martin Tuohy

FURTHER READING: Jebsen, Harry, Jr. "Blue Island, Illinois: The History of a Working Class Suburb." Ph.D. diss., University of Cincinnati. 1971. ■ Jebsen, Harry, Jr. "Preserving Suburban Identity in an Expanding Metropolis: The Case of Blue Island, Illinois." *Old Northwest* 7.2 (Summer 1981): 127–45. ■ Volp, John H. *The First Hundred Years, 1835–1935: Historical Review of Blue Island, Illinois.* 1938.

Bolingbrook, IL, Will and DuPage Counties, 26 miles SW of the Loop.  Few communities demonstrate the interstate highway system's profound influence on suburban development as well as Bolingbrook. The opening of Interstate 55 in the early 1960s made the farm fields of northern Will County more accessible to Chicago, attracting developers and resi-

dents. Incorporated in 1965, Bolingbrook grew from thinly settled farmland to the second-largest community in Will County (behind JOLIET) in less than 10 years.

The Potawatomi lived in this area from the late 1700s. In 1816 the Indians ceded a 10-mile-wide area on both sides of the Des Plaines River to the U.S. government. The northern line of the "Indian Boundary" passed through what is now Bolingbrook. The area's first white residents settled west of Bolingbrook where the DuPage River splits into its east and west branches.

Captain John Barber came west from Vermont in 1832. Barber and his family claimed 211 acres near the intersection of two Indian trails (today's Route 53 and Boughton Road), where they operated a dairy farm. Barber named the area Barber's Corners, a designation that lasted until Bolingbrook's incorporation in 1965. Other settlers, many from Vermont, made their homes in Barber's Corners and established sawmills and gristmills, a tavern, a post office, and a cheese factory. Agricultural ways of life continued into the first half of the twentieth century.

While other communities developed in proximity to railroads or the Illinois & Michigan Canal, the Bolingbrook area relied on roads for transportation. Fittingly, roads propelled the region's transformation after President Dwight Eisenhower signed the Interstate Highway Act into law in 1956. The legislation prompted the replacement of U.S. Route 66, which ran just south of Bolingbrook, with a limited-access superhighway. The expressway, designated Interstate 55, was constructed closer to the town, allowing faster travel to and from Chicago.

Dover Construction Company developed Westbury, Bolingbrook's first subdivision, west of Route 53 and north of I-55 on Briarcliff Road. Colonial Village, an even larger development east of 53, followed. An attempt to incorporate the two subdivisions in 1963 failed by more than a three-to-one margin; a second effort, in 1965, succeeded. Bolingbrook's affordable housing, combined with its newfound access to Chicago, attracted thousands of residents. By 1972, 15,000 called Bolingbrook home.

In 1975 the Old Chicago entertainment complex opened for business in Bolingbrook. Touted as "the world's first shopping center/amusement ride park," Old Chicago combined vaudevillian themes with county fair–type rides and two hundred stores. The complex never lived up to expectations and closed in 1980.

Bolingbrook participated in the area's massive growth into the twenty-first century. New subdivisions have pushed the population to over 50,000, with large areas of open land still available for development.

Aaron Harwig

Bowmanville, neighborhood in the LINCOLN SQUARE Community Area, first developed in 1850 by a local hotel keeper.

Boys Town, area within the LAKE VIEW Community Area, between about 3100 and 3800 N. Halsted Street. The unofficial designation of Boys Town dates back to 1970, when residents marched here in Chicago's first annual Gay Pride Parade.

In 1997 the city of Chicago proposed a $3.2 million facelift for the area that included a plan to recognize Boys Town's gay and lesbian residents. Eleven pairs of art deco pillars with rainbow rings, erected in 1998, mirror similar gateways to Chicago's ethnic-identified neighborhoods..

Erik Gellman

FURTHER READING: Engelbrecht, P. J. "Proud Pylons Rise over Boys Town." *Outlines,* October 7, 1998. ■ Reed, Christopher G. "There's No Place Like Home: Making Chicago's 'Boys Town.'" In *(A) Way Stations: The Architectural Space of Migration,* ed. Paul duBellet Kariouk and Mabel Wilson. 2002. ■ Wockner, Rex. "America's First Official Gay Neighborhood Debuts." *Stonewall Journal,* January 1999.

Brainerd, neighborhood in the WASHINGTON HEIGHTS Community Area, developed in the 1880s and named after a local farm family.

Bricktown, neighborhood in the AVONDALE Community Area.

Bridgeport, Community Area 60, 3 miles SW of the Loop. Before the Fort Dearborn Massacre, Charles Lee owned a farm along the South Branch of the Chicago River. In April 1812 Indians raided Lee's farm and killed two whites at a place known as Hardscrabble, all within the bounds of present-day Bridgeport.

60
Bridgeport

The beginning of construction of the Illinois & Michigan Canal in 1836 gave birth to Bridgeport. Canal commissioners probably named the new town, which included the northern terminus of the canal, to distinguish it from an earlier privately planned settlement, Canalport. First Irish laborers, and then Germans and Norwegians, arrived to work under chief engineer William Gooding. Many lived along Archer Avenue, named after William Beatty Archer, who supervised construction on the project. The canal opened in 1848 and guaranteed Bridgeport's position as an industrial center. Lumberyards, manufacturing plants, and packinghouses opened along both the river and canal. Drovers bringing livestock to Bridgeport packers often crowded Archer Road, a thriving commercial strip.

Most packers relocated to the Union Stock Yard after 1865, but the meatpacking industry remained a major employer of Bridgeport residents. Also in 1865 the Union Rolling Mill began operation. Other manufacturers arrived, and in 1905, the Central Manufacturing District opened in the western section of Bridgeport.

In 1850 enough Irish lived along Archer Avenue to organize St. Bridget's, the first of four Irish Roman Catholic parishes. The district soon attracted other immigrant groups. Germans settled in the neighborhood originally called Dashiel north of 31st Street and east of Halsted Street. The First Lutheran Church of the Trinity (1863), Holy Cross Lutheran Church (1886), St. Anthony Catholic Church (1873), and Immaculate Conception Catholic Church (1883) were all originally German congregations. Czech Catho-

THE GREAT CHICAGO SEWER.—THE RIVER AT ITS JUNCTION WITH THE ENLARGED ILLINOIS AND MICHIGAN CANAL.

"The Great Chicago Sewer," Bridgeport, 1871. Artist: Unknown. Source: The Newberry Library.

lics organized St. John Nepomucene parish in 1871. Poles and Lithuanians settled along Morgan Street. The Poles established St. Mary of Perpetual Help parish (1886) and St. Barbara's (1910), while the Lithuanians opened St. George Church in 1892. Frame and brick cottages and two-flats with small backyards made up the majority of the housing stock. Small stores, saloons, fraternal halls, and schools soon joined the churches lining the streets. After 1880, as streetcars made their way up and down Halsted and 35th Streets, the intersection of those two thoroughfares developed into a small but important shopping strip, eventually replacing Archer Avenue as the neighborhood's commercial district.

Bridgeport residents, while primarily working in local industries, often looked beyond the factories. After the Civil War the Irish in particular saw the expanding municipal government as an opportunity for upward mobility. Bridgeport politicians actively pursued patron-

age jobs as options for their constituents. When the Democratic machine came to power in 1931 under Mayor Anton Cermak, Bridgeport politicians provided an important part of the coalition. After Cermak's death two Bridgeport natives, Patrick A. Nash and Edward J. Kelly, dominated city government. In 1955 Richard J. Daley, who hailed from the Bridgeport neighborhood of Hamburg, took office. As mayor and chairman of the Cook County Democratic Party, Daley controlled one of the most powerful machines in urban America until his death in 1976. Bridgeport's disproportionate share of patronage provided a stable economic base for the neighborhood. In 1989 his son, Richard M. Daley, became the fifth mayor of Chicago born in Bridgeport.

Bridgeport once stood as a bastion of white ethnic parochialism. Racial and ethnic strife has always been part of its history. An almost legendary clash between the Germans and the Irish occurred in 1856. During the Civil War

Mr. Dooley Explains Our "Common Hurtage"

In the late 1890s, Finley Peter Dunne's newspaper columns in Irish dialect brought to life a fictional Bridgeport bartender, Mr. Dooley. During the Spanish-American War, Dunne used his sharp humor to critique a notion of imperialism based on the superiority of the Anglo-Saxon race. Living among Chicagoans drawn from around the globe, Mr. Dooley extended his definition of Anglo-Saxon to include most of his ethnic neighbors:

> Schwartzmeister is an Anglo-Saxon, but he doesn't know it, an' won't till some wan tells him. Pether Bowbeen down be th' Frinch church is formin' th' Circle Francaize Anglo-Saxon club, an' me ol' frind Dominigo that used to boss th' Arrchey R-road wagon whin Callaghan had th' sthreet conthract will march at th' head iv th' Dago Anglo-Saxons whin th' time comes. There ar-re twinty thousan' Rooshian Jews at a quarther a vote in th' Sivinth Ward; an', ar-rmed with rag hooks, they'd be a tur-r-ble think f'r anny inimy iv th' Anglo-Saxon 'lieance to face. Th' Bohemians an' Pole Anglo-Saxons may be a little slow in wakin' up to what the pa-apers calls our common hurtage, but ye may be sure they'll be all r-right whin they're called on.

pro-Confederate rallies were held in the neighborhood. In the twentieth century Polish and Lithuanian gangs often clashed along Morgan Street. While in the 1990s African Americans made up less than 1 percent of the community area's population, the number of Mexican and Chinese residents has grown. Meanwhile the traditional white ethnic population has grown older and smaller. Bridgeport is adjacent to the booming Chinese community in ARMOUR SQUARE, and lies just to the south of PILSEN, home to the city's largest Mexican community. In addition, while Bridgeport remains largely working-class, its proximity to the city's expanding LOOP puts it in the direct line for future investment and development. Already new housing—expensive town houses and single-family

houses—has appeared in the district, and older housing has been restored and modernized.

Dominic A. Pacyga

FURTHER READING: Holt, Glen, and Dominic A. Pacyga. *Chicago: A Historical Guide to the Neighborhoods: The Loop and South Side.* 1979. ■ Pacyga, Dominic A., and Ellen Skerrett. *Chicago, City of Neighborhoods: Histories and Tours.* 1986. ■ Pierce, Bessie Louise. *A History of Chicago.* 3 vols. 1937–1957.

Brighton, platted in 1840, now part of the MCKINLEY PARK Community Area.

Brighton Park, Community Area 58, 6 miles SW of the Loop. Brighton Park, named for the Brighton livestock market in England, is bounded roughly by the Stevenson Expressway and 48th, Western, and Kimball Streets. Construction of the Illinois & Michigan Canal and Archer Avenue drew early settlers. Henry Seymour subdivided land north of Pershing Road in 1835. By 1851 there was a small settlement named Brighton Park near the Blue Island Avenue Plank Road (now Western Avenue). In 1855 Mayor Long John Wentworth opened the Brighton Race Track.

58
Brighton Park

In the late 1850s Brighton became a livestock trading center. A stockyard was built in 1857 at the corner of Archer and Western, and in 1861 a state fair was organized by the U.S. Agricultural Society. The completion of the Union Stock Yard in 1865 forced the closing of Brighton's yards. Instead, Brighton Park attracted other industries, including the Northwestern Horse Nail Company, a cotton mill, a silver smelting and refining company, and the Laflin and Rand Company, a firm that manufactured explosives. On August 29, 1886, lightning struck one of Laflin and Rand's warehouses, leaving a 20-foot crater and damaging property for miles around. After heated meetings, the citizens ordered all powder mills to leave the area. The mills relocated to BLUE ISLAND, Illinois.

The Chicago & Alton Railroad established a roundhouse in the community, and industrial employment attracted German and Irish workers. By the 1880s and 1890s infrastructure and transportation improvements drew even more diverse populations. In 1887 the Santa Fe Railroad moved in, building its Corwith Yards, then the busiest in the nation. In 1889 Brighton Park was annexed to the city of Chicago as part of Lake Township.

Much of the ethnic character of the community was carried by the churches. The first churches in the community were Protestant, serving the Yankees who owned and managed the early firms. The Brighton Park Baptist Church dates from 1848, and the McKinley Park Methodist Church first met in 1872. In 1878 Irish Roman Catholics established St. Agnes Church. By 1892 French Catholics had established St. Jean Baptiste church at 33rd and Wood Streets. Eastern European Jews also arrived. Later, Italians, Poles, and Lithuanians found jobs and homes in Brighton Park. They developed their own churches, including Five Holy Martyrs in 1908 (Polish); Immaculate Conception in 1914 (Lithuanian); St. Pancratius in 1924 (Polish); and St. John's Polish National Parish, also in 1924.

Industrial parks such as the Central Manufacturing District opened in 1905, and the Kenwood Manufacturing District opened on the southern border of Brighton Park around 1915. The Crane Manufacturing Company opened a plant in 1915, providing more jobs. By 1930 Brighton Park's population had peaked, at 46,552 people, 37 percent being of Polish descent. Deindustrialization, exemplified by the closing of Crane's in 1977, weakened the area's economy, and population declined by one-third between 1930 and 1980.

Although the community remains largely residential, there is a growing commercial section. The community maintains monuments to its European connections, including the Balzekas Museum of Lithuanian Culture and the Polish Highlander Alliance. By 2000 the population had rebounded to 44,912, 69 percent of Mexican origin.

Clinton E. Stockwell

FURTHER READING: Chicago Fact Book Consortium, ed. *Local Community Fact Book: Chicago Metropolitan Area, 1990.* 1995. ■ Hamzik, Joseph. "Brighton Park History." Binders, 1952–1976. Brighton Park Public Library. ■ Hamzik, Joseph. "Gleanings of Archer Road." December 1961. Brighton Park Public Library.

Bronzeville, community centered in the GRAND BOULEVARD Community Area. This South Side region was the cultural, business, and political center of African American life through much of the twentieth century.

Brookfield, IL, Cook County, 13 miles SW of the Loop. This middle-class bedroom community has little industry or major business, although the Brookfield Zoo draws substantial numbers of visitors. Major settlement of the area began in 1889 when the Chicago real-estate developer S. E. Gross opened his Grossdale subdivision. The first building Gross erected was a train station. Easy access to downtown Chicago via the Chicago, Burlington & Quincy Railroad (now Metra) made the community popular as a suburban home site. (In 1981 the station was moved across the tracks and now houses the Brookfield Historical Society. It is on the National Register of Historic Places.) Gross later added the subdivisions of Hollywood (1893) and West Grossdale (1895), each with its own train station. Residents voted to incorporate as the village of Grossdale in 1893.

In the early years the community was heavily influenced by Gross. He named numerous streets in the subdivisions after family members and in 1895, against residents' wishes, changed the name of the Hollywood subdivision to East Grossdale. In 1901 the community's ambivalence about his strong presence generated an unsuccessful attempt to change the village's name to Montauk. Support for a name change persisted and became the platform of the victorious Independent Party in the 1905 election. A contest to choose a new name yielded "Brookfield" in respect for Salt Creek, which runs through the area. During this period East Grossdale reverted to the name Hollywood and West Grossdale was renamed Congress Park.

Housing stock in the village ranges from Victorian homes built by Gross in the late nineteenth century to bungalows built in the 1920s and more modern homes from the post–World War II building boom. The village board system of government continued in Brookfield until a 1947 ordinance called for a village manager, a structure permanently adopted in 1951. In 1952 Brookfield received an All-American City award from the National Municipal League and *Look* magazine, in recognition of "intelligent, purposeful, citizen action." The village's main claim to fame, however, is the Chicago Zoological Park, commonly known as Brookfield Zoo. The zoo is located on land given to the Cook County Forest Preserve District by Edith Rockefeller McCormick in 1919. The village's population reached a high of over 20,000 in the 1960s, declining slightly to 19,085 in 2000.

Emily Clark

FURTHER READING: Mary Green Kircher, ed. *Brookfield, Illinois: A History.* 1994.

Brookline, neighborhood in the GREATER GRAND CROSSING Community Area, dating to the 1890s.

Bucktown. Part of the WEST TOWN and LOGAN SQUARE Community Areas. Roughly bounded by North, Ashland, Western, and Fullerton Avenues, Bucktown supposedly takes its name from the goats that roamed its streets at the turn of the twentieth century. Originally a primarily Polish working-class area of small homes, saloons, and churches, it has experienced significant gentrification in recent years.

Steven Essig

FURTHER READING: Fremon, David. *Chicago Politics Ward by Ward.* 1988.

Budlong Woods, neighborhood in the NORTH PARK Community Area.

Buena Park, early residential subdivision in the UPTOWN Community Area, dating to 1860.

Buffalo Grove, IL, Cook and Lake Counties, 26 miles NW of the Loop. New Englanders established the first farms in the area, followed in the 1840s by Melchior Raupp and other Germans. Early farmers carried their harvest in wagons along 34 miles of dirt roads to Chicago. Mainly Roman Catholics, these German settlers raised $300 and donated seven acres of land to build St. Mary's Church in 1852. A few years later arsonists destroyed the church, but it was rebuilt in 1899 at Buffalo Grove and Lake-Cook Roads. Additions enlarged the structure in the 1980s.

Around the turn of the century dairy farming was extensive, prompting J. B. Weidner to build a cheese factory. When the price of milk rose, the cheese factory closed. In 1899 Little Mike's Place located across from St. Mary's Church, with a bar, dining room, dance hall, sleeping rooms, and stable for horses. More than a century later, the establishment remains in operation, with its original bar intact, as part of the regional chain Lou Malnati's Pizzeria.

In the 1930s Dundee Road became the first state concrete road in northern Illinois, improving automobile access. Development began in earnest in 1957, when builder Al Frank purchased 100 acres of farmland and began building ranch-style houses, generally without basements.

Following incorporation in 1958, the village grew from 164 to 1,492 residents within two years. Other developers, including William Levitt, who built Long Island's Levittown, entered the market. New subdivisions included Strathmore and the Woodlands at Fiore. In the 1970s Jewish families flocked to the area, and by the early 1990s there were six synagogues in Buffalo Grove. At the end of the twentieth century Jews constituted approximately 30 percent of the village's population.

Growth has not been limited to residential subdivisions. The Buffalo Grove Commerce Center was developed in 1981 with 50 acres of light industrial park at Lake-Cook Road and the Soo Line Railroad tracks. In the mid-1980s Corporate Grove industrial park was established to the east and Buffalo Grove Business Park to the west. Expansion continued into the 1990s to the north with Arbor Creek Business Centre at Aptakisic Road and Barclay Boulevard, and Covington Corporate Center on Busch Road.

By the end of the twentieth century the village had grown from 67 acres at incorporation to approximately 5,000 acres. Population in 2000 stood at 42,909.

Marilyn Elizabeth Perry

FURTHER READING: Clipping file. Indian Trails Public Library, Wheeling, IL. ▪ Polzin, Michael. "Charging Ahead." *North Shore Magazine*, July 1991, 38–41, 93–102. ▪ Stritch, Samuel Alphonsus Cardinal. *Solemn Blessing and Dedication of St. Mary's School, Buffalo Grove, Illinois.* 1947. Booklet, Indian Trails Public Library, Wheeling, IL.

Burnside, Community Area 47, 11 miles S of the

47
Burnside

Loop. Burnside, the smallest of Chicago's community areas, is a distinctive and difficult-to-access triangle bounded entirely by railroads: the Illinois Central Railroad on the west, the Rock Island (Chicago, Rock Island & Pacific Railroad) on the south, and the New York Central on the east. Prior to the mapping of community areas in the early twentieth century, the area was known as Stony Island and subsequently the Burnside Triangle. The area earlier Chicagoans knew as Burnside occupied a different physical place, almost entirely within the community areas of ROSELAND and CHATHAM.

Situated on the low, swampy land surrounding Lake Calumet, the Burnside Triangle initially seemed more suited to industrial than residential development. When the Illinois Central (IC) established its Burnside station, named after former company official and Civil War general Ambrose Burnside, in 1862, what little development occurred took place west of the tracks. Not until the 1890s, when the IC began building a roundhouse and repair shops south of 95th Street (on what is now the site of Chicago State University), did developer W. V. Jacobs purchase and subdivide land in the Triangle. Settlement there proceeded slowly compared to the rest of Burnside. By 1911, when the entire area was embroiled in a strike against the IC, the Triangle had become home to a small population of the newest immigrants— primarily Hungarians, Italians, Ukrainians, and Poles—who occupied the least skilled jobs in the IC's Burnside shops, the New York Central Stony Island shops, the Calumet & South Chicago street railway shops, the Pullman Car Works, Burnside Steel, and other factories nearby.

With their 400 homes and boardinghouses spread sparsely over the 30 blocks of Burnside, residents had to build many of their own institutions; with the exception of Perry Public School, most existing facilities were located west of the IC tracks. Two churches were among the most important: the Hungarians' Our Lady of Hungary Roman Catholic Church and the Ukrainians' Sts. Peter and Paul Church. These, along with the Burnside Settlement and the school, offered citizenship classes, educational programs, and a variety of other opportunities and services. Saloons, some with meeting halls, provided another venue where residents who lived in adjoining wooden homes and boardinghouses could meet.

Clearly defined physical boundaries (enhanced when the railroads were raised in the 1920s), small size, and residents' ethnic ties and common work experiences made Burnside a socially cohesive community in the years between the world wars. They also meant Burnside attracted little outside attention. Even in the political arena, where it moved between the Ninth and Tenth Wards, it garnered little clout and few rewards.

Only after World War II did the vacant residential land in Burnside attract the attention of developers and potential new residents. New single-family homes began to appear, especially in the most northerly, undeveloped areas. Homes for the middle class, they gradually changed the nature of Burnside, first by class and then, beginning in the 1960s, by race, as middle-class African Americans built their own homes or occupied those of residents of European descent who left the neighborhood. In the mid-1970s, Burnside, like other South Side neighborhoods, suffered from the scandals associated with Federal Housing Authority loans that led to a high number of foreclosures.

By the end of the twentieth century, Burnside had again become a comfortable residential community, still well defined by the railroads that created it and still underserved by City Hall.

Janice L. Reiff

FURTHER READING: City of Chicago, Department of Planning and Development. *Demographic and Housing Characteristics of Chicago and Burnside: Community Area #47 Profile.* 1994. ■ Davis, Berenice Davida. "Housing Conditions in the District of Burnside." M.A. thesis, University of Chicago. 1924.

Burr Ridge, IL, DuPage County, 17 miles SW of the Loop. Burr Ridge's gently rolling hills were carved by glaciers at the end of the last ice age; most of the village lies on the Valparaiso Moraine. Flagg Creek, a tributary of the Des Plaines River, runs through town.

Joseph Vial erected a log cabin near Wolf and Plainfield Roads in 1834. Vial also ran a hotel on the stagecoach line, and the Vial family was actively involved in Lyons Township politics and the creation of the Lyonsville Congregational Church. The first Democratic convention in Cook County was held here in 1835. After 1848 farmers shipped their goods to Chicago along the Illinois & Michigan Canal. A small settlement of German farmers also inhabited Flagg Creek by the 1880s.

In 1917 the International Harvester Company purchased 414 acres for an experimental farm, where it tested the world's first all-purpose tractor, the Farmall. Also in 1917, the Cook County Prison Farm (also known as the Bridewell Farm) began operation in what is now Burr Ridge.

In 1947 developer Robert Bartlett, whose company also developed BEVERLY SHORES and Countryside, established Hinsdale Countryside Estates on the site of a former pig farm. In 1956 these residents incorporated as the village of Harvester, in honor of International Harvester.

In the 1940s Denver Busby bought 190 acres that became known as the Burr Ridge dairy farm, named for a group of bur oaks on a ridge. He later launched the Burr Ridge Estates, with five-acre home sites. In 1961 Burr Ridges Estates and the International Harvester farm merged with Harvester, and the community's name was changed to Burr Ridge. By 1963 the population had more than doubled, to 790, and by 1975 it had soared to over 2,200.

In 1969 Chicago mayor Richard J. Daley floated a proposal to build low-income subsidized housing on the prison farm property, but Republican-dominated DuPage County squashed the idea. The prison farm site instead became the Ambriance Subdivision, a gated community of multimillion-dollar homes. Other farms gave way to the Carriage Way subdivision, and in 1971 additional farmland became the Braemoor neighborhood. An area known as Valley View, once owned by a Chicago industrialist and later by the Chicago chapter of the Boy Scouts of America, was developed in the early 1970s as the Burr Ridge Club. The village also has five corporate parks. As with other towns in the industrial corridor southwest of Chicago, close proximity to Interstates 294 and 55 spurred development in Burr Ridge.

By 1990 the population had risen to 7,669, a 100 percent increase over 1980. In the 1990s Burr Ridge continued to aggressively annex surrounding land, growing to include seven square miles. The 1998 median home value was $470,000. An $8 million project at the turn of the century upgraded water mains, with water coming via Bedford Park. The Robert Vial home, relocated to Pleasant Dale Park, now houses the Flagg Creek Historical Society.

Ronald S. Vasile

FURTHER READING: "Farmers Till the Rich Soil." *Doings,* September 3, 1981. ■ "Village of Burr Ridge: A Very Special Place." 1998 Calendar and Annual Report. ■ McCullough, Purdie. "A Very Special Place." Burr Ridge Bicentennial Committee, 1976.

Bush, early mill neighborhood in the SOUTH CHICAGO Community Area.

Cabrini-Green, neighborhood in the NEAR NORTH SIDE Community Area. Formerly "Swede Town" and then "Little Hell," the site of the Cabrini-Green public housing complex was notorious in the early twentieth century for its inhabitants' poverty and dilapidated buildings. During World War II, the Chicago Housing Authority razed Little Hell and built a low-rise apartment project for war workers, naming it the Frances Cabrini Homes after the first American canonized by the Catholic church. CHA further transformed the area with the high-rise Cabrini Extension (1958) and William Green Homes (1962). The original population of Cabrini-Green reflected the area's prior ethnic mix—poor Italians, Irish, Puerto Ricans, and African Americans lived among the war workers and veterans—but racial segregation overtook Cabrini-Green by the early 1960s.

The large new apartments and swaths of recreation space failed to mend the area's poverty. Blacks had difficulty finding better, affordable housing elsewhere and so became a permanent population. CHA failed to budget money to repair buildings and maintain landscaping as they deteriorated. Cabrini-Green's reputation for crime and gangs rivaled Little Hell's; the mur-

ders of two white police officers in 1970 and of 7-year-old resident Dantrell Davis in 1992 drew national attention.

Increasing real-estate values in the late twentieth century led housing officials to begin replacement of the complex with mixed-income housing. Residents argued that such a move would displace them permanently but were unable to prevent the demolition of the high-rises, which completed the slum removal effort begun with the building of Cabrini Homes half a century earlier.

Amanda Seligman

FURTHER READING: Bowly, Devereux, Jr. *The Poorhouse: Subsidized Housing in Chicago, 1895–1976.* 1978. ■ Marciniak, Ed. *Reclaiming the Inner City: Chicago's Near North Revitalization Confronts Cabrini-Green.* 1986.

Calumet City, IL, Cook County, 19 miles S of the Loop. Calumet City is adjacent to Chicago at the Indiana state line, east of the Bishop Ford Freeway between 143rd and 163rd Streets. It is north of Lansing and southeast of Dolton. Originally known as West Hammond, Calumet City is separated from HAMMOND, Indiana, by State Line Road.

Founded in 1893 with a population consisting mainly of German Lutheran farmers, the early community depended heavily on the factories and commerce of Hammond. The 1900 population of 2,935 grew to 7,492 by 1920. By that time, Poles outnumbered Germans, with residents of Irish ancestry in third place. A Polish American was elected village president in 1900, and in 1902 one municipal party was able to field a slate made up completely of candidates with Polish names.

When Indiana went dry in 1916, West Hammond became an attractive watering hole for the drinkers of northwest Indiana. Bootleggers like Al Capone built on this base when Prohibition was enacted, and the town of West Hammond, just 30 minutes from downtown Chicago, gained a reputation as a "Sin City," where gam-

Frances Cabrini Homes, Near North Side, ca. 1942. Photographer: Unknown. Source: University of Illinois at Chicago.

bling, prostitution, and illegal booze joints constituted a proto–Las Vegas strip on State Street. Hardworking residents were so dismayed by the town's bad reputation that they voted in 1923 to change the name to Calumet City. Despite the city's notoriety, the population grew from 7,500 to 12,300 during the 1920s, reaching 25,000 in 1960, 32,956 in 1970, and 39,697 in 1980. From the 1920s on various mayors and citizen groups battled to shut down the State Street bars, with varying success; Mayor Jerry Genova's efforts in the 1990s seemed to bring that chapter of the city's history to an end.

In 1966 investors spent $35 million and built the 80-store River Oaks Shopping Center. The center's excellent location, on U.S. Route 6 a few miles from the Bishop Ford Freeway, brought customers from Chicago's South Side, and a renovation in the early 1990s (completely enclosing the previously open-air mall) maintained its drawing power.

In 2000 Calumet City's population was 39,071, with 54 percent African American and 11 percent Hispanic. Thirteen percent of Calumet City residents reported Polish ancestry, with smaller percentages of German, Irish, and Italian ancestry.

Dominic Candeloro

FURTHER READING: McGahen, Adeline. "Calumet City Centennial Celebration." 1993. Calumet City Public Library.

Calumet Heights, Community Area 48, 11 miles SE of the Loop. Calumet Heights lies on Chicago's Southeast Side, bounded by 87th Street on the north, South Chicago Avenue on the east, and railroad lines on the west and south (along 95th Street). The community takes its name from the nearby Calumet River and from the ridge of Niagara limestone that runs through the area.

48
Calumet
Heights

The swampy Calumet Heights region remained largely unoccupied throughout much of the nineteenth century. Though travelers passed through, few settled. In the 1870s the Calumet and Chicago Canal and Dock Company acquired property in what was by then part of the incorporated Township of Hyde Park, holding it for future use. In 1881 the New York, Chicago & St. Louis Railroad built rail yards at the area's western border, and a settlement began to develop nearby. A new quarry near 92nd Street prompted further settlement. Real-estate developer Samuel E. Gross purchased a portion of the Calumet and Chicago land in 1887, creating the new Calumet Heights subdivision. Though Chicago annexed the entire Hyde Park Township just two years later, and the adjacent Stony Island and South Chicago Heights subdivisions followed in 1890 and 1891, residential growth remained slow for several decades.

By 1920 Calumet Heights had 3,248 residents, many of them, especially in the eastern section, foreign-born. During the following decade, the community experienced a surge in residential building, and population more than doubled, to 7,343 by 1930. The large foreign-born population included many Poles, Italians, Irish, and Yugoslavians. The new housing included many single-family homes, though an area of apartments also developed west of Stony Island Avenue, between 87th and 91st Streets. Building slowed dramatically, however, during the Great Depression, and much of Calumet Heights remained vacant.

The postwar years saw renewed growth. The 92nd Street quarry was filled in and a group of small homes constructed there. A shopping area developed around Stony Island Avenue and 87th Street. The community's population grew to 9,349 in 1950, and surged to 19,352 by 1960.

Between 1960 and 1980 the Calumet Heights community experienced a sea change in its population. A few African Americans began to move in during the early 1960s. By 1970 they made up 45 percent of the population; by 1980, more than 86 percent. Louis Rosen, whose family remained in Calumet Heights well after most of its white neighbors, documented this change in *The South Side: The Racial Transformation of an American Neighborhood* (1998).

Throughout the last decades of the twentieth century, Calumet Heights remained solidly middle class, with many professionals and oth-er white-collar workers drawn to its well-kept homes. In 1990 nearly three-quarters of the homes were single-family, and of these, four of five were owner-occupied.

Calumet Heights comprises two distinct residential areas. The Stony Island Heights neighborhood occupies the eastern two-thirds of the community. More affluent is the Pill Hill neighborhood, said to be named for the large number of doctors from nearby South Chicago Hospital who own spacious homes atop the Stony Island ridge.

Elizabeth A. Patterson

FURTHER READING: Chicago Fact Book Consortium, ed. *Local Community Fact Book: Chicago Metropolitan Area, 1990.* 1995. ■ Kouri, Charles. "Upwardly Mobile: Calumet Heights a 'High-End' Community." *Chicago Tribune*, November 22, 1991. ■ Richardson, Cheryl Jenkins. "Communities: At Home in Calumet Heights." *Chicago Tribune*, November 23, 1998.

Canalport, an early settlement, planned but undeveloped, along the Illinois & Michigan Canal in what is now the McKINLEY PARK Community Area. It was a predecessor to BRIDGEPORT.

Central Park, neighborhood built by Chicago & North Western Railway workers in the 1870s, now in the WEST GARFIELD PARK Community Area.

Central Station, neighborhood established in 1990 on former rail yards in the NEAR SOUTH SIDE Community Area.

Chatham, Community Area 44, 10 miles S of the Loop. African American middle class. Defined by a jagged boundary—roughly 79th and 95th Streets, the Illinois Central Railroad, and the Dan Ryan Expressway— Chatham has, since the mid-1950s, been a stronghold of Chicago's African American middle class and is home to several of the most successful black-owned businesses in the country.

44
Chatham

More suitable for duck hunting than for human habitation, the swampy area was known as Mud Lake to hunters and as Hogs Swamp to the farmers who began to settle the western portion of Chatham during the 1860s. The first buildings in the area were corncribs assembled by the Illinois Central in 1860 along the tracks between 75th and 95th Streets. Industrial development began to the north after 1876 when Paul Cornell, founder of HYDE PARK, established the Cornell Watch Factory at 76th and the Illinois Central tracks. By 1900 steel mills, built along the lakefront and the Calumet River, provided work for European immigrants settling in Chatham.

Population growth and residential expansion in Chatham began in earnest in the 1880s with the subdivision of three small areas that constituted the community. The first permanent residents in the eastern portion of Chatham were Italian stonemasons, who in the mid-1880s built frame houses in what is now AVALON PARK. When Chatham was annexed to Chicago as part of Hyde Park Township in 1889, Hungarian and Irish railroad workers inhabited the Dauphin Park subdivision, also in the eastern portion of what is now Chatham. With the 1914 subdivision of central Chatham as Chatham Fields, strict zoning codes and property standards became a characteristic feature of the entire community.

The 1920s brought dramatic increases in both property values and the population of Chatham. As new residents, most of Swedish, Irish, or Hungarian origin, took occupancy in numerous bungalows, the population swelled from 9,774 to 36,228 by the end of the decade, and the community evolved from working class to middle class. Another boom started in Chatham toward the end of the Great Depression with the development of the Chatham Park housing complex in 1941, which stimulated the growth of Cottage Grove Avenue as a shopping district. By 1959 the mostly Jewish occupants of Chatham Park converted the complex into what was claimed to be the first cooperative rental property in Illinois.

As in many other Chicago neighborhoods, ra-

cial transition occurred in Chatham quite rapidly. In 1950 African Americans made up less than 1 percent of Chatham's population. By 1960 the figure had jumped to 63.7 percent. That transition, however, entailed relatively little confrontation. While the West Chatham Improvement Association attempted to keep the area reserved for whites, other community leaders wanted to avoid the violence that had occurred just to the north in GREATER GRAND CROSSING. Several area churches, for example, welcomed blacks into their congregations, and the Chatham–Avalon Park Community Council began in 1955 to include African American residents in its organization. Owing partly to the scare tactics of some real-estate agents, however, whites left Chatham in large numbers in the 1950s and 1960s. The 1990 census reported 99 percent of Chatham's residents as African American.

Chatham has the distinction of being perhaps the only neighborhood in Chicago that developed from a European American middle-class community into one composed of middle-class African Americans. Middle-class African Americans were, in fact, drawn to the area precisely because of its strict property standards, high levels of community organization, and good schools, and worked diligently to maintain the middle-class character of their community.

Successful black businesses located in Chatham have included the Johnson Products Company (Ultra Sheen Hair Products), the Independence Bank of Chicago, Seaway National Bank of Chicago, and a branch of the Illinois Service Federal Savings and Loan Association. Independence Bank was one of the nation's largest black-owned banks until 1995, when it was acquired by another corporation.

Toward the end of the 1990s Chatham seemed on the brink of another transition, as reports of crime, property neglect, and economic instability were on the rise. More important, the declining population—down from a 1970 high of 47,287 to 37,275 in 2000—was aging. Community leaders and residents, however, devoted their energies to a number of revitalization projects designed to assure that Chatham would remain, in the words of real-estate developer Dempsey Travis, "the jewel of the Southeast Side of Chicago."

Wallace Best

FURTHER READING: Gregory, Mae. "Chatham 1865–1987: A Community of Excellence." Special Collections, Harold Washington Library, Chicago. ■ Mayer, Harold M., and Richard C. Wade. *Chicago: Growth of a Metropolis.* 1969. ■ Neufeld, Steve, and Annie Ruth Leslie. "Chatham." In *Local Community Fact Book: Chicago Metropolitan Area, 1990,* ed. Chicago Fact Book Consortium. 1995.

Chatham Fields, established with a 1914 subdivision in the CHATHAM Community Area.

Cheltenham Beach, neighborhood in the SOUTH SHORE Community Area.

Chesterton, IN, Porter County, 36 miles SE of the Loop. When Indiana became a state in 1816, the northern portion, which bordered on Lake Michigan, was a densely forested area inhabited largely by Potawatomi. The first non-Indian settler in what is now the town of Chesterton was Jesse Morgan, who built a cabin on the Detroit–Fort Dearborn Post Road. His house became a stopping place for the stagecoach, and a post office from 1833 to 1853.

In the early 1830s William Thomas bought a large tract of land originally owned by a Potawatomi Indian woman, Mau-Me-Nass. A settlement known as Coffee Creek grew up around his cabin, sawmill, and general store. In 1852 the town was platted with the name of Calumet. The Michigan Southern Railroad (New York Central) ran through the town toward Chicago on land donated by William Thomas II. In succeeding years other railroads crossed the area, and Calumet became a busy railroad center.

Railroad construction drew Irish workers in the 1850s, followed in the 1860s and 1870s by Swedes and Germans. Many of the Swedish settlers stayed to own homes, farms, and businesses.

In 1869 Calumet was incorporated as the town of Chesterton, the name apparently derived from that of Westchester Township, in which it was located. The incorporation failed in 1878, owing to an inadequate tax base. Reincorporation occurred in 1899; this time planners were careful to take in sufficient territory to raise the necessary taxes. Annexation brought in additional land in later years.

By 1880 Chesterton was a well-established town with several small factories. The Hillstrom Organ Factory relocated from Chicago in 1880 and became the town's main industry. A growing preference for pianos over organs resulted in the sale of the factory to private investors by the Hillstrom estate in 1898, and the eventual closure of the factory in 1920. Other small industries included a china factory and a glass factory. The *Chesterton Tribune* has been published continuously since 1884. The Chesterton State Bank was founded in 1890 by George Morgan (son of Jesse Morgan) and Joseph C. Gardner. In the early 1900s electricity and telephones became available, along with transportation to nearby towns. The Chicago, South Shore & South Bend Interurban still serves the area.

Since World War II growth has been rapid in Chesterton. The opening of Burns Harbor and the establishment of Bethlehem Steel's Burns Harbor Division in the early 1960s increased the economic health of Westchester Township. Through the efforts of U.S. senator Paul Douglas of Illinois and various interested groups, the Indiana Dunes National Lakeshore was established in 1966. This park, together with the Indiana Dunes State Park, which opened to the public in 1926, preserves the remaining dunes of the south shore of Lake Michigan for recreational use.

With a population of 10,488 in 2000, Chesterton is the largest town in Westchester Township. Since 1980 business development has occurred largely at the junction of Indian Boundary Road and State Highway 49. Sand Creek Country Club and the

Sand Creek residential development, the largest of many new subdivisions, are nearby, located in the area originally settled by Jesse Morgan.

Margaret D. Doyle

FURTHER READING: *History of Porter County.* 1912. ■ Local History Archives. Westchester Public Library, Chesterton, IN. ■ Moore, Powell A. *The Calumet Region: Indiana's Last Frontier.* 1959.

Chicago Heights, IL, Cook County, 26 miles S of the Loop. Chicago Heights is located six miles from the Indiana border at the crossroads of Lincoln Highway (Route 30) and Dixie Highway (Hubbard's Trail). Absalom Wells built  a cabin on the ridge above Thorn Creek in the 1830s and was the first farmer in the area, which by the 1840s was called Thorn Grove. The First Presbyterian Church established a place of worship and a cemetery for the rural community.

In the early 1890s a group of Chicago developers led by Charles Wacker determined to establish "Chicago Heights" as an outer-ring industrial suburb. They recruited large-scale heavy industries such as Inland Steel and built the impressive Hotel Victoria (designed by Louis Sullivan). Community growth and development progressed rapidly. By 1920 Chicago Heights boasted a population of 19,653. Italian, Polish, Slovak, Lithuanian, Irish, and African American workers poured into the East Side and Hill neighborhoods to be close to the heavy industries. The downtown area served as the retail, banking, transportation, and entertainment center for nearby communities and rural settlements in a 15-mile radius. Local pride (and commerce) swelled when, in 1916, city fathers persuaded the Lincoln Highway Association to route the first transcontinental highway through the city, making it "the Crossroads of the Nation." The city gained some notoriety as a stomping ground for top bootleggers during the Prohibition era and, because of its industrial base, was hit hard by the Great Depression in the 1930s. Chicago Heights factories worked around the clock during World War II to produce steel, chemicals, and war materials of every sort. This period set the stage for a golden era that saw residential expansion to the north and west, prosperity for downtown retailers, and (in the mid-1950s) the coming of a new Ford stamping plant that provided employment for thousands. In the 1950s Bloom Township High School also gained a high level of recognition in sports and academics.

Changing retail patterns, including competition from nearby Park Forest Plaza, brought challenges to the commercial center in the 1970s. Heavy manufacturing employment became less reliable as well.

The diverse population of Chicago Heights peaked at 40,900 in 1970 and declined to 32,776 in 2000, with the percentage of African Americans and Hispanics on the rise. The prosperity of the late 1990s brought stabilization of the industrial base, a movement for renewal of the old East Side and Hill neighborhoods, a preservation movement, and continued challenges in the commercial sector.

Dominic Candeloro

FURTHER READING: Beeson, F. S. *History of Chicago Heights, Illinois, 1833–1938.* 1938. ■ Candeloro, Dominic, and Barbara Paul. *Images of America: Chicago Heights.* 1998. ■ Candeloro, Dominic. "Suburban Italians: Chicago Heights 1890–1975." In *Ethnic Chicago,* ed. Melvin Holli and Peter d'A. Jones. 1981.

Chicago Junction, developed in the 1850s around a rail stop and cluster of rail junctions in what is now the WEST ENGLEWOOD Community Area.

Chicago Lawn, Community Area 66, 8 miles SW of the Loop. Locals call Chicago Lawn "MARQUETTE PARK" because the 300-acre park by that name dominates the southern portion of the neighborhood. It remained mostly farmland with some  **66** Chicago Lawn scattered settlements until the 1920s, when developers constructed bungalows and lured managers and skilled stockyard workers to the community, chiefly from BACK OF THE YARDS and ENGLEWOOD. Germans and Irish were followed by Poles, Bohemians, and Lithuanians. Between 1920 and 1930 the population increased from 14,000 to 47,000. Most residents belonged to Protestant denominations, but Chicago Lawn also was home to many Roman Catholic churches and schools as well as a Carpatho-Russian Orthodox church. The Great Depression did not entirely stop the growth of this thriving urban neighborhood. By 1940 its population reached 49,291.

Chicago Lawn's residents formed tightly knit communities around their respective churches and schools. The Lithuanians established an especially notable presence, earning their community the label of Lithuanian Gold Coast. Their network of institutions included some of the richest savings and loans in the city; Holy Cross Hospital (1928) and Maria High School (1952), both founded by the Lithuanian Sisters of St. Casimir; and the Lithuanian Youth Center, just to the north in GAGE PARK.

Chicago's changing racial demographics had a profound impact on Chicago Lawn. By 1960 its population swelled to over 51,000 as whites fled Englewood and WEST ENGLEWOOD. In the mid-1960s Chicago Lawn became a target for open-housing marches by civil rights groups. A 1966 march led by Martin Luther King Jr. into Marquette Park met a violent reaction. King himself was hit by a rock. Violence also erupted in the neighborhood when Gage Park High School attempted integration. The American Nazi Party opened a headquarters in Chicago Lawn, aiming to capitalize on the racial tension, but it did not find the sympathetic reception it expected; many Eastern European immigrants in particular had their own horror stories about the German Nazis. Resistance to integration was driven primarily by fear of declining property values among people who had put their life savings into their homes and of disruption of ethnic bonds, especially among the Lithuanians. As they saw it, Chicago had no workable precedent for integrated neighbor-

hoods, and Chicago Lawn would disintegrate with racial change.

By 1990 African Americans accounted for 27 percent of the population, members of Hispanic groups for 28 percent. Arabs had also taken up residence. Some Irish, Poles, and Lithuanians still remain; most, however, have moved further south and west, many Lithuanians having resettled in LEMONT. A number of groups have worked to keep the area economically vital, and a tenuous peace exists in this ethnically and racially diverse neighborhood.

Eileen M. McMahon

FURTHER READING: Pacyga, Dominic A., and Ellen Skerrett. *Chicago, City of Neighborhoods: Histories and Tours.* 1986.

Chinatown. In 1890, 25 percent of the city's 600 Chinese residents lived along Clark between Van Buren and Harrison Streets. After 1910 Chinese from the LOOP moved to a new area near Cermak Road and Wentworth Avenue, mainly in search of cheaper rent. Chinatown expanded into ARMOUR SQUARE in the 1970s and by 1990 into BRIDGEPORT. In 2000 Chicago had 32,187 Chinese residents, 33 percent of whom lived in Chinatown and adjacent areas.

Chinese have also concentrated in the so-called New Chinatown, centered along Argyle Street between Sheridan Road and Broadway in UPTOWN. That area was home to more Vietnamese than Chinese in 2000, with smaller numbers of Koreans as well.

For decades, Chinatown has been a unique tourist attraction in Chicago. A colorful gate decorated with a Chinese inscription ("The world is for all") stands at the intersection of Cermak Road and Wentworth Avenue. Nearby is a landmark of Chinese architecture, the former Chinese Merchants Association Building. Adorned with red and green pagodas, flowers, and lion sculptures, the building houses a library, meeting rooms, and a shrine. The Chinatown Square mall, near Archer and Wentworth Avenues, has a pagoda structure and 12 statues representing the

Parade in Chinatown, 1928. Photographer: Unknown. Source: Chicago History Museum.

animals of the Chinese zodiac. Tourists can shop for oriental gifts or groceries or enjoy Chinese food; along Wentworth Avenue between 22nd and 24th Streets there are at least 30 Chinese restaurants. Printers and bakeries are found in the commercial areas along Wentworth Avenue and Cermak Road.

Chinatown is fragmented by many transportation lines. The New York Central Railroad and the Dan Ryan Expressway run near its east boundary. The Santa Fe Railroad parallels the South Branch of the Chicago River, which forms its northwest boundary. The Pennsylvania Railroad cuts Chinatown from north to south along Canal Street. And the Stevenson Expressway cuts from east to west along 26th Street.

Chinatown is overcrowded. Residential areas consist mostly of two-story structures, both old and new. High-rises include Archer Courts and the Chinatown Elderly apartments for low-income seniors. In response to a critical shortage of open space, the city of Chicago built Ping Tom Memorial Park, a 12-acre park along the east bank of the South Branch of the Chicago River from 16th to 21st Streets. The park has an indoor swimming pool, playing fields, a Chinese teahouse pavilion, and a rose garden.

Ying-cheng (Harry) Kiang

FURTHER READING: Kiang, Harry. *Chicago's Chinatown.* 1992.

Cicero, IL, Cook County, 7 miles W of the Loop.

The town of Cicero, bordered on the north and east by Chicago, is the suburb nearest to downtown. Named for a town in New York State, Cicero has the only town form of government in Cook County and is governed by a board of trustees.

Ogden Avenue, a former Indian trail, was one of

Crowd at Cicero's Hawthorne Race Track on Derby Day, 1924. Photographer: Unknown. Source: Chicago History Museum.

the early thoroughfares through Cicero. The area's first homesteaders settled on the highest and driest land (now part of OAK PARK). Other families settled along Ogden Avenue, Lake Street, and Cermak Road (22nd Street). When the Galena & Chicago Union Railroad was built westward from Chicago in 1848, Cicero became the first western suburb connected to the city by rail.

In 1857 inhabitants formed the township of Cicero in order to levy taxes for roads and drainage ditches. In 1869 Cicero was incorporated as a town, and that same year Chicago annexed 11 square miles along Cicero's eastern edge; the town's population of 3,000 dropped 50 percent as a result.

Cicero's location on several rail lines influenced the Chicago & North Western Railway and the Chicago & Alton Railroad companies to establish manufacturing and repair shops there. Small communities began to develop around these and other industries, such as the Brighton Silver Smelting & Refining Company and the Brighton Cotton Mill.

During the 1880s new residents were drawn to the industries in the northern part of the town along the Galena & Chicago Union tracks. As these communities expanded they began to meld. Some of these areas later separated from Cicero; others, such as Clyde and Hawthorne, remained as names of railroad stops.

In 1889 Chicago again annexed territory along Cicero's eastern border, and by 1897 street railways ran from the city into Cicero. In 1899 Chicago annexed its last portion of Cicero, including the AUSTIN area. Cicero ceded the Hawthorne Race Track to Stickney in 1900, and in 1901 Oak Park and BERWYN separated from Cicero. Present-day Cicero, 5.5 square miles, is less than one-sixth of its original 36-square-mile area.

Western Electric established a telephone equipment manufacturing plant in Cicero in 1904 that employed more than 20,000 people—more than the number then living in Cicero. The suburb's population, only 14,557 in 1910, more than quadrupled over the next 20 years, with the majority of newcomers Eastern European immigrants. Yet there was still enough open land in the 1920s for Cicero Field, one of Chicago's earliest airfields.

Cicero's position at the edge of Chicago attracted criminal elements wishing to evade the city's law enforcement agencies. In the mid- to late 1920s the gangster Al Capone established his headquarters in Cicero. At the end of the twentieth century government officials were convicted on charges of corruption that recalled the town's earlier reputation.

Racial tensions flared throughout the 1950s and 1960s as Cicero residents resisted African Americans moving into their community. At the end of the century, Cicero had virtually no black residents, although people of Hispanic or Asian ancestry contributed to its mixture of ethnic cultures. Ethnic tensions surfaced in town politics as an entrenched Republican organization reluctantly shared power with an emerging Hispanic majority.

Betsy Gurlacz

FURTHER READING: Anderson, Alan B., and George W. Pickering. *Confronting the Color Line: The Broken Promise of the Civil Rights Movement in Chicago.* 1986. ■ Clark, Eugene. "History of Cicero by a Ciceronian." Cicero Library Reference Desk, Cicero, IL. ■ Spelman, Walter Bishop. *The Town of Cicero: History, Advantages, and Government.* 1923.

Clearing, Community Area 64, 10 miles SW of the Loop. Chicago annexed much of the area known as Clearing in 1915, with other segments added in 1917 and 1923. It is bounded by 65th Street to the south, 59th Street to the north, Harlem to the west, and Cicero to the east and includes about half of Midway Airport.

64
Clearing

Dutch and German farmers lived in the area by the mid-nineteenth century. The most extensive landholder was Long John Wentworth, a congressman and mayor of Chicago whose 4,700 acres included land in what eventually became Clearing, GARFIELD RIDGE, and SUMMIT. Wentworth built a house in 1868 at the corner of what is now 55th and Harlem. Clearing received its name from a proposed railway-switching yard. A. B. Stickney, president of the Chicago Great Western Railroad, laid out a plan in 1888 for a one-mile circle that would allow workers to load and unload goods while avoiding the rail congestion closer downtown. The scheme failed, so the enterprising Stickney tried to cut a deal in 1891 with the upstart Chicago National Stockyards to rival the Union Stock Yard. This effort also failed, in part because of the national economic depression of 1893–1897. What was to have been "Stickney's Circle" turned into "Stickney's Folly."

In 1909 George Hill established a hardware store, one of the first businesses in Clearing. Three years later residents voted to incorporate as a village. By 1915 the Chicago Transfer and Clearing Company connected the freight car switching hub with 18 industrial companies, and Clearing was annexed to the city.

From those 18 companies in 1915 the Clearing Industrial District grew to more than 90 by 1928. Land in Clearing and Garfield Ridge owned by the Chicago Public schools was leased to the city in 1926 for the purpose of building an airport on the Southwest Side. In 1927 Mayor William Hale Thompson dedicated the Chicago Municipal Airport. In 1928 there were 4 runways, expanding to 16 by 1941. By 1949 the airport was renamed Midway Airport to honor victories at Midway Island during World War II.

Clearing enjoyed a postwar residential and economic boom, and its population grew from 6,068 in 1940 to a peak of 24,911 in 1970. By 1970 some 300 firms had located in what is now known as the Bedford-Clearing Industrial District. During the economic recession from 1974 to 1984, over half of those companies left Clearing for other locations, reducing the number of firms to 175 and the number of workers from 50,000 to just over 19,000. Since 1985, with the resurgence of Midway Airport, some stability has returned.

Clinton E. Stockwell

FURTHER READING: Chicago Fact Book Consortium, ed. *Local Community Fact Book: Chicago Metropolitan Area, 1990.* 1995. ∎ Hill, Robert Milton. *A Little Known Story of the Land Called Clearing.* 1983. ∎ Swanson, Stevenson. *Chicago Days: 150 Defining Moments in the Life of a Great City.* 1997.

Cleaverville, company town built by Charles Cleaver in 1850s for his slaughterhouse and soap factory, now in the OAKLAND Community Area.

Colehour, early industrial neighborhood in the EAST SIDE Community Area.

Crystal Lake, IL, McHenry County, 43 miles NW of the Loop. In her memoir *Wau-Bun,* Juliette Kinzie described seeing in 1830 "a beautiful sheet of water, now known as Crystal Lake." Ziba Beardsley's 1835 description of the lake as "clear as crystal" named both lake and community. Beman Crandall and Christopher Walkup platted the east-shore village in 1840.

In 1855 residents believed that the Illinois & Wisconsin Railroad would follow the Big Foot Trail through the hamlet even without local investment. However, without any Crystal Lake investors, the railroad chose a route more than a mile to the north. Meanwhile, the Fox River Valley Railroad (Chicago & North Western Railway), building northward from Algonquin, skirted the village to the east. The rival track gangs attacked each other at the crossing point, with peace established only after the Illinois & Wisconsin agreed to construct a bridge over the Fox River's rails.

The consolidated line known as the Chicago & North Western erected a station near the junction and laid a spur to Crystal Lake. The village of Nunda developed at the junction. The two villages incorporated independently in 1874, but in 1908 Nunda became North Crystal Lake, and in 1914 the two communities merged, with most commercial activity in the expanded city of Crystal Lake shifting to the station area.

In 1863, at the end of the Crystal Lake rail spur, Charles Dole of Chicago grain warehouser Armour, Dole & Co. established an expansive estate that included the lake bottom. Dole had ice cut from the lake, which he shipped to Chicago even during summer months; well-insulated ice houses lined the shore of Crystal Lake. Popular in Chicago as Knickerbocker Ice, its quality attracted many vacationers to the lake. Resorts and boardinghouses rose around the north shore while the Dole family hosted picnics and public outings along their beachfront. In 1912 citizens took legal action to ensure public access to the lake, and in 1921 the Crystal Lake Park District was established. Unfortunately, lake bottom ownership was not clearly resolved.

Crystal Lake's reputation as a resort lasted throughout the 1920s, and wealthy vacationers built homes in the woods along the lake's south shore. Facing unwanted expansion from the city of Crystal Lake, south shore residents incorporated as Lakewood in 1933.

The area's population remained stable from the 1930s through the 1950s. When the Ladd family's large Coventry Subdivision quickly sold out to pilots based at Chicago's expanding O'Hare Airport in the early 1960s, Crystal Lake became the center of a land rush. Between then and 1980, the city's population doubled, reaching 18,590, and the commercial activity of the retail center moved away from the railroad. By 2000 the population had grown to 38,000. As crowding increased, the city of Crystal Lake, the Crystal Lake Park District, the village of Lakewood, and a lakeshore property owners group continued to contest ownership and control of the lake. To alleviate the problem, the city of Crystal Lake devised a plan to create a new lake from a large gravel pit on the southeast side of the city for recreational use.

Craig L. Pfannkuche

FURTHER READING: Heisler, James, Susan Riegler, and Roberta Smith, eds. *Crystal Lake, Illinois: A Pictorial History.* 1986. ■ *McHenry County in the Twentieth Century, 1968–1994.* McHenry County Historical Society, 1994. ■ Nye, Lowell A., ed. *McHenry County, Illinois, 1832–1968.* 1968.

Dauphin Park, neighborhood in the eastern CHATHAM Community Area.

Dearborn Park. The Dearborn Street Station once served as a major national rail terminus in the NEAR SOUTH SIDE Community Area. Downtown business leaders convinced George Halas in 1977 to bestow 51 acres of railroad yards for redevelopment as Dearborn Park. The resulting complex of apartments and town houses along tree-lined walkways was hailed as a model of urban renewal.

Erik Gellman

FURTHER READING: Wille, Lois. *At Home in the Loop: How Clout and Community Built Chicago's Dearborn Park.* 1997.

Deerfield, IL, Lake County, 22 miles NW of the Loop. Deerfield lies in the prairie of northern Illinois, surrounded by farmlands and forests. The Potawatomi once inhabited the area and used the nearby Des Plaines, Fox, and Chicago Rivers as a means of transportation. Jacob Cadwell settled in 1835, and the area became known as Cadwell's Corner. Farmers were attracted by the availability of land and fertile soil, and by the close proximity of rivers. The waterways allowed residents to ship goods such as timber, venison, and

wheat to the markets in Chicago, as well as to bring supplies to the area.

In 1840 the village was renamed Le Clair. Although many of the original settlers were of Irish descent and favored the name Erin, in honor of their homeland, in 1849 a settler named John Millen encouraged people to change the name to Deerfield, after his hometown in Massachusetts and because of the area's heavy deer population. The opening of the Milwaukee Railroad (Chicago, Milwaukee, St. Paul & Pacific Railroad) in 1872 attracted new residents who commuted to work in the city. The village was incorporated in 1903, but in 1910 Deerfield was still a small town with a population of only 476.

The completion of the Edens Expressway in 1959 enticed Chicagoans just as the proximity of rivers had attracted settlers a century before. The population of Deerfield increased from 7,009 people in 1957 to 11,786 people in 1960. By 2000 the number of people living in the village stood at 18,420, of whom 96 percent were white. The median household income was $107,194.

The village faced a setback in 1991 when the area's main industry, the food company Sara Lee Corp., moved after 27 years of operation in Deerfield. The area's economy continued to thrive, however, because of Deerfield-based medical supplier Baxter International, as well as the growth of the real-estate and service industries.

Thomas A. Auger

FURTHER READING: Deerfield, Bannockburn, Riverwoods Chamber of Commerce. "A Look at . . . Deerfield, Bannockburn, Riverwoods." 1990. ■ Reichelt, Marie Ward. *History of Deerfield, Illinois.* 1928.

Des Plaines, IL, Cook County, 17 miles NW of the Loop. Des Plaines is a suburban transportation hub. The Des Plaines River (variously known as Le Plein, Aux Plaines, and Oplain until Germans settled in the village and called it Des Plaines) provided the earliest means of

transportation. Today trains, buses, and highways provide a network bringing commuters and visitors from Chicago to Des Plaines and beyond.

In 1835 Socrates Rand settled on the river's west bank; in 1837 he opened his home for Episcopal services and in 1838 operated the first school in the cheese room of his cabin. An important community member, Rand helped to build the railroad by providing timber for a sawmill, and he became the first township chairman. In 1857 the first subdivision was named for him.

The Illinois & Wisconsin Railroad (later known as the Chicago & North Western Railway) came through Des Plaines in 1854 with a depot located near the river. Train service and the extension of the North West Plank Road brought industry and laborers. In 1869 the town became Des Plaines by act of the state legislature. In 1873 the settlement was incorporated as a village. The 1880 census figured population at 818.

Flooding posed a constant threat. Although 10 bridges crossed the river in Des Plaines, their wood construction made them temporary. Spring floods could wash them away, and the Great Flood of 1881 hindered travel for many weeks. The addition of brick culverts only somewhat secured the bridges. The first steel bridge crossed the river in 1900.

The Des Plaines Methodist Camp Ground, established in 1860, drew Methodists from across the region. Northwestern Park's pavilion provided another attraction when it opened for dancing in the early 1900s. In 1918 Cook County's Forest Preserve District created favorable water levels for boating, swimming, and fishing by constructing a dam two miles north of Des Plaines. In the summer months the idyllic river setting enticed Chicagoans to board trains for Des Plaines to picnic or camp. As many as 8,000 people came in a day, disrupting the quiet community and annoying townspeople, whose flower gardens were trampled by visitors.

Growth accelerated in the 1920s and the population more than doubled, to 8,798 in 1930. A city form of government was adopted in 1925

and the village of Riverview was annexed. Orchard Place was added in 1949, with adjacent land becoming part of O'Hare International Airport. Des Plaines grew to eight square miles, as a center for both suburban residential growth and light industry.

In 1955 Des Plaines became home to the McDonald's Corp.'s first restaurant. In 1969 the community welcomed Oakton Community College. Population reached 57,239 in 1970 but declined to about 53,000 over the following two decades. By 2000 the population had rebounded to 58,720, with 17 percent Hispanic, 8 percent Asian, and 1 percent African American.

Connections for workers continue to make Des Plaines an attractive community for commuters. Next door to O'Hare Airport, townspeople have access to numerous daily trains, extensive bus lines, major roads such as Rand Road and Northwest Highway, and tollroads and expressways.

Marilyn Elizabeth Perry

FURTHER READING: Henkes, Mark. *Des Plaines: A History.* 1975. ▪ Johnson, Donald S. *Des Plaines, Born of the Tallgrass Prairie: A Pictorial History.* 1984. ▪ Smith, Hermon Dunlap. *The Des Plaines River, 1673–1940: A Brief Consideration of Its Names and History.* 1940.

Douglas, Community Area 35, 3 miles S of the

35
Douglas

Loop. In 1852 Stephen A. Douglas, lawyer, politician, and land speculator, purchased 70 acres of land fronting the lake between 33rd and 35th Streets. Douglas built a house at 34 E. 35th Street and donated land to the Baptists who opened the first University of Chicago in 1860. At the beginning of the Civil War (1861), the Union army set up Camp Douglas between 31st and 33rd Streets, first as a training facility for the Illinois regiment and subsequently as a prisoner of war camp for Confederate soldiers, 4,100 of whom died because of poor conditions at the camp.

Access to both a commuter stop of the Illinois Central Railroad and a growing number of street-

A short five blocks east of the epicenter of "the Stroll," the Plantation Café's bright neon sign at 35th and Calumet. Photographer: Unknown. Source: Chicago History Museum.

car lines drew a wide range of Chicagoans. After the war, wealthy citizens like Joy Morton, founder of the Morton Salt Company, lived in Groveland Park and Woodland Park, while upper-middle-class families purchased homes along Dearborn, State, Wabash, Indiana, and Michigan Avenues.

The area attracted many of the city's leading Jewish families, who in 1881 built a hospital with $200,000 from the estate of Michael Reese. Less than a decade later, the Jewish community completed the Kehilath Anshe Mayriv Synagogue (1890) at 33rd and Indiana. Designed by Dankmar

Adler and Louis Sullivan, it has housed the Pilgrim Baptist Church since 1922.

Working-class families employed in the nearby meatpacking industry, railroad shops, and breweries constructed small balloon-frame houses and a few brick cottages along Federal Street. Irish workers built and worshiped at St. James Church (1880) at 29th and Wabash. In 1869 the Sisters of Mercy relocated their Mercy Hospital to 26th and Calumet. In 1889 the Irish helped to establish De La Salle Institute, a Catholic academy for young men. Mayors Martin Kennelly, Richard J. Daley, Michael Bilandic, and Richard M. Daley graduated from this school.

African Americans made their way along the boulevards from the LOOP to Douglas. By the 1890s the boundaries of the South Side black community had expanded southward along a narrow strip known as the "Black Belt," and black institutions began to play a prominent role in the community. Olivet Baptist Church, with the city's largest African American congregation, moved from the Loop to 27th and Dearborn in 1893, later purchasing the First Baptist Church at 31st and South Parkway (now King Drive). As an outgrowth of the economic strength of the area, businessman Jesse Binga opened Chicago's first black-owned bank in 1908.

During the 1920s through the 1940s, Douglas, along with GRAND BOULEVARD, to the south, became Chicago's center of black business and cultural life. Popularly known as the Black Metropolis or Bronzeville, the area exhibited an amazing diversification of professional and commercial interests. By day black people transacted business in companies housed in the Jordan, Overton Hygienic, and *Chicago Bee* Buildings, and at night they went to clubs where they heard musicians like King Oliver, Louis Armstrong, and Jelly Roll Morton. After the stock market crash of 1929, most of the black-owned banks and insurance companies went out of business.

Many middle-class houses were converted into apartments and fell into disrepair. In 1941 the Chicago Housing Authority (CHA) built the Ida B.

Wells housing project at 37th and Vincennes. In 1950 the Dearborn Homes at 27th and State were opened. In 1952 the CHA completed Prairie Avenue Courts and in 1961 added the Clarence Darrow Homes. In between, it constructed STATEWAY GARDENS at 35th and State and the ROBERT TAYLOR HOMES to the south, replacing all that remained of the worker cottages and tenements along Federal Street.

This new housing and the existing single-family dwellings were not enough to accommodate the 30,000 black newcomers who arrived in the area during World War II, but the city's segregated real-estate market—backed by restrictive covenants, violence, and intimidation by whites—limited options for black people interested in moving out of the community.

Even as public housing was being constructed along Douglas's western border, private developments for middle- and upper-income groups were being erected along the eastern border. Michael Reese Hospital and the Illinois Institute of Technology (created by the merger of the Armour and Lewis Institutes) played pivotal roles in these initiatives. The Lake Meadows apartment complex (between 31st and 35th Streets east of King Drive), Prairie Shores (adjacent to Michael Reese), and South Commons (Michigan Avenue south of 26th Street) were completed by the mid-1960s.

Since the late 1980s there has been a concerted effort to bring the old Black Metropolis back to life. The Mid-South Planning and Development Commission and a number of local community organizations have been in the forefront of this renaissance. The majority of the rebirth has taken place in the area called the GAP, a national historic landmark district located between the Prairie Shores and Lake Meadows high-rise developments (31st to 35th Streets and King Drive to Michigan Avenue). The demolition of Stateway Gardens and the Robert Taylor Homes began in the late 1990s.

Adrian Capehart

FURTHER READING: Drake, St. Clair, and Horace R. Cayton. *Black Metropolis: A Study of Negro Life in a Northern City.*

Rev. ed., 1993. ■ Pacyga, Dominic A., and Ellen Skerrett. *Chicago, City of Neighborhoods: Histories and Tours.* 1986. ■ Spear, Allan. *Black Chicago: The Making of a Negro Ghetto, 1890–1920.* 1967.

Downers Grove, IL, DuPage County, 21 miles W of the Loop. The village of Downers Grove takes its name from the community's first landowner, Pierce Downer, who came from New York State in 1832 to join his son Stephen, a stonemason who was working on the first Chicago lighthouse. Downer staked his claim to 160 acres of prime grove surrounded by prairie, turning it into a successful dairy farm. The Downers were followed by others like Walter Blanchard, Israel Blodgett, Henry Carpenter, Henry Lyman, Henry Puffer, and Dexter Stanley, who created a community around their grove.

The year before the Chicago, Burlington & Quincy Railroad came through town in 1864, Samuel Curtiss established the first subdivision in what would become the southeastern side of the central business district. In 1873 local leaders incorporated as the village of Downers Grove.

Growth continued near the village's three railroad stations at Main Street, Belmont, and East Grove. In 1890 E. H. Prince platted an attractive subdivision north and west of the Main Street station. In 1892 just north of the Belmont station, Chicago businessmen, including Marshall Field, founded the first nine-hole golf course west of the Appalachian Mountains. North of the East Grove station, immigrant families from Gostyn, Poland, purchased lots, creating the largest ethnic neighborhood in town. In 1891 they founded St. Mary's of Gostyn, the village's oldest Roman Catholic church.

Given its proximity to Chicago and its large rail siding, the village became a major site for mail-order housing sold by Sears, Roebuck & Co. between 1908 and 1940. With up to two hundred possible Sears houses identified, Downers Grove has one of the largest concentrations of existing Sears houses in the world.

The Tivoli Theatre, built in 1928, was the second theater in the nation constructed specifically for sound motion pictures.

With the advent of the expressway system in the post–World War II era, the automobile accelerated Downers Grove's expansion, just as the railroad had done almost a century earlier. The village annexed adjoining unincorporated land, and the East-West Toll Road provided easy access. By 2000 the village of Downers Grove comprised 13 square miles, with 48,724 residents. Its diverse economy included corporate headquarters, light industry, service, and retail businesses.

Residents of Downers Grove have often had an impact on the state, the nation, and the world. Arthur C. Ducat served as an inspector general of the Union army during the Civil War, and later established the 800-acre Lindenwald Estate on the west side of town. James Henry Breasted became an internationally renowned Egyptologist at Chicago's Oriental Institute. Lottie Holman O'Neill was the first woman elected to the state legislature, where she served from 1923 to 1963. Art Chester made newspaper headlines in the 1930s and 1940s as an air race champion and aircraft designer. And Cammi Granato captained the U.S. women's Olympic hockey team, winning a gold medal in 1998 and a silver in 2002.

Mark S. Harmon

FURTHER READING: Dunham, Montrew, and Pauline Wandschneider. *Downers Grove, 1832 to 1982.* 1982. ■ Herrick, Bartle R. *What You Didn't Know about Downers Grove and Didn't Know Who to Ask.* 1982.

Dunning, Community Area 17, 10 miles NW of the Loop. In 1851 this remote prairie location seemed ideal for Cook County's plans to erect a poor farm and asylum for the insane. The county purchased from Peter Ludby 160 acres hemmed in by Irving Park Road and Narragansett, Montrose, and

17
Dunning

7280 Irving Park Blvd., Dunning, Ill.

ELM TREE GROVE.

A picnic grove called the Elm Tree Grove, on West Irving Park Boulevard, 1908. Photographer: Curt Teich & Co. Source: Curt Teich Archives, Lake County Discovery Museum.

Oak Park Avenues. Both facilities were housed in a three-story building situated atop a ridge.

Residents of the poor farm lived with their families, growing vegetables, washing their clothes, and attending school on the premises. After 1863 the institution also admitted tuberculosis patients. The county built a separate building for the insane asylum in 1870. The construction of two more buildings in the 1880s added enough space to accommodate the more than 1,000 patients.

Following the Civil War, Andrew Dunning purchased 120 acres just south of the county property to start a nursery and lay the groundwork for a village. He set aside 40 acres for the settlement, but proximity to the insane hospital kept settlers away.

Initially transportation links were poor. Although trains brought employees and commuters from the city, visitors had to walk two and a half miles from the depot to the county farm. After a single three-mile track was extended to the facilities in 1882, the Chicago, Milwaukee &

St. Paul (Chicago, Milwaukee, St. Paul & Pacific) "crazy train" brought patients, supplies, and medicines. The county built a station, naming it for Dunning.

In the 1880s and 1890s Dunning's rolling landscape remained sparsely settled. The Scandinavian Lutheran Cemetery Association bought 65 acres south of Dunning's property in 1886, which became Mount Olive Cemetery. Jewish families purchased 40 acres between the Scandinavian cemetery and Addison for burials.

Around the turn of the century Henry Kolze inherited a tavern and wooded acreage at Narragansett and Irving Park, which he turned into a picnic grove. The idyllic scenery enticed visitors, as did the tavern. With the advent of the Irving Park Boulevard street railway, clubs, churches, and companies held picnics in the grove.

The infirmary, poorhouse, and asylum eventually became overcrowded. Minimal heat in winter, no hot water, and poor ventilation contributed to the deaths of many patients and inmates. In 1886 an official investigation found misconduct, gambling, patient abuse, and "influence" in the hiring of medical personnel. After 1910 the poor farm was moved to Oak Forest, and two years later the state bought the mental hospital and property for one dollar. Although it was called the Chicago State Hospital, many continued to refer to the institution simply as Dunning.

Outside the state facility, the population had grown to only 1,305 by 1909. In 1916 the first housing boom occurred when Schorsch Brothers Real Estate bought a tract west of Austin and south of Irving Park. They called the area West Portage Park to remove the stigma of association with Dunning.

Following World War I the population rose to 4,019, with residents primarily of Swedish, German, and Polish descent. In 1934 Wright Junior College was built in the eastern portion. Population peaked at 43,856 in 1970 but fell to 36,957 by 1990. The State Hospital property stood in shambles, and in the 1970s nearly half the buildings were razed. In 1965 the Chicago-Read Mental Health Center was established, incorporating the old hospitals.

Dunning moved toward a revival of institutional, commercial, and residential growth in the 1980s and 1990s. The neighborhoods of Schorsch Village, Belmont Heights, Belmont Terrace, and Irving Woods became more desirable. On Narragansett north of Irving Park, Ridgemoor Estates boasted luxury homes near a golf club. New modern facilities were constructed at Chicago-Read Mental Health Center. Wright Junior College expanded with futuristic-style buildings and a learning resource center at Narragansett and Montrose. By 2000 the population had grown again, to 42,164.

Marilyn Elizabeth Perry

FURTHER READING: Johnson, Charles B. *Growth of Cook County*, vol. 1. 1960. ■ Ryan, David Joseph. "The Development of Portage Park from the Earliest Period to the 1920s." Senior History Seminar, Northwestern University. May 24, 1974. ■ State Commissioners of Public Charities. *Special Report of an Investigation of the Management of the Cook County Hospital for the Insane.* 1886.

East Garfield Park, Community Area 27, 4 miles W of the Loop. East Garfield Park was annexed to Chicago in 1869; that same year its western section was designated as the site of Central Park, one of three large West Side parks. This prompted a

27 East Garfield Park

flurry of real-estate dealing, but after subdividing the property south and east of the park for sale, developers provided neither buildings nor infrastructure. Intense trading lasted until the 1871 fire, after which speculators looked outside the city, beyond the reach of the fire limits. A quarter century elapsed before the area was thickly populated. Like the residential land, Central Park remained barren, as the corrupt West Park Board ignored William Le Baron Jenney's original designs. Not until 1905, under Jens Jensen's supervision, was the landscaping of the renamed Garfield Park undertaken. A few churches (Our Lady of Sorrows, Warren Avenue Congregational) and schools (Marshall) served the small population.

Unreliable transportation service further diminished the West Side's appeal to potential residents. Instead, the railroads that described East Garfield Park's northern, eastern, and southern boundaries attracted manufacturers expanding westward from the NEAR WEST SIDE at the turn of the century. The most notable of these industrial developments was the four-block-long Sears plant along the border with NORTH LAWNDALE. Commercial development likewise followed the tracks of the new Lake Street Elevated after 1893. Two-flats and small apartment buildings were erected to house the population working in local industry. East Garfield Park's early residents were mostly Irish and German, later joined by Italians and Russian Jews. By 1914 modest homes, commercial buildings, and industry intermixed in East Garfield Park.

A brief prosperity visited the area after World War I. The success of the Madison-Crawford shopping district in WEST GARFIELD PARK spilled eastward along Madison Street. A high-class residential hotel, the Graemere, opened just east of Garfield Park. Flower Technical High School, a vocational school for Chicago's girls, moved from the South Side to 3545 W. Fulton in 1927. But during the Great Depression and World War II, many homes were converted into smaller units, crammed with boarders, and allowed to deteriorate. By 1947 the area was so needy that the Daughters of Charity opened Marillac House at 2822 W. Jackson to serve the local poor.

Although Marillac House's original clients were whites, East Garfield Park's racial composition soon began to change. The building of the Congress (Eisenhower) Expressway during the 1950s displaced residents from a southern stretch of the neighborhood. African Americans, crowded out of the South and Near West Sides, bought and rented homes in East Garfield Park. Finally, a cluster of Chicago Housing Authority (CHA) projects—Harrison Courts, Maplewood Courts, and Rockwell Gardens—delineated the western edge of family public housing in Chicago and the eastern edge of East Garfield Park by 1960.

Many institutions welcomed black participation. Warren Avenue Church and Central Presbyterian Church invited interracial membership. The Midwest Community Council sponsored block clubs and promoted urban renewal. Marillac House created Neighbors at Work to teach organizing skills. The Institute of Cultural Affairs founded the Fifth City Human Development Project in 1963 to develop local leadership. At the same time, physical conditions deteriorated: absentee landlords ignored tenants' requests for repairs, and vacant lots became increasingly common.

In 1966 Martin Luther King's northern civil rights drive built antislum organizations in several neighborhoods. The East Garfield Park Union to End Slums led rent strikes and pickets against neglectful landlords. Participants also organized the East Garfield Park Cooperative to obtain groceries and housing. A coalition of residents and clergy successfully fended off the CHA's attempt to build more high-rise public housing, arguing that the area already had its share. This promising spurt of activism was undermined by rioting along Madison Street following King's assassination in 1968. Businesses left when they lost their insurance, and federal open-occupancy legislation enabled the dispersal of black residents who wished to leave. Burned buildings were not replaced, as both people and money flowed out of the area.

East Garfield Park lost more than two-thirds of its population to out-migration, falling from a high of 70,091 in 1950 to 20,881 in 2000. In the 1970s and 1980s, as endemic poverty and unemployment overtook the area, a drug economy and associated criminal activity such as prostitution filled the economic void. Sporadic reinvestment included the expansion of Bethany Hospital, the building of Ike Sims Village for senior citizens, and the arrival of St. Stephen AME Church.

Amanda Seligman

FURTHER READING: Bennett, Larry. *Fragments of Cities: The New American Downtowns and Neighborhoods.* 1990. ■ East Garfield Park Community Collection. Special Collections, Harold Washington Library, Chicago. ■ *Local Community Fact Book* series.

East Side, Community Area 52, 13 miles SE of the Loop. The modern history of the East Side was shaped by the entrance of heavy industry into the Calumet area in the 1870s. Prior to this time, Native Americans had lived off the land, hunting and fishing for their food. Located just south of SOUTH CHICAGO and east of SOUTH DEERING, the region's natural port and its proximity to railroads attracted many firms. By the

52
East Side

1920s the East Side, until then known by the names Taylorville, Goosetown, and Colehour, was significant for iron and steel production.

As industry flourished, settlement exploded. Germans and Swedes established themselves in the late 1800s. The first religious congregation, the Colehour German Lutheran Church, opened in 1874, and a succession of congregations soon followed. When Croatian, Slovene, and Serbian immigrants began to arrive in the 1880s, Germans and Swedes asserted their "American-ness" before their new neighbors. These first nationalist divisions set the pattern for a trend that would continue into the next century.

New settlers were quick to organize their own congregations. Croatians formed the Sacred Heart Catholic parish at 96th and Escanaba. Italians entered the area in 1914; together with the Slavs, they inhabited the older neighborhoods near the Calumet River. Shortly thereafter, Calumet Park was constructed on the lakefront; it influenced the eastward migration of the community. Today it is considered a great resource of the East Side, home to local athletics, a beach, and other public entertainment.

The East Side's geography, bordered by water on three sides and shielded by miles of mills, corresponds with its voluntary social isolation. The East Side has long been considered a suburb of South Chicago, and its residents have a profound sense of social cohesiveness; family and friendship ties tend to remain stable for many years. There have, however, been ethnic tensions, as noted above. As new immigrants entered the area, they often met with antagonism from the older inhabitants. Following World War I, ethnic differences began to subside as immigration slowed and a process of Americanization influenced the population. The attempted entry of African Americans into the area, however, produced particularly bitter and often violent resistance from East Siders. Race riots exploded at Calumet Park and in the nearby area of Trumbull Park in South Deering following attempts by African American families to move

in after World War II. Between 1980 and 2000 the Hispanic population grew from 13 to 68 percent, and the area remained a predominantly working-class enclave.

Industrial conflict arising from the hegemony of local steel has plagued the area since the 1930s. Republic Steel had built a specialty plant and was one of the area's chief employers when, in 1937, the Steel Workers Organizing Committee (SWOC) launched a campaign to unionize the Republic steelworkers. With great support from by local iron- and steelworkers, SWOC organized a Memorial Day march on the plant. As 1,000 people approached the mill gates, Chicago police ordered their retreat; the crowd capitulated, yet police began shooting at the strikers, killing 10 and maiming many more. The massacre sidetracked the drive for unionization; Republic Steel was eventually organized in 1941. SWOC was transformed into the United Steelworkers of America in 1942.

The decline of the Chicago steel industry had profound effects on the East Side community. Calumet-area steel producers suffered greatly from depressed economic conditions and international competition. Republic Steel dismissed half its employees in the 1980s. In 1984 the company merged with Jones and Laughlin to form LTV Steel, becoming the country's second largest steel producer, but in 1986 LTV declared bankruptcy, closing operations in Chicago. Layoffs reverberated throughout the East Side, decimating the local economy. In 1982 the area became an official "enterprise zone," part of the city's effort to revitalize the local economy. These efforts have not proved very successful. Two decades later, the East Side remained an embattled and struggling community, attempting to re-create its sense of cohesion. In 2000 the Ford Motor Company announced plans to expand onto the site of the former Republic Steel.

David Bensman

FURTHER READING: Bensman, David, and Roberta Lynch. *Rusted Dreams: Hard Times in a Steel Community.* 1988. ∎ Kornblum, William. *Blue Collar Community.* 1974.

Edgebrook, commuter rail settlement established in 1880s, now in the FOREST GLEN Community Area.

Edgewater, Community Area 77, 7 miles N of the Loop. Although it was an

77
Edgewater

elite nineteenth-century suburb, Edgewater was not recognized as distinct when scholars laid out the community areas in the 1920s. Instead, Edgewater was merged into UPTOWN. In the 1970s, however, Edgewater's property owners persuaded the city of Chicago to make a rare change in its community area maps and recognize Edgewater as a separate entity.

Few people lived in the Edgewater area before the late nineteenth century. Scattered settlers farmed celery. Edgewater's residents were mostly German and Irish. Swedes gathered along Clark Street in an area they called ANDERSONVILLE.

John Lewis Cochran (1857–1923) purchased land near Lake Michigan in the town of LAKE VIEW in 1886. There he developed a subdivision he advertised as "Edgewater." He first built mansions on the lakefront for wealthy families and later had smaller houses built to the west. In contrast to other suburban developers, Cochran installed improvements such as sidewalks, sewers, and streetlights before customers moved in. Cochran also founded the Edgewater Light Company to ensure that his buyers could use the most modern conveniences. Cochran's final task was to provide adequate transportation to the area. He persuaded the Chicago, Milwaukee & St. Paul Railroad (Chicago, Milwaukee, St. Paul & Pacific) to open a stop on Bryn Mawr Avenue and was instrumental in the creation of the Northwestern Elevated Railroad, which in 1908 opened up a connection through to Howard Street. The availability of transportation encouraged the erection of apartment buildings, a development Cochran had not intended. This strip of "common corridor" buildings and residential hotels, concentrated between Winthrop

and Kenmore, increased Edgewater's population density.

During the twentieth century, Edgewater solidified its status as one of the most prestigious residential areas in Chicago. In 1898 the exclusive Saddle and Cycle Club relocated to Foster Avenue, on the lakefront. The Edgewater Beach Hotel (1916) and the Edgewater Beach Apartments (1929), finished in sunrise yellow and sunset pink, served as local landmarks. Residential Edgewater's wealth reinforced the glamour of recreational Uptown.

During the citywide housing crisis of the 1940s, these apartment buildings were subdivided into smaller units. The area began to become overcrowded and landlords collected increasing rents while allowing their properties to deteriorate. When building resumed, more large apartment buildings replaced older ones. Along the Winthrop-Kenmore corridor, most new structures were four-plus-one low-rise apartments. Along Sheridan Road, most of the old mansions were razed and replaced with high-rises, giving the street the feel of a canyon.

These developments disturbed some Edgewater residents. They regarded the Winthrop-Kenmore corridor as an eyesore that attracted transients, the ill, and the elderly. Single people who would not stay long in the area rented in the Sheridan Road high-rises. Alarmed at the prospect of social and physical blight, property owners created the Edgewater Community Council in 1960. The ECC sought a variety of local improvements. For example, in conjunction with the Organization of the Northeast, they arranged a moratorium on the opening of new residential health care facilities. During the 1970s ECC's strategy shifted to separating its identity from Uptown, which Edgewater residents regarded as the source of their plight. The opening of the Edgewater branch of the Chicago Public Library in 1973 was a major victory in this battle, which culminated in 1980 when the city government ratified the separation of Edgewater from Uptown by designating it Community Area 77.

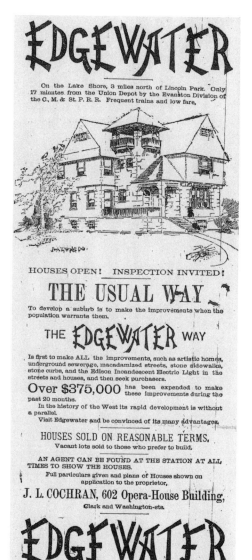

Advertisement for the Edgewater subdivision, 1888.
Source: Chicago History Museum.

The success of the rehabilitation was reflected in Loyola University's increasing involvement in Edgewater. Although it had been oriented to Rogers Park, by the late 1970s Loyola began encouraging its faculty and students to recognize, and even to live in, Edgewater.

At the same time, the smaller commercial strips within Edgewater promoted their own distinctive flavors. What began as a promotion

of "Chinatown North" on Argyle Street evolved as Edgewater's population shifted to include diverse Asian Americans. Among the shop owners on Argyle were Vietnamese, Thai, Japanese, Koreans, Indians, Pakistanis, and also Spanish-speakers, Greeks, and Albanians. Along Clark Street, merchants revived Andersonville's Swedish past during the 1960s, successfully marketing the area as a clean and friendly place to shop for curiosities. Later, merchants from other ethnic groups and enterprises run by lesbian women supplemented Andersonville's Swedish flavor.

Amanda Seligman

FURTHER READING: Marciniak, Ed. *Reversing Urban Decline: The Winthrop-Kenmore Corridor in the Edgewater and Uptown Communities of Chicago.* 1981. ■ Pacyga, Dominic A., and Ellen Skerrett. *Chicago, City of Neighborhoods: Histories and Tours.* 1986.

Edison Park, Community Area 9, 13 miles NW

9
Edison Park

of the Loop. Edison Park lies in the far northwest corner of Chicago, a little more than a mile west of the Chicago River, along a Metra commuter line. The area has changed from a home to various Indian groups to a farming community to a railroad suburb to a Chicago neighborhood. At each transition, new residents and land uses have confronted old ones, reshaping the landscape.

The wooded areas along the river provided summer camps for Native Americans before the 1830s, when German farmers staked claim to the land. Among this group were members of the Ebinger family, who regularly met Native Americans who continued to move along the old trail (now Milwaukee Avenue) near the farms. A tavern along Milwaukee Road served both farmers and Indians as they traveled in the vicinity and on their way to Chicago. An evangelical church and cemetery were among the institutions founded by these farmers.

After the arrival of the railroad in the early 1850s, developers tried to breathe life into two

Children standing in front of an anti-German sign posted in the Edison Park neighborhood, 1917. Photographer: Unknown. Source: Chicago History Museum.

paper suburbs that today are part of Edison Park: Canfield and Ridgelawn. It was not until the 1890s that Edison Park grew, claiming to be the first Northwest Side community with electricity. Area residents organized as a village in 1896 and touted artesian water, a volunteer fire company, a hotel, a large railroad depot, and dozens of large houses. Located between two successful railroad suburbs, PARK RIDGE and NORWOOD PARK (later annexed to Chicago), Edison Park joined the competition. By 1910 there were 300 residents.

New residents and established farm families created a park district and a grammar school (part of Maine Township), improved roads and water provision, and established new churches and clubs. In addition, several religious institutions established homes for children on former farmland. Residents often traveled to JEFFERSON PARK on the railroad for shopping.

One problem that area residents faced was the distance to a high school. Living in Maine Township, area students had to travel many miles to the new Maine West High School. Residents decided to merge with Chicago in 1910, so that their children could attend Carl Schurz High School (accessible by rail). The village trustees disbanded the government and Edison Park began the slow process of integration into the city.

After World War I, Edison Park experienced a major building boom. Businesses and industry began locating nearby and automobile travel made the area attractive to workers. Chicago bungalows and Dutch colonials soon outnumbered the older, larger houses. Second-generation immigrants, many of them Roman Catholic or Lutheran, moved into the area as the population grew to 5,370 in 1930. Little farmland remained, but the Ebinger name was memorialized in the name of the new local school.

During the 1950s builders constructed brick

bungalows on remaining empty lots in the neighborhood. The neighborhood had an Italian flavor, with ethnic grocery stores and bakeries in the business center. The construction of the Kennedy and Edens expressways, the O'Hare rapid transit line, and the Tri-State Toll Road have diffused the importance of the railroad line to Edison Park residents. Residents in recent years find work, leisure, and shopping opportunities in all directions, both within the city and in surrounding suburban areas.

Ann Durkin Keating

FURTHER READING: Scholl, Edward T. *Seven Miles of Ideal Living*. 1957.

Elgin, IL, Kane County, 35 miles NW of the Loop.

The future site of Elgin was well known to the Potawatomi, for here the Fox River could be forded at many times of the year, and there was good fishing in the shallows. Hezekiah Gifford apparently gave Elgin its name after the 1833 Black Hawk War. By 1837 it already had a bridge and a mill or two, and was beginning to enjoy a certain importance as a stage on the coach route from Chicago to the lead mines of Galena. In 1849 the Galena & Chicago Union Railroad reached Elgin; later, railroads running along both banks of the Fox River would link the growing town to Chicago and other urban centers. Elgin showed great promise in the 1850s, and in 1856 the Elgin Academy was founded. The town continued to thrive during the 1860s, both as a center of military production during the Civil War and because industrial enterprises began to use the water power of the swiftly flowing Fox River.

The most important venture founded at this time was the Elgin National Watch Company, organized in 1864 to compete with the American Waltham Watch Company of Waltham, Massachusetts. From its small beginnings it became, for a time, the world's largest watch-manufacturing complex, spreading the name Elgin across much of the industrialized world. In 1866 Gail Borden founded a condensed-milk factory, whose product also became widely known. Other Elgin industries included a large shoe factory and a number of grain mills. The population of Elgin grew from 5,441 in 1870 to 17,823 in 1890, when the city was divided into seven wards. It had expanded far out from its origins by the ford, especially along the timbered east bank of the river. In 1872 it attracted a major state institution, the Northern Illinois State Mental Hospital.

During the twentieth century, Elgin has continued to thrive modestly. For a time during the 1920s it was one of the centers for a great network of interurban rail lines, which linked together the towns of the Fox River Valley and their neighbors to the east. This remarkable system might have continued to grow and to serve the region well, but it was dismantled during the great expansion in automobile travel in the 1950s.

Today the town continues to grow along Interstate 90 to the north. Most of its heavy industries have disappeared, but it enjoys a quiet prosperity as a center for commuters and, increasingly, for companies such as Motorola and Bank One. Redevelopment of the downtown area has included the opening of the Grand Victoria Casino.

David Buisseret

FURTHER READING: Alft, E. C. *Elgin: An American History, 1835–1935.* 1984. ∎ Alft, E. C. *South Elgin: A History of the Village from Its Origin as Clintonville.* 1979.

Elk Grove Village, IL, Cook and Lake Counties,

20 miles NW of the Loop. Elk Grove Village differs from many other suburban towns in that it did not emerge as a nineteenth-century market town or around a railroad depot; indeed, it did not come into existence as a center of settlement until around 1940, roughly at the place where Touhy Avenue intersects with route

Holiday Inn of Elk Grove Village-Centex Industrial Park

Holiday Inn of Elk Grove Village–Centex Industrial Park, 1968. Photographer: Curt Teich & Co. Source: Curt Teich Archives, Lake County Discovery Museum.

53. This was in the southeastern corner of the old Elk Grove township, which took its name from the huge grove that is now the Ned Brown Forest Preserve. Bounded on the west by Salt Creek and on the east by the line of the present-day Arlington Heights Road, this forested area attracted not only Potawatomi hunters but also, from the mid-1830s onward, Yankee settlers. The open prairie areas tended to be marshy, but the early Yankee farmers were joined in the late 1840s by Germans, and together they eventually drained much of the area round the future site of Elk Grove Village.

No railroad traversed this part of the country, and it remained very rural right down to World War II; indeed, it is only on the map of 1941 that we begin to discern the development of a town. At that time the future O'Hare Airport, a mile or so to the southeast, was beginning to emerge as a center for the manufacture of Douglas transport aircraft; eventually it would become the major hub of United Airlines, which would make its headquarters in Elk Grove Village.

All this lay in the future in 1941, and as late as 1956, when Elk Grove Village was incorporated, the population numbered only 125. After that, however, development was rapid. Following a plan proposed by the Centex Corporation of Dallas, Texas, curvilinear streets were laid out, and by the late 1950s and 1960s a whole suburb had come into being, complete with schools, churches, and shopping centers; in 1958 this growth was much encouraged by the construction of the Northwest Tollway, which cut across the northern edge of the town.

The Northwest Tollway also clipped off the northern section of the old grove. But in general the Elk Grove Forest Preserve, established in 1924, succeeded not only in resisting such encroachments but even in recovering land previously lost. By 1994 the great grove had largely recovered its historic outline. And by 2000 Elk Grove Village had reached the limits of territorial expansion, with 34,727 inhabitants.

David Buisseret

FURTHER READING: Buisseret, David, and James A. Issel. *Elk Grove Village and Township.* 1996. ■ Wajer, Mary Hagan. *Elk Grove: The Land and the Settlers, 1834–1880.* 1976.

Elmhurst, IL, DuPage County, 16 miles W of the
Loop. Elmhurst shares the
agricultural roots of its Du-
Page neighbors but also
served as an elegant center
for great estate owners during the late nineteenth century and was, in the 1920s,
DuPage's largest city.

York Township's early residents came mainly
from New York or Europe to live along Salt Creek.
Germans, such as Frederick Graue, settled in the
north near the Elmhurst-Addison boundary, while
those of predominantly English ancestry resided
in the south near today's Butterfield Road; the village remained bilingual for decades.

Gerry Bates, referred to as Elmhurst's founder,
brought a sense of community to the area when his
Hill Cottage Tavern opened in 1843 as inn, stage
stop, and local gathering place. In 1849 the Galena
& Chicago Union Railroad arrived, and the community was officially named Cottage Hill, after
the tavern. York Street became the village's main
thoroughfare. In 1850 School District No. 1 was organized, with both English and German spoken in
the classroom. The German Evangelical Synod of
the Northwest established a proseminary in 1871,
which later became Elmhurst College.

Thomas Barbour Bryan, a Virginia-born lawyer, purchased a thousand acres from Bates and
built a country house. His contributions to the
town led residents to refer to him as "the Father
of Elmhurst." In 1862 he organized the first Protestant church as an Episcopal lay reader (St. Mary's
Roman Catholic Church was founded the same
year). Bryan's brother-in-law, Jedediah H. Lathrop, joined with other estate owners in planting
a large number of elm treees along Cottage Hill,
from which Elmhurst acquired its present name
in 1869.

The 1871 Chicago Fire brought wealthy refugees
to Elmhurst and marked the onset of Elmhurst's
gilded age, an era of elegant socializing that lasted into the twentieth century. By the turn of the
century, what is now the site of York High School

"Old Main," Elmhurst College, 1943. Photographer: Curt
Teich & Co. Source: Curt Teich Archives, Lake County
Discovery Museum.

had served as both the Elmhurst Golf Club and
the original Hawthorne racetrack (since relocated
to CICERO).

Elmhurst was incorporated in 1882, serving not
only these wealthy estate owners, but also farmers,
local businessmen, and owners of area industries.
In 1883 Adolph Hammerschmidt and Henry Ass-
man founded Elmhurst-Chicago Stone Company
near the village's western limits to quarry dolomite limestone.

During the 1920s Elmhurst became DuPage's
largest city, with paved streets, a city planning
commission, and the founding in 1926 of the
Elmhurst Memorial Hospital. The city-man-
ager form of government was adopted in 1953.
Elmhurst grew as a railroad suburb with many
urban amenities, including Elmhurst College
(whose campus is an accredited arboretum), the
Lizzadro Museum of Lapidary Art (1962), the

Swenson's Greenhouse, 5 York Street, Elmhurst, early twentieth century. Photographer: Unknown. Source: DuPage County Historical Museum.

Elmhurst Art Museum, a public library, a park district, the Wilder Park conservatory (1923), the Elmhurst Historical Museum (1956), and the Elmhurst Symphony Orchestra (1960). Though essentially landlocked by the 1990s, Elmhurst engaged in ongoing redevelopment.

Jane S. Teague

FURTHER READING: Russell, Don. *Elmhurst: Trails from Yesterday.* 1977. ■ Thompson, Richard A., ed. *DuPage Roots.* 1985.

Elsdon, neighborhood established by railroad workers in the 1880s, now in the GAGE PARK Community Area.

Englewood, Community Area 68, 7 miles S of the Loop. In 1852 several railroad lines crossed at what became known as Junction Grove, stimulating the growth, in what had been an oak forest with much swampland, of what we know today as Englewood.

68
Englewood

The earliest settlers to Englewood were Germans and Irish who worked initially on truck farms and the railroads, and later at the Union Stock Yard. By 1865 Junction Grove was annexed to the town of Lake and in 1889 to Chicago. In 1868 Henry B. Lewis, a wool merchant in the LOOP and a board of education member, suggested a new name, Englewood, deriving from his association with Englewood, New Jersey. Also in 1868, developer L. W. Beck gave 10 acres to Englewood for the Cook County Normal School (later Chicago State University), a teacher's college that would serve the Chicago region. Normal Park developed around the school, paving the way for incoming middle-class home buyers. In the 1870s Englewood High School was opened.

The first religious mission to the area was begun by the Presbyterians, but the first church was St. Anne's Roman Catholic Church, established in 1869. In the 1870s Protestants of every variety established churches. By 1880 Germans, Irish, and Scots were the largest ethnic groups, but were supplanted at the turn of the century by Poles and other Eastern European immigrants. By 1887 horsecar lines connected Engle-

Beck's American Band, Englewood (no date). Photographer: Unknown. Source: Chicago History Museum.

wood to downtown, followed by electric trolleys in 1896 and the elevated line in 1907. By 1922 Englewood was served by 2,900 street railway, elevated, and suburban train runs daily.

The construction of apartment buildings in the 1910s and 1920s created problems of density and economic segregation. By 1920 the population soared to 86,619 and Englewood's shopping district at Halsted and 63rd was the second busiest in the city. In 1929 Sears developed a $1.5 million store here. The Great Depression did not affect the operation of the larger stores, but many smaller ones suffered and several banks in Englewood closed.

The 1940s witnessed a decline of real-estate values in Englewood. Buildings were 40 years old,

and the expanding Black Belt population from the east resulted in rapid turnover. Materials necessary to redevelop Englewood were scarce owing to World War II, and later practices of redlining and disinvestment sealed Englewood's future as a low-income community with a declining housing stock. In 1959 a *Chicago Sun-Times* writer interviewed a banker about lending in Englewood. His reply illuminates attitudes among lenders at the time: "When a lender makes a loan on a house, he looks at the total financial position of the borrower. The rate is determined by risk. The Negro has to pay a *higher rate* because he is not as secure in his job."

While economic gains by African Americans gave some the opportunity to purchase larger houses in Englewood, many low-income residents rented in crowded conditions. In 1940 blacks constituted just 2 percent of the population, but this increased to 11 percent in 1950, 69 percent in 1960, and 96 percent by 1970. In 1960 the population peaked at over 97,000 people, despite the exodus of 50,000 whites. Public works projects such as the Dan Ryan Expressway, coupled with patterns of housing abandonment and deterioration, led to a massive loss of housing stock. Further, attempts at restoring the shopping district through public funds were unsuccessful. This is due in part to competition from nearby shopping centers built in the 1960s (such as Evergreen Park and Ford City). By the 1970s Sears and Wieboldt's had closed, and Chicago State University had moved to 95th Street in ROSELAND. By the end of the century about 100 shops were still operational, with over 75 percent managed by Korean and Pakistani merchants. Englewood's population declined to 59,075 by 1980 and to 40,222 by 2000, despite 200 housing units built by the Antioch Baptist Church and some publicly funded apartments for elderly and handicapped persons. Few communities in Chicago have lost as much population or housing stock in the twentieth century.

Clinton E. Stockwell

FURTHER READING: Hill, Barbara Rector. *Englewood, 1912–1950: In Celebration of Chicago's Sesquicentennial.* 1988. ▨ Pacyga, Dominic A., and Ellen Skerrett. *Chicago, City of Neighborhoods: Histories and Tours.* 1986. ▨ Sullivan, Gerald E., ed. *The Story of Englewood, 1835–1923.* 1924.

Essex, early neighborhood in the SOUTH SHORE Community Area.

Evanston, IL, Cook County, 12 miles N of the Loop. On the shore of Lake Michigan just north of Chicago, the area that is now Evanston was home to Potawatomis until the 1830s, when they were moved west to Iowa. During the 1840s the area became thinly settled by farmers

from upstate New York and elsewhere in the eastern United States and by German-speaking immigrants from the region where today the Netherlands, Belgium, Luxembourg, and Germany converge.

In 1853 the embryonic Northwestern University purchased and surveyed more than three hundred acres of swampy land, which is now central Evanston. Northwestern held its first Evanston classes two years later. Two other educational institutions also opened that year: the Garrett Biblical Institute and the Northwestern Female College.

Incorporated as a village in 1863, the town (named in honor of John Evans, a central founder of Northwestern) initially grew slowly. But the Chicago Fire of 1871 led thousands of well-to-do Chicagoans, fearing another fire, to build homes in Evanston. To meet their needs an influx of servants and tradesmen swelled Evanston's population. The village of North Evanston merged with Evanston in 1874, and in 1892 residents of South Evanston voted to join with Evanston.

Evanston's African American community, which predated the Civil War, also grew. Most African Americans were employed as domestic servants or manual laborers until the opening of light manufacturing on Evanston's west side, which included in its workforce both African Americans and Polish immigrants.

During the first two decades of the twentieth century, rapid transit access to Chicago's LOOP stimulated a boom in the construction of large apartment buildings. In the 1920s a real-estate boom led to the development of northwest Evanston as a wealthy enclave. By the 1940s Evanston had become the home of numerous national organizations and nationally known firms.

By the 1960s Evanston's African American population had become largely concentrated in the city's west and south-central neighborhoods. Immigrants from Haiti and Jamaica began arriving in sizable numbers, as did a large number of former residents of Chicago's HYDE PARK neighborhood. Growing racial tensions led to conscious efforts to ensure racial balance in the Evanston Public Schools.

The opening of the Old Orchard Shopping Center in adjacent Skokie in the early 1960s drained vitality from Evanston's central business district. Many retail shops were replaced by restaurants, making Evanston one of metropolitan Chicago's premier dining centers, a development anticipated in 1972 when the city dropped a ban on the sale of alcoholic beverages that had its antecedents in an 1855 temperance amendment to Northwestern's charter.

Town-gown conflicts had surfaced periodically since 1874 because of the tax exemption that was granted to the university by the Illinois state legislature in 1855. In the late 1990s high property taxes and high rents threatened to diminish Evanston's long-standing appeal for middle-class residents. A joint Northwestern-Evanston Research Park failed to fulfill its promises of new jobs and renewed economic vitality. But successful retail and residential developments have helped Evanston remain one of Chicago's most stable and attractive suburbs.

Patrick M. Quinn

FURTHER READING: Ebner, Michael. *Creating Chicago's North Shore*. 1988. ■ Perkins, Margery Blair. *Evanstoniana: An Informal History of Evanston and Its Architecture*. 1994. ■ Sheppard, Robert D., and Harvey B. Hurd. *History of Northwestern University and Evanston*. 1906.

Fernwood, subdivision adjacent to a rail stop, built in the 1880s and an independent incorporated suburb until 1891, when it was annexed to Chicago. Now part of the Washington Heights Community Area.

Flossmoor, IL, Cook County, 24 miles S of the Loop. Flossmoor, a small residential town in the southern suburbs, is situated in the Calumet River watershed and lies in the townships of Bloom and Rich. Excavations at the Horton site (near Brookwood and Western) during 1966 and 1967 indicated that Native Americans occupied the site in a large structure (about 30 feet wide) several hundred years ago.

The town is to a great extent the creation of the Illinois Central Railroad, which bought 160 acres in the area in 1893. The company's plan was to strip away the black dirt and use it as fill at the World's Columbian Exposition, but the soil proved unsuitable. When the railroad later decided to sell its land, it received an unexpected boost.

In 1898 a group of investors conceived the idea of building a golf course in the area. They asked the Illinois Central to extend service beyond Homewood, then the southernmost stop on the commuter line, and to erect a station near the site of the proposed course. When the railroad agreed, the investors established the Homewood County Club (renamed Flossmoor in 1914). The venture was such a success that other country clubs soon followed, notably Ravisloe, in Homewood (1901); Idlewild, in Flossmoor (1908); Olympia Fields, in Olympia Fields (1915); and Calumet, in Homewood (1917).

The Illinois Central broke its land into lots, platted the subdivision in 1901, and in 1903 built a half dozen houses. The U.S. Post Office selected the name Flossmoor from a list the Illinois Central had assembled through a contest to name the place. The railroad vigorously promoted Flossmoor, even running free-lunch excursions for prospective buyers from Chicago, and steadily built ridership by touting the country clubs and providing special services for golfers. Residential construction picked up after 1910, and by World War I the upper-middle-class community was firmly established and home to some of the railroad's executives. Electrification of the commuter train lines in 1926 further increased the desirability of the area.

Flossmoor incorporated as a village in 1924. Among the first local laws was an ordinance that prohibited industry within the town limits, thus guaranteeing the village's residential character. It also implicitly screened in new residents who worked elsewhere. By 1967 Flossmoor and neighboring Homewood were among a handful of suburbs where more than half the workers commuted to jobs in Chicago.

In the post–World War II period Flossmoor and Homewood formed some significant partnerships. Homewood-Flossmoor Community High School in Flossmoor opened its doors in 1959 and has proven exceptionally successful, winning awards from the U.S. Department of Education in 1982–83, 1994–95, and 2001–2. A joint park district was incorporated in 1969.

Flossmoor's population at incorporation was 265, and by 1930 it had grown to 808. The village grew steadily through World War II and then in the 1950s surged 156 percent, to 4,624 in 1960. Population topped 8,400 in 1980 and reached 9,301 by 2000.

John H. Long

FURTHER READING: Adair, Anna B., and Adele Sandberg. *Indian Trails to Tollways: The Story of the Homewood-Flossmoor Area.* 1968. ■ League of Women Voters. *Know Your Town: Homewood, Flossmoor, Olympia Fields.* 1967. ■ Wagner, Susan F. *A History of the Village of Flossmoor, 1851–1974.* 1974.

Ford City, neighborhood initially centered around factories at 77th Street and Cicero Avenue in the WEST LAWN Community Area.

Ford Heights, IL, Cook County, 26 miles S of the Loop. The village of Ford Heights sits on a rise of land that stretches northeast into areas along Deer Creek. Farmers came in 1848 and grew onion sets and maintained fruit or-

chards. Both black and white families farmed in the area before 1900.

After 1920 more residents came to live on newly subdivided land called the "Park Addition" on a farm road from CHICAGO HEIGHTS to Indiana. Acting together in 1924, 40 families successfully petitioned for electrical service. That same year, the main east-west road became a two-lane concrete highway, designated as U.S. Route 30 in 1926 and later known as the transcontinental Lincoln Highway. By the 1930s the Park Addition had telephone service and was known as East Chicago Heights.

Early settlers included the family of Alberta Armstrong, whose grandmother was one of the first black residents. Also important and memorable was Isabella "Grandma" Greenwood. She and her husband, both born into slavery, built a small house in the village in 1893. Alberta Armstrong and others organized black and white women to raise funds for a fire truck, and by 1948 this group became the East Chicago Heights Citizens Association.

In 1949 East Chicago Heights incorporated with a growing African American population. Then as now, however, its small population and minimal commercial activity limited the financial base for local government initiatives. Such dilemmas were complicated by race. For decades, racism across the metropolitan area severely limited housing choices, and East Chicago Heights was a forced option. This fostered the success of the Sunnyfield subdivision (1964) as a suburban place for middle-class black families, but it also brought families with limited resources to the village. In the 1960s, 63 acres with substandard housing were cleared in an urban renewal project, leaving vacant land and the loss of over 60 families. New public housing further taxed village resources.

Once referred to as the "poorest suburb in America," the community has taken many steps to strengthen its future. In 1987 the village changed its name to Ford Heights.

Larry A. McClellan

FURTHER READING: Hayes, Jack. "The Poorest Suburb in

America." *Chicago Reader,* September 18, 1987. ■ McClellan, Larry A. *A History of Ford Heights, Written and Compiled to Celebrate the 50th Anniversary of the Village Incorporated as East Chicago Heights in 1949.* 1999.

Forest Glen, Community Area 12, 10 miles NW of the Loop. Forest Glen is perhaps the most stereotypically suburban of Chicago's community areas. This well-to-do and well-kept area contains the prestigious Edgebrook and Sauganash neighborhoods. Many city administrators, upper-echelon police and fire officials, lawyers, judges, and politicians live here. This secluded area, on the city's far Northwest Side, is separated from surrounding portions of the city and suburbs by a ring of forest preserves, parks, golf courses, and cemeteries. Here, the monotonous flatness of the Chicago lake plain gives way to heavily forested and gently rolling terrain. The North Branch of the Chicago River forms part of the area's southern boundary and wriggles from northwest to southeast through the community's eastern portion. The uniqueness of the area is further enhanced by a complex street pattern that, thanks to the serpentine wanderings of the river, departs markedly from the rigorous rectangular grid of most of Chicago's streets.

12
Forest Glen

The woods to the east of the river are thicker than those to the west since, from early times, the river protected them from fires blown eastward by the prevailing west winds. These flower-dappled woods once provided summer campgrounds and prime hunting territory for the Miami and Potawatomi Indians. Artifacts of their presence are still occasionally found here, and streets with Indian names invoke their memory. Indeed, the nearly 2.5-square-mile area occupied by Sauganash and Edgebrook was once the preserve of Billy Caldwell, a colorful chief of the Potawatomi. Caldwell, whose Indian name was Sauganash (meaning Englishman), mediated the treaties between the Indians and the United States. In 1828, in recognition of his help, the federal government ceded Caldwell the tract of land.

As Chicago grew outward, more and more distant areas were drawn into the urban web, particularly with the expansion of commuter rail lines. Railroad stops at Forest Glen and Edgebrook encouraged commuter settlement by the 1880s. Residential development began in that decade when Captain Charles Hazelton founded the first church in the area, built a home (which still stands), and subdivided 10 acres for additional development. Milwaukee Railroad (Chicago, Milwaukee, St. Paul & Pacific Railroad) executives created a residential retreat alongside a golf course at Edgebrook. Initially a part of Jefferson Township, this area was largely annexed to Chicago in 1889. The relative remoteness of Forest Glen from the city center and the limited transportation facilities probably contributed to its sluggish development. It was not until the 1920s that home building began in earnest.

By 1940 Forest Glen began to exhibit the character it shows today as a wealthy and powerful community of fine homes. By this time, the original residents, of English and Swedish stock, had been joined by neighbors whose nationalities were German, Czech, and Irish. Roman Catholics founded new parishes alongside older Protestant churches. The community reached its highest population of 20,531 in 1970. Mayor Richard J. Daley's insistence that city workers live in the city led many to live in Forest Glen.

At the end of the twentieth century, Forest Glen had a scattering of industry along the rail tracks and limited commercial facilities near major intersections on Cicero, Devon, and Lehigh Avenues. Even so, the area was overwhelmingly residential in character, and most of the housing consisted of owner-occupied, single-family dwellings. Although there were virtually no apartments or town houses, the housing stock was diverse. Within the community area, the various neighborhoods were rather stratified, with bungalows in Forest Glen, midrange housing in Edgebrook, and palatial dwellings in Sauganash. Some of these vintage homes have remained in the same families for generations.

The community is stable, comfortable, and wealthy relative to most of Chicago, and it holds an aura of political power. The population has retreated slightly from its 1970 high as younger residents have moved out to establish their own families. In 2000 the area continued as an overwhelmingly white, Roman Catholic community.

David M. Solzman

FURTHER READING: Alexander, Lois Ann, et al. *Sauganash: A Historical Perspective.* 1999. ■ Chicago Fact Book Consortium, ed. *Local Community Fact Book: Chicago Metropolitan Area.* Based on the 1970 and 1980 censuses. ■ Solzman, David M. *The Chicago River: An Illustrated History and Guide to the River and Its Waterways.* 1998, 2006.

Forest Park, IL, Cook County, 9 miles W of the

Loop. Forest Park extends from Harlem Avenue on the east to the Des Plaines River and First Avenue on the west, and from Madison Street and the North Western Railway tracks on the north to Cermak Road on the south. The village's earliest inhabitants settled along the Oak Park spit, a high sand ridge along Des Plaines Avenue. In 1839 Leon Bourassa, a French Indian trader, purchased 160 acres along the Des Plaines River in present-day Forest Park, which was then part of Noyesville. Ferdinand Haase, a German immigrant, bought a 40-acre tract from Bourassa in 1851, which he eventually enlarged to 240 acres and turned into a popular park for residents and city dwellers. In 1856 the Galena & Chicago Union Railroad opened a shop and roundhouse at today's Des Plaines Avenue and Lake Street, bringing 25 men and their families to settle there. In the same year, John Henry Quick purchased a large tract of land in Forest Park and the east end of River Forest, and named the entire area Harlem after his hometown in New York.

Since the 1870s Forest Park's main industry has been several large cemeteries—Jewish Waldheim (1870), Concordia (1872), German Waldheim (1873), Forest Home (1876), and Woodlawn (1912)—which cover most of the town's acreage. Forest Home, which merged with the adjacent German Waldheim Cemetery in 1968, has a long history of burials, as evidenced when two mounds containing Native American artifacts and skeletons were unearthed in 1900. Forest Home is also the final resting place for the four men hanged in 1887 for their presumed role in Chicago's Haymarket Riot. In 1893 these men were honored as martyrs to the labor movement with a large monument over their graves. In later years, a number of other prominent labor leaders, anarchists, socialists, and communists were buried in the so-called Radicals' Row area of the cemetery.

Leisure has also figured in Forest Park's history. An amusement park that operated there from 1907 to 1922 featured a giant safety coaster that was the highest ride in the nation at the time. Other top attractions included a fun house, beer garden, casino, swimming pool, and skating rink. The park closed in 1922. A thoroughbred racetrack was built by John Condon in 1894, a year after the Hawthorne track, but the track was unable to rebound following a fire in 1904. Between 1912 and 1938 the Harlem Golf Course was located on the site, which is now occupied by the Forest Park Mall.

Incorporated as the town of Harlem in 1884, the village was renamed Forest Park in 1907, as another post office named Harlem existed near Rockford. Historically composed of mainly Germans and Italians, the town's ethnic composition has diversified in recent decades. Today Forest Park enjoys a strong tax base—industrial and commercial—which includes a major shopping mall at Roosevelt and Des Plaines and bustling commercial life on historic Madison Street. As a result, low property taxes are fueling real-estate sales—luring empty nesters to Forest Park's condominiums as well as young people looking for affordable housing.

Jean Louise Guarino

FURTHER READING: "History of Forest Park," scrapbook no. 1. (compilation of early newspaper articles). Forest Park Library, Forest Park, IL. ■ *The Chronicles of Forest Park, 1776–1976.* 1976. ■ *The Village of Harlem, Fiftieth Anniversary of the Settlement, 1856–1906.* 1906.

Fox Lake, IL, Lake County, 46 miles NW of the

Loop. When the Wisconsin glacier melted, it left behind a chain of lakes— Pistakee, Nippersink, Fox, Grass, Petite, and others— in the Fox River Valley. Although some dairy and hay farming did occur, the area remained sparsely settled into the 1880s as the wet areas made travel difficult during most of the year.

Some large hunting and fishing lodges that were built along the eastern shores of the lakes in the 1880s were generally reached by steam launches based in MCHENRY. A visit by boat to Fox Lake's "Egyptian Lotus" beds became a popular excursion for vacationing Chicagoans in the 1890s.

The railroad entered the chain of lakes in 1901 when the Milwaukee Road (Chicago, Milwaukee, St. Paul & Pacific Railroad) crossed the chain at its narrowest point, between Pistakee and Nippersink Lakes, on its way to Janesville, Wisconsin. A station built near the east side of the crossing called Nippersink Point became the center of the Fox Lake community. With rail access, the vacation trade mushroomed and numerous small resorts blossomed next to such large, older resorts as the Bay View, the Illinois, the Waltonian, and a stately, 79-guest-room beauty, the Mineola. So much money flowed into the area from tavern licenses that area farmers paid no property taxes.

The county's leaders, living almost entirely in eastern Lake County, soon ordered raids on the numerous unlicensed drinking and gambling resorts around Fox Lake, adding the fines to the county's coffers. Unhappy with those actions, Fox Lake's resort leaders united their community to maintain local control through incorporation in 1907. The new government placed few restraints on its resorts and, with Prohibition-era enforcement at a minimum, Chicagoans flocked to enjoy the summer water amenities, drinking, and gambling.

The war to control the lucrative Fox Valley beer and gambling trade came to Fox Lake with a vengeance on June 1, 1930, when three men friendly to anti-Capone interests were machine-gunned to death at the Manning Hotel and George Druggan, brother to mobster Terry Druggan, was wounded.

The permanent population of Fox Lake grew slowly between 1930 and 1950. The Depression-era trend of turning summer cabins into permanent housing expanded as soldiers returning from World War II found affordable housing in a resort setting. The paving of Rand Road (now U.S. 12) through Fox Lake after the war allowed the village to remain a popular vacation destination for Chicagoans even as the permanent population grew.

Fox Lake began to modernize its infrastructure in the 1960s under five-term president Joseph Armondo, preparing the village for its present role as a middle-class residential community in a resort setting. Today, Fox Lake is a haven for many water sports enthusiasts; the area remains one of the busiest aquatic vacation sites in the United States. While the renovated Mineola Resort and the Manning Hotel remain to remind the community of its past, the numerous commuter trains that end their runs at Fox Lake speak to the community's new residential identity.

Craig L. Pfannkuche

FURTHER READING: *Fiftieth Year History of the Fox Lake Volunteer Fire Department.* 1958. ▪ *The Fox Lake Region.* 1928. ▪ *Preliminary Planning Report: Fox Lake, Illinois.* N.d.

Franklin Park, IL, Cook County, 13 miles W of

the Loop. Franklin Park has more than met the expectations of Lesser Franklin, who settled in the area in the 1890s. He envisioned an industrial center that would blend with residential neighborhoods. A century later, Franklin Park boasted over 1,200 industries and related businesses covering 60 percent of the community land area.

German farmers settled in the 1840s. By the mid-1870s the Atlantic & Pacific Railroad (Milwaukee Road tracks of the Chicago, Milwaukee, St. Paul & Pacific Railroad) laid tracks and built a station on Elm Street. The Minneapolis, St. Paul & Sault Ste. Marie (Soo Line) and the Indiana Harbor Belt Railroads followed.

In the early 1890s Franklin, a real-estate broker, purchased four farms totaling 600 acres. At the railroads' intersection he built the community's center. He named the town Franklin Park and enticed prospective buyers with parades along LaSalle Street in Chicago. He offered free Sunday train rides to the property. A pavilion was built on Rose Street where potential customers received free food and beer, heard speeches, danced, and participated in contests. Lot sales exceeded a million dollars.

The community was incorporated in 1892. Before the turn of the twentieth century the first industry was founded. Lesser Franklin donated land for an iron foundry in 1900 and offered another parcel to the Siegel, Cooper Company to build a factory in 1905. Records from the 1923 foundry and school rosters listed the majority of workers and residents as Polish, Italian, and Slavic immigrants. World War II and a national preparedness program brought Douglas Aircraft and Buick Motors into the area. By 1948, 40 manufacturing firms called Franklin Park home. During the next decade 155 new companies were added. The Chamber of Commerce and the Northwest Suburban Manufacturing Association have continually supported the efforts of businesses.

Population increased from 3,007 in 1940 to 18,322 by 1960. Town government promoted industrial development with zoning laws favoring its growth. During this period a central alarm at the fire department gave both residents and industries access to heat- and smoke-detection systems. Water reserves provided large users with millions of gallons daily.

The village has remained in search of land for industrial expansion. In 1990 Franklin Park annexed 65 acres, giving it the fourth largest in-dustrial area in Illinois. By 2000 population was at 19,434, with a Hispanic population of about 38 percent. Most residents were blue-collar workers employed by the complex of industries. Good location and easy access to O'Hare Airport cargo terminals, railroad freight terminals, major ex-pressways for routing, and spur tracks accessing the rear of buildings have made Franklin Park a desirable place for industry.

Marilyn Elizabeth Perry

FURTHER READING: *The History of Franklin Park, Illinois in Words and Pictures: Centennial Commemorative Book, 1892–1992.* 1992. ■ Kunstman, John William. "The Industrialization of Franklin Park, Illinois." Ph.D. diss., Northwestern University. 1964. ■ League of Women Voters. *Know Your Town: Franklin Park, Illinois.* 1971.

Fuller Park, Community Area 37, 5 miles S of the Loop. Fuller Park is the neighborhood due south of U.S. Cellular Field, the home of the American League Chicago White Sox baseball team. One of Chicago's small-est community areas, this narrow two-mile strip is bounded on the east by the Dan Ryan expressway and the Rock Island Railroad Metra lines (Chicago, Rock Island & Pacific Railroad) and on the west by the Chicago & Western Indiana Railroad. The northern and southern borders are Pershing Road and Garfield Boulevard. The community derives its name from a small park named for Melville W. Fuller, Chicago attorney and U.S. chief justice.

 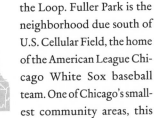

37
Fuller Park

After the Civil War, people of Irish descent lived here, many of them employed by either the railroads or the stockyards. In 1871 a railroad round-house was built in the community by the Lake Shore & Michigan Southern Railroad (New York Central). Because of the Great Fire in that year, residential growth increased in Fuller Park (then a part of Lake Township) as developers built be-yond the city limits to avoid expensive building codes. Survivors of the 1870s include frame houses at 4463 S. Wells and 4233 S. Princeton. In the mid-1880s, Chicago architect Henry Newhouse designed and built a series of modest Queen Anne–style houses at 5029–5045 S. Princeton.

In 1889 the town of Lake was annexed to the city of Chicago. Germans and Austrians joined the Irish as residents in the 1890s, and African Americans began moving into the community after 1900. In the early 1900s a public health movement among settlement house leaders sought a plan to give residents access to light, air, and exercise. Consequently, Fuller Park opened in 1912, with a field house designed in Greek revival style by Daniel H. Burnham and Company.

By 1920 African Americans, Mexicans, and Slavic workers had replaced the Irish and Germans. Fuller Park has always been home to the poor: in 1950, 24 percent of the community lacked indoor toilets. In the 1950s the community was overrun and split by the Dan Ryan Expressway, which displaced one-third of the population. The 1950s also saw the erosion of the local economy as trucking and interstate highways rendered the centralized Union Stock Yard unnecessary.

The stockyards continued to decline in the 1960s and closed in 1971, eliminating many jobs in the area. During the same period, thousands of southern African Americans migrated north each year and encountered a segregated housing market that restricted them to areas of the city's South and West Sides. Fuller Park saw its population change from 80 percent white in 1945 to 97 percent black in 1970, with total numbers falling from 17,174 in 1950 to 4,364 by 1990. From 1975 to 1990, there was a net loss of 41.5 percent of jobs in the stockyards area, including nearly 45 percent of all manufacturing jobs. During the 1980s Fuller Park received fewer bank loans for home improvement purposes than any other neighborhood in Chicago.

While there are many longtime home owners who either cannot or do not want to leave, over two-thirds of the community's 2,000-unit housing stock is rental. The poverty rate is over 40 percent, and single mothers head a large number of families. Yet renewal efforts persist as the Neighbors of Fuller Park attempt to recover the neighborhood's rich architectural history. These efforts include the rehabilitation of the park, including its central fountain, courtyard, and field house. In the early 1990s, a shopping center was developed between the Dan Ryan Expressway and the Metra tracks just west of the ROBERT TAYLOR HOMES, which were demolished in the following years.

Clinton E. Stockwell

FURTHER READING: Chicago Historic Resources Survey. *An Inventory of Architecturally and Historically Significant Structures.* 1996.

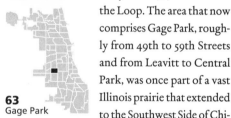

Gage Park, Community Area 63, 7 miles SW of the Loop. The area that now comprises Gage Park, roughly from 49th to 59th Streets and from Leavitt to Central Park, was once part of a vast Illinois prairie that extended to the Southwest Side of Chicago. In the 1840s Germans settled there as farmers, and in 1865 the area was incorporated as the town of Lake, which was annexed to Chicago in 1889. At that time, there were but 30 wood-frame cottages in Gage Park, and no paved streets or public transportation. Between 1900 and 1910, however, the electric trolley extended its service to Western and Kedzie Streets, contributing to a building boom. In 1911 the Bartlett Realty Company developed Marquette Manor, which provided economic stimulus for further neighborhood development. Between 1905 and 1919 Western and Garfield Boulevards were laid out, and residential and industrial development escalated. The neighborhood was named after the Gage family, which owned much property in the area.

While Protestants tended to settle in CHICAGO

63
Gage Park

LAWN (also known as MARQUETTE PARK), Roman Catholics settled in Gage Park; many came from nearby BRIDGEPORT and BACK OF THE YARDS. By 1920 there were 13,692 people in Gage Park, mostly Bohemian and Polish, and mostly employees of the Union Stock Yard. The community supported three movie theaters, including the Colony, which was built in 1925 in classical Gothic style at 5842 S. Kedzie. Slavic immigrants were lured to the area as national churches were created. St. Simon's was organized by Slavic Catholics in 1926, while Lithuanians organized the Nativity of the Blessed Virgin Mary parish in 1927, the largest Lithuanian parish outside Lithuania. Also in 1927, Poles organized St. Turibius parish.

In 1922 Ben F. Bohac, a Czech American, organized one of the largest savings and loan institutions in Illinois, Talman Home Federal Savings and Loan, at 51st and Talman Streets. Talman merged with the LaSalle National Bank in 1992. Bordered on three sides by railroads, Gage Park attracted other important employers, including Central Steel and Wire Company, Royal Crown Bottling Company, and World's Finest Chocolate.

In the 1960s the Marquette Park–Gage Park area became a center of testing for open housing for African Americans. Martin Luther King Jr. led a march to Marquette Park, where he met violent resistance from counterdemonstrators, a minority of whom were sympathizers of the Ku Klux Klan and the American Nazi Party. In 1972 Gage Park High School was integrated, despite much protest, including a boycott by white parents. In the 1970s and 1980s several neighborhood organizations were formed to stabilize the area and to ease racial tensions: the Southwest Community Congress sought to improve race relations with bordering neighborhoods, whereas the Southwest Parish and Neighborhood Federation sought to curb real-estate blockbusting tactics and to maintain middle-class stability. A subsidiary, the Southwest Community Development Corporation, has sought to revitalize the area commercially.

Thanks to these efforts, Gage Park has retained its middle-class character as it grows racially di-

verse. The 1990 census showed that the community had 26,957 residents, of whom 70 percent were white and 5 percent black; 39 percent identified themselves as Hispanic. Ten years later the population had grown to 39,193, of whom 45 percent were white, 7 percent African American, and 79 percent Hispanic. In 1993 the Orange Line elevated rapid transit line was finished, connecting the LOOP to Midway Airport, two miles from Gage Park. As a result, home values appreciated 70 percent, from an average of $50,000 in 1985 to $86,450 in 1996.

Clinton E. Stockwell

FURTHER READING: *Chicago Historic Resources Survey: An Inventory of Architecturally and Historically Significant Structures.* 1996. ■ Orr, Kathy. "Gage Park Again." *Daily Southtown,* December 20, 1996. ■ Pacyga, Dominic A., and Ellen Skerrett. *Chicago, City of Neighborhoods: Histories and Tours.* 1986.

Galewood, industrial neighborhood established in the 1880s, now in the BELMONT CRAGIN Community Area.

Gano, neighborhood in the WEST PULLMAN Community Area, originally settled by Pullman Company workers in the 1880s.

Gap, neighborhood in the DOUGLAS Community Area, a national historic landmark district bounded by 31st and 35th Streets, King Drive, and Michigan Avenue.

Garfield Ridge, Community Area 56, 10 miles SW of the Loop. Garfield Ridge, formerly Archer Limits, is a relatively young and well-ordered neighborhood of single-family houses along the western boundary of the city. It takes its name from Garfield Boulevard (55th Street), a main east-west thoroughfare, and a rather inconsequential topographic rise left behind in the retreat of glacial Lake Michigan. Limited agricultural development of the soggy prairies came in the nineteenth cen-

56
Garfield Ridge

tury. Industrial development, first around the area and then within it, prompted residential development after 1900. By 1950 residential development overtook the industrial as block after block filled with the middle-class brick bungalows that typify the area. On the farthest reaches of the city on the Southwest Side, once remote Garfield Ridge has over the last century steadily grown into its urban status.

Speculators and farmers purchased the lands from the 1830s to the 1850s, but few stayed. Like Native Americans, whites at first just wanted to pass through and did so on Archer Road, the Illinois & Michigan Canal (completed 1848), and the Chicago & Alton Railroad (1850s). William B. Archer, I&M Canal commissioner, land speculator, and namesake of Archer Avenue, was among the earliest speculators, buying 240 acres adjoining present-day Harlem and Archer Avenues in 1835. In 1853 "Long John" Wentworth, onetime mayor of Chicago, farmer, and fellow land speculator, purchased several tracts just to the east of Archer's holdings. A park named for Wentworth occupies ground he once owned. Chicago annexed the area in bits and pieces in 1889, 1915, and 1921.

Among the first to settle permanently were Dutch farmers who specialized in market gardening, and in 1899 the Archer Avenue Reformed Church, formerly of SUMMIT, tended 275 parishioners. Intensive residential use began in the northeast section of the area, in what was known as the Sleepy Hollow neighborhood. More substantial growth came in the 1920s. During that decade, the population jumped from 2,472 to 6,050, with Eastern European immigrants, especially Poles, accounting for the bulk of the increase. The expanding industrial base around Garfield Ridge, in CLEARING and Argo (Summit) especially, offered jobs and incentive to settle in the area. Archer Avenue, with its streetcar line, evolved into the main commercial corridor for the community. With the opening of the Chicago Municipal Airport (later Midway) in 1926, the neighborhood's essential economic infrastructure was set in place. Nevertheless, the rural character of the area lingered. In 1936 residents commented on the still villagelike appearance of the section west of Central Avenue, with dirt roads, farmhouses, haystacks, and grazing animals filling the landscape.

The pace of development slowed during the Great Depression, but the population almost doubled between 1940 and 1950, from 6,813 to 12,900, then tripled to 40,449 during the following decade. Again, industrial growth, fostered in part by activity at Midway Airport, led to residential growth, predominantly single-family houses that during the 1940s filled in the western portion of the community.

At the beginning of 1950 the community was entirely white. In 1960 Garfield Ridge maintained a high rate (almost 40 percent) of foreign-born residents, but for the first time also included a sizable African American population (6.6 percent). Blacks lived exclusively in LeClaire Courts, a low-rise public housing project along Cicero Avenue just south of the Stevenson expressway, completed by the Chicago Housing Authority in 1950 and expanded in 1954. Garfield Ridge's population peaked in 1970 at 42,998.

The decline of Midway traffic as airlines moved to O'Hare Airport led to declines in businesses, jobs, and population. Most of the residents who left were white, while lesser numbers of blacks and Hispanics, many of them out-migrants from LITTLE VILLAGE and PILSEN, took their places. Of the 36,101 residents of Garfield Ridge in 2000, 77 percent were white (more than one-third of Polish ancestry) and 12 percent black; about 4 percent were Hispanic, predominantly of Mexican heritage. The African American community had by then expanded beyond LeClaire Courts into surrounding middle-class homes.

In the 1990s with the renewed interest and investment in Midway Airport and the arrival of rapid transit to downtown, the community continued on its path to urban maturity.

Jonathan J. Keyes

FURTHER READING: *Local Community Fact Book* series. ■ Municipal Reference Collection. Harold Washington Library, Chicago.

Gary, IN, Lake County, 25 miles SE of the Loop.

Founded in 1906 on the undeveloped southern shore of Lake Michigan 30 miles east of Chicago, Gary was the creation of the U.S. Steel Corporation, which had been searching for a cheap but convenient Midwestern site for a massive new steel production center. The city was named after industrialist Elbert H. Gary, chairman of the board of U.S. Steel. Anticipating a large population of steelworkers, Gary Land Company, a U.S. Steel subsidiary, laid out a gridiron city plan, built a variety of houses and apartments, and advertised its new creation far and wide as the "Magic City" or the "City of the Century." Real-estate speculators and private builders came to control the new city's south side, however, where shoddy building of small houses and barracks-type apartments contradicted modern planning principles and led to rapid slum development. Partially planned but partially abandoned to land speculators, Gary quickly came to be known as one of the new "satellite cities," or industrial suburbs, growing up in Chicago's widening sphere of economic influence.

The new Gary Works of U.S. Steel supplied the steel demands of the Midwest's expanding industrial economy in the early twentieth century. The city of Gary became home to a rapidly growing population of European immigrants and, by the 1920s, southern blacks and immigrants from Mexico. Its population grew to about 55,000 in 1920 and over 100,000 in 1930. Immigrants and their American-born children made up 45 percent of the population in 1930, while blacks constituted almost 18 percent. The mostly unskilled immigrant steelworkers came primarily from Southern and Eastern Europe—from Italy, Greece, Poland, Russia, and the Balkans—while the company's skilled workers and managerial staff were primarily English, Irish, German, or native-born. African Americans from the American South began migrating to Gary after the outbreak of World War

I and the cessation of European immigration. In the 1920s, as immigration restriction became permanent, Mexican workers were imported by U.S. Steel to fill unskilled jobs in the mills. By 1930 over 9,000 Mexicans resided in Gary and nearby East Chicago, Indiana.

Throughout its first half century, Gary served as a testing ground for the assimilation of European immigrants. Many of the city's institutions—its schools, churches, workplaces, settlement houses, political system, and newspapers—focused on the struggle to Americanize the immigrant steelworkers and their families as rapidly as possible. Gary's nationally famous "work-study-play" or "platoon school" system, implemented by longterm school superintendent William A. Wirt, sought to Americanize immigrant children and prepare them for industrial work. By contrast, blacks and Mexicans were marginalized and isolated behind powerful walls of discrimination, segregation, and racism.

Gary's network of settlement houses and Protestant churches worked also to Protestantize the newcomers. However, Gary's immigrants established their own communal networks and ethnic institutions designed to preserve language, culture, and customs. The conflict between native culture and immigrant newcomer was highlighted in the Great Steel Strike of 1919, when the mostly foreign-born steelworkers were depicted as radicals and revolutionaries—a portrayal used to justify mobilization of federal soldiers to put down the strike, ultimately delaying the unionization of the steelworkers until the late 1930s, when New Deal legislation protected organizing efforts.

Gary grew substantially in the 1920s, as a nativeborn booster elite worked with U.S. Steel leaders to transform the city physically and plan its future growth. At the same time, ethnicity, race, and class shaped relationships among the city's diverse and socially fragmented cultures. Throughout the 1920s the city's apparent economic prosperity remained dangerously dependent on a single industry, a condition that backfired during the Great Depression when the steel mills cut back production by 80 percent, unemployment soared, most banks failed, and the city government faced bankruptcy. The city was dominated politically by the local Republican Party until the 1930s, but an emerging New Deal political coalition prompted the ascendancy of a Democratic Party machine that retained power until well into the 1990s.

The economic demands of World War II revived the steel industry and pulled Gary out of the Depression. After the war, however, racial segregation and strife, labor problems in steel, industrial pollution, and political corruption (which had been persistent since the 1920s) earned Gary a national reputation as a troubled town. The city's population continued to grow moderately, reaching 133,911 in 1950 and 175,415 in 1970. But the composition of population changed more markedly: African Americans made up 18 percent of the population in 1930, 29 percent in 1950, and 53 percent in 1970.

Population and politics were related. A succession of white ethnic mayors in the 1950s and 1960s ended in 1967 with the election of Richard G. Hatcher, one of the nation's first big-city black mayors. White flight to nearby suburbs had already begun in the 1960s, but Hatcher's election and confrontational approach to governing speeded the process considerably, and white business too fled the city. As descendants of European immigrants emptied out of the city, the population declined dramatically, to 116,646 by 1990, while the proportion of African Americans rose to over 80 percent. With a secure black power base, Hatcher was reelected four times, unusual for big-city administrations, and served a total of 20 years as Gary's mayor.

Blacks anticipated better times under Hatcher, but disappointment gradually replaced political euphoria. The Hatcher years were accompanied by steel company disinvestment—Gary had over 30,000 steelworkers in the late 1960s but fewer than 6,000 in 1987. Hatcher also faced the consequences of national policy shifts as the urban development programs of the Great Society years wound under President Nixon and succeeding administrations. Hatcher worked hard to reverse long-standing patterns of institutional racism and to initiate various economic development strategies, but the task was difficult given continued white political and business opposition at the county and state level.

In 1987 Thomas A. Barnes, another black Democrat but with a less confrontational style, ousted Hatcher and began two uneventful terms. In 1995 two black candidates divided the African American vote in the Democratic mayoral primary, permitting white attorney Scott King to win the mayor's office. Blacks continued to control the city council, which blocked many of King's proposals for governmental change and economic development. Created early in the twentieth century on a wave of optimism for the future, Gary came to exemplify in many respects the troubled state of urban America at the end of the century.

Raymond A. Mohl

FURTHER READING: Catlin, Robert A. *Racial Politics and Urban Planning: Gary, Indiana, 1980–1989.* 1993. ▪ Hurley, Andrew. *Environmental Inequalities: Class, Race, and Industrial Pollution in Gary, Indiana, 1945–1980.* 1995. ▪ Mohl, Raymond A., and Neil Betten. *Steel City: Urban and Ethnic Patterns in Gary, Indiana, 1906–1950.* 1986.

Gold Coast, neighborhood in the NEAR NORTH SIDE Community Area. "Gold Coast" refers to a stretch of expensive lakefront property occupied by the city's wealthiest residents. Because it was isolated from the downtown business district, only a few wealthy families, including the Cyrus McCormicks, the Potter Palmers, and the Joseph T. Ryersons, lived here before the construction of the Michigan Avenue Bridge in 1920.

The opening of the bridge brought the development of Michigan Avenue north of the river as a luxury shopping district. A new architectural form, the luxury apartment building, sprang up in the area, dispelling fears that apartment dwellers had to be poor, and some of Chicago's elite took up residence in new residential hotels such as the Drake. The district became the heart of the upper crust of Chicago society. So-

Gold Coast aerial view, 1929. Photographer: Underwood & Underwood Source: The Newberry Library.

ciologist Harvey Warren Zorbaugh, who claimed that college boys returning from the East Coast dubbed the area the "Gold Coast," immortalized it in *The Gold Coast and the Slum*. The density of wealth in the Gold Coast buffered it against the deterioration that threatened other portions of the North Side in the 1950s. Developer Arthur Rubloff's projects, particularly the revitalization of the MAGNIFICENT MILE and SANDBURG VIL-LAGE, sparked a new round of investment that protected the Gold Coast through the end of the twentieth century.

Amanda Seligman

FURTHER READING: Zorbaugh, Harvey Warren. *The Gold Coast and the Slum: A Sociological Study of Chicago's Near North Side.* 1929.

Goose Island, neighborhood in the NEAR NORTH SIDE Community Area. William B. Ogden created Goose Island in the 1850s when he had a canal cut to bypass a meander in the Chicago River's North Branch between North Avenue and Chicago Avenue. The waterfront site drew noisome industries, including tanneries, breweries, and soap factories. Some Irish factory workers took up residence on the island, which took its name from the geese they kept. In the 1890s a few Polish workers made their homes there, but Goose Island's 160 acres were primarily industrial.

In the late twentieth century, Goose Island's industries declined. Rising land values in the Near North Side and nearby LINCOLN PARK prompted speculation over transforming the vacant factories into luxury residential lofts. In 1990, however, Mayor Richard M. Daley declared Goose Island the city's first Protected Manufacturing District, leading to new development that now includes the Wrigley Global Innovation Center and Kendall College's Riverworks Campus.

Amanda Seligman

FURTHER READING: Winslow, Charles S. *Historic Goose Island.* 1938. Typescript. Newberry Library, Chicago.

Goosetown, early industrial neighborhood in the EAST SIDE Community Area.

Grand Boulevard, Community Area 38, 5 miles S of the Loop. Originally called the Forrestville Settlement, the Grand Boulevard community became a part of Hyde Park Township in 1861, and was annexed as part of HYDE PARK to Chicago in 1889. The area is bounded by 39th and 51st Streets

38
Grand
Boulevard

to the north and south, and by Cottage Grove Avenue and the Chicago, Rock Island & Pacific Railroad tracks to the east and west. Until 1874, when the South Parks Commission lined with trees a thoroughfare they called Grand Boulevard (now Dr. Martin Luther King Jr. Drive), the area was a combination of prairie and thick woods. This street, situated at the center of the community, became a popular carriage route along which many of Chicago's wealthy built elegant mansions. The population of the Grand Boulevard community grew steadily throughout the latter part of the nineteenth century, attracting not only the wealthy, but middle- and working-class American-born whites of Irish, Scottish, and English origin, German Jews, and a few African Americans.

Excellent transportation providing easy access to and from Chicago's LOOP sparked the commercial and residential development of Grand Boulevard. Cable cars running along Cottage Grove Avenue reached 39th street by 1882 and 63rd street in 1887. East-west lines were also added. In 1896 the South Side "L" established stops in Grand Boulevard at 43rd, 47th, and 51st streets, around which small commercial strips of mostly Jewish-owned businesses developed. By the turn of the century, good transportation and the construction of a large number of multifamily dwellings transformed Grand Boulevard into a solidly middle- and working-class neighborhood, one of Chicago's most desirable.

There had been a small African American community in Grand Boulevard since the 1890s, but by 1920 blacks, many of them southern migrants, constituted 32 percent of the area's 76,703 residents; by 1930 African Americans made up 94.6 percent of the total population of 87,005. Like other areas of rapid racial transition in Chicago, Grand Boulevard experienced resistance and violence, but the influx of African Americans continued, and by 1950 blacks accounted for 99 percent of the community's 114,557 residents.

Grand Boulevard became the hub of "Bronzeville," the name the *Chicago Bee* gave to Chicago's South Side African American commu-

Philanthropist Julius Rosenwald funded the construction of the Michigan Boulevard Garden Apartments in 1928. Photographer: Mildred Mead. Source: Chicago History Museum.

nity. A thriving center of successful black businesses, civic organizations, and churches, Bronzeville was in every way "a city within a city." The large number of black intellectuals, politicians, sports figures, artists, and writers who made their homes in Bronzeville made it a cultural mecca, the central institution of which was the famed Regal Theater, located at 47th and Grand Boulevard.

The Grand Boulevard community has also maintained a rich tradition of diverse religious institutions, housed in some of the city's most beautiful edifices. Irish Roman Catholics established St. Elizabeth of Hungary at the corner of 41st and Wabash in 1881. Corpus Christi Catholic Church, at 49th and Grand Boulevard, followed later. Sinai Temple was built on the corner of 46th and Grand Boulevard in 1915, but within a decade congregants moved out of the neighborhood in the wake of racial transition; the building was sold

in 1944 to Corpus Christi to become a high school for African American Catholics. It was sold again in 1962 and became the Mt. Pisgah Missionary Baptist Church. Temple Isaiah at 4501 Vincennes Avenue, built in 1899 and the last major work of Chicago architect Dankmar Adler, became the Ebenezer Baptist Church in 1921.

Once a place of wealth and grandeur, Grand Boulevard has been characterized in the latter decades of the twentieth century by physical deterioration, poverty, unemployment, and public housing. The loss of stockyard and steel mill jobs, as well as numerous black-owned businesses, sent the community into a tailspin of economic decline. Along with a poverty rate of two-thirds by the 1990s, Grand Boulevard contained the densest population of public housing in the country. The demolition of the ROBERT TAYLOR HOMES, located primarily in Grand Boulevard, dramatically re-

African American residential neighborhood, 49th Street and Champlain, ca. 1925. Photographer: Webb. Source: Chicago History Museum.

duced the presence of public housing in the area. Since the mid-1980s numerous individuals, as well as community-based organizations like Centers for New Horizons, have worked to address to the needs of Grand Boulevard and its people.

Wallace Best

FURTHER READING: Bowly, Devereux, Jr. *The Poorhouse: Subsidized Housing in Chicago, 1895–1976.* 1978. ■ Holt, Glen E., and Dominic A. Pacyga. "Grand Boulevard." In *Chicago: A Historical Guide to the Neighborhoods: The Loop and the South Side.* 1979. ■ Reed, Christopher R., and Annie Ruth Leslie, "Grand Boulevard." In *Local Community Fact Book: Chicago Metropolitan Area, 1990,* ed. Chicago Fact Book Consortium. 1995.

Greater Grand Crossing, Community Area 69, 8 miles S of the Loop. As the name implies, Greater Grand Crossing encompasses several neighborhoods: Grand Crossing, Park Manor, Brookline, Brookdale, and Essex. The original Grand

69
Greater
Grand
Crossing

Crossing community consisted of the southeast corner of the present community area. The entire area was annexed to Chicago in 1889 as part of Hyde Park Township.

Development began after a train accident in 1853 that killed 18 people and injured 40 others. The accident occurred at what is now 75th Street and South Chicago Avenue when Roswell B. Mason, who was to become a Chicago mayor, secretly had intersecting tracks built for the Illinois Central across the rail lines of the Lake Shore & Michigan Southern Railroad (New York Central). The intersection remained dangerous for many years after the 1853 accident, but industry developed around it as it became required for all trains to make a complete stop there.

Chicago real-estate developer Paul Cornell thought that the area surrounding the intersection, although it was mostly prairie and swampland, would be ideal for suburban development because transportation to Chicago was assured via the railroads. Cornell began buying large tracts of land in 1855. Through the early 1870s he subdivided the area and offered lots for sale. Initially calling the subdivision Cornell, he changed the name to Grand Crossing after learning of an existing village named Cornell.

The early residents were of Irish, English, and Scottish descent and developed railroad settlements in the southeast portion of Greater Grand Crossing, just south of Oakwoods Cemetery. Factory workers, farmers, and craft workers of German origin followed in the 1890s, building frame cottages in the Brookline section of Greater Grand Crossing.

The World's Columbian Exposition of 1893 further stimulated growth. Between 1895 and 1912 single-family frame and brick homes, two-flats, and apartments began to appear in the area to accommodate a steady population increase. There were improvements to infrastructure as well. The Calumet electric street railway at 63rd and Grand Boulevard (now Dr. Martin Luther King Jr. Drive) was extended to Cottage Grove and 93rd, and in 1912 the dangerous train intersection that had given rise to the community was elevated. White City, an amusement park that opened in 1904, towered over the northern part of Greater Grand Crossing from Grand Boulevard to Calumet Avenue and from 63rd to 67th Streets until it was closed in 1933. The park was finally torn down in 1950 to make way for the Parkway Gardens, a public housing project.

Though there had been some industry in the area since the mid-nineteenth century, by 1920 the community, with a population of 44,538, was largely residential. By the 1930s people of Swedish and Italian descent joined those of Irish and German origin. At the same time, however, African Americans began coming to the community in larger numbers, and European immigrants, along with native whites, began to move out. During the 1950s the black population of Greater Grand Crossing increased from 6 percent to 86 percent. Since 1980 the community has been 99 percent African American.

Apart from Parkway Gardens, there has been little construction in Greater Grand Crossing since the 1930s, and the community has undergone significant depopulation since the 1960s. In 1960 the population stood at 63,169. Between 1980 and 1990 the population dropped from 45,218 to 38,644. Although as of 1990 a fifth of the population, 56 percent of whom were African American women, lived at or below poverty level, a third of the residents of Greater Grand Crossing were second- and third-generation property owners.

Wallace Best

FURTHER READING: Chicago Fact Book Consortium, ed. *Local Community Fact Book: Chicago Metropolitan Area, 1990.* 1995. ■ Drury, John. "Historic Chicago Sites." Greater Grand Crossing clipping file, Chicago History Museum, Chicago. ■ Hutchinson, O. N. *Grand Crossing, 1871–1938.* ■ Chicago Communities: Greater Grand Crossing. Special Collections, Harold Washington Library, Chicago.

Greektown. In the late nineteenth century, Chicago's Greek population began to coalesce in the area surrounded by Halsted, Harrison, and Blue Island Streets in the NEAR WEST SIDE Community Area, where the campus of the University of Illinois at Chicago is now located. Greektown (also known as "the Delta") was the largest and best-known urban community of Greeks in the United States for much of the early twentieth century.

Max Grinnell

FURTHER READING: Kourvetaris, George A. *First and Second Generation Greeks in Chicago.* 1971. ■ Steiner, Edward A. *On the Trail of the Immigrant.* 1906.

Gurnee, IL, Lake County, 37 miles N of the Loop.

The village of Gurnee hugs the banks of the Des Plaines River, just west of the port city of WAUKEGAN. Prior to 1835 the area offered the Potawatomis a convenient ford in the river as well as portage access between the Great Lakes and the continental interior via the Mississippi River system. In 1836 the area was designated as a stopping point on the Chicago-Milwaukee stage line, which crossed the river on a bridge built at the site of the Potawatomi ford. The opening of the east-west McHenry-Waukegan toll road made it an important crossroads in the area. Water-powered industries serving the needs of local farmers opened almost immediately, including a gristmill in 1835 and a sawmill three years later. These were followed closely by mercantile trade and taverns catering to coach passengers. In 1850 the area organized as Warren Township to prevent annexation by Waukegan, the larger neighbor to the east.

The arrival of the railroad in 1873 not only linked Warren with the regional markets in Chicago but also provided the first village of the township with its name. The depot at Warren was named for railroad land agent and former Chicago mayor Walter S. Gurnee, who purchased the right-of-way for the Chicago, Milwaukee & St. Paul line (Chicago, Milwaukee, St. Paul & Pacific Railroad). The relatively quick rail trip to Chicago encouraged local farmers to produce for the growing urban population. The Bowman Dairy Company furnished the city with a regular "milk train," and a stockyard developed near the depot. The overwhelming importance of the train to local life shifted the physical location of the town's center from the stage line to the rail depot.

When Gurnee was incorporated in 1928 it had only 200 residents. The village remained a largely rural, agricultural town on the Chicago periphery until well into the latter half of the twentieth century. In the 1960s the construction of a new toll road, Interstate 94, brought Gurnee into a tighter orbit of Chicago.

In 1976 Gurnee became home to Great America, one of the largest amusement parks in the Midwest, and 1991 the largest shopping mall in the Chicago area opened in Gurnee. The concomitant growth of local industry and suburbanization led to a veritable population explosion, from 7,179 in 1980 to 28,834 in 2000.

Mark Howard Long

FURTHER READING: Haines, Elijah M. *Historical and Statistical Sketches of Lake County, State of Illinois.* 1852. ■ Lawson, Edward S. *A History of Warren Township.* 1974.

Hammond, IN, Lake County, 20 miles S of the Loop. In 1851 Ernest and Caroline Hohman purchased 39 acres of land along the Grand Calumet River, where they operated a stagecoach stop. The area remained unsettled until 1869, when the George H. Hammond Company purchased 15 acres from the Hohmans for a slaughterhouse. Initially a small operation, the slaughterhouse prospered, employing 1,500 workers by 1895. Marcus Towle, one of Hammond's partners, platted the first subdivision, established the first newspaper and cemetery, and built an expensive hotel, a roller skating rink, and an opera house. He also created a variety of small industries to diversify the economy. When the city incorporated in 1883, Towle served as Hammond's first mayor.

From its inception Hammond was a German, working-class city, with a large percentage of home owners among both skilled and unskilled workers. Local support for labor climaxed in 1894, when Hammond played a major role in the Pullman Strike. During the strike, local workers refused to handle Pullman cars, making Hammond the last stop for westbound rail traffic entering Chicago. City officials supported the strikers. But after violence erupted, federal troops occupied Hammond. On July 7, 1894, the troops shot and killed a local carpenter. Outraged, a mass meeting of citizens condemned President Grover Cleveland for having employed troops.

Support for labor diminished after 1901, when fire destroyed the Hammond Company and eliminated its 1,500 jobs. The city faced a crisis. To attract new industries, local officials promised to protect capital from labor agitators. The promise allowed Hammond to attract new industries. The most significant came in 1906 with the arrival of

Standard Steel Car Company, which employed 3,500 men. But the city never became as industrial as its neighbors WHITING, East Chicago, and GARY.

Instead, Hammond developed an impressive regional downtown with department stores, office blocks, and movie palaces. In addition, the 1920s produced a housing boom. A few of the new subdivisions south of downtown were exclusive, like Woodmar, which promised to move residents "out of the smoke zone and into the ozone" and provided work for local architects L. Cosby Bernard and Addison Berry. But most new homes were modest bungalows. The Great Depression halted construction, which resumed at a fever pitch during the 1950s. By 1960 Hammond had no room for expansion.

The creation, in 1966, of River Oaks shopping mall in CALUMET CITY challenged Hammond's 70-year history as a center for retailing. During the next decade, long-established family businesses closed and a wave of demolition gutted the once-prosperous downtown. Major industries also closed, including American Steel Foundries in 1973, Pullman-Standard in 1981, and Rand McNally in 1981. Only Saint Margaret's Hospital and the First Baptist Church continued to prosper downtown.

From 1970 to 1990 Hammond's population declined 22 percent, from 107,983 to 84,236. In 1980, 47 percent of the workforce remained in manufacturing occupations, 40 percent in technical sales and service, and 13 percent in managerial and professional occupations. By 2000 the population of 83,048 remained 72 percent white, primarily of German, Polish, and Irish ancestry; Hispanics and African Americans accounted for 21 percent and 15 percent of the population, respectively.

Joseph C. Bigott

FURTHER READING: Bigott, Joseph C. "With Security and Comfort for All: Working-Class Home Ownership and Democratic Ideals in the Calumet Region, 1869 to 1929." Ph.D. diss., University of Delaware. 1993. ■ Moore, Powell A. *The Calumet Region: Indiana's Last Frontier.* 1959. Reprinted with an afterword by Lance Trusty, 1977. ■ Trusty, Lance. *Hammond: A Centennial Portrait.* 1984.

Hanson Park, neighborhood in the BELMONT CRAGIN Community Area, first developed in the 1880s around area industries.

Harrison Courts, neighborhood in the EAST GARFIELD PARK Community Area, built by the Chicago Housing Authority.

Harvard, IL, McHenry County, 63 miles NW of the Loop. In 1855 the Chicago & North Western Railway built toward Janesville, Wisconsin, from Cary. Calculating where trains from Chicago would have to stop for servicing in the days of wood fuel, Elbridge Gerry Ayer and two other North Western stockholders platted a community in southeastern Chemung Township on land that they had purchased without mentioning their railroad affiliation. In April 1856 the railroad accepted Ayer's town plat as a station named Harvard. When the North Western's Kenosha-Rockford line entered Harvard in 1859, the railroad built engine-handling facilities there.

As railroad employment expanded, Harvard's population ballooned. In 1868 voters incorporated the community and elected Ayer as president.

Bounded on the north by fertile corn-growing land and on the south by wet prairies called the Islands, where masses of wild, fodder-quality hay grew, Harvard quickly became the center of a thriving dairy industry. The railroad cheaply transported fresh milk products to Chicago.

Hay-handling equipment manufacturer Hunt, Helm, and Farris (later the Starline Corporation) expanded job opportunities in the community when it arrived in 1883. By April 1891 Harvard had become so populous that voters acted overwhelmingly to form a city with ward divisions. The first mayor was N. B. Helm.

In 1939 the Kenosha Rail Line was torn out, marking the beginning of economic change in Harvard. The railroad's shift to diesel power in the late 1950s brought many layoffs. The Admiral

Corporation, which opened a large radio assembly plant in 1947, expanded during the 1950s, but television usage and the success of Japanese electronics forced the plant to close in the 1970s.

In 1942 the city instituted an annual celebration called Harvard Milk Days. A lavish parade down whitewashed streets presided over by a large plastic Holstein cow named Harmilda attracted thousands. Celebrations aside, dairy farming declined as farmers found it easier and as profitable to supply metropolitan Chicago's supermarkets with produce. Many Mexicans who came to work as temporary pickers and processors remained in Harvard as landscape laborers, significantly changing the community's population makeup.

With urban expansion overrunning eastern McHenry County in the late 1960s, Harvard's rural setting became a model to many who opposed that growth. They lobbied county government to adopt land-use plans to preserve agricultural areas. Nonetheless, Harvard's rising property taxes coupled with resident demands for shopping amenities and infrastructure improvements drove the city to annex agricultural lands for industrial development. Harvard's leaders achieved their goal in 1996 when the Motorola Corporation opened a major facility to manufacture cellular telephones north of the city. However, in 2003 the plant closed.

Craig L. Pfannkuche

FURTHER READING: Behrens, Paul L. *The KD Line.* 1986. ■ *Harvard Area, 1829–1976.* 1984. ■ *History of McHenry County, Illinois.* 1885.

Harvey, IL, Cook County, 19 miles S of the Loop.

In 1889 Turlington Harvey, a wealthy Chicago lumberman and banker, organized a real-estate syndicate to promote the industrial suburb of Harvey, Illinois. The Harvey Land Association advertised in the nation's religious press, promoting the suburb as a temperance community offering steady work for skilled labor. To achieve this

goal, the association induced a handful of manufacturers to establish factories in town. The Illinois Central Railroad tracks divided the residential and industrial sections of the community.

The founders envisioned Harvey as a model town, a blend of capitalism and Christianity. Investors provided residents with a high quality of city services, similar to nearby PULLMAN. But unlike Pullman, Harvey encouraged home ownership by offering potential residents a variety of house plans. In 1895 residents voted by a slight majority to license saloons, ending the temperance experiment. By 1900 the town contained 5,395 residents, a bank, and 11 industries.

Throughout the first decades of the twentieth century, industrialists and local merchants functioned in tandem. By their efforts, Harvey acquired a fine public school system with Thornton Township High School as its centerpiece. In the 1920s industrialist Frederick Ingalls endowed a community hospital whose board brought together the prestigious members of the community. The development of a Young Men's Christian Association also united the interests of industrial outsiders and the local community.

During the 1920s Harvey's population grew from 9,216 to 16,374. The development produced a modest downtown and housing for various grades of industrial workers as well as finer residences for local merchants and white-collar commuters to Chicago.

The first Roman Catholic church, Ascension, established in 1899, was a small, predominantly Irish parish. Polish residents attended mass in nearby Posen until 1914, when they established St. John the Baptist. Despite the growth of the Catholic community, however, Harvey remained, to a great extent, an evangelical Protestant community. Protestants retained control of the city thanks to the adoption in 1912 of a commission form of government, which replaced ward-elected aldermen with commissioners elected at large.

During the 1930s Harvey suffered an economic crisis. Two local banks closed, and the city could not maintain basic services, since most residents could not pay their property taxes. But the high school basketball team, led by Lou Boudreau, became state champions with an amazing run of victories.

Development resumed after World War II. In 1948 Sinclair Oil established a 38-acre research facility for developing new products. By 1960 Harvey's population reached 29,071, with many residents employed by local industries. In 1966 Dixie Square shopping mall opened on the western edge of the city, providing space for 41 stores.

From 1960 to 1980 Harvey changed dramatically as the African American population rose from 7 to 66 percent. The turnover led to racial violence at Thornton Township High School and to race riots in 1969. Simultaneously, Harvey lost its industrial and commercial base. The closing of Dixie Square became a symbol of the city's escalating social problems. Many residents with loans from the federal Department of Urban Development could not meet mortgage payments, leading to abandoned residences. Harvey's rates of crime, unemployment, and poverty were among the suburbs' highest. The city struggled to redevelop industrial properties and improve its reputation as a residential city.

Joseph C. Bigott

FURTHER READING: Gilbert, James. *Perfect Cities: Chicago's Utopias of 1893.* 1991. ■ *History: The City of Harvey, 1890–1962.* 1962. ■ Rahn, Carol. "Local Elites and Social Change: A Case Study of Harvey, Illinois." Ph.D. diss., University of Chicago. 1980.

Heart of Chicago, neighborhood between PILSEN and SOUTH LAWNDALE in the LOWER WEST SIDE Community Area that has been home to successive waves of immigrant workers.

Hegewisch, Community Area 55, 16 miles SE of the Loop. Early maps indicate that a natural water passage existed from the present location of HAMMOND, Indiana, to the western banks of Wolf Lake through Hyde Park Lake. Native Americans

55
Hegewisch

settled on sand dunes and traveled along this passage for trade purposes. Waterfowl also followed this natural route during migratory periods as the primary feeder to the Mississippi flyway.

Immigrant laborers and other settlers built the first railroads across this terrain into Chicago in the 1850s. Originally part of Lake Township, it became part of Hyde Park Township in 1867.

Adolph Hegewisch, president of U.S. Rolling Stock Company, hoped to establish "an ideal workingman's community" when he laid out the town along a rail line in 1883. He moved his company about 10 miles east to border the new town and announced plans to build two major canals as an incentive for other factories to locate near the town. The first canal would have shortened the Calumet River; the second would have stemmed from the first to connect Wolf Lake to Lake Michigan. Owing to a lack of capital, these plans never came to fruition, and the town of Hegewisch fell dramatically short of its estimate of 10,000 residents by 1885—only 500 names were listed in the town directory in 1889.

In 1889 Hegewisch was annexed to Chicago along with the rest of Hyde Park Township. Adolph died a few years later, and the Rolling Stock Company became part of the Pressed Steel Car Company before World War I. During these decades, Joseph H. Brown and other industrialists developed steel mills in and around Hegewisch. New residents included many Polish, Slavic, Swedish, and Irish workers.

In 1935 the Congress of Industrial Organizations (CIO) created the Steel Workers Organization Committee (SWOC) to organize workers for better pay, hours, and conditions. In 1937 Carnegie-Illinois, a major subsidiary of U.S. Steel located in Hegewisch, signed a contract with the SWOC that limited hours, increased pay, and provided vacation time. The other "Little Steel" plants around the area did not follow suit, which prompted a strike against Republic Steel and other plants in May. On Memorial Day, off-duty police officers hired by Republic opened fire on the nonviolent demonstrators, killing 10 and injuring hundreds. The violence succeeded in breaking the union until the emergence of the United Steelworkers in the 1940s. This event has since become known as the Memorial Day Massacre; a plaque commemorates the victims at 117th Street and Avenue O.

The steel mills in and around Hegewisch remained the mainstays of the community over the next half century. The Pressed Steel Car Company switched its manufacturing operation from railroad cars to Howitzer tanks and other vehicles during World War II. After the Vietnam War, steel manufacturing waned across America, Hegewisch included. After the closure of Wisconsin Steel in 1980, the population declined because of layoffs. However, the remaining residents focused new energies on community activism and successfully blocked plans for both a Calumet airport and designation of landfills in the area. In the 1980s residents of Hegewisch initiated a renewal project that included successful lobbying for a Metra stop, a branch of the Chicago Public Library, and a $300,000 block grant to repair infrastructure. Since the 1960s Hegewisch has balanced out some of its population losses with the relocation of a significant number of Mexican Americans into the area. Adjacent to the Bishop Ford Expressway (I-94) and numerous railway lines, industry (including DMC, a major Midwest distributor of Ford automobiles since 1998) and nearby Indiana casinos constitute the employment base for the residents of Hegewisch.

Erik Gellman

FURTHER READING: Sellers, Rod, and Dominic A. Pacyga. *Chicago's Southeast Side*. 1998.

Hermosa, Community Area 20, 6 miles NW of the Loop. Hermosa is defined by railroad tracks and embankments. The Chicago & North Western Railway line forms its western boundary east of Cicero Avenue while the east and south borders are hemmed by two lines of the Chicago, Milwaukee & St. Paul Railroad (Chicago, Milwaukee, St. Paul & Pacific Railroad). To the north, six blocks of Belmont Avenue were initially the tiny hamlet's main access into neighboring communities.

20
Hermosa

As early as 1875 the CM&SP had a depot in Hermosa, but it was not a regular stop until 1886. Scottish immigrants settled here in the 1880s, calling the area of woods and prairie Kelvyn Grove after the eighth Lord Kelvyn. Not long after, German and Scandinavian farmers established themselves in the northwest and southern parts of what became Hermosa.

The Dreyer Company tried to establish a factory for locomotive works in 1882 where the two CM&SP lines intersected, but two years later when the building had still not been occupied, it was sold to the Laminated Wood Company. By 1886 a number of other companies, such as the Expanded Metal Company, the Eclipse Furnace Company, and a warehouse belonging to the Washburn and Moen Manufacturing Company, located along the rails.

To accommodate factory workers, real-estate developers built in an area to the southwest, naming the subdivision Garfield after the recently assassinated president. One of the development companies, J. F. and C. P. Keeney, erected cottage-style houses and guaranteed each of the 150 home buyers that if they died before completion of the contract, their heirs would receive a free deed to the property. James F. Keeney took a special interest in the community. He joined in local politics, persuaded the railway to add a stop at Garfield, and then donated money for a depot, which was named after him. Chicago annexed the area in 1889 under the name Hermosa, a name whose origin is disputed.

Although railroads brought some industry, and annexation slowly added municipal service and street improvements, accelerated growth did not occur until 1907 when streetcar lines extended along North, Armitage, and Fullerton Avenues. Polish, Irish, and Italian populations then moved into the Swedish and German community. The population stood at 15,152 in 1920, with construction booming in the vicinity of the newly created Kelvyn Park. Industrial growth along the railroads actually impeded residential construction, however.

Growth continued until the Great Depression. By 1942 frame and brick bungalows and two-flats predominated. Dead-end streets, a product of the rail lines, isolated residents from adjacent communities but also gave them a sense of security. Many homes had 25-foot frontages, and the narrow distance between houses generated a neighborliness on the block.

Hermosa's population fluctuated only slightly from 1970 to 1980 but rose in the next decade from 19,547 to 23,131. Ethnically the area changed as Hispanics became the dominant group, growing from 31 percent in 1980 to 68 percent in 1990 and 84 percent in 2000. More than half of the Hispanic population were Puerto Rican, while most of the rest were Mexican.

Criminal activity concerned residents as early as the 1970s when the community's crime rate increased significantly. A 17.4 percent poverty rate in 1989 and an unemployment rate of 10.9 percent in 1990 accounted for a decrease in home buyers and an increase in renters.

Working to prevent any further deterioration, residents banded together in block clubs, church groups, and other organizations. Groups such as United Neighbors in Action formed in 1982 to voice their concerns over proposed subsidized housing. To ensure safety and combat escalating gang problems, some groups began policing their blocks. Kelvyn Park occupants formed the Kelvyn-Ken-Wel Community Organization to encourage redevelopment of two vacant properties where gangs were engaging in drug deals. Other projects included developing a neighborhood reinvestment program to encourage area banks to work with potential home buyers.

Marilyn Elizabeth Perry

FURTHER READING: Karlen, Harvey M. *Chicago's Crabgrass Communities: The History of the Independent Suburbs and Their Post Offices That Became Part of Chicago.* 1992. ■ Kruggel, Adam. "Federation Partnership Puts Community First." *National Training and Information Center Reports*

(January, February, March 1997): 2, 4. ■ Skeris, Peter, and Maria T. Armendariz. *Hermosa: A Study of a Community in Transition.* 1971.

Highland Park, IL, Lake County, 23 miles N of the Loop. Highland Park's

bluffs, lake vistas, ravines, and accessibility to Chicago support the foresight of nineteenth-century developers who envisioned this picturesque suburb as a retreat for Chicago's affluent professionals.

Indian trails and mounds indicate that before the Black Hawk War, Potawatomi traversed the forested acres that became Highland Park. German immigrants founded two village ports, St. Johns (1847) and Port Clinton (1850), in hopes of opening the hinterlands for trade.

By 1855 Walter S. Gurnee, former Chicago mayor, North Shore real-estate speculator, and president of the Chicago & Milwaukee Railroad (Chicago, Milwaukee, St. Paul & Pacific Railroad), took control of the Port Clinton Land Company and platted the area for residential settlement. Gurnee surmised that rail offered the best link to Chicago and that residential development, rather than commercial, would succeed.

The city of Highland Park incorporated with about 600 residents, a school, a hotel, and a religious association in March 1869. Purchase or public consumption of alcohol was prohibited. To heighten the picturesque appeal of the area, developers hired landscape architects Horace W. S. Cleveland and William French to plat the streets. Prairie School architects left their mark on the summer and year-round estates of elite professionals who settled along the lake bluffs. Away from the water, developers built more modest homes for residents who provided services to the suburb.

Residents supported investment in a public library (1887) and annexed the village of Ravinia, south of Highland Park, in 1899. By the turn of the century, Highland Park's population was 2,806 and socially, if not economically, diverse. Institu-

One of Highland Park's characteristic ravines, 1912. Photographer: C. H. Warren & Co. Source: Curt Teich Archives, Lake County Discovery Museum.

tions such as the Gads Hill Summer Settlement House encampment, the Railroad Men's Home, and Wildwood, a resort for German-Jewish families excluded from suburban country clubs, attest to this diversity. Unlike many of its suburban neighbors, Highland Park welcomed a sizable Jewish population after World War II.

The city experienced two growth spurts: in the 1920s, when the population grew by 98 percent to 12,203, and in the 1950s, when it leapt 52 percent to 25,532. Careful planning has protected the area's appeal by promoting its village character and building on its strengths of private and public amenities. The Ravinia Music Festival is one such legacy. What began as a recreational park and cultural center established in 1904 by A. C. Frost, now hosts, each summer, tens of thousands of visitors for classical and popular concerts in a wooded outdoor setting, including performances by the Chicago Symphony Orchestra.

Derek Vaillant

FURTHER READING: Ebner, Michael. *Creating Chicago's North Shore*. 1988.

Hinsdale, IL, DuPage and Cook Counties, 16 miles W of the Loop. Hinsdale, a commuter village along the Chicago, Burlington & Quincy Railroad, roughly encompasses the area between Kingery Highway, 59th Street, Interstate 294, and Ogden Avenue. The village sits on elevated prairie land. A valley runs east to west, splitting Hinsdale's morainic hills, some of which rise to over 70 feet above Lake Michigan.

Shortly after the Black Hawk War ended in 1833, a settlement developed north of present-day Hinsdale in an area along the Southwest Plank Road (Ogden Avenue) near the banks of Salt Creek. This area, known as Brush Hill for its abundance of hazelnut bushes, grew into a thriving community of taverns, mills, and feed stores. By 1851 Ben Fuller had acquired most of Brush Hill, which he platted and renamed Fullersburg.

In 1858 Fuller petitioned the Chicago, Burlington & Quincy Railroad to build a line

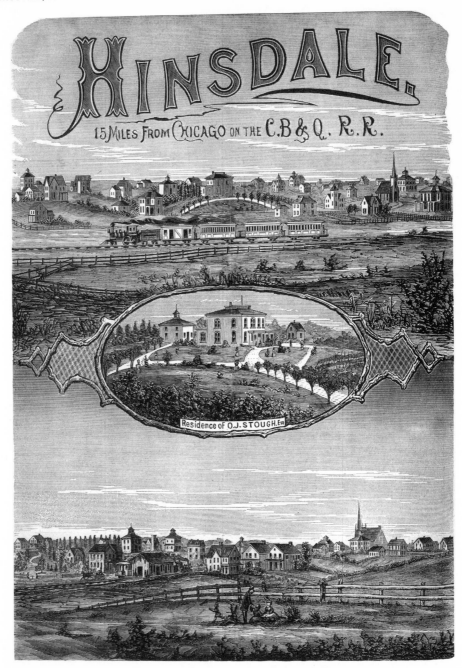

Advertisement for Hinsdale, 1873. Artist: Unknown. Source: The Newberry Library.

through Fullersburg. Because of topographical problems, however, the line was built one mile south through Hinsdale's valley instead. In 1862 William Robbins bought 640 acres of what is now south Hinsdale. The tracks through Hinsdale were completed on May 20, 1864, and Robbins hired landscaper Horace W. S. Cleveland to plat the village south of the tracks. Robbins planted elm and maple trees along proposed streets and built a school.

Hinsdale was incorporated in 1873, with Judge Joel Tiffany as its first president. The Hinsdale Library Association was incorporated in 1887. During the 1890s Hinsdale installed a water pumping station, wood and brick-paved roads (1892), electric streetlights (1896), and a telephone exchange (1896). The Hinsdale Golf Club set up links on Anson Ayres's property in the 1890s.

The Hinsdale Sanitarium was started in 1903. Improvements in the 1920s included the Ruth Lake Country Club (1922), the Madison school (1924), and the Hinsdale Theater (1925). The Woodlands, an area east of County Line Road, was annexed in 1917, and Fullersburg was annexed in 1923. In 1924 the Hinsdale Plan Commission was formed to consider zoning ordinances. The colonial-style Memorial Building, which today houses village offices, was built in 1928, funded entirely by private donations.

From 1960 to 1975 Hinsdale carried out eight annexations, eventually reaching its present borders. In 1975 Hinsdale annexed Katherine Legge Memorial Park, which had been donated to the village by International Harvester. Since the 1980s Hinsdale has restored many of its historic structures; builders have been encouraged to use the Georgian style of colonial architecture in keeping with the Hinsdale Plan of early civic leaders.

In 1870, 43 percent of Hinsdaleans were originally from the northeastern United States. The remaining 50 percent consisted of German, English, and other northwestern European immigrants. In 2000 Hinsdale's population was 17,349, twice what it had been in 1950.

Tom Sterling

FURTHER READING: Sterling, Tom, and Mary Sterling. *Hinsdale and the World: One Hundred Years.* 1996. ■ Thompson, Richard A., ed. *DuPage Roots.* 1985.

Homewood, IL, Cook County, 22 miles SW of the Loop. Central to Homewood's evolution from a whistle-stop farming center to a substantial suburb of a large city is its location on the Illinois Central Railroad. There is no evidence of a Native American settlement in Homewood, but the Vincennes Trace (now Dixie Highway) ran through the town. The area drains into the Calumet River. Homewood lies in four townships: Bloom, Bremen, Rich, and Thornton. It formally organized as a village in 1893.

Immediately after federal surveyors marked the section lines around Homewood in 1834, settlers bought land and started farms. In 1852, a year after the first store opened, the business district was platted as Hartford. The next year the Illinois Central Railroad commenced service with a stop called Thornton Station, because  most passengers were traveling to or from nearby THORNTON. In 1869 the U.S. postmaster general assented to a petition from local residents and officially changed the name to Homewood.

Through the nineteenth century the town grew slowly. Farmers shipped their produce to Chicago, and local businesses and some industry developed to serve their needs, including a flour mill that operated from 1856 into the 1880s. The population in 1900 was 352.

In the twentieth century recreation began to draw visitors, some of whom became residents. Five early golf clubs still operate: Flossmoor Country Club, in neighboring FLOSSMOOR (organized in 1898 as Homewood Country Club; name changed 1914); Ravisloe (1901); Idlewild, in Flossmoor (1908); Olympia Fields, in Olympia Fields (1915); and Calumet (organized in 1901 in Chicago; relocated to Homewood in 1917). The Illinois Central offered special schedules and created special stops just for golfers—the origin of the stops that became Calumet, Flossmoor, and Olympia Fields. The railroad attracted more new residents to both towns by selling real estate in Flossmoor and, in 1926, by electrifying its commuter service. Homewood's population grew from 713 in 1910 to 1,389 in 1920 and 3,227 in 1930.

Relatively little direct benefit accrued from

another recreational attraction, Washington Park Race Track, which opened on grounds located west of Halsted Street, just outside the village bounds, in 1926. Few of the horse racing patrons shopped or ate in Homewood, because the Illinois Central built a spur line linking the track directly to Chicago. During the Great Depression, however, the Illinois Jockey Association helped Homewood pay for infrastructure built during the optimistic, prosperous 1920s. Washington Park went out of business after its grandstand burned in 1977; in 1992 Homewood bought the site and turned it into a commercial and retail development.

In the postwar period, Homewood and Flossmoor established institutional partnerships. Homewood-Flossmoor Community High School opened its doors in 1959, and a joint park district was incorporated in 1969.

The Great Depression and World War II merely slowed growth. There were 4,078 people in 1940, but a surge pushed the total to 13,371 in 1960. Total population hit 18,871 in 1970 and since then has held steady between 19,000 and 20,000. By the 1970s Homewood had become a virtual bedroom for Chicago—in 1967 Homewood and Flossmoor formed one of only three outlying suburban zones where half or more of the workers commuted to jobs in Chicago—and the trend continued into the twenty-first century.

John H. Long

FURTHER READING: Adair, Anna B., and Adele Sandberg. *Indian Trails to Tollways: The Story of the Homewood-Flossmoor Area.* 1968. ▪ Hinko, Michael J. *History of Homewood.* 1976.

23
Humboldt
Park

Humboldt Park, Community Area 23, 5 miles NW of the Loop. Chicago's Humbolt Park community, on the city's Northwest Side, centers on the 207-acre park named for the naturalist Alexander von Humboldt in 1869. Annexed to Chicago the same year, the sparsely settled prairie settle-

ment experienced dramatic gains in real-estate value during the early 1870s amid the avid promotion of parkside areas. In 1886 the street railway arrived, followed by branches of the elevated railway in the 1890s. Two-flat houses became popular between 1900 and 1920, together with new brick bungalows and one- and two-story frame dwellings. Later small apartment buildings went up.

As the downtown business district expanded during the 1870s, Chicago's Danish and Norwegian communities extended northwest along the Milwaukee Avenue corridor, moving to Humboldt Park in considerable numbers during the 1880s and 1890s. By 1900 the Danish community stretched along North Avenue from Damen Street west to Pulaski, in a band six to eight blocks wide. Over two dozen Norwegian churches were located in and around the Humboldt Park and LOGAN SQUARE areas.

Ethnic residential succession, from the waves of Germans and Scandinavians arriving during the last quarter of the nineteenth century through the presently dominant Puerto Ricans, is evident in the use of the park itself, which quickly became a magnet for political and cultural activities. Statues (transplanted elsewhere after the dissolution of the particular national community) were first raised by the Germans to Alexander von Humboldt (1892) and author Fritz Reuter (1893). In 1901 some 50,000 flag-waving North Side Scandinavian Americans flocked to Humboldt Park for the unveiling of Sigvald Asbjornsen's statue of the heroic adventurer Leif Erikson. In 1904 Poles erected at the park's entrance an equestrian statue of Thaddeus Kosciuszko, a political exile who had served with distinction as a general in the American Revolutionary army. Parades and other nationalistic events were regularly held at the statue's base at the peak of the Polish influx in the first two decades of the twentieth century; 100,000 Polish Americans gathered in June 1918 to celebrate the anniversary of the creation of the Polish army in France..

During the 1920s and 1930s Italian Americans and German and Russian Jews, who had recently entered the community to take advantage of the newer and larger apartments, enjoyed the park's bicycling, boating, and skating facilities, as well as the rose garden and the Prairie-style boathouse and shelter (designed in 1905 by Danish immigrant Jens Jensen). The more exotic Division Street locale offered sidewalk music and soapbox political oratory, a setting from which the writers Saul Bellow, Nelson Algren, and Studs Terkel emerged. By 1960 most of the Jewish residents of Humboldt Park had moved out, with many going to ALBANY PARK and NORTH PARK. Italians were the largest remaining European ethnic group, followed by Poles.

The next entrants were Puerto Ricans, who moved in from WEST TOWN and points east. The period 1950 to 1965 saw the first massive migration of Puerto Ricans to Chicago. In June 1966 a three-day riot erupted after a policeman shot and wounded a young Puerto Rican man in West Town. Community leaders rallied in the park to devise strategies to calm the crowds. Deteriorating economic conditions facing Puerto Ricans and incoming African Americans embodied many aspects of the national urban crisis while ethnic conflicts, especially those between young Puerto Ricans and Polish Americans, prevailed during the transition period. For Puerto Ricans the Division Street area (*La División*, in local parlance), with its stores and restaurants, has anchored settlement since the 1960s. Humboldt Park still remains the symbolic nucleus of Puerto Rican Chicago. Park thoroughfares have been renamed in honor of notables (such as former governor of Puerto Rico Luis Muños Marín and nationalist leader Pedro Albizu Campos), reflecting abiding concerns for the homeland not unlike those displayed by earlier groups.

In smaller but increasingly significant numbers, Mexican immigrants have also joined the community mix; by 1980 they represented almost one-third of Humboldt Park's 29,000 Latinos (Latinos in turn constituted 41 percent of the total population). By 2000 Latinos were 48 percent of the population, and half were of Mexican origin. Meanwhile, the black population has steadily

increased to equal the size of the Latino population. Most recently, the arrival of Dominican immigrants in the northwestern section reflects the community's ongoing ethnic evolution.

David A. Badillo

FURTHER READING: Cutler, Irving. *The Jews of Chicago: From Shtetl to Suburb.* 1996. ■ Latino Institute. *Latinos in Metropolitan Chicago: A Study of Housing and Employment.* 1983. ■ Padilla, Felix M. *Puerto Rican Chicago.* 1987.

Huntley, IL, McHenry and Kane Counties, 45 miles NW of the Loop.  Platted beside the Galena & Chicago Union Railroad in 1851 by Thomas Huntley and incorporated in 1872, Huntley remained an agricultural village until the 1980s. Suburban sprawl and Sun City, a massive senior residential area on the village's south side, caused the population to grow from 2,453 in 1990 to 5,730 by 2000.

Craig L. Pfannkuche

FURTHER READING: *McHenry County in the Twentieth Century, 1968–1994.* McHenry County Historical Society. 1994. ■ Nye, Lowell A., ed. *McHenry County, Illinois, 1832–1968.* 1968.

Hyde Park, Community Area 41, 6 miles SE of the Loop.  The development of the Hyde Park community began in 1853 when Paul Cornell, a New York lawyer, purchased 300 acres of property between 51st and 55th Streets. Always a shrewd investor, Cornell deeded 60 acres to the Illinois Central Railroad in exchange for a train station and the promise of daily trips to the heart of Chicago's commercial core. The community continued to prosper over the next 30 years, as residential construction expanded and the transportation network grew dense. By the late 1880s transportation options in the area included the Cottage Grove cable car and dozens of trains leaving from the South Park station at 57th Street for the LOOP.

Statue of the Republic and Grand Basin, at the 1893 World's Columbian Exposition. Photographer: Unknown. Source: Chicago History Museum.

Despite such improvements, the transformation of the built environment of Hyde Park remained modest until two major events of the early 1890s. The first was the creation of the University of Chicago and the second was the World's Columbian Exposition of 1893. The University of Chicago emerged from the philanthropy of John D. Rockefeller, who was interested in launching an institution of higher learning in the Midwest, specifically one to serve the educational needs of the American Baptist community in Chicago. The university also benefited from the good will of Marshall Field, who donated a significant amount of land for the new campus. The Columbian Exposition stimulated the construction of hundreds of residential and commercial buildings in Hyde Park and WOODLAWN and the development of the South Side Elevated line, which reached southward from the Loop to 39th Street by 1892 and finally reached the exposition in Jackson Park in the middle of 1893.

After a significant building slump immediately following the exposition, construction continued vigorously until the late 1920s. A variety of prominent architects worked in the area, including Frank Lloyd Wright, who designed the Heller and Robie houses on South Woodlawn Avenue. Through the first two decades of the twentieth century, a mixed-use pattern of six-flat walk-up apartment buildings interspersed with larger structures and a wide variety of commercial uses became commonplace throughout Hyde Park.

During this period, the community also became increasingly ethnically diverse. Jewish residents became an important part of the area's social fabric and began to set up a variety of social

James Farmer: A Chicago Lunch Counter Sit-In

James Farmer came to Chicago in 1941 to work as the race-relations secretary with the Fellowship of Reconciliation, a pacifist organization. Farmer, a recent graduate of Howard University, convened an inter-racial group, mostly University of Chicago graduate students, to study Gandhi and his pacifist model for social change. This group evolved into the Committee of Racial Equality (CORE), which became an important force in the civil rights movement.

CORE set about fighting segregation in Chicago through direct-action techniques. Its first success was at the Jack Spratt Coffeehouse, a restaurant on 47th Street in Kenwood that refused to serve African Americans. Farmer explained CORE's direct action:

We went in with a group of about twenty—this was a small place that seats thirty or thirty-five comfortably at the counter and in the booths—and occupied just about all of the available seats and waited for service. The woman was in charge again [the manager they had encountered on a previous visit]. She ordered the waitress to serve two whites who were seated at the counter, and she served them. Then she told the blacks, "I'm sorry, we can't serve you, you'll have to leave." And they, of course, declined to leave and continued to sit there. By this time the other customers who were in there were aware of what was going on and were watching, and most of these were university people, University of Chicago, who were more or less sympathetic with us. And they stopped eating and the two people at the counter she had served and those whites in the booth she had served were not eating. There was no turnover. People were coming in and standing around for a few minutes and walking out. There were no seats available.

Ultimately, CORE succeeded in desegregating this restaurant and fought for equal treatment in other public venues. CORE's techniques would later play a significant role in attacking racial segregation in the Deep South.

Raines, Howell. *My Soul Is Rested.* 1977.

and civic institutions, including a Jewish community center and several synagogues. Many older Jewish residents preferred to live in the taller apartment buildings that were becoming commonplace throughout east Hyde Park, which was rapidly developing into a popular hotel and resort area. By the early 1930s Hyde Park had over one hundred hotels, and the lakefront was home to almost a dozen of these increasingly elaborate and well-appointed structures, many of which were later converted into apartment buildings. Some of the older hotels built for the Columbian Exposition persevered, but others soon began to cater to a more transient population, a condition that would become problematic by the late 1940s.

Beginning in the early 1930s, concerns arose about certain changes taking place in Hyde Park. Numerous studies were commissioned to examine the growing crime problem in the area, along with the citywide phenomenon of illegal residential conversions. While many in the community were concerned about the viability of an integrated community in light of a rapidly expanding African American population, other groups were concerned with the safety of the University of Chicago's campus and its physical plant, valued at many millions of dollars. In order to coordinate efforts to sustain and renew the community, the university in 1952 helped establish the South East Chicago Commission, which was charged with monitoring building code violations and local crime.

By the late 1950s the first federally sponsored urban renewal plan was under way in Hyde Park. The plan attracted severe criticism from community residents who stood to be displaced and from outsiders, including Monsignor John Egan of the Roman Catholic Church. The plan, which took almost a decade to execute, transformed many older, densely built-up areas of Hyde Park into a state of semisuburbia.

Max Grinnell

FURTHER READING: Beadle, Muriel. *The Hyde Park–Kenwood Urban Renewal Years.* 1964. ■ Block, Jean F. *Hyde Park Houses: An Informal History, 1856–1910.* 1978. ■ Grinnell, Max. *Hyde Park, Illinois.* 2001.

Ida B. Wells Homes, neighborhood built by the Chicago Housing Authority in the 1930s in the OAKLAND Community Area.

Irving Park, Community Area 16, 7 miles NW of

16
Irving Park

the Loop. Irving Park's past and present are tied to preservation of its historic houses. Building fine houses was the concept that businessman Charles T. Race decided upon after purchasing acreage in 1869 from Major Noble, whose father had bought the land in 1833. Race had intended to become a gentleman farmer, but his land was close to the Chicago & North Western Railway and he realized there would be more profit in beginning a settlement. After Race paid for a depot, the rail company agreed to stop at the settlement, which was first called Irvington as a tribute to author Washington Irving, but was soon renamed Irving Park.

Race built himself a three-story brick house with basement and "French roof." Joined by associates, he organized the Irving Park Land Company, bought additional land, and subdivided it into lots. Advertisements promoted the area's easy access to downtown via hourly trains. Boasting an idyllic setting comparable to that of suburbs such as EVANSTON and OAK PARK, the ad pointed to Irving Park's "shady streets, fine schools, churches and stores," and homes of varied designs. The Irving Park subdivision was followed by Grayland, Montrose, and Mayfair.

The commuter suburb attracted many wealthy residents who sought larger homes of seven to ten rooms and such amenities as closets and drinking water from artesian wells. Race and his associates turned a 600 percent profit on the land. Other, less affluent residents came to the area to remove their families from the dangers of the city. Rich or

---

Ida B. Wells: African Americans at the World's Columbian Exposition

Ida B. Wells grew up in the post–Civil War South and became a fierce opponent of lynching. She came to Chicago in 1893 to protest the exclusion of African Americans from exhibits at the World's Columbian Exposition. The Haitian building stood in as a center for Americans of color. Frederick Douglass, the noted abolitionist and advocate for equal rights, represented the Haitian government at the fair. Wells described Haiti's pavilion as "one of the gems of the World's Fair, and in it Mr. Douglass held high court."

Wells and Douglass wrote and published "The Reason Why the Colored American Is Not in the World's Columbian Exposition." As Wells described it, the pamphlet

> was a clear, plain statement of facts concerning the oppression put upon the colored people in this land of the free and home of the brave. We circulated ten thousand copies of this little book during the remaining three months of the fair. Every day I was on duty at the Haitian building, where Mr. Douglass gave me a desk and spent the days putting this pamphlet in the hands of foreigners.

Ultimately, the fair officials offered to sponsor a special day for African Americans. Wells and many other African Americans considered Negro Day little more than a gesture and were reluctant to participate. Frederick Douglass, however, took the opportunity to spotlight the problems that people of color faced in the United States. Douglass died in 1895, but Wells moved permanently to Chicago and became involved in a wide range of civic and club activities.

Duster, Alfreda M., ed. *Crusade for Justice: The Autobiography of Ida B. Wells.* 1970.

---

middle-class, the population of Irving Park was generally native-born, Protestant, and white-collar. Residents participated in community events and activities of a literary and musical nature. Both men and women were active in neighborhood organizations. The Irving Park Woman's Club formed in 1888 with an agenda of cultural and reform activities.

Suburban paradise was not without problems, however. In the 1880s heavy rains produced floods, and poor drainage turned unpaved streets to mud. In 1881 complaints were heard of raw sewage floating down Irving Park Road from the Cook County poor house and insane asylum in DUNNING.

Although Irving Park was annexed to the city of Chicago as part of Jefferson Township in 1889, in the 1890s streets were still unpaved and unlighted. As improvements were added, the main thoroughfare became a construction zone; streets were updated and public transportation was created. A residential boom between 1895 and 1914 added more than 5,000 new buildings, of which 1,200 were multifamily residences. New structures changed the housing composition of the area, leading to concerns about community standards.

Germans and Swedes had begun arriving around the turn of the century but in the 1920s were largely replaced by Poles and Russians. Population peaked at 66,783 in 1930, and commercial interests sprang up along the major roads, but until 1940 construction was mainly residential. Most notable architecturally were the bungalows of the VILLA DISTRICT; Old Irving Park with its Queen Anne, Victorian, and Italianate houses, farmhouses, and bungalows; and Independence Park with many homes of turn-of-the-century vintage.

A new emphasis on neighborhood unity and the preservation of area houses began in 1983 with the founding of the Old Irving Park Association (OIPA). The organization broke into two groups a year later, with the OIPA focusing on rehabilitating old houses, fund-raising for charity, helping needy residents, and sponsoring forums for political candidates. The second association, the Old Irving Park Historical Society (OIPHS), began conducting an area house walk in 1985. Its members also worked on preservation. A number of structures have been cited as landmarks, including Carl Schurz High School and the Steven Race House. In the 1980s the Chicago Landmark Commission named 43 other buildings as potential landmarks.

Irving Park's population grew from 49,489 in 1980 to 58,643 in 2000. During those two decades the Hispanic population increased from 9 percent to 43 percent and included immigrants from Central and South America along with larger numbers of Mexicans and Puerto Ricans. Filipinos and Indians predominated among Asians, who constituted 8 percent of the population in 2000.

Marilyn Elizabeth Perry

FURTHER READING: Drury, John. "Old Chicago Neighborhoods, XXII: Irving Park." *Landlord's Guide* (February 1949): 12–13. ■ Mayer, Harold. "Zoning Is Irving Park, Albany's Best Protection." *Real Estate*, June 28, 1941, 12–18. ■ Posadas, Barbara M. "Suburb into Neighborhood: The Transformation of Urban Identity on Chicago's Periphery—Irving Park as a Case Study, 1870–1910." *Journal of the Illinois State Historical Society* 76 (Autumn 1983): 162–176.

Jackson Park Highlands, neighborhood established in 1905 by residents who would also found the South Shore Country Club, now part of SOUTH SHORE Community Area.

Jefferson Park, Community Area 11, 10 miles NW of the Loop. Jefferson Park continues to live up to its nickname, "Gateway to Chicago." Located at the northwest edge of the city, the community long has been an important transportation link and hub. Indian trails were already well traveled by traders and hunters when John Kinzie Clark built his cabin in the early 1830s. By 1836 a hotel had been erected, a school district established, and farmers, mostly English, had settled. To get their produce to the Chicago markets they traveled on often mud-filled Indian trails.

11
Jefferson Park

After 1849 farmers moved their goods more quickly on two plank roads, the North West Plank Road (later Milwaukee Avenue) and the Lower Road (Elston Avenue).

In 1850 the state formed Jefferson Township, named after President Thomas Jefferson, and in 1855 residents platted a village near Milwaukee Avenue and Higgins Road, naming it Jefferson. Farmers traveling to and from the city often stopped to water their horses, pick up supplies, or rest. In 1855 a resident recorded that the town consisted of approximately 50 buildings. When the Chicago, St. Paul & Fond du Lac Railroad (Chicago & North Western) laid tracks and built a depot near the town's center, population grew. The town of Jefferson was incorporated in 1872 and annexed by Chicago in 1889. In 1884 an estimated 500 persons lived in Jefferson Township with most incoming residents Polish and German immigrants. About this time the area became known as Jefferson Park.

By 1900 a web of street railway lines extended on Lawrence, Milwaukee, and Elston Avenues. With new means of transportation came an influx of laborers, artisans, and tradesmen. Immigrants of Polish, German, Russian, Italian, Czech, and Slovakian backgrounds brought ethnic diversity into the area. Growth mushroomed in the 1920s, bringing larger numbers of Germans, Poles, and Italians. By 1930 the population stood at 20,532. As the neighborhoods grew, Victorian graystones, A-frames, and bungalows predominated.

As plans for an expressway were implemented in the 1950s, some residents of Jefferson Park objected, not only to the expressway but to a proposed tollbooth, until the 1956 Interstate Highway Act made tolls unnecessary. The Northwest Expressway (later the Kennedy Expressway) was completed in 1959, slicing diagonally through Jefferson Park and giving denizens an added means of transportation.

In 1970 the Chicago Transit Authority (CTA) constructed a terminal in Jefferson Park that connected CTA and Regional Transportation Authority bus routes, a Greyhound bus stop, a Chicago & North Western commuter railroad station, and an elevated line. In the 1980s the Northwestern rapid transit line was extended to O'Hare Airport, running through Jefferson Park along the median of the Kennedy Expressway. Despite this access to transportation, relatively little industry developed in Jefferson Park. A complex of offices and small retailers located at the intersection of Higgins Road and Lawrence and Milwaukee Avenues, the original nucleus of the community, remained the center of activity.

In 1990 nearly half of the 23,649 population was of Polish descent. Many congregate at Copernicus Center, a Polish cultural and study organization, based in the former Gateway Theater. Asians and Hispanics also are a significant presence in the community. Although seniors constituted approximately 22 percent of the population in 1990, the end of the decade saw a trend toward younger residents. Transportation continued to attract newcomers: the Metra station served 10,000 commuters a day, and on weekdays 800 buses traveled Jefferson Park's main arteries.

Marilyn Elizabeth Perry

FURTHER READING: Drury, John. "Old Chicago Neighborhoods: Jefferson Park." *Landlord's Guide* 38.3 (September 1947) and 41.8 (August 1950). ■ Karlen, Harvey M. *Chicago's Crabgrass Communities: The History of the Independent Suburbs and Their Post Offices That Became Part of Chicago.* 1992. ■ Posadas, Barbara M. "A Home in the Country: Suburbanization in Jefferson Township, 1870–1889." *Chicago History* 8.3 (Fall 1978): 134–149.

Jeffrey Manor, neighborhood in the SOUTH SHORE Community Area.

Joliet, IL, Will County, 35 miles SW of the Loop.

In 1673 Louis Jolliet and Father Jacques Marquette paddled up the Des Plaines River and camped on a huge mound a few miles south of present-day Joliet.

In 1833, following the Black Hawk War, Charles Reed built a cabin along the west side of the Des Plaines River. Across the river in 1834 James B. Campbell, treasurer of the canal commissioners, laid out the village of "Juliet," a name local settlers had been using before his arrival.

The Juliet region was part of Cook County until 1836, when it became the county seat of the new Will County. Just before the depression of 1837, Juliet incorporated as a village, but to cut tax expenses residents soon petitioned the state to rescind that incorporation.

In 1845 local residents changed the community's name from "Juliet" to "Joliet." Joliet was reincorporated as a city in 1852. Soon its transportation arteries included the Des Plaines River, a road that followed the Sauk Trail, the Illinois & Michigan Canal (1848), and the Rock Island Railroad (Chicago, Rock Island & Pacific Railroad, 1852), which ran through the business district. Today Joliet is served by several railroads, as well as Interstates 55 and 80, which intersect a few miles southwest of the city.

The quarrying of limestone, with a bluish-white tinge, earned Joliet the nickname "City of Stone." The Illinois & Michigan Canal was both a consumer of stone, for the building of locks, bridges, and aqueducts, and, after its completion in 1848, an artery for shipping stone to regional customers.

In 1858 the state of Illinois located a new penitentiary in Joliet, in part because of the abundance of stone for prison walls and cell houses. The Chicago Fire of 1871 spurred demand for stone, and by 1890 Joliet quarries were shipping over three thousand railroad carloads of stone per month to Chicago and other cities.

The "City of Steel" emerged with the construction of the Joliet mill in 1869. The Bessemer converters installed at the mill in the 1870s were among the earliest used in the United States. While canal construction drew Irish immigrants, the steel mill attracted thousands of southeastern Europeans. These new immigrants also found jobs on the railroad that serviced the steel mill, the Elgin, Joliet & Eastern Railway.

The city's large labor force and its steel mill

attracted other industries. Wire mills, coke plants, stove companies, horseshoe factories, brick companies, foundries, boiler and tank companies, machine manufacturers, can companies, bridge builders, plating factories, steel car shops, and many others established plants in the Joliet area. Other Joliet industries have ranged from the production of greeting cards and calendars to the bottling of 7-Up, from the manufacture of Hart, Schaffner & Marx clothing to the brewing of beer. Pianos, windmills, wallpaper, and barrels have been manufactured in Joliet, as have building materials, oil and chemical products, and Caterpillar scrapers. Joliet Junior College, founded in 1901, is the nation's oldest public community college. Joliet's economy entered a period of decline in the late 1970s, and by 1983 its unemployment rate stood at 26 percent.

During the 1990s Joliet's economy rebounded. Millions of people visit Joliet's riverboat casinos and its new drag-racing and NASCAR tracks. The millions of dollars in new tax receipts have been used to revitalize the downtown city center. Population leapt from 76,836 in 1990 to 106,221 in 2000.

Robert E. Sterling

FURTHER READING: Sterling, Robert E. *Joliet Transportation and Industry: A Pictorial History.* 1997. ■ Sterling, Robert E. *Joliet: A Pictorial History.* 1986. ■ Woodruff, George H. *The History of Will County, Illinois.* 1973 [1878].

Junction Grove, settlement founded in 1852 at the crossroads of several rail lines, now part of the ENGLEWOOD Community Area.

Kelvyn Grove, area around a rail stop named by area Scottish residents, near Kelvyn Park in what is now the HERMOSA Community Area.

Kenilworth, IL, Cook County, 15 miles N of the
Loop. In 1889 Joseph Sears
planned a North Shore village in the image of the bucolic English countryside,
in contrast to his urban
mansion on PRAIRIE AVE-
NUE. He purchased 223
acres of woodland, pasture, and wetlands located
between WILMETTE and WINNETKA, one of the
last undeveloped tracts of farmland lying along
Lake Michigan just north of Chicago. Much of
the land was covered with native oak, hickory,
and butternut trees and overgrown with wild
blackberry bushes. Its woodlands attracted serious botany students from Northwestern University, and its grassy pasture provided the neighborhood milk cows with daily forage. A settler's cabin
from the 1830s still stood near the lakeshore,
though any Native American presence had long
since vanished.

The Kenilworth Company's plan limited the
number of building lots in the new village and
used restrictive covenants to sell land to whites
only. In 1896 Kenilworth incorporated and ordinances were adopted that set 100 by 175 feet as
the minimum size for lots. The village name was
taken from a town in the midlands of England.
In 1899 the local women's club selected, and the
village adopted, street names such as Abbotsford
and Essex, taken from Sir Walter Scott's novel *Kenilworth*. In 1920, when the nearby North Shore
golf course went out of business, village residents
bought the 40 acres west of the railroad to ensure
compatible development. No additional expansion of village boundaries was possible.

The Kenilworth Company built municipal features that made the village especially attractive to
potential home owners and protected the existing
trees. Though in the 1960s Kenilworth lost many
elms to disease, other mature specimen trees remain outstanding landscape features. Commercial development was limited and today is found
only along Green Bay Road, which parallels the
railroad.

In 2000 Kenilworth's population was 2,494,
small in comparison to its neighbors and relatively
unchanged over time. For most of the twentieth
century, houses here were among the most expensive on the North Shore. Residents traveled
outside the village for employment. Kenilworth's
good location and physical comforts attracted
prominent residents, including utility magnate
Samuel Insull in the 1920s and U.S. senator Charles
Percy in the 1960s and 1970s. Kenilworth remains
a largely white community, although high income
is the prerequisite, not race.

The village contains houses designed by a number of esteemed architects. Kenilworth has the
largest collection of buildings by George W. Maher, a contemporary of Frank Lloyd Wright. Maher lived in Kenilworth and saw nearly 40 of his
designs constructed between 1893 and 1926. He
also fashioned the limestone pillars that mark the
Sheridan Road entrances to the village and the
town's central fountain. Consistent with the overall English theme of the village, Maher's buildings
are strongly influenced by the English architects
of the Arts and Crafts movement. Other designs
reference the Prairie School. Maher's work plus
Kenilworth's distinctive stone commuter train
station, built in 1890, its numerous Tudor revival
residences, and the Old English–style streetlamps
continue to evoke the pastoral image of an earlier
time and vision of community.

Jan Olive Nash

FURTHER READING: Ebner, Michael H. *Creating Chicago's
North Shore*. 1988. ■ Kenilworth Historical Society. *George
Washington Maher in Kenilworth*. 1993. ■ Kilner, Colleen
Browne. *Joseph Sears and His Kenilworth*. 1969.

Kensington. Born as a railroad town named
Calumet Junction, Kensington grew up where
the Illinois Central and Michigan Central Railroads connected in 1852. The town grew slowly
until, by 1880, 400 German, Irish, Scandinavian,
and Yankee residents lived there, servicing the
railroads and the population of farmers in the
vicinity. Despite the presence of churches, stores,
and schools, Kensington became notorious for its

saloons, leading the Dutch in neighboring ROSE-LAND to nickname it "Bumtown."

When George M. Pullman announced in 1880 that his model town would be built just north of Kensington, the small settlement boomed. Board-inghouses, taverns, and small stores opened to serve the construction crews and visitors to the site, who initially took the train to Kensington and walked to PULLMAN. The relationship be-tween the two communities remained close: Pull-man workers lived in Kensington; Kensington businessmen lived in Pullman. Pullman workers relaxed in Kensington taverns and billiard halls; Kensington saloonkeepers delivered beer in Pull-man. Kensington even figured prominently in the Pullman Strike. Its Eiche Turn-Verein (a German club dedicated to cultural education and physi-cal exercise) served as strike headquarters and its largest store, Secord and Hopkins, owned by Chicago mayor John P. Hopkins, offered credit and support to strikers and their families.

Changes in Pullman hiring policies and the opening of Illinois Terra Cotta brought Italians to Kensington, which gradually became a center of South Side Italian life. Employment bureaus, travel agencies, and grocery stores reflected the regional diversity within the Italian community. Nowhere was that diversity more apparent than in the three altars in San Antonio de Padua Roman Catholic Church. The first altar, like the church itself, was named for the patron saint selected by the Venetians; the second was named for San Ales-sandro by the Calabrese; and the third was named for the Virgin of the Rosary by the Sicilians.

When University of Chicago sociologists di-vided the city into community areas, they split Kensington among WEST PULLMAN, Roseland, and RIVERDALE. Roseland's Michigan Avenue business district grew south into Kensington's. Its Italian and Polish populations linked it socially to Pullman's ethnic communities. By the 1960s Kens-ington's unique identity was sustained primarily by the taverns that still lined its main streets, the Kensington police station, and St. Anthony's.

As industries began to close in the 1960s and

1970s, Kensington's population also began to change. Mexicans and African Americans returned for the first time since the 1920s, and by the 1980s African Americans came to dominate the commu-nity. The Fifth District police station moved away, as did many of the stores along Michigan Avenue and 115th Street. The Salem Baptist Church lo-cated in the former St. Salomea building. In 1998 the last remnant of Kensington's nineteenth-cen-tury identity gave way as well. Led by members of Salem Baptist Church, precincts in what had once been Kensington voted themselves dry. The Chicago papers heralded what they called the Roselanders' victory, though ultimately it was the residents of Kensington who had achieved their century-old goal. "Bumtown" was no more.

Janice L. Reiff

FURTHER READING: Andreas, A. T. *History of Cook County, Illinois.* 1884. ■ Greater Calumet Community Collection. Special Collections, Chicago Public Library, Chicago IL. ■ Vecoli, Rudolph J. "Chicago's Italians Prior to World War I: A Study of Their Social and Economic Adjustment." Ph.D. diss., University of Wisconsin. 1963.

Kenwood, Community Area 39, 5 miles SE of the

39
Kenwood

Loop. Kenwood, much like its bucolic counterparts to the north of the city, was set-tled in the 1850s by individu-als seeking respite from the increasing congestion of Chi-cago. The first of these resi-dents was Dr. John A. Kennicott, who built his home near the Illinois Central Railroad tracks at 48th Street. He named the home Kenwood after his ancestral land in Scotland, and when the Illi-nois Central built a small depot near 47th Street, they named the station Kenwood as well. Shortly afterward, the name Kenwood came to be applied to the area of land between 43rd Street and 51st Street, and from the lake west to Cottage Grove Avenue.

By the early 1860s Kenwood was fast becoming a fashionable place for many of Chicago's most prominent residents. Enticed by the promise of transportation improvements (most notably the

Bigger Thomas: A Tale of Two Neighborhoods

Richard Wright came to Chicago in 1927, one of thousands of African American migrants. Living on the South Side, Wright saw firsthand the dramatic racial and class divides that separated blacks and whites. He described this chasm through the eyes of his character Bigger Thomas in *Native Son* (1940). The novel opens with Bigger Thomas awaking in the single room in Douglas that he shares with his brother, sister, and mother to the sight of a huge black rat. Later, Bigger journeys south into Kenwood, an affluent, all-white neighborhood, in search of work, and he chooses to go armed:

He was going among white people, so he would take his knife and his gun; it would make him feel that he was the equal of them, give him a sense of completeness. Then he thought of a good reason why he should take it; in order to get to the Dalton place, he had to go through a white neighborhood. He had not heard of any Negroes being molested recently, but he felt that it was always possible.

Bigger Thomas walks south to 46th Street.

[The] houses he passed were huge; lights glowed softly in windows. The streets were empty, save for an occasional car that zoomed past on swift rubber tires. This was a cold and distant world; a world of white secrets carefully guarded.

Wright, Richard. *Native Son*. 1940.

Illinois Central and, in the 1870s, horse railway lines), residents of note included U.S. senator Lyman Trumbull; Norman Judd, President Lincoln's ambassador to Prussia; and William Rand, of the Rand McNally map corporation. In 1874 one publication dealing with Chicago suburbs stated that "Kenwood is the LAKE FOREST of the south, without the exclusiveness of its northern rival."

Kenwood continued to prosper through the 1880s and 1890s, and several new concentrations of large single-family homes emerged along Drexel Boulevard and between 45th and 50th Streets

from Drexel Boulevard to Blackstone Avenue. What little retail development the area had during this period was concentrated along 47th Street. Wealthy residents continued to commission large homes in a variety of architectural idioms, including the Prairie and Queen Anne styles. These residents included lumber merchant Martin Ryerson, meatpacker Gustavus Swift, and Julius Rosenwald, the chief executive of Sears, Roebuck & Co. The area had few apartment buildings.

While Kenwood residents had a variety of transportation options for decades, the "L" finally reached the community in 1907, and the terminus of the Kenwood branch was built out to 42nd Place and the lake in 1910. This new rapid transit facility attracted LOOP office workers to the northern part of Kenwood, and rooming houses and kitchenette apartments proliferated. Numerous walk-up apartment buildings were constructed west of the Illinois Central tracks in the 1910s, and the population of the area increased to 21,000 by 1920. East of the railroad tracks some vacant land remained, but the late 1920s saw the addition of two impressive art deco elevator apartment buildings along with the increased popularity of the Chicago Beach Hotel at Hyde Park Boulevard and Lake Michigan.

By the early 1930s there were signs of deterioration within the community, as the population, which continued to grow significantly, was accommodated by the conversion of older homes into rooming houses and the subdividing of existing apartment units. As transient residents began to populate the half of Kenwood north of 47th Street, home owners in the southern half gradually began to move elsewhere. This transformation accelerated between 1940 and 1960, as the population increased 41 percent without new construction of residences. Conventional wisdom pointed to the influx of African Americans moving out of the Black Belt as the cause of community deterioration and blight in the area.

The late 1940s saw the creation of the Hyde Park–Kenwood Community Conference, a group committed to maintaining a stable and integrated neighborhood in Kenwood. While much of the group's efforts were focused on the more pressing problems in HYDE PARK, Kenwood benefited from the urban renewal funds that became available in the late 1950s as well, and several housing projects were developed as a result of the group's efforts. Kenwood experienced a renaissance in the late 1970s, as several segments of the neighborhood were designated as historic districts by the city and new residential construction began to replace vacant lots. By the late 1990s families were moving back into the area, and an educational partnership between the Chicago Board of Education and the University of Chicago resulted in the formation of a charter school.

Max Grinnell

FURTHER READING: Abrahamson, Julia. *A Neighborhood Finds Itself.* 1959. ▪ Hyde Park Historical Society. *Some Residential Structures of Historical and Architectural Significance in Hyde Park and Kenwood.* 1978. ▪ *Kenwood District.* Commission on Chicago Historical and Architectural Landmarks. 1979. ▪ Pattillo, Mary, *Black on the Block: The Politics of Race and Class in the City.* 2007.

La Grange, IL, Cook County, 13 miles W of the Loop. Throughout the mid-nineteenth century, the expansion of the rail system around Chicago laid the framework for a sprawling metropolis. As railroads reached into new areas,

real-estate developers bought land and built towns along the lines, offering affluent Chicagoans the chance to move out of the increasingly congested central city.

Like his fellow speculators, Franklin Dwight Cossitt sought to take advantage of middle- and upper-class Chicagoans' "suburban fever." In 1870 Cossitt purchased a 600-acre tract of farmland

and uncultivated prairie adjacent to the recently completed Chicago, Burlington & Quincy line through western Cook County. Cossitt named his tract La Grange, after a Tennessee cotton farm that he had owned before the Civil War. French for "the barn," La Grange had been the name of the ancestral home of Marquis de Lafayette, a Revolutionary War hero.

Cossitt sought to distinguish his small, ordered village from what he saw as the overcrowded chaos of metropolitan Chicago by planting hundreds of elm trees, restricting the sale of liquor, building large single-family houses, setting aside property for schools and churches, contributing to the construction of a rail depot, and laying out a street plan that allowed for large lots. He advertised La Grange as a utopian retreat from the perceived dangers of the city, promising investors not only a cleaner, more orderly, and more "natural" physical environment but also a less threatening population. For some, the high concentration of foreign-born workers in Chicago contributed to a perception of danger. Although La Grange's population, like that of many other railroad suburbs, represented a mix of upper-income professionals and lower-income service employees, many of its residents were native-born and few worked as industrial laborers.

The Chicago Fire of 1871 reinforced the image of La Grange (and other communities in Cook County) as a suburban sanctuary. By forcing refugees to seek shelter outside the city and by further convincing middle-class and wealthy Chicagoans that the city had become too dangerous, the fire accelerated the process of suburbanization and the expansion of the metropolitan area begun by the railroads, Cossitt, and other real-estate developers. By the end of the nineteenth century, when the suburban electric railway reached La Grange, the village had been integrated within the expanding geographic entity of metropolitan Chicago.

La Grange continued to grow in the first decades of the twentieth century, both demographically and geographically, annexing and developing surrounding land in order to accommodate a population that rose from 6,525 in 1920 to 10,103 in 1930. Unable to find open and affordable land in Chicago, manufacturers like General Motors and the Aluminum Company of America moved into La Grange during the 1930s and 1940s. In the mid-twentieth century, as suburbanization and the exodus from Chicago accelerated, the population of La Grange continued to rise, to nearly 17,814 by 1970. Zoning laws that restricted housing density and limited multiple-dwelling units prevented even greater population increases. By 2000 the population of La Grange had leveled off to 15,608.

Sarah S. Marcus

FURTHER READING: Andreas, A. T. *History of Cook County, Illinois.* 1884. ■ Chamberlin, Everett. *Chicago and Its Suburbs.* 1874. ■ Cromie, William J., ed. *La Grange Centennial History.* 1979.

Lake Bluff, IL, Lake County, 30 miles N of the

Loop. Lake Bluff, settled in 1836 by Catherine and John Cloes, is the most distant suburb on the North Shore. First known as Dwyer Settlement, it was subsequently renamed Oak Hill (1848), Rockland (1859), and then Lake Bluff (1882).

Location on the transportation corridor connecting Chicago to WAUKEGAN and Milwaukee, first by stagecoach (1836) and then by rail (1855), proved paramount to development. Walter S. Gurnee, mayor of Chicago (1851–1852) and speculator, foresaw this place as another railway suburb. His early vision went unfulfilled for another 40 years.

The Lake Bluff Camp Meeting Association (1874) took form instead, at a summer gathering place established by Methodists. The association's founders appreciated its assets: lovely beaches, a railroad, and the cachet of the North Shore. Guests summered in tents through 1882. The five-story Hotel Irving (1883) advanced its attractions, embracing worldly activities including

art, bathing, boating, dancing, and other recreational pursuits.

By the late 1880s, however, Lake Bluff was becoming a residential suburb, with the construction of modest cottages. In 1895 the village incorporated and erected a two-story public school. Hastening its transformation, a fire in 1897 destroyed the hotel, and the camp meeting association dissolved two years later. Soon after came the building of a commuter station (1904) and a graceful village hall (1905). When the nearby Great Lakes Naval Training Station, completed in 1911, sought to designate Lake Bluff as its postal address, civic leaders lobbied in opposition. The NORTH CHICAGO post office was chosen instead.

Citizens contemplated consolidation into LAKE FOREST in 1895, 1908, 1912, and 1930, although never proceeding to referendum. After 1900 Lake Bluff became the site for country-style estates constructed by prominent Chicago families (Armour, Clow, Durand, Field) as well as the exclusive Shore Acres Country Club (1916).

Lake Bluff reflected the nationwide suburban trend after 1945. Population increased: 2,000 in 1950, 5,008 in 1970, and 6,056 in 2000. A large subdivision known as the Terrace, straddling Green Bay Road, started in 1961, contributing to Lake Bluff's largest population advance in any decade, 1,514 new residents between 1960 and 1970. The former estate of Phillip D. Armour III, also along Green Bay Road, was subdivided, yielding the more distinctive Armour Woods and Tangley Oaks, designed to conserve woodlands and ponds.

At the end of the twentieth century, Lake Bluff encountered challenges as well as opportunities. Its traditional housing stock east of Sheridan Road was its cherished coin, heightening interest in historic preservation. Median home value for Lake Bluff in 1990 was $285,200—above comparable countywide statistics but lower than in the nearby suburbs of Bannockburn, Lake Forest, and Mettawa. Knollwood, an unincorporated residential neighborhood west of Lake Bluff but within Lake Bluff's park and school districts, made unsuccessful petitions for annexation in 1978, 1982, and 1996. Lake Bluff did expand to the southwest, developing a commercial and light manufacturing district plus a retail complex featuring a modern supermarket. Knauz Motors, conducting business in Lake Forest since 1934, relocated all its new-car dealerships to western Lake Bluff by 2001. At the same time, the economic vitality in the original retail center diminished, stirring the village board to contemplate ambitious plans designed to foster downtown rejuvenation.

Michael H. Ebner

FURTHER READING: Mellinger, Barbara A. "History of Lake Bluff." Unpublished senior thesis, Cornell College, Mt. Vernon, IA. 1978. ■ Nelson, Janet, Kathleen O'Hara, and Ann Walters. *Lake Bluff, Illinois: A Pictorial History.* 1995. ■ Vliet, Elmer B. *Lake Bluff: The First 100 Years.* Ed. Virginia Mullery. 1985.

Lake Forest, IL, Lake County, 27 miles N of the Loop. Lake Forest, a favorite retreat of Chicago's upper class, is tied to the network of suburbs north of Chicago along Lake Michigan regarded as the North Shore. Earliest white habitation, circa 1834, was for farming. The area was initially beyond Chicago's reach, but starting in 1855 railroads enabled daily commuting.

Presbyterians established Lake Forest in 1857. Almerin Hotchkiss's design resembled a park, featuring curvilinear lines. Incorporated in 1861, it attained high regard among wealthy Chicagoans by offering cultivated landscapes, abundant land, and the prospect of social order. The founders simultaneously organized Lake Forest College, anticipating its centrality in their community.

The population of 877 in 1880 advanced to 1,203 in 1890, then nearly doubled, to 2,215, by 1900. Chicagoans constructed country-style estates, often occupied seasonally (Cyrus H. McCormick Jr.'s Walden, Louis F. Swift's Westle-

igh, J. Ogden Armour's Mellody Farm). But the crowning glory was the Onwentsia Club, established in 1895 as a private country club.

Market Square was completed in 1917. This sublime commercial center designed by Howard Van Doren Shaw complemented the sumptuous private dwellings. Rectangular in form, it opened upon the railway station. Anticipating the automobile age, the tree-lined square enabled access for motorists. Capitalized and operated privately through a land trust, it became a lasting civic expression. In 1978 it was listed on the National Register of Historical Sites as the nation's first planned shopping center.

Population reached 6,554 by 1930, with much of the growth occurring in the 1920s. Skokie Highway, completed in 1931, connected Lake Forest to other population centers. Local services and facilities required attention: infrastructures for utilities, a new city hall, a professional fire department, the first freestanding post office as well as library, new schools, a youth center, a movie theater, a public golf course, and a modern hospital. To preserve the historic scale, a municipal zoning ordinance was enacted in 1923. In 1926 voters approved the annexation of a largely uninhabited 10-square-mile expanse on Lake Forest's western boundary, tripling the town's size to 15 square miles.

Change accelerated in the second half of the twentieth century. Population surpassed 10,000 in 1960 and reached 20,059 in 2000. During these postwar decades the prevailing residential expression shifted from castles to ranch houses. While the east side remained largely unchanged (save for new apartment complexes), single-family homes proliferated in the southern and western reaches. Lake Forest also became a center of employment, especially in financial services: within its central business district, office space increased by more than 300,000 square feet (a 286 percent gain) between 1974 and 1999, and private-sector employment citywide advanced 203 percent between 1978 and 1998, in part due to an office park acquired through further annexation. Local gov-

Ida Honore Grant, Grace Brown Palmer, and Bertha Honore Palmer, at Lake County Fair, Lake Forest, July 1916. Photographer: Unknown. Source: Chicago History Museum.

ernment again encountered challenges: vehicular congestion, water service, school construction, recreation (especially beachfront development), services for senior citizens, and cultural affairs. Advocacy for historic preservation and land conservation intensified. So did opposition to the town's governing regime, in place since the 1940s. The premium placed on real estate bearing a Lake Forest address threatened to lead to overbuilding; municipal officials responded with the nation's first building-scale ordinance in 1989 to regulate the demolition of residences and the construction of oversize replacements. For 1999 the average sale price of single-family homes was $821,316.

Michael H. Ebner

FURTHER READING: Arpee, Edward. *Lake Forest, Illinois, History and Reminiscences, 1861–1961.* 1963; rev. ed. 1991. ■ Dart, Susan. *Market Square, Lake Forest, Illinois.* 1984. ■ Miller, Arthur H., and Shirley M. Paddock. *Lake Forest, Estates, People, and Culture.* 2000.

Lake Meadows, neighborhood built on urban renewal lands in the DOUGLAS Community Area in the 1960s.

Lake View, Community Area 6, 4 miles N of the Loop. Over the past century and a half, the name Lake View has referred in turn to the first of Chicago's North Shore suburban developments, an independent township, a city in its own right,

6
Lake View

and a Community Area within Chicago. All of the Lake Views have occupied land between two and eight miles north of Chicago's center. As one official incarnation of Lake View gave way to the next, it gradually transformed from a loose agglomeration of large parcels of land occupied by farms and estates into distinct neighborhoods housing many single young adults, childless married couples, and gay men.

Lake View's early residents followed the lead of nearby LINCOLN SQUARE's first property owner, Conrad Sulzer, in truck farming. Farmers from Germany, Sweden, and Luxembourg made celery Lake View's most important local crop. In 1854 James Rees and Elisha Hundley built the Lakeview House near Lake Shore Drive and Byron Street as a resort for potential investors in local land. (According to legend, Walter Newberry stood on the hotel's veranda and, admiring its view, suggested that it be called "Lake View House.") Wealthy Chicagoans seeking summer retreats from the city's heat and disease bought up land in the eastern sector of the area. New railroad lines prompted development of more residential land and added suburban characteristics to Lake View's resort atmosphere.

With increasing settlement came legal identity: in 1857 the area presently bounded by Fullerton, Western, Devon, and Lake Michigan was organized into Lake View Township; in 1872 residents built a town hall at Halsted and Addison; and in 1887 Lake View was incorporated as a city. In 1889, however, despite a controversial vote and the recalcitrance of Lake View officials, the city was annexed to Chicago.

The urbanizing Lake View attracted not only new residents, but also visitors to its burgeoning commercial and recreational facilities. A baseball park at Clark and Addison, later known as Wrigley Field (1914), attracted Chicagoans who lived outside Lake View. Wieboldt's Department Store (1917) anchored a new shopping district at the intersection of Lincoln, Belmont, and Ashland Avenues. Southwestern Lake View's working-class residential character merged with that of neighboring NORTH CENTER, as factory workers sought homes near their jobs. They occupied such subdivisions as Gross Park, which was laid out by Samuel Eberly Gross. Developers also built apartment buildings to accommodate residents who could not afford homes of the sort preferred by the old, suburban elite. In the mid-twentieth century, high-rise apartments and four-plus-ones (multiunit low-rises), both of which attracted single people and childless couples, were popular solutions to the growing housing problem.

The apparent changes in the family and architectural structures of Lake View alarmed some residents, who organized the Lake View Citizens Council in the 1950s to fight potential blight. LVCC quickly realized that Lake View was too well off for designation as a government conservation area, so it encouraged private redevelopment and rehabilitation instead. Residents and merchants used different strategies to preserve distinctive neighborhoods within Lake View. In the early 1970s, for example, East Lake View became known as New Town for its trendy shops and counterculture denizens. The elegant Alta Vista Terrace attained landmark status. A real-estate frenzy during the early 1980s drove neighborhoods such as Wrigleyville into public view.

The physical preservation of Lake View, however, did not reconfigure the area into a family-centered community. While some of the new residents, such as World War II Japanese American

Lake View town hall, built in 1872 at the corner of Halsted and Addison. Photographer: Unknown. Source: Chicago History Museum.

refugees from California and the increasing Latino population, did arrive in family units, most of Lake View's new population were single, childless young adults. As early as the 1950s, an identifiable gay male population resided in the Belmont Harbor area. According to the 1990 census, more than 22,000 residents of Lake View were between the ages of 25 and 44 and lived in "nonfamily" households.

Amanda Seligman

FURTHER READING: Andreas, A. T. *History of Cook County, Illinois, from the Earliest Period to the Present Time.* 1884.∎ Clark, Stephen Bedell. *The Lake View Saga.* 1985 [1974].

Lathrop Homes, neighborhood of public housing built by the Chicago Housing Authority in 1938 in the NORTH CENTER and LINCOLN PARK Community Areas. Named for the social reformer Julia C. Lathrop.

LeClaire Courts, low-rise public housing project along Cicero Avenue just south of the Stevenson Expressway in the GARFIELD RIDGE Community Area.

Lemont, IL, Cook, DuPage, and Will Counties,  24 miles SW of the Loop. Lemont lies in the Des Plaines River Valley, on the south bank of the Illinois & Michigan Canal. Few of Chicago's suburbs have been as strongly influenced by topography. The Des Plaines River at Lemont is deeply incised into surrounding glacial uplands. The village, established largely in response to impending development of the canal, was nestled between valley bluffs to the southeast and the river to the north. The I&M Canal, constructed along the south side of the river in 1848, left areas between the two waterways to be developed for industrial purposes. Lemont's downtown and residential districts grew between the canal and the valley walls.

The first attempt at settlement after the displacement of Indians was the "paper town" of Keepataw, platted in 1836, followed by Athens in 1839. Lemont proper was not incorporated until 1873, on land previously occupied by the defunct Keepataw.

Early development was guided by farseeing commercial magnates such as Nathaniel Brown and Horace Singer, who along with other major landowners controlled both the residential district and the flatlands in the floodplain. When canal digging revealed "Athens marble" not far beneath the valley's floor, Lemont became famous for its quarries. Used at first for the canal and local construction, the easily worked rock (a form of

Niagaran dolomite) soon became a major export. Chicago's Water Tower is built of this stone.

Work in the quarries and on area transportation links required a large labor force, supplied by European immigrants. The Irish came first, followed in the 1880s by Poles, Germans, and Scandinavians. Each group left its mark, perhaps none more indelible than that of the Polish congregation led by Father Moczygemba. Sent in 1882 to minister to the Polish settlers, this priest established the cohesive residential community of Jasnagora that sits above Lemont today.

Life was not easy for the immigrant laborers, who struggled against low pay and poor working conditions. Employers quashed several strikes with the assistance of state militia between 1885 and 1893. Competition from better-quality, cheaper Indiana stone, along with labor conflict, contributed to the decline of the quarries. Lemont was rescued from stagnation, however, by a manufacturing base that included activities as diverse as dairying, soda and beer bottling, cement and tile making, and clothing and shoe manufacturing. As the high-tech industry of its time, the Illinois Pure Aluminum Company (established 1892) provided a mainstay of employment for exactly a century. In 1922 the Globe Oil and Refining Company opened what was then the largest refinery in the state.

Lemont became noted during the 1920s for an abundance of large institutional landholdings. Forest preserves, golf courses, cemeteries, and ecclesiastical retreats began to cluster nearby. After World War II, these were joined by research installations such as the Argonne National Laboratory. More recently, the Lithuanians World Center and the Hindu Temple of Greater Chicago have added to the village's cosmopolitan flavor. Although they did not radically alter village life, these developments marked the start of a new era. Well into the 1960s, Lemont retained its identity as a small, spatially distinct canal town; with the growth of these religious and recreational functions, it began to attract people from throughout the Chicago area and to merge with the expanding metropolitan fringe.

Argonne National Laboratory, 1956. Photographer: Hubert Henry, Hedrich-Blessing. Source: Chicago History Museum.

In the 1970s Lemont suffered from industrial obsolescence and economic recession. At the same time, however, it drew on new resources from white-collar and professional families moving from Chicago to an expanding suburbia. With its inexpensive land and accessibility to employment centers, Lemont shared in the massive, area-wide growth of subdivision development.

Lemont moved to bring these subdivisions within its borders by actively annexing land to the south. A greater population required more services, leading to the emergence of a new urban core on the southern edge of town. This new center was unabashedly modern in tone, with shopping malls and parking lots designed for an automotive public. No longer contained by its valley, Lemont shed the uniquely isolated character of the older village.

John D. Schroeder

FURTHER READING: Buschman, Barbara, ed. *Lemont, Illinois: Its History in Commemoration of the Centennial of Its Incorporation.* 1972. ■ Conzen, Michael P., and Carl A. Zimring, eds. *Looking for Lemont: Place and People in an Illinois Canal Town.* 1994.

Levee, vice district around Cermak and State into the early twentieth century, in the NEAR SOUTH SIDE Community Area.

Libertyville, IL, Lake County, 33 miles NW of the Loop. George Vardin settled on a low ridge of ground on the west side of the upper Des Plaines River along the Chicago-Milwaukee Road in 1835. He thought that he could profit by platting a village on his farm site and called his plat "Vardin's Grove." When a post office was

established there in 1837, Vardin's Grove became known as Independence Grove. After postal authorities rejected that name, Archimedes Wynkoop rechristened the settlement as Libertyville.

When Lake County was split from McHenry County in 1839, some merchants worked to bring the county seat to Libertyville under the new name of Burlington. Their hope collapsed when Waukegan took the honor, and the name Libertyville was retained.

In the late 1860s Ansel Brainerd Cook, later a sidewalk contractor and president of the Chicago City Council, constructed a large, porticoed house in Libertyville along the Milwaukee Road. The house, which still stands as Libertyville's centerpiece, was located on Cook's horse farm, which provided power for Chicago horsecar lines.

The Chicago, Milwaukee & St. Paul Railroad (Chicago, Milwaukee, St. Paul & Pacific Railroad) built a line between Milwaukee and Chicago in 1872 that bypassed Libertyville. Walter C. Newberry, nephew of the founder of the Newberry Library and, like Cook, a Lake County real-estate speculator and Chicago politician, persuaded Libertyville's merchants to fund a three-mile spur line into town in 1880. The resulting railroad boom led Libertyville leaders to incorporate their community in 1882.

The architectural nature of Libertyville changed after a massive fire destroyed the business center in 1895 and the village board decreed that only brick buildings could be constructed in the downtown area.

In 1906 Samuel Insull purchased 160 acres south of the village. Unhappy with irregular electrical service in the area, Insull brought a number of rural generating plants together under the name of Commonwealth Edison in a successful experiment to improve reliability.

Insull acquired the Chicago & Milwaukee Electric line (renamed the Chicago, North Shore & Milwaukee), which had built a spur from Lake Bluff to Libertyville in 1903. Not only was this interurban line a major electricity consumer, but it also simplified Insull's commute from Chicago to his landholdings. By 1921 Insull's holdings around Libertyville grew to 4,445 acres, which he christened the Hawthorne-Mellody Farms.

In the mid-1930s the Great Depression left Insull's empire in ruins, and portions of the Hawthorne-Mellody Farms were sold to successful Chicagoans such as John F. Cuneo, owner of Cuneo Press; and Adlai Stevenson, Chicago attorney and later two-time presidential candidate.

When suburbanization intensified in the 1960s, owners of estates around Libertyville, many carved from the Hawthorne-Mellody Farms, successfully resisted efforts to subdivide the area.

In 2000 Libertyville was a commercial center for over 20,000 residents who enjoy a suburban commuter lifestyle in spacious conditions thanks to the historic acquisitions of Cook and Insull.

Craig L. Pfannkuche

FURTHER READING: *Libertyville Illustrated*. 1993. ■ *The Past and Present of Lake County, Illinois*. 1877. ■ Turner, Elisha R. *The Growth and Development of Libertyville*. 1974.

Lilydale, African American neighborhood in the Roseland Community Area.

Lincoln Park, Community Area 7, 3 miles N of

7
Lincoln Park

the Loop. During the nineteenth century, the inhabitants of the future Lincoln Park Community Area ranged from affluent residents focused on the park and the Loop, to German farmers and shopkeepers oriented toward North Avenue, to industrial workers living near the factories along the North Branch of the Chicago River. Most of the early European residents were German truck farmers, whose products earned the area the nickname "Cabbage Patch." By 1852 the German community was well enough established to begin work on St. Michael's Roman Catholic Church, which was named for the patron saint of local brewer and land donor Michael Diversey. The city of Chicago made the southeastern portion of the area its cemetery in 1837, but the

Girls' race at Adams Playground, 1919 N. Seminary, Chicago Special Park Commission, 1907. Photographer: Unknown. Source: Chicago Public Library.

graves proved such a health hazard that the cemetery was moved and the land redesignated Lake Park in 1864. It was renamed Lincoln Park the next year for the assassinated president. This recreational center attracted such cultural institutions as the Chicago Academy of Sciences, the Lincoln Park Zoo, and the Chicago History Museum (formerly the Chicago Historical Society). In 1863 Cyrus McCormick sponsored the opening of the Presbyterian Theological Seminary of the Northwest in northwestern Lincoln Park; the school was later renamed for its benefactor.

In 1871 the Great Fire swept through the North Side, including much of Lincoln Park, and destroyed most of the structures there. Residents rebuilt swiftly, with many finding housing in temporary wooden shacks before the city extended fire limits to the city boundaries in 1874. Dur-

ing the next decades, industrial plants such as furniture factories and the Deering Harvester Works concentrated along the North Branch of the river. Italians, Poles, Romanians, Hungarians, and Slovaks worked in these factories and established the working-class character of west Lincoln Park. The eastern sector remained an enclave of families of middle-class commuters, with expensive mansions fronting the park. Among the new institutions of the late nineteenth century was Crilly Court, an apartment complex designed by Daniel F. Crilly, who selected artists for tenants. In 1898 St. Vincent's College, renamed DePaul University in 1907, opened near the McCormick Seminary. By the early twentieth century, Lincoln Park was firmly established as a residential neighborhood that hosted some of Chicago's major cultural institutions.

Picnic Groves: Ogden's Grove

Ogden's Grove, Wright's Grove, Brand's Park, Hoffman Park, and Schutzenpark are among the picnic groves that dotted the Chicago metropolitan area well into the twentieth century. Many were located along rivers and streams, which provided a picturesque backdrop for summer outings. Popular especially among German immigrants, these groves were the scene of special events sponsored by churches, businesses, unions, and clubs. In July 1896, the Desplaines Hall Workers Club sponsored a picnic in Ogden's Grove, near North and Halsted, which was covered in the German-language newspaper Der Westen:

> Sunshine, woodland green and woodland shade, the sound of horns! on a Sunday afternoon, what more could a German heart possibly wish for?!—A good mug of beer!—
> "Fellow countryman," I asked the cashier as he accepted my 15 cents, "would you have a drop of beer, too?"
> "Oh, plenty!" answered the man from Holstein . . . "not to mention spirited company!"
> The Desplaines Hall Workers Club was having a picnic under the oak columns at Ogden's Grove. There was a large group with many women and children and there were so many other people there that all the tables and benches were taken.
> Cheerful groups everywhere, families and their friends taking of Sunday afternoon nectar, extra-strong coffee, and the ambrosia without which it wouldn't be complete in the form of "Stippels"-Topfkuchen [sweet bread made with yeasted dough, similar to coffee cake] and buttered almond cake. There, in all the different dialects of the dear German homeland, chatting and blabbering . . . and groups of young and old men and boys drinking beer . . . Ha! The Germans like nothing better than a party under the oaks! The life our forefathers had in the woods still clings to us.

Keil, Hartmut, and John B. Jentz. *German Workers in Chicago: A Documentary History of Working-Class Culture from 1850 to World War I.* 1988.

ern section of Lincoln Park, worried that their neighborhood hovered on the verge of becoming a slum. They formed the Old Town Triangle Association in 1948, which inspired Lincoln Park residents to create a similar organization in 1950. In 1954 the Lincoln Park Conservation Association was organized to cover the entire community area. LPCA pursued neighborhood renewal by encouraging private rehabilitation of property and the use of government tools such as federal urban renewal funds and enforcement of the housing code. In 1956 Lincoln Park was designated a conservation area, and in the 1960s the city began implementing its "General Neighborhood Renewal Plan." Although the LPCA had consciously tried to avoid the wholesale demolition that took place in HYDE PARK, it nonetheless incurred the wrath of poor people who lived in the southwestern quarter of Lincoln Park. The Concerned Citizens of Lincoln Park argued that Puerto Ricans and African Americans were being displaced from their homes and priced out of the renewing neighborhood. Developers bought land near the park and built high-rise apartment buildings, to the consternation of LPCA, which had hoped to keep the district congenial to families.

In the last quarter of the twentieth century, land values increased dramatically, making it difficult for people and institutions in financial straits to remain in Lincoln Park. Most of the poor left. In 1973 the struggling McCormick Seminary sold its land to DePaul and moved to Hyde Park. Single professionals and childless couples moved into the new high-rises and rehabilitated old houses. By the end of the century, the combination of public and private urban renewal efforts had made Lincoln Park one of the highest-status neighborhoods in the city.

Amanda Seligman

FURTHER READING: Bennett, Larry. *Fragments of Cities: The New American Downtowns and Neighborhoods.* 1990. ■ Ducey, Michael H. *Sunday Morning: Aspects of Urban Ritual.* 1977. ■ Pacyga, Dominic A., and Ellen Skerrett. *Chicago, City of Neighborhoods: Histories and Tours.* 1986.

During the Great Depression, Lincoln Park's housing stock deteriorated as owners subdivided and neglected their properties. After World War II, residents of OLD TOWN, in the southeast-

Lincoln Square, Community Area 4, 7 miles N of the Loop. The Lincoln Square Community Area has hosted a wide array of unrelated enterprises. The RAVENSWOOD residential subdivision was so influential that its name at one time stood for the whole area. Only after the vacant commercial spaces filled up after World War II did local merchants promote Lincoln Square as a cohesive neighborhood with a shopping district at its heart.

4
Lincoln
Square

Early commercial agriculture in the Lincoln Square area emphasized truck farming and the mass production of flowers, pickles, and celery. In 1836 Swiss immigrant Conrad Sulzer bought property near the present intersection of Montrose and Clark. Truck farmers, mostly of German and English descent, followed his example. They drove their produce in wagons down the old Little Fort Road (Lincoln Avenue) to market in Chicago. The celery crop gained such broad distribution that local growers proudly called the area the nation's celery capital. The Budlong brothers opened a successful pickle factory in 1857 and expanded into the flower business with the opening of Budlong Greenhouses in 1880. They employed Polish workers from Chicago on a seasonal basis. The increasing traffic along the old Little Fort Road encouraged the opening of many taverns for thirsty travelers.

Other investors promoted nonagricultural land use in Lincoln Square. Bowmanville, one of its first residential subdivisions, was developed in 1850 by a local hotel keeper who disappeared before his customers discovered that he did not own the land he had sold. Rosehill Cemetery, which occupies almost one quarter of the land in Lincoln Square, opened in 1859 around the site of Hiram Roe's tavern. The entrance faced the North Western Railroad stop at Rosehill Drive as an encouragement to mourners and picnickers to make day-long outings to the area. In 1868 the opening of another flag stop about a mile south of the cemetery inspired the building of the Ravenswood subdivision, an exclusive commuter suburb that encompassed Sulzer's original property. Ravenswood's success encouraged other real-estate speculators to create more local developments, such as Summerdale and Clybourn.

Electric street railways began running through Lincoln Square in the 1890s, and the Ravenswood Elevated opened in 1907. Both brought new residents to Lincoln Square. The area's farmland gradually began to fill up with bungalows, two-flats, and small apartment buildings; the names of two of the new developments, Ravenswood Gardens and Ravenswood Manor, traded on the area's residential history. Some land intended for residential use lay undeveloped until after World War II. Among the new residents were Greeks, whose many small businesses and St. Demetrios church (1929) set the stage for Lincoln Square to become the "new Greektown" when the old GREEKTOWN was displaced by construction of the Congress (now Eisenhower) Expressway and the University of Illinois at Chicago. An industrial corridor developed along the North Western Railway tracks on Ravenswood Avenue. One of the largest interests to locate there was Abbott Laboratories, founded in 1888 by local physician and pharmacist Wallace Calvin Abbott (1857–1921).

The common use of the name "Ravenswood" reflected Lincoln Square's residential image. Beginning in 1949, the Lincoln Square Chamber of Commerce promoted the area's commercial identity. The intersection at Lincoln, Lawrence, and Western Avenues had never been as popular as other regional shopping districts, and the growing number of empty storefronts after World War II made some merchants worry about their ability to attract customers. In 1956 they erected a statue of the late president Abraham Lincoln, for whom the area and its major street were named. In 1978 they developed the Lincoln Square mall, a pedestrian plaza that required a controversial rerouting of local traffic. The chamber tried to evoke an Old World flavor with European-style shops and a lantern imported from Hamburg, Germany. Many of the empty storefronts did indeed fill in; an increasing number of proprietors, however, were not of European descent, reflecting the fact that Latinos and Asians in Chicago found the family-friendly housing of Lincoln Square as attractive as previous generations had.

Amanda Seligman

FURTHER READING: Lake View–Ravenswood Historical Collection. Sulzer Regional Library, Chicago. ▪ Vivien M. Palmer Documents. Chicago History Museum, Chicago. ▪ Zatterberg, Helen. *An Historical Sketch of Ravenswood and Lake View.* 1941.

Lincolnwood, IL, Cook County, 10 miles NW of the Loop. Lincolnwood is an ethnically diverse, 2.5-square-mile suburb. Potawatomi originally settled the wooded area but vacated the land after the Indian Boundary Treaty of 1816. Rural development proceeded slowly on treacherous plank roads along present-day Milwaukee and Lincoln Avenues. Johann Tess, for whom the village was originally named, came with his family from Germany in 1856, purchasing 30 acres of barren land in the area. Population slowly increased, and the first commercial establishment, the Halfway House Saloon, was established in 1873.

The agrarian population grew after the establishment of a Chicago & North Western Railway station in nearby SKOKIE in 1891 and the completion of the North Shore Channel in 1909, which made the easily flooded prairie land manageable. More saloons and taverns soon appeared, specifically along Crawford and Lincoln Avenues. Because only organized municipalities could grant liquor licenses, 359 residents incorporated in 1911 and named the village Tessville. Tessville annexed land throughout the 1920s, finally stretching to Central Avenue on the west and Kedzie Avenue on the east. During Prohibition, Tessville became a haven for speakeasies and gambling facilities.

Tessville was reputed for drinking and gambling until the 1931 election of its longest-serving mayor, Henry A. Proesel, a grandson of George Proesel, one of the area's original American settlers. In 1932 Lincoln Avenue, formerly a plank toll road, became a state highway. Proesel then worked with the federal government's Public Works Administration and hired the community's entire unemployed workforce to plant 10,000 elm trees on the village streets. Most important, the community passed a law, in 1934, that limited the number of liquor licenses available within the city limits and became a model ordinance for other communities. Proesel finally changed Tessville's image when he renamed the village Lincolnwood in 1936.

Lincolnwood's institutions, industries, and clubs continued to grow along with the suburb. The Bryn Mawr Country Club (1919), the East Prairie Welfare Club, later to become the Lincolnwood Woman's Club (1927), the Lincolnwood Afternoon Club (1953), and American Legion Post #1226 (1952) helped create a sense of community in the village. School District 74 formed in 1938, and the Lincolnwood Public Library (1978) provided residents with quality education and offered much needed services. Bell & Howell's relocation to east Lincolnwood (1942) spurred growth and increased other industry relocation to the village. The Lincolnwood Jewish Congregation (1958) and St. John's Lutheran Church (1942) served residents' religious needs.

Significant population growth in Lincolnwood occurred with the opening of the Edens Expressway (1951). The village rapidly matured as a suburb, growing from 3,072 in 1950 to 12,929 in 1970. In 2000 Lincolnwood's population was 75 percent white, highly educated, and had a median household income of $71,234.

Laura Milsk

FURTHER READING: Lamm, Shirley, W. "Lincolnwood, Illinois: A Thesis." Master's thesis, Northeastern Illinois University. 1969. ▪ League of Women Voters of Skokie and Lincolnwood. *The Village of Lincolnwood.* 1973. ▪ *Lincolnwood Seventy-fifth Diamond Jubilee Celebration, 1911–1986.*

Little Italy. Chicago's Little Italy developed in the NEAR WEST SIDE around Halsted and Taylor Streets near Jane Addams's Hull House in the late nineteenth century. Upon their arrival in the area, Italians quickly established their own cultural, social, and religious institutions, such as Our Lady of Pompeii and the Holy Guardian Angel Roman Catholic churches. While Italians were never a majority in the area, they maintained a strong presence in the commercial and political fabric of the area throughout the twentieth century.

Max Grinnell

FURTHER READING: Cipriani, Lisi. *Italians in Chicago and the Selected Directory of the Italians in Chicago.* 1933. ■ DeRosa, Tina. *Paper Fish.* 1980. ■ Holli, Melvin G., and Peter A. Jones, eds. *Ethnic Chicago: A Multicultural Portrait.* 1995.

Little Village. Known by its residents as the "Mexico of the Midwest," Little Village, in the SOUTH LAWNDALE Community Area, has over the past 35 years joined PILSEN as a point of entry for Latino immigrants to Chicago. A gateway on 26th Street proclaims "Bienvenidos a Little Village." Neighborhood organizations like the United Neighborhood Organization have sought to curb gang violence and foster a sense of community solidarity. Little Village hosts the largest annual Latino parade in Chicago, drawing hundreds of thousands of spectators each September.

Erik Gellman

FURTHER READING: Adelman, William J. *Pilsen and the West Side: A Tour Guide to Ethnic Neighborhoods, Architecture, Restaurants, Wall Murals, and Labor History with Special Emphasis on Events Connected with the Great Upheaval of 1877.* 1977. ■ Padilla, Felix M. *Latino Ethnic Consciousness: The Case of Mexican-Americans and Puerto Ricans in Chicago.* 1985.

Lockport, IL, Will County, 30 miles SW of the  Loop. Lockport, located in the Des Plaines River Valley, grew initially as the headquarters for the Illinois & Michigan Canal and as an agricultural processing center. The agricultural

CHICAGO

Lockport

promise of the area increased when a local farmer developed a steel plow in 1835.

The original town of the 1830s and 1840s was mainly populated by Yankees, and a part of the town was called "Yankee Settlement." The other element was recently emigrated Irish farmers and laborers. By the 1860s there was an increasing number of German emigrants who were merchants and farmers. The late nineteenth century brought an influx of Scandinavians and a few African Americans who worked on the Sanitary and Ship Canal. Italians, mostly from northern Italy, worked in factories in the area. The town's population remained stable until the late 1980s when new residences were built for an influx of urbanites and close-in suburbanites.

Lockport was platted and named by the Illinois & Michigan Canal commissioners in 1837 as the canal headquarters. Chief engineer William Gooding saw the water-power potential of the site, which is 40 feet higher than JOLIET, four miles to the south. Gooding supervised construction of a headquarters building and stone warehouse. The canal opened in 1848, and in 1853 Lockport residents incorporated as a town.

The canal grain trade dominated the town's early economy, and the 1858 arrival of the Chicago & Alton Railroad did little to change this. Hiram Norton oversaw an extensive canal operation devoted to grain shipping and processing. His water-powered flour mill was one of the largest in northern Illinois, and along with other hydraulic-powered production facilities and a number of canal boats, made him one of the wealthiest residents in the 1860s.

The construction of the Sanitary and Ship Canal after 1895 halted the grain trade on the old canal, and the Norton Company went bankrupt. The construction of the Calumet-Sag Channel north of Lockport, which began in 1911, cut off most of the water power to the town, and the remaining mills closed.

The area's economy revived after 1911 when the Texas Company (Texaco), built its first refinery outside the Southwest on the northern boundary of Lockport. In addition, area railroads began running commuter trains to Chicago; the 1901 opening of the Chicago & Joliet Electric Railway encouraged commuting between Lockport, Joliet, and Chicago.

In the 1980s the closure of the Texaco refinery and other industrial plants in the area signaled yet another economic and social shift. History became a focus of commercial development. In 1968 the Will County Historical Society had opened a canal museum in the old I&M Canal headquarters building. The Gaylord Building, built in 1837 to store canal construction materials, was acquired by the National Trust for Historic Preservation and is now operated as a museum by the Canal Corridor Association. The old downtown was made a historical district in 1974 and Lockport began calling itself "the Old Canal Town." In the 1980s restaurants, antique shops, and specialty retailers opened in the historic district. In addition, population shifts in the metropolitan area drew residential developers. The closing decades of the twentieth century brought not only history but also strip malls, fast-food outlets, and other elements of urban sprawl. Population grew from 9,401 in 1990 to 15,191 in 2000.

John Lamb

FURTHER READING: Conzen, Michael, and Adam Daniel, eds. *Lockport Legacy: Themes in the Historical Geography of an Illinois Canal Town.* 1990. ■ Lamb, John. *Lockport, Illinois: The Old Canal Town.* 1999. ■ LeBaron, W. *History of Will County.* 1878.

Logan Square, Community Area 22, 5 miles NW

22
Logan Square

of the Loop. Logan Square is a large, densely populated community. Long home to immigrant populations, it is now predominantly Hispanic. Logan Square is graced with a system of tree-lined boulevards and squares, including the one for which the community is named. The area is bounded on the east by the North Branch of the Chicago River and bisected diagonally by Milwaukee Avenue, one of Chicago's main commercial thoroughfares.

The open prairie that would become Logan Square lay beyond Chicago's borders in 1836, when New Yorker Martin Kimbell laid claim to 160 acres there. Other settlers soon joined Kimbell in what was then the town of Jefferson. Beginning in 1850, farmers in Logan Square and beyond could haul their produce to market along the North West Plank Road (later Milwaukee Avenue), which followed the path of an Indian trail angling northwest out of Chicago. Several years later, the Chicago & North Western Railway laid its tracks just west of the river. Industries soon followed. In 1863 Chicago annexed the territory east of Western Avenue and south of Fullerton. (This neighborhood—now BUCKTOWN—was known as Holstein for its population of German factory workers.) Six years later, the area just to the north (east of Western, between Fullerton and the river) became part of the city.

Logan Square grew more rapidly after the fire of 1871. Because the area lay outside Chicago's fire limits, moderately priced frame houses immediately appeared, especially in suburban Maplewood, south and west of the Chicago & North Western Railway's new Maplewood station at Diversey Avenue, and along Milwaukee Avenue. By 1884 Maplewood's population had reached 6,000. (A second early subdivision, Pennock, in northwestern Logan Square, failed to thrive until the following decade.) With the extension of the Milwaukee Avenue street railway line to Armitage and then Belmont, German and Scandinavian immigrants increasingly moved northwestward into the area.

Chicago annexed the remainder of Logan Square in 1889. The "L" arrived the following year, and new homes quickly encircled the Fullerton and Milwaukee Avenue stations. Shortly thereafter, the city paved and planted the boulevard system, planned years before by the West Park Commission. The solid graystone two- and three-flats and substantial single-family houses of upwardly mobile Scandinavians and Germans soon lined Logan, Kedzie, and Humboldt Boulevards and Logan and Palmer Squares.

After World War I, Logan Square boomed. Even as earlier-arriving immigrants moved further out Milwaukee Avenue, Poles and Russian Jews arrived to take their place. Construction of rental apartments and flats continued unabated. In 1925 developers claimed the last sizable tract of open land, the Logan Square Ball Park at Milwaukee and Sawyer.

Vibrant Logan Square began to fade shortly thereafter. Population fell gradually after 1930. Older frame residences on the community's industrial eastern edge deteriorated. In the late 1950s construction of the Northwest (Kennedy) Expressway effectively severed this district from the rest of Logan Square, prompting residents to depart. Construction of the Dearborn/Milwaukee subway (now the Blue Line) disrupted commercial life in central Logan Square in the following decade.

In the early 1960s, however, Logan Square saw the first signs of a resurgence that has lasted into the twenty-first century. In 1963 area residents formed the Logan Square Neighborhood Association, a group that has worked ever since to improve housing and community spirit. In the succeeding decades, young urban professionals purchased and rehabilitated many of the fine houses along the boulevards, obtaining recognition of the corridor as a National Register district in the 1980s. The oldest portion of Logan Square, the Bucktown neighborhood in the community's southeast corner, has become a haven for artists.

Today Logan Square exhibits a vital ethnic and economic diversity. Its population has fallen less rapidly than that of Chicago as a whole, thanks to an influx of Hispanics since 1960. By 1990 Hispanics made up almost two-thirds of Logan Square's population, comprising the largest Puerto Rican, Cuban, and South and Central American populations in Chicago, together with a sizable Mexican community. Yet Polish can still be heard in the streets alongside English and Spanish. And while upper-middle-class professionals own the solid houses along the boulevards and new and rehabilitated town houses in gentrifying Bucktown, the majority of Logan Square's residents continue to live in the community's many rental flats and apartments.

Elizabeth A. Patterson

FURTHER READING: Andreas, A. T. *History of Cook County Illinois.* 1884. ■ Chicago Fact Book Consortium, ed. *Local Community Fact Book: Chicago Metropolitan Area, 1990.* 1995. ■ Newspaper clippings in hardcopy and on microfilm. Municipal Reference Collection, Harold Washington Library, Chicago.

Lombard, IL, DuPage County, 20 miles W of the  Loop. Lombard shares its early history with Glen Ellyn. Brothers Ralph and Morgan Babcock settled in a grove of trees along the DuPage River. In what was known as Babcock's Grove, Lombard developed to the east and Glen Ellyn to west. In 1837 Babcock's Grove was connected to Chicago by a stagecoach line that stopped at Stacy's Tavern at Geneva and St. Charles Roads. Fertile land, the DuPage River, and plentiful timber drew farmers to the area.

Sheldon and Harriet Peck moved from Onondaga, New York, to this area in 1837. They claimed 80 acres of land, which they farmed. Sheldon Peck was also an artist and primitive portrait painter who traveled to clients across northeastern Illinois. The Peck house also served as the area's first school and has been restored by the Lombard Historical Society.

In 1849 the Galena & Chicago Union Railroad ran two trains daily each way through Babcock's Grove. Farmers began to send their goods to Chicago along the railroad, quickly putting the stagecoach line out of business. Soon a post office, a general store, and a hotel emerged near the train station. German farmers joined the early Yankee and New York settlers.

Josiah Lombard, a Chicago banker, purchased 227 acres of land in 1868 and headed a group of capitalists who registered the first plat and spearheaded the incorporation of Lombard in 1869. Lombard hoped the area would develop as a commuter center. Stylish Victorian homes appeared on North Main Street (the Lombard Historical Museum maintains a house museum in the style of one of these homes, circa 1870s). The Maple Street Chapel, which is now on the National Register of Historic Places, was constructed in 1870 to serve a growing population.

While commuters came, industry also developed. The Lombard train station was a "milk stop" for area farmers, and a cheese factory and creamery operated for many years. Conflicts between farmers and commuters included temperance. After attempts to shut down saloons in Lombard were rejected numerous times in the nineteenth century, temperance advocates prevailed in 1911.

In 1910 William R. Plum, a retired Chicago lawyer, Civil War veteran, and Lombard resident, began collecting lilacs. The Plum garden became known as Lilacia, where over two hundred varieties of the flowering bush grew. In 1927 William and Helen Plum donated their estate to the village. The garden became a park, their home a public library. In 1929 the landscape artist Jens Jensen was hired by the Lombard Park District to design the park. The first Lilac Festival was held the following year and continues annually during May.

Between 1906 and 1957 the Chicago, Aurora & Elgin Railway provided passenger service on its interurban line. By 1920 the number of residents increased to 1,331. During the 1920s a new high school, a paving program, and the development of the Lombard Park District increasingly made Lombard attractive to new residents. The DuPage Theatre opened in 1928 with a starlit sky and gilded pillars. A significant population increase occurred after World War II. Throughout the 1950s new homes and shopping centers were built, and by 1960 the population reached 22,561. Lombard remained primarily residential until the 1970s, when the 75-acre Yorkbrook Industrial Park and the 200-acre Clearing Industrial District were developed. The population reached 42,322 by 2000.

Elizabeth M. Holland

FURTHER READING: Budd, Lillian. *Footsteps on the Tall Grass Prairie: A History of Lombard, Illinois.* 1977. ■ Fruehe, Margot. "Lombard." In *DuPage Roots,* ed. Richard A. Thompson, 191–99. 1985. ■ Knoblauch, Marion, ed. *DuPage County: A Descriptive and Historical Guide, 1831–1939.* 1948.

Long Grove, IL, Lake County, 29 miles NW of the Loop. The 1838 survey maps show large groves of oaks standing in bluestem prairie along the southern boundary of Lake County, one of them labeled "Long Grove." Before 1840, a Yankee, John Gridley, settled at a minor trail crossing deep in the grove.

German immigrants to the area in the mid-1840s discovered that the open prairie had already been claimed and made their claims within the wooded area. A post office established in 1847 under the name Muttersholz ("Mother's Woods") highlights the area's strong German influence. By the early 1850s immigrant families who had split from the Roman Catholic parish at BUFFALO GROVE founded their own St. Mary's parish at Muttersholz. An Evangelical Lutheran congregation formed at the same time.

Recruitment during the Civil War and industrial opportunities in Chicago drained away most of the area's remaining Yankee families, leaving German as the most commonly spoken language. Most families had their origins in the Rhineland and spoke in a Plattdeutsch dialect until nativist hostility to German culture during World War I impelled residents to make greater use of English. Muttersholz then became Long Grove once again. The cultural isolation of the small community, which had grown from 161 in 1870 to only 640 in 1960, deepened as the area's major roads, Routes 53 and 83, bypassed the still rural country crossroad.

Many of the community's young men who left to fight in World War II stayed away, leaving behind old farms filled with German-crafted oak furniture and tools. When the Fanning family opened their Farmside Store in Long Grove in 1947, they found that well-to-do Chicagoans were interested in acquiring antiques from their resale store, and Long Grove quickly established a reputation as a center for the growing antique trade.

This commerce drew the attention of developers. In the early 1950s area property owners formed an association to oppose a major development plan, countering with a village plat that would require a minimum lot size of three acres, with the aim of preserving the area's historic character. Following litigation between developers and the association, a referendum was passed in 1956 that incorporated the village of Long Grove. Guy Reed became the village's first president. After Reed's death in 1959, new president Robert Coffin pushed to retain the village's antique style through ordinances prohibiting neon signs and the development of convenience and chain stores. Any new business construction had to feature 1880s-style facades.

The hundreds of daily visitors who come to Long Grove's numerous craft and antique shops generate so much sales tax revenue that, as of the mid-1990s, no property taxes were levied and all municipal services were contracted. The low-density development objectives set forth in the village's 1973 comprehensive plan were reflected in the community's growth from 2,013 residents in 1980 to 6,735 in 2000.

Craig L. Pfannkuche

FURTHER READING: Michaelson, Mike. "One of a Kind." *North Shore Magazine*, July 1992, 81–94. ■ Park, Virginia L. *Long Grove Lore and Legend*. 1978. ■ Wittner, Dale. "Long Grove." *Chicago Tribune*, November 6, 1977.

Loop, Community Area 32. The Loop is the popular name for the Chicago business district located south of the main stem of the Chicago River. The name apparently derives from the place where the electrified loops powering cable cars turned around on a pulley in the center of the

32
Loop

city. The concept was extended to the ring of elevated rail tracks for rapid transit lines connecting downtown with the neighborhoods. Completed in 1897, this loop created an integrated intracity transportation system that helped insure the dominance of Chicago's historic core in the development of the metropolis. All of Chicago's nineteenth-century railroad depots were located at the edges of the central business district, creating a circle of stations around the hub of the city.

Jean Baptiste Point de Sable established a trading post on the north bank of the Chicago River in the late 1780s. Fort Dearborn followed on the opposite side in 1803–1804. South Water Street, along the south bank, became a hub of activity in the 1830s, with Lake Street, a block to the south, soon picking up the character of a retail street. In the period of the walking city the Loop area accommodated all of the functions of the city near the main stem of the river.

The diversity of the population in the center city meant that most of Chicago's older ethnic groups can point to origins in the city's historic core. As early as the 1850s the area south and west from State and Madison Streets had a German character, although people of every background lived there, including Irish and African Americans. As the commercial district expanded toward the railroad stations, it pushed areas of blight, vice, and transient housing just ahead of it, often creating pockets of inexpensive housing just beyond the depots.

The Civil War brought rapid growth downtown, encouraged by the use of streetcars, which first appeared along State Street in 1859. At the war's end Potter Palmer engineered the shift of retail commerce from Lake Street to State Street by erecting a splendid hotel, a large commercial emporium, and other mercantile buildings along State Street. This reorientation of the business district was well under way when the 1871 fire destroyed most residential buildings, as well as historic church and school buildings, in the heart of the city.

The rise of the skyscraper in the 1880s rein-

Clark Street at Jackson Boulevard, 1929. Photographer: Underwood & Underwood. Source: The Newberry Library.

forced the trend toward commercial growth, creating a distinct character for the downtown district and establishing a skyline as the symbol for the entire city.

Improvements in transportation enabled the residents of the expanding city to maintain contact with the center. State Street's horsecars were replaced by cable cars in 1882, and these in turn yielded to electric trolleys in 1906. Gasoline buses joined the trolleys in 1927, and construction began on the State Street subway in 1938. Until 1950 citizens of Chicago had two neighborhoods: their particular residential area and downtown, a common destination for work, recreation, government, and shopping. The number of passengers entering and leaving the Loop peaked in 1948, reaching almost a million per day in each direction, with a quarter of the total traveling by private automobile.

After 1950 the outward pull of suburban development in the new automobile metropolis reduced the importance of the Loop in the daily lives of many Chicagoans. It no longer functioned as a second neighborhood for so many citizens, and retail sales downtown accounted for a much smaller portion of the metropolitan total. An extension of the central business district northward along Michigan Avenue kept a luxury shopping district close by, and a return of residential buildings downtown brought back aspects of the old walking city. Cooperation between the city government, led by Richard J. Daley, and business leaders, supported by a steady flow of state and federal funds, produced a building boom of unprecedented scale to provide offices for corporations, banks, and governmental agencies, as well as hotel rooms for visitors and expanded facilities for cultural and educational institutions.

Gerald A. Danzer

FURTHER READING: Duis, Perry. *Chicago: Creating New Traditions.* 1976. ■ Holt, Glen E., and Dominic A. Pacyga. *Chicago: A Historical Guide to the Neighborhoods: The Loop and South Side.* 1979. ■ Johnson, Earl Shephard. "The Natural History of the Central Business District with Particular Reference to Chicago." Ph.D. diss., University of Chicago. 1941.

Lower West Side, Community Area 31, 3 miles SW of Loop. The Lower West Side has served as a point of entry to Chicago for working-class immigrants from a broad range of ethnic groups. The area is bounded on the south and east by the

31
Lower
West Side

Chicago River, and on the north and west by the Burlington Northern Railroad tracks. Though the area remained somewhat isolated for much of its history, its neighborhoods—especially PILSEN and Heart of Chicago—have been vibrant and dynamic enclaves for generations of Bohemians, Germans, Poles, and Mexicans.

The oldest sector was settled predominantly by Bohemians displaced by the Chicago Fire of 1871 and was dubbed "Pilsen" after one of the largest cities in their homeland. Pilsen grew into a major manufacturing center and remained heavily industrial into the twentieth century. Germans and later Slavs worked alongside Czechs and Bohemians in diverse industries: from Schoenhofen Brewery (18th and Canalport) and the lumberyards along the river to Chicago Stove Works Foundry (22nd and Blue Island) and McCormick Reaper Works (22nd and Western). Neighborhood residents unionized in the 1880s, founded Roman Catholic and Protestant churches, published newspapers in several languages, organized meetings of Freethinkers, and formed benevolent groups (Thalia Hall, 18th and Allport, 1892; Gads Hill Social Settlement House, 22nd and Robey/Damen, 1898) to aid newly arriving immigrants.

The area around Cermak Road and Damen (originally Robey) Street, lying between Pilsen and SOUTH LAWNDALE, was known as Heart of Chicago. First settled by Germans and Irish in the 1860s and 1870s, its population was largely Polish (with lesser numbers of Slovenians and Italians) by the turn of the century. Like their immigrant neighbors, Germans established their own schools, churches, and newspapers. In 1889 they founded St. Paul Federal Savings and Loan, which made home ownership possible for many generations of immigrants throughout the Chicago area. Like the Bohemians who moved to South Lawndale, many Poles moved westward from Pilsen as they accumulated resources, buying property in Heart of Chicago and establishing their own ethnic institutions. Some charitable associations and churches even returned to help poorer Pilsen neighbors

Migrants to Chicago

Thea Kronborg was a rather incurious migrant to Chicago in Willa Cather's *The Song of the Lark* (1915):

> During this first winter Thea got no city consciousness. Chicago was simply a wilderness through which one had to find one's way. She felt no interest in the general briskness and zest of the crowds. The crash and scramble of that big, rich, appetent Western city she did not take in at all, except to notice that the noise of the drays and street-cars tired her. The brilliant window displays, the splendid furs and stuffs, she scarcely noticed.

In contrast, the heroine of Theodore Dreiser's *Sister Carrie* (1900) is interested in Chicago from the moment she debarks a train from Wisconsin:

> The entire metropolitan center possessed a high and mighty air calculated to overawe and abash the common applicant, and to make the gulf between poverty and success seem both wide and deep.
> Into this important commercial region the timid Carrie now wended her way. She walked east along Van Buren Street through a region of lessening importance until it deteriorated into a mass of shanties and coalyards and finally verged upon the river. She walked bravely forward, led by an honest desire to find employment and delayed at every step by the interest of the unfolding scene, and a sense of helplessness amid so much evidence of power and force which she did not understand. These vast buildings, what were they? These strange energies and huge interests—for what purposes were they there?

through missions, including the Bethlehem Congregational Church missions (1890), which advocated temperance, and Howell Neighborhood House (1905).

Until the 1930s the Lower West Side continued as a center of ethnic group development with fairly stable working-class populations. The hardships of the Great Depression and the housing crisis during World War II, however, strained community and individual resources. In the 1950s many of the industries that formed the economic backbone of these neighborhoods closed their plants, including International Harvester; others relocated to the suburbs of Chicago.

Just as the prospects for Lower West Side residents began to look bleak, urban renewal in the NEAR WEST SIDE coupled with the completion of the Stevenson Expressway (1964) to revitalize the area. Mexican families, many of whom had lived on the Near West Side since the 1920s, resettled further south in Pilsen, while the Stevenson provided ready access to the LOOP and other parts of Chicago. As the meatpacking houses of the stockyards district shut down (1950s), many Mexican residents migrated north into Pilsen and LITTLE VILLAGE. Throughout the 1960s and 1970s, Mexicans from the southwestern United States, Puerto Ricans, and African Americans (many from NORTH LAWNDALE) also settled there. Like previous groups, Mexicans set up their own institutions and practices. Howell Neighborhood House became Casa Aztlán; Benito Juárez High School was created in 1977; and the Mexican Fine Arts Center Museum opened in 1987. Mexican and Chicana/o artists painted numerous murals celebrating Mexican culture. Fiesta del Sol celebrations have been held since 1973; street parades annually celebrate Mexican Independence Day (September 16); and Posada processions are held during the Christmas season.

Pilsen retains its character as a point of entry for poor and working-class migrants. Restaurants and bodegas line 18th Street, its commercial center, and evoke the residents' homelands: the many regions of Mexico and other Latin American countries including El Salvador, Guatemala, Chile, Puerto Rico, and Cuba. Legal aid and mutual benefit societies continue to struggle against poverty and discrimination. And some still follow the westward drift of previous residents.

Gabriela F. Arredondo

FURTHER READING: Casuso, Jorge, and Eduardo Camacho. *Hispanics in Chicago*. 1985. ■ Pacyga, Dominic A., and Ellen Skerrett. "Lower West Side." In *Chicago, City of Neighborhoods: Histories and Tours*. 1986. ■ Reichman, John J. *Czechoslovaks of Chicago: Contributions to a History of a National Group*. 1937.

Lyons, IL, Cook County, 11 miles SW of the Loop.

The marshy region at what is now 47th and Harlem separates waters that flow into the Great Lakes from those that flow into the Mississippi River. During wet seasons Native Americans could travel from the South Branch of the Chiacgo River to the Des Plaines River through an area called Mud Lake.

The origin of the town name is uncertain; local lore suggests a relation to Lyon, France, a town at the confluence of two rivers, similarly defined by its relation to bodies of water. David and Bernardus Laughton established a trading post and tavern in the late 1820s near the confluence of Salt Creek and the Des Plaines River. Construction on the Illinois & Michigan Canal brought workers to the region. German farmers settled here, but growth was slow, in part owing to fear of prairie fires. A large brewery began operations in 1856, and two years later Lyons joined with other towns in petitioning for a railroad to be built through their towns.

By the early 1880s a thriving limestone quarry and lime kilns, a flour mill, and numerous taverns constituted the town's major commercial enterprises. Harvesting ice from the Des Plaines River provided seasonal employment. A Roman Catholic church opened in 1876, and a Lutheran church served the large German community. By the 1880s Polish immigrants arrived in significant numbers.

Formal incorporation came in 1888, and in 1897 the small town of Cooksville was transferred to Lyons from adjoining RIVERSIDE. In the early twentieth century one commentator referred to Lyons as "bibulous . . . the chosen abode of Bacchus and Terpsichore." A more restrained observer characterized Lyons as "quaint" and traditional, and noted that there were "unlimited possibilities" for the development of the town.

Progressive-era reformers targeted the town for change, but in 1908 a vote to abolish saloons lost by a lopsided 244–14 margin. Not surpris-

ingly, one of the most influential men in town was a brewer, George Hofmann Jr. In 1908 he built a dam on the Des Plaines River in order to generate water power, and adjacent to the dam he erected the Hofmann Tower, the center of a park complete with boat rides on the river.

The paving of Ogden Avenue in 1914 expedited auto travel, and the Chicago & Joliet Electric Railway made the town even more accessible. Amusement parks and taverns continued, even during Prohibition. Residential development boomed after 1945, when most of the town's available land was converted to housing. The last amusement park closed in the 1970s, as did the red-light district.

The population of 10,255 in 2000 was ethnically varied, although there were relatively few African Americans. Lyons's reputation as a residential, blue-collar town has not diminished over the years, and there are still many taverns. Metra's Burlington Northern Santa Fe line provides easy access to Chicago. The Chicago Portage National Historic Site, located in Ottawa Trail Woods, is a place where the Native American and French pasts mingle with the present. Hofmann Tower remains a local landmark and is on the National Register of Historic Places.

Ronald S. Vasile

FURTHER READING: Andreas, A. T. *History of Cook County Illinois.* 1884. ■ Benedetti, Rose Marie. *Village on the River, 1888–1988.* 1988. ■ *Lyons Diamond Jubilee, 1888–1963.* 1963.

Madison-Crawford, major mid-twentieth-century shopping district in the WEST GARFIELD PARK Community Area.

Magnificent Mile. Chicago's North Michigan Avenue, one of the city's most prestigious com-

Plan of Chicago: Michigan Avenue northward. From a rendering by Jules Guerin. Source: Chicago History Museum.

mercial and residential thoroughfares, extends north from the Loop to Oak Street and the Drake Hotel in the Near North Side Community Area. Named the Magnificent Mile in the 1940s by developer Arthur Rubloff, it includes the Wrigley Building, Tribune Tower, London Guarantee Building, Palmolive Building, and the John Hancock Center.

The Magnificent Mile was proposed in Daniel Burnham's 1909 *Plan of Chicago* and constructed in the 1920s. The avenue replaced the former Pine Street, which was lined with warehouses and factory buildings near the river, then large mansions and row houses as it passed through the neighborhoods of McCormickville and Streeterville. Its most famous monuments, the Water Tower and Pumping Station, are among the oldest structures in Chicago.

Buildings constructed on the avenue during the economic boom of the 1920s were characterized by historicist architectural styles that ranged from Beaux Arts classicism and Gothic revival to vertical-style modernism. As the buildings soared to new and unprecedented heights, each with a different stylistic elaboration and tower profile, there evolved a new definition of urban context and design compatibility.

A renewed surge of development occurred in the late 1940s after the Great Depression and war years amid escalating property values, growing rental demands, and liberalized zoning laws that allowed for even greater building heights. Much of the interest in the avenue was due to a strategic marketing campaign initiated by Rubloff, who proposed a plan by the architectural firm Holabird & Root for the construction of new buildings, the renovation of many existing ones, the addition of a park, and a more efficient traffic and parking system. Rubloff and a New York partner, William Zeckendorf, bought or gained management control of much of the property along the avenue, still at Depression-level prices, and proceeded to develop and promote it as the most prestigious address in the city, a distinction it continues to hold today.

John W. Stamper

FURTHER READING: Burnham, Daniel H., and Edward H. Bennett. *Plan of Chicago.* 1909. ■ Condit, Carl W. *Chicago, 1910–29: Building, Planning, and Urban Technology.* 1973. ■ Stamper, John W. *Chicago's North Michigan Avenue: Planning and Development 1900–1930.* 1991.

Maplewood, post–1871 fire commuter rail suburb, now part of the LOGAN SQUARE Community Area.

Markham, IL, Cook County, 20 miles S of the Loop. Comprising five square miles, Markham is bordered by Posen and Midlothian to the north, HARVEY to the east, Hazel Crest and Country Club Hills to the south, and Oak Forest to the west. Markham shares a history with all of these communities, especially Harvey, which contains the Markham Yards of the Illinois Central Railroad.

Interstate 57 traverses the community, northeast to southwest, along a line that has both geological and historic significance. Markham is located on a lake plain formed by glacial Lake Chicago (12,000 years ago), and Interstate 57 follows the line of the Tinley Moraine. Native Americans had long lived on the Tinley Moraine. Archaeologists have investigated the Oak Forest site, which was occupied in the 1600s. Interstate 57 also runs along the route of an Indian Boundary Line. The Potawatomi ceded the lands northwest of this line to the United States government in the 1816 Treaty of St. Louis.

Yankee farmers arrived in the mid-1830s, followed in the 1840s and 1850s by German and Irish immigrants. The settlers bypassed the marshy areas that today are Markham's most celebrated natural features: the Old Indian Boundary Prairies. German immigrants planted 60 pine seedlings from the Black Forest, one of which survived until 1985 and is depicted on Markham's city seal.

Both the Illinois Central and the Rock Island (Chicago, Rock Island & Pacific) Railroads run near Markham, enabling farmers to ship their produce by rail. In the early twentieth century, new residents were drawn by railroad and industrial jobs found in northern neighbor Harvey. They built houses and incorporated Markham in 1925, naming their town in honor of Charles H. Markham, then president of the Illinois Central Railroad.

African Americans moved into Markham during the second half of the twentieth century, as they took up the industrial jobs European immigrants had held earlier in the century. By the 2000 census, 80 percent of Markham's population of 12,620 was African American, and 84 percent of homes were owner-occupied.

Dave Bartlett

FURTHER READING: "Featuring Bremen Township." *Where the Trails Cross* 7.1 (Fall 1976): 1–3. ■ Bluhm, Elaine A., and Gloria J. Fenner. "The Oak Forest Site." In *Chicago Area Archaeology,* 2nd ed., ed. Elaine Blum, 139–161. 1983. ■ *History of Oak Forest.* 1972.

Marquette Manor, streetcar suburb developed after 1911 in what is now the GAGE PARK Community Area.

Marquette Park. Residents of CHICAGO LAWN often refer to their neighborhood as Marquette Park, after the 300-acre park at Marquette Road (6700 south) and California Avenue.

Matteson, IL, Cook County, 26 miles S of the Loop. The village of Matteson is located along the Metra Electric commuter rail line and sits astride Interstate 57 and the Lincoln Highway. Although a largely residential community, the village is the site of several corporate office buildings and the Lincoln Mall (1973), one of the largest shopping centers in the south suburbs.

In the mid-1850s, German settlers established the village at the junction of the recently constructed Illinois Central and Michigan Central Railroads, naming it after then Illinois governor Joel Matteson. When Matteson was formally incorporated in 1889, there were fewer than 500 residents in the village, which served area farmers.

After World War II Matteson grew steadily, reaching a population of 3,225 in 1960. By 1970 the village numbered 4,741, a figure that more than doubled, to 10,223, by 1980. In 2000 there were 12,928 people living in Matteson.

Population growth brought greater diversity. In 1970 the census listed only one African American in the community. By 1990, when the total population had climbed to 11,378 people, the 5,000 African American residents accounted for nearly half the population. In 2000 the 8,098 African American residents outnumbered white residents nearly two to one.

In the mid-1990s Matteson gained national media attention, and some notoriety, after the village board initiated an advertising campaign to seek new white residents. Village officials claimed it was simply an effort to maintain an integrated community and asserted that there were similar programs in other suburbs. Critics noted that many of the African Americans who were moving into the community were wealthier and better educated than the white former residents.

As Matteson has flourished over the last 50 years, there have been some substantial alterations in its geography. Originally platted on a 40-acre parcel, the village has grown a hundredfold, through the annexation of several housing subdivisions, and now occupies more than 7 square miles. In 2000 there were some 4,712 housing units in the village, nearly two-thirds of them constructed in the last 30 years. Old Matteson, as the community's original center is sometimes called, has some of the feel of a traditional village, especially near Main Street and the railroad. Most of the village's stores, however, are located along the heavily commercialized Lincoln Highway and in two large shopping centers. In the late 1990s Matteson officials created a "village commons" with a village hall and a bridge over Interstate 57.

Matteson is not the most exclusive of Chicago's south suburbs, but its median household income is substantially higher than in either the city of Chicago or Cook County. More than 80 percent of the houses in the village are single-family. As is the case in other nearby suburbs, new houses tend to be more expensive than the smaller older residences.

Ian McGiver

FURTHER READING: Andreas, A. T. *History of Cook County, Illinois.* 1884.

Maxwell Street For a century, Maxwell Street, located in the NEAR WEST SIDE Community Area, was one of Chicago's most unconventional business and residential districts. About a mile long and located in the shadow of downtown skyscrapers, it was a place where businesses could grow selling anything from shoestrings to expensive clothes.

Immigrants arrived from several continents and many countries shortly before the turn of the century. First to come were Germans, Irish, Poles, Bohemians, and, most prominently, Jews, especially those escaping czarist Russia, Poland, and Romania. In the 1940s southern blacks worked in Maxwell Street's stores and entertained its crowds with Delta blues. Later, Mexicans, Koreans, and Gypsies joined its teeming environment. From the area's poverty-stricken homes came both the famous—Arthur Goldberg, William Paley, Benny Goodman, Barney Ross—and the infamous—Jake Guzik and Jack Ruby.

Goods on card tables and blankets competed with goods in sidewalk kiosks and stores. Sunday was its busiest day since the Jews worked on the Christian Sabbath, when stores were closed in most other parts of the city.

Merchants battled city officials to keep Maxwell Street alive despite its reputation for crime and residential overcrowding. Its eastern section was destroyed in the mid-1950s for the Dan Ryan Expressway. In the 1980s and 1990s virtually all of the rest was razed for athletic fields for the University of Illinois at Chicago. What remained of the market was moved several blocks to a place with none of the flavor of the old street.

Ira Berkow

FURTHER READING: Berkow, Ira. *Maxwell Street: Survival in a Bazaar.* 1977.

Maywood, IL, Cook County, 11 miles W of the

Loop. A planned community from the outset, Maywood lies on the west bank of the Des Plaines River, stretching from Roosevelt Road on the south to just beyond Augusta Street on the north. Maywood was originally part of a larger area known as Noyesville, named after one of Proviso Township's early settlers, who established the area's first post office in the mid-1830s.

In 1869 a group of Vermont businessmen formed the Maywood Company and purchased the village's original plat—a narrow, one-and-three-quarters-mile strip along the Des Plaines River. Company president William T. Nichols named the village after his daughter May, and immediately began subdividing the land and creating improvements necessary to "build up a neat, desirable suburb." In 1870 wide streets were laid out, 20,000 trees were planted, and building commenced on the north side of the Chicago & North Western Railway tracks, which bisected the community. That year, an advertisement boasted easy access to the city via regular train service, along with such amenities as a school, churches, a post office, a grocery store, a hotel, and a beautiful park.

Since its incorporation as a village in 1881, Maywood's economic development has hinged on light industry, starting in 1884 with Chicago Scraper and Ditcher, a manufacturer of agricultural machinery. In 1885 Norton Can Works (later the American Can Company) moved to Maywood. Industries located primarily within the factory district along the north side of the railroad tracks. Maywood gained a major institution in 1920 when the Edward Hines Jr. Memorial Hos-

pital was established for the care of war veterans. These businesses and their workers were served by excellent transportation, including the Chicago & North Western train (1870), electric street railways (1893), and Chicago's rapid transit system. During the 1920s Checkerboard Field (now Miller Meadow) provided air service.

In the 1970s several industries transferred out of the region, including the village's major employer, American Can Company. Maywood's retail base also declined, as Montgomery Ward and Sears, Roebuck department stores left the main shopping street, Fifth Avenue. Somewhat offsetting these losses, in 1969 Maywood had gained the Loyola University Medical Center, including the Stritch School of Medicine.

In the 1990s Maywood began to rebound from the economic decline of the previous decades. Trying to attract new industry and businesses, the village established a tax increment financing district on the site of American Can Company plant, which was leveled in 1997. Economic change has been accompanied by demographic shifts; Maywood's African American population increased from 3 percent in 1930 to 19 percent in 1960 to 82 percent in 2000. Whites and Hispanics constitute 10 and 11 percent of the population, respectively, and live primarily in the village's northeastern section.

Jean Louise Guarino

FURTHER READING: *Festival of Progress, Maywood, Illinois, Seventieth Year, September 23rd to October 1st.* 1938. Maywood Public Library, Maywood, IL. ■ *Maywood and Its Homes.* 1904. Maywood Public Library, Maywood, IL. ■ *Maywood, a Suburb of Chicago, As It Is in 1870.* 1870. Maywood Public Library, Maywood, IL.

McHenry, IL, McHenry County, 46 miles NW of

the Loop. In 1832 Major William McHenry led an expeditionary force through northern Illinois during the Black Hawk War. Settlement of the Fox River Valley began over the next few years, and on the river's west bank, at the site of an old Indian ford, the hamlet of McHenry developed.

The McLean, Wheeler, McCullom, and Boone families were influential in the community's early years. A sawmill, hotel, and ferryboat were in operation by 1837. Legislation creating McHenry County was passed that year, and the village served as county seat until 1844.

Gristmills started along newly dammed Boone Creek, and a wagon road entered town from the south in 1851. In 1864 the famed Riverside Hotel was built and still stands.

George Gage, who served as the region's first state senator (1854–1858), owned the lands west of the millpond and was able to secure the route of the Fox River Valley Railroad (afterward a branch of the Chicago & North Western) from Chicago in 1854. Consequently, Gagetown (later West McHenry) began to eclipse the older east side of town. Their rivalry can still be detected in the disjunct commercial pattern that characterizes McHenry.

The village incorporated in 1872. Though there were fewer than 800 inhabitants, commerce flourished. By 1876 there were seven churches and over 80 enterprises, including flour mills, harness makers, a pickle factory, a brewery, seven saloons, and a newspaper. The newspaper, the *McHenry Plaindealer,* was in publication from 1875 to 1985.

Over the next 50 years McHenry grew slowly. During the 1920s the town became known as a resort destination. Bands played at local pavilions, trainloads of visitors arrived to tour the famous lotus beds, and summer cottages proliferated along the Fox River. A boat-building industry thrived; marine recreation still remains important.

With the advent of the automobile, State Route 120 crossed the Fox on a new two-lane bridge. The old wagon trail, now Highway 31, doglegged along the same route for a critical half mile before turning north toward Wisconsin. These configurations effectively relocated the city's commercial center to Route 120, and had the unintended side effect of isolating the original business districts (West Main, Riverside Drive, and Green Street).

A new wave of industry, including the manufacture of automotive components, electronics, and metalworking, swept into town after World War II. The Northern Illinois Medical Center, begun in 1956 as a 23-bed community hospital, evolved into a regional trauma center serving two states. Beginning in the late 1940s, subdivisions were annexed on all sides of the city. By this time, many residents were commuting to work in other localities, including Chicago. McHenry's population tripled from 2,080 in 1950 to 6,772 in 1970, and tripled again, to 21,501, in 2000.

McHenry continues to grow in all directions. In 1995 the city's corporate boundaries leapt east of the Fox for the first time. The city now has seven separate commercial centers but no distinct core. Traffic continues to be a problem, and there is insufficient access to the city's major scenic resource, the river.

John D. Schroeder

FURTHER READING: *History of McHenry County.* 1885. ∎ *McHenry County in the Twentieth Century, 1968–1994.* 1994. ∎ Meyer, Barbara K., ed. *McHenry, 1836–1986: A Proud Past and Progressive Future.* 1986.

McKinley Park, Community Area 59, 4 miles SW of the Loop. McKinley Park has been a working-class area throughout its long history. This tradition began around 1836 when Irish workers on the Illinois & Michigan Canal took squatter's rights to small tracts of land. By the 1840s a few farmers had purchased and drained land and sent the Irish squatters packing. Canalport, one of the first attempts at town building, died stillborn, but Brighton was platted in 1840 and incorporated in 1851.

59
McKinley Park

The completion of the Illinois & Michigan Canal in 1848 and the coming of the Chicago & Alton Railroad in 1857 spurred further subdivision of the area. The rails amplified the transportation advantages of the area, and during the Civil War industries located along the waterways and the railroad. The Union Rolling Mill was founded in the early 1860s along the South Fork, a tributary to the South Branch of the Chicago River later known as "Bubbly Creek," and produced 50 tons of rails per day. Eventually, the firm became part of U.S. Steel.

Many steelworkers lived in the triangle formed by Archer and Ashland Avenues and 35th Street in an area called Mt. Pleasant. The name was probably ironic because of the adjacent steel mills and because much of the area was swampy and undrained. Standing water bred hordes of mosquitoes, and spring flooding was so severe that many houses were built on stilts. Not surprisingly, a portion of McKinley Park was called Ducktown. Some landowners desperate to elevate their holdings invited scavengers to dump ashes and thereby fill low areas. Unfortunately the scavengers dumped not only ashes but garbage as well. Thus the area was not only wet, but fetid. Even with these problems, McKinley Park was annexed to Chicago in 1863.

The Chicago Fire of 1871 displaced numerous industrial operations and many relocated to this area. Within five years after the fire 11 factories opened—most in iron and steel—along with 27 brickyards. During this same period, meatpacking operations just to the south moved into high gear. The result was the creation of the solid working-class community that still exists today.

The packinghouses fouled the environment and dumped wastes directly into the South Fork, creating a hellish mess of decomposing material that came to be known as "Bubbly Creek." Ultimately the stream's upper reaches were filled in to rectify the problem.

If industries created pollution, they also created many good jobs and led to a period of unprecedented growth and prosperity. Irish, Germans, Swedes, English, and native-born Americans filled the industrial jobs of the 1870s. Even after 1900, when Poles and other Eastern Europeans came to the area, English prevailed as the street language, and the area was the most American of all settlements in the stockyard districts. Transportation had always been poor, but the 1880s and 1890s saw improvement and extension of the car lines on Archer Avenue and on 35th Street. As time passed, steel mills and brickyards closed and industries changed, replaced by new activities. The Central Manufacturing District was begun in 1905 on some 260 acres along the South Fork. In the late 1990s it was still operating, Pepsi-Cola was opening a new bottling plant, and the Wrigley Company was still making chewing gum. Meanwhile, the *Chicago Sun-Times* was building a mammoth printing and distribution plant west of Ashland along the Chicago River.

The beginning of the twentieth century led, after years of complaints by residents, to the creation of a park, which was named for President McKinley after his assassination. The 69-acre park now boasts a swimming pool and ice-skating rink. It is the area's showplace and lent its name to the entire community.

After years of decline, the population grew during the 1990s from 13,297 to 15,962, with Mexicans joining the ethnic mix. Well-kept two- and four-flat buildings dominate the landscape, but new infill housing has begun to appear. Two stops on the CTA Orange Line rapid transit have boosted property values and spurred development of a new restaurant, shopping mall, and drugstore.

David M. Solzman

FURTHER READING: Chicago Fact Book Consortium, ed. *Local Community Fact Book: Chicago Metropolitan Area, Based on the 1970 and 1980 Censuses.* 1984. ■ Solzman, David M. *Waterway Industrial Sites: A Chicago Case Study.* 1966. ■ Solzman, David M. *The Chicago River: An Illustrated History and Guide to the River and Its Waterways.* 1998, 2006.

Melrose Park, IL, Cook County, 12 miles W of the Loop. Melrose Park is one of Chicago's many pre–World War II suburbs that do not fit the mythology of suburban affluence. Its origins may be dated to 1873, when the Melrose Land Company subdivided a large tract almost due west of Chicago, well beyond the city limits. The company initially gave away a pair of 26-foot lots

to anyone who agreed to build a dwelling valued at $500 or more. Within a year 50 people had accepted the offer. No services were provided, however, and settlement slowed. By 1880 the population was barely 200, and in 1882 only 38 votes were cast to establish the village of Melrose. The village grew steadily during the 1880s, however, adding "Park" to its name in 1894. By the turn of the century it was home to 2,592 people.

Melrose Park evolved into an industrial suburb. Stagnating after 1900, it boomed after World War I as a number of manufacturers established or greatly expanded operations. These included National Malleable and Steel Castings, the American Brake Shoe and Foundry Company, and the Edward Hines Lumber Company. At first, like other industrial suburbs, Melrose Park functioned almost as a self-contained entity. One of the larger companies in the early 1920s was Richardson's, a manufacturer of asphalt shingles, roll roofing, and composition battery casing. In the mid-1920s three-quarters of its workforce of more than 500 lived within the village. During the 1920s demand for homes supported the activities of many small builders and at least one large one. In 1925 the Sol Bloch Real Estate Improvement Company was building more than a hundred homes in Melrose Park and adjacent suburbs, selling some for as little as $500 down, with the balance to be paid over a period of 7 to 12 years.

The opening of the huge Proviso freight yards in 1926 reinforced the character of Melrose Park as an industrial, working-class suburb. By 1940 the town offered 38 jobs for every 100 residents (including children), two-thirds of which were in manufacturing. These ratios were higher than for more diversified suburbs such as BLUE ISLAND, but lower than for industrial suburbs and satellites such as CICERO and CHICAGO HEIGHTS. Wartime growth sparked more of the same sort of development, notably the construction of a Buick airplane motor plant along the Indiana Harbor Belt Railroad. Other businesses in Melrose Park after World War II included Zenith (which closed its factory in 1998), Alberto-Culver, a Ford

automobile parts facility, and the headquarters of Jewel Food Stores. Melrose Park was also the site of the region's oldest amusement park, Kiddieland, founded in 1929.

The ethnic composition of Melrose Park has included many Italians, with smaller numbers of Germans, Irish, and Poles. Since 1894 the Feast of Our Lady of Mt. Carmel has been an annual Italian American celebration. In the latter part of the twentieth century many Hispanic immigrants were also attracted to Melrose Park by its jobs and inexpensive housing. In 2000, 54 percent of the village's population was Hispanic, while less than 3 percent was black.

Richard Harris

FURTHER READING: Christgau, Eugene F. "Unincorporated Communities in Cook County." M.A. thesis, University of Chicago. 1942. ■ Harris, Richard. "Chicago's Other Suburbs." *Geographical Review* 84.4 (1994): 394–410. ■ Keating, Ann Durkin. *Building Chicago: Suburban Developers and the Creation of a Divided Metropolis*. 1988.

Merrillville, IN, Lake County, 33 miles SE of the

Loop. Known as "Downtown Northwest Indiana," the town of Merrillville, just south of GARY, embraces a large number of restaurants, banks, malls, and businesses typical of American suburbia in the late twentieth century.

In the mid-1830s, Potawatomi and Miami regularly visited the Merrillville area. Calling it McGwinn's Village, Indians would hold intertribal councils and conduct ceremonies and dances. Over 15 Indian trails crisscrossed the region, connecting with the Sauk Trail, a major east-west route through Indiana and into Illinois. In addition, the site included a Native American burial ground with over a hundred graves.

In 1835 as American settlers pushed west into northwest Indiana, Jeremiah Wiggins purchased a claim just south of Turkey Creek and named it Wiggins Point. Other settlers arrived soon after, changing the name to Centerville because of its location in the county. In 1848 the post office renamed the settlement Merrillville, after residents Dudley and William Merrill. At that point, the village included a store, a blacksmith shop, a cheese factory, and the California Exchange Hotel. Railroads pushed through Merrillville in 1876 (Chesapeake & Ohio) and in 1880 (Chicago & Grand Trunk), opening links to the Chicago markets. Through World War II, Merrillville remained a typical Midwestern farming community.

Beginning in the 1950s, however, several phenomena combined to cause striking changes in the Merrillville landscape. As in other areas of the country, urban residents began their outward march to suburbia; in northwest Indiana, residents of the industrial cities of Gary, HAMMOND, and East Chicago began to buy new homes in central Lake County. The 1967 election of Richard Gordon Hatcher, Gary's first African American mayor, accelerated the white flight begun a decade earlier. Finally, Interstate 65 opened in 1968, connecting Interstate 80/94 in Gary to U.S. 30 in Merrillville. Almost overnight, the town experienced tremendous commercial and residential growth. Most of the retail and bank establishments relocated from downtown Gary and Hammond to Merrillville, and suburban malls and office complexes sprang up in the cornfields.

Efforts to incorporate Merrillville began in the 1950s but were unsuccessful until 1971, when Indiana's General Assembly passed legislation exempting Lake County from the state's "buffer zone" law, which prohibited incorporation in areas within three miles of larger cities (such as Gary and neighboring Hobart).

Although Merrillville experienced a commercial and residential boom, little of that prosperity reached town government. In 1972 Indiana passed legislation freezing local budget increases at 5 percent per year. Merrillville's budgets quickly fell relative to inflation, and the town struggled to maintain services. To compound matters, neighboring Hobart annexed a large portion of unincorporated Ross Township in 1994, including the profitable Southlake Mall and other retail malls.

At the end of the twentieth century, Merrillville continued to serve as northwest Indiana's commercial hub. Its population stabilized and became more diverse, as African Americans and other minorities began to buy houses and attend schools.

Stephen G. McShane

FURTHER READING: Clemens, Jan. *A Pictorial History of Merrillville.* 1978. ■ Goodspeed, Weston A., and Charles Blanchard. *Counties of Porter and Lake Indiana.* 1882. ■ Moore, Powell A. *The Calumet Region: Indiana's Last Frontier.* 1959.

Michigan City, IN, LaPorte County, 41 miles E of the Loop. Michigan City, Indiana, lies at the mouth of Trail Creek, on Lake Michigan's southeastern shore. Envisioned by nineteenth-century boosters as a commercial and transportation center, this small city is now best known as a tourist hub for the Indiana Dunes territory.

When federal surveyors arrived in the Lake Michigan dunes, they saw the low, swampy site at the mouth of Trail Creek as the ideal location for a major harbor at the end of the Michigan Road, then being built northward through Indiana. In 1831, armed with inside knowledge of the harbor plans, Major Isaac C. Elston, a real-estate speculator from Crawfordsville, Indiana, began to buy land in the area, and in 1832 he laid out the town of Michigan City. The first settlers arrived the following year. By 1836 the town's population had swelled to nearly 3,000.

Between 1837 and 1844 the town served as the principal grain market for northern Indiana. Several rail lines arrived in the 1850s, bringing their repair shops with them. The Haskell & Barker Car Company, established in 1852, quickly became the city's largest employer. The Northern State Prison began supplying local manufacturers with convict labor shortly after it opened in the early 1860s.

Harbor construction finally moved forward after the Civil War. In 1867 and 1868 the Michigan City Harbor Company built two piers and dredged a deep channel between them. With an infusion of federal funds, the harbor was soon ready to accept large vessels. Michigan City became one of Indiana's largest lumber markets. Industry boomed.

Michigan City's fortunes began to recede after 1900. Profitable convict labor was outlawed. The lumber trade gradually died out. The Michigan Central Railroad moved its shops at the close of World War I, and Haskell & Barker became Michigan City's sole large employer. Hoosier Slide, the town's once-towering sand dune, was completely mined out by the 1920s.

Fortunately for Michigan City, Lake Michigan tourism surged at about the same time. Though lake steamer excursions declined after 1915, when the Michigan City–bound *Eastland* rolled over in the Chicago River, other modes of tourist transportation took their place. The Dunes Highway opened in 1923. Shortly thereafter, utilities magnate Samuel Insull upgraded the Chicago, South Shore & South Bend Railroad. Both the highway and the electric interurban provided Chicagoans with easy access to Michigan City and the dunes beaches. (They also provided Michigan City residents a convenient means of commuting into Chicago.) Michigan City's lakeshore Washington Park, established in 1891 and improved in the 1930s, aimed to draw the tourist trade. The creation of the Indiana Dunes National Lakeshore in the 1960s fortified the tourism industry. By the end of the twentieth century, downtown Michigan City, which had experienced decline in the face of urban renewal, housed a popular outlet mall and a casino boat moored in Trail Creek.

Elizabeth A. Patterson

FURTHER READING: Greening, Elwin G., ed. *A Pictorial History of Michigan City, Indiana, 1675–1992.* 1992. ∎ Nicewarner, Gladys Bull. *Michigan City, Indiana: The Life of a Town.* 1980. ∎ Packard, Jasper. *History of LaPorte County, Indiana, and Its Townships, Towns, and Cities.* 1876.

Midway Park, historic core of the AUSTIN Community Area around Central and Lake, now a National Register historic district.

Montclare, Community Area 18, 9 miles NW of the Loop. First attracted by the rolling landscape, William Sayre in 1836 laid claim "by right of possession" to 90 acres in what is now the Montclare Community Area. Unable to gain title to the land because of an inaccurate government survey, he bought the acreage at the Jefferson Township land sales in 1838. A year later he married Harriet Lovett, daughter of another area settler, in the first marriage of the township. They set up housekeeping in a newly built frame house in 1840.

18
Montclare

Sayre and his neighbors cleared fields of hay and tended crops of oats and corn. Farmers used Grand Avenue as their main thoroughfare to the downtown markets in Chicago, where many hawked their produce from wagons at the Randolph Street Market. The return home was sometimes dangerous: along the dark, lonely road, farmers faced the threat of robbery and by the 1880s risked having their wagons hit by a train.

In 1872 Sayre allowed the Chicago & Pacific Railroad Company right-of-way over his property, and Sayre Station was built on the farm. A year later another family farm in the area was platted by developers, who sold lots for $250 to $500. The town and the depot were named Montclare after Montclair, New Jersey.

In 1873 the rail line failed and was taken over by the Chicago, Milwaukee & St. Paul Railroad (Chicago, Milwaukee, St. Paul & Pacific Railroad). As a result, the only form of commuter transportation was a single daily train, reducing the desirability of the area. Lots remained vacant. Undaunted by a lack of settlers, the 120 or so residents went about their farming. Two schools were in evidence in 1884. Social activities focused on family, church, and Sunday school. Most residents were native-born, English, or German.

Montclare was annexed by the city of Chicago in 1889, but the first spurt of growth did not occur until 1912, when the Grand Avenue streetcar line extended service to the area. The Sayre family contributed acreage for community use in 1916, which, along with another piece of donated property, later formed Rutherford-Sayre Park. The park was bisected by the railroad tracks, which marked the neighborhood's southern boundary.

Settlement concentrated in the southeastern section, near the depot, but was hampered until utilities and paved streets were added in the 1920s. Single-family structures, mainly standard bungalows, predominated in the area. Some residents found employment at light industrial plants along the CM&SP railroad lines that bounded Montclare on its eastern and southern edges; most workers crossed into neighboring communities where factories were more plentiful.

Housing extended north of Diversey Avenue in the 1930s, a combination of bungalows, ranches, and Tudor houses. Hugging Chicago's western edge, Montclare retained an identity more suburban than urban. Pre–World War II commercial development was minimal; the only shopping was a retail strip at Grand and Harlem. In the 1960s the strip experienced decline and deterioration as stores left and newer shopping centers were built in nearby areas. But residential areas remained intact owing to good construction and property upkeep by conscientious residents.

The 1970 census showed a population of 11,675, of which Poles, Italians, and Germans constituted a majority. The figure decreased to 10,573 by 1990, with Greeks, Ukranians, Lithuanians, Lebanese, and a growing number of Hispanics (11 percent) added to the mix. In the late 1980s a few African Americans moved into the neighborhood, prompting racially motivated incidents; groups such as the Galewood-Montclare Community Organization subsequently devoted their efforts to reducing tensions. At the close of the twentieth century Montclare still had only 297 African American residents, but the proportion of Hispanics stood at 38 percent.

Marilyn Elizabeth Perry

FURTHER READING: Edwards, Brian. "Frontier Bargains: Tiny Montclare Offers Quiet Family Living Way Out West." *Chicago Tribune*, August 24, 1990. ■ Karlen, Harvey M. *Chicago's Crabgrass Communities: The History of the Independent Suburbs and Their Post Offices That Became Part of Chicago*. 1992, 163–166. ■ Melaniphy & Associates, Inc. *Chicago Comprehensive Neighborhood Needs Analysis*, vol. 2. 1982, 16–23.

Morgan Park, Community Area 75, 13 miles S of the Loop. Laid out in the 1870s by Thomas F. Nichols, Morgan Park, with its winding streets, small parks, and roundabouts, evokes images of an English country town.

75
Morgan Park

In 1869 the Blue Island Land and Building Company purchased property from the heirs of Thomas Morgan, an early English settler, and subdivided the area between Western and Vincennes Avenues that falls within the present community area of Morgan Park. Although the Chicago, Rock Island & Pacific Railroad laid tracks through the area in 1852, regular commuter service to downtown was not established until the suburban line opened in 1888.

To spur residential development, the Blue Island company donated land and helped finance buildings for Mt. Vernon Military Academy (1873), the predecessor of Morgan Park Academy; Morgan Park Baptist Church (1874); and the Chicago Female College (1875). But the company's greatest success occurred in 1877, when the Baptist Theological Union agreed to relocate. By 1879 its well-regarded faculty included William Rainey Harper, who in 1891 became the first president of the University of Chicago.

Reflecting its origins as a Baptist community, Morgan Park prohibited the sale of liquor in the area between Western and Vincennes Avenues when it was incorporated as a village in 1882. Its middle-class character was further reinforced by the construction of mainline Protestant churches, among them Methodist (1888), Episcopalian (1889), Congregational (1890), and Presbyterian (1891). Equally important was the completion in 1890 of a substantial brick structure for Esmond Public School and the imposing library donated by Charles Walker, president of the Blue Island Land and Building Company.

Despite these clear signs of growth, Morgan Park lost its bid to become the home of the University of Chicago, which settled in HYDE PARK. After the Baptist Theological Union left Morgan Park in 1892, its buildings were used by Morgan Park Military Academy.

Although Morgan Park cultivated an identity as a white Anglo-Saxon Protestant community, it also included a small settlement of African Americans as well as French immigrants. Beth Eden (1891) was the first of more than 19 churches organized by black families who lived in the segregated district east of Vincennes, near the main line of the Rock Island Railroad. On the other side of the tracks, near 117th Street, French Roman Catholics who worked in the local Purington brickyard established Sacred Heart Church (1904).

The battle over annexation to Chicago, in 1911, sharply divided the community and dragged on in court until 1914. At a time when they were denied the franchise in national elections, women voted overwhelmingly in favor of annexation because it meant better police and fire protection as well as a new high school.

By 1920, 674 of Morgan Park's 7,780 residents were African American. The official report published in the wake of the city's 1919 race riot noted that, while whites and blacks in Morgan Park "maintain a friendly attitude," nevertheless "there seems to be a common understanding that Negroes must not live west of Vincennes Road, which bisects the town from northeast to southwest." Public institutions such as the new Morgan Park High School (1916) and the Walker Branch Library remained integrated.

But African Americans were not the only residents in Morgan Park to live on the periphery. Between 1930 and 1960 the community's population

more than doubled, from 12,747 to 27,912, as new subdivisions were built up with homes. Whereas Morgan Park's mainline Protestants tended to live and worship in the oldest part of the neighborhood, the largely Irish Roman Catholic parishes of St. Cajetan (1927) and St. Walter (1953) drew most of their congregations from the area west of Western Avenue. Reflecting the reality of urban segregation, African American Catholics established Holy Name of Mary (1940) at the east end of the neighborhood.

Racial integration in the larger Morgan Park area did not occur on a large scale until the late 1960s. By then, however, the west leg of Interstate 57 had effectively isolated the older black settlement east of Vincennes. Perhaps the greatest change to occur in Morgan Park involved the construction of nearly 400 "section 235" subsidized housing units between 1969 and 1974, the largest number for any Chicago neighborhood.

With support from the BEVERLY Area Planning Association (1947), Morgan Park has marketed its historic homes, worked to keep its public schools integrated, and strengthened area shopping strips. The Walker branch of the Chicago Public Library, enlarged and renovated in 1995, remains a showplace, and the Beverly Arts Center's new complex for the performing arts (2002) has sparked redevelopment at the intersection of 111th and Western Avenue. Morgan Park claims one of the city's pioneer African American communities, and since 1979 its Irish American community has sponsored an event billed as the largest neighborhood-based St. Patrick's Day parade outside Dublin.

Ellen Skerrett

FURTHER READING: Mayer, Harold M., and Richard C. Wade. *Chicago: Growth of a Metropolis.* 1969. ■ Pacyga, Dominic A., and Ellen Skerrett. *Chicago, City of Neighborhoods: Histories and Tours.* 1986.

Mount Greenwood, Community Area 74, 14 miles SW of the Loop. Mount Greenwood is a two-square-mile community area bounded by eight cemeteries and the suburbs of OAK LAWN, Alsip, Evergreen Park, and Merrionette Park. Because of the prevalence of cemeteries, the area was once known as Seven Holy Tombs.

German and Dutch truck farmers were active in the area by the Civil War. In 1879 George Waite  received a state land grant of 80 acres and named the area Mount Greenwood after the presence of trees on an elevated ridge. It seemed ideally suited for a cemetery. By 1897 taverns and restaurants emerged on 111th and Sacramento Streets to serve mourners following funerals, which were all-day horse-driven affairs. Dog and horse racing tracks were also close by, so an assortment of customers patronized 111th Street. Irish saloons served corned beef and cabbage, while German saloons served sauerbraten and dumplings.

74
Mount
Greenwood

The first religious congregations in the community were Methodist and Reformed, respectively attracting German and Dutch Protestants. These populations were later joined by other European immigrant groups, including Irish, Welsh, English, Poles, Lithuanians, Swedes, Norwegians, and Danes.

In the early 1900s Protestant temperance crusaders sought to close down the saloons and make the community dry like nearby MORGAN PARK. But the opposition succeeded in incorporating Mount Greenwood in 1907 as part of a strategy to remain wet. In 1927 Mount Greenwood voted for annexation to Chicago, hoping for improvements such as sewers, water mains, hard-surfaced streets, streetlights, and a new public school, but such changes were slow to arrive. It was not until 1936 that the Works Progress Administration finally laid sewage systems and paved and lighted community streets. As late as the 1960s, the Mount Greenwood Civic Association was still fighting the city for curbs and gutters.

From 1930 to 1950 Mount Greenwood experienced its first spurt of residential growth, with population increasing from 3,310 to 12,331. These young families required new schools, parks, and public recreation areas. In the first years after

World War II, from 1945 to 1953, 4,000 new homes were built. However, population declined from 23,186 in 1970 to 19,179 in 1990.

By the 1980s Mount Greenwood was home to the last surviving farm in the city, which was developed as the Chicago High School for Agricultural Sciences. The magnet school stirred controversy in the late 1980s, when black students were bussed into the overwhelmingly white community. This led to a community protest and increased racial hostility. By 2000 the population had declined to 18,820, of whom 94 percent were white, with African Americans and Hispanics each accounting for less than 4 percent.

Clinton E. Stockwell

FURTHER READING: "The Tallest Fence: Feelings on Race in a White Neighborhood." *New York Times,* June 21, 1992. ■ Chicago Fact Book Consortium, ed. *Local Community Fact Book: Chicago Metropolitan Area, 1990.* 1995. ■ DeZutter, Hank. "The Last Farm in Chicago." *Chicago Reader,* August 15, 1981.

Mount Prospect, IL, Cook County, 20 miles NW of the Loop. Yankee  farmers established homesteads in what became the heart of downtown Mount Prospect after signing a treaty with the Potawatomi in 1833. New Englanders cleared and farmed the land until 1843. Many then moved west in search of larger claims and were replaced by German immigrants, who planted the roots of a small rural community.

By 1854 the Illinois & Wisconsin Railroad (later renamed the Chicago & North Western Railway) ran through Mount Prospect, but it did not stop there until 1886. As a result, the remaining Yankee families, who wanted access to broader markets, moved to the neighboring railroad towns of ARLINGTON HEIGHTS and DES PLAINES. Meanwhile more German and Irish immigrant families bought up the available homesteads.

In 1871 real-estate agent Ezra Carpenter Eggleston built a four-block residential subdivision on farmland south of the railroad. Eggleston named the area Mount Prospect because the village sat on the highest point in Cook County. Eggleston went bankrupt, since the area failed to prosper until a railroad station was established.

In 1900 the community still fell short of the 300 people required for incorporation. A group of small businessmen known as the Mount Prospect Improvement Association pushed for official empowerment to solicit funds through taxation. In May 1917 the village immediately incorporated when a newborn infant became Mount Prospect's three hundredth resident.

William Busse, a local storeowner, served as the first president from 1917 to 1929. During this period, Mount Prospect experienced business expansion and population growth that increased the number of residents to 1,225 by 1930. Although the area remained predominantly farmland, a small industrial district appeared north of the railroad tracks, which included a creamery, farm machinery retailers, a hardware store, a coal yard, and a general store.

The village's post–World War II population growth was similar to that in neighboring communities, with an influx of white, middle-class Chicagoans. During the 1950s the population increased 370 percent to 18,906, prompting village officials to adopt a council-manager form of government. In this period of growth, the Randhurst Corporation opened an enclosed and air-conditioned mall, Randhurst Shopping Center (1962). The village also attracted new industry and light manufacturing with the addition of the Kensington Center (1974).

During the late 1970s village president Carolyn Krause contested the Metropolitan Housing Development Corporation's efforts to rezone for the building of multifamily housing for minorities and the elderly. A federal agreement, however, allowed the construction of low-income housing on unincorporated land between Arlington Heights and Mount Prospect. Although village leaders continued to promote some light industry, they maintained Mount Prospect as a residential community made up primarily of middle-class white

families. Most white-collar residents worked for large companies in the area (such as Centel, Mitsubishi Electronics, and Eastman Kodak) or commuted to Chicago. By 1992 the village's Chamber of Commerce began a downtown revitalization campaign that sought to "keep the small in small town."

David MacLaren

FURTHER READING: Chicago Fact Book Consortium, ed. *Local Community Fact Book: Chicago Metropolitan Area, Based on the 1970 and 1980 Censuses.* 1984. ▪ *Chicagoland's Community Tour Guide.* 20th ed. 1983/84. ▪ Murphy, Jean Powley, and Mary Hagan Wajer. *Mount Prospect: Where Town and Country Met, An Illustrated History.* 1992.

Mundelein, IL, Lake County, 33 miles NW of the  Loop. The area that is now Mundelein was once known as Mechanic's Grove, a name said to have been inspired by an 1850s settlement of English millwrights three miles west of LIBERTYVILLE. When the Wisconsin Central Railroad built through the area to Chicago in 1880, local farmer John Holcomb donated land for a station and village plat, which he named after himself. To honor the line's most notable stockholder, the railroad renamed the station after William Rockefeller in 1885.

Little changed in the tiny community until after the Chicago & Milwaukee Electric Interurban terminated its LAKE BLUFF spur line there in 1904. Anticipating a boom, residents planned an incorporation referendum for January 1909. There were too few residents to meet the legal requirements, but settlers around nearby Diamond Lake were included in the vote with the understanding that they could withdraw from the new village. The referendum was successful, and Sylvester L. Tripp was named village president in March. Diamond Lake residents withdrew shortly thereafter.

Meanwhile, Chicagoan Arthur Sheldon purchased a large holding on the east side of Rockefeller called Mud Lake. Hoping to prepare and sell home-study business school courses, he erected large buildings and hired numerous employees, primarily women. Sheldon even persuaded villagers in mid-1909 to change Rockefeller's name to Area, an acronym for his company's motto: Ability, Reliability, Endurance, and Action.

Sheldon's business failed—perhaps as a result of World War I—and his property fell vacant. By 1920 George Cardinal Mundelein, seeking to realize his dream of building a world-renowned theological seminary, purchased these holdings, renaming Mud Lake as St. Mary's Lake. In 1924 Area was renamed Mundelein in honor of the cardinal. As a grand complex of buildings rose, the village played host to the 28th International Eucharistic Congress in 1926, which over 500,000 people attended.

The size of the crowds interested Samuel Insull, Chicago capitalist and electricity mogul, who attempted to organize a large, planned community with underground utilities and decentralized shopping centers. The failure of his economic empire and the Great Depression derailed his dream, and Mundelein's population grew to only 1,328 by 1940.

As suburbanization swept into Lake County, Mundelein, which had been planned to accept growth, mushroomed from 3,186 in 1950 to over 12,000 in 1962. Even with such a population base, the Chicago, North Shore & Milwaukee Electric interurban ceased operating in January 1963.

Still, Mundelein's population continued to rise, to 17,053 in 1980 and 30,935 in 2000. Community and other area leaders worked with Metra to acquire a rail commuter route, which opened in 1996 as the Metra North Central line from Chicago through Mundelein to ANTIOCH.

Craig L. Pfannkuche

FURTHER READING: "Mundelein." *Waukegan News-Sun,* October 2, 1995. ■ "Twenty-fifth Anniversary Edition." *Mundelein News,* June 27, 1968. ■ Purcell, Connie. *Memories of Mundelein.* 1984.

Munster, IN, Lake County, 24 miles S of the Loop. In 1850 most of the site of the future town of Munster, Indiana, lay under the turbid waters of Cady Marsh or was seasonally flooded by the Little Calumet River. But for centuries Native Americans, most recently the Potawatomi, had lived on the abundant fish, wildlife, and countless migratory birds found along the dry and sandy ridge. After 1840 a scattering of European American families moved in and as often drifted away. Beginning in 1845, a succession of innkeepers, among them Allen Brass and Johann Stallbohm, welcomed travelers to a rambling wooden structure beside Ridge Road.

Dutch immigrants arrived in 1855 and by 1900 had established a tidy farm community. Jabaays, Kooys, Schoons, Jansens, and Bakkers raised potatoes, cabbages, beans, and flowers along the ridge for local families and regional wholesalers, and onion sets for the national market.

Peter Klootwyck and town postmaster Jacob Munster operated small stores. Late in the century Aaron Norton Hart channeled through the ridge to the Little Calumet, drained Cady Marsh, and created hundreds of acres of valuable farmland. In 1927 Burns Ditch minimized the annual floods of the Little Calumet and made north Munster habitable.

The 7.5-square-mile town of Munster was organized in 1907 with a population of 500. After 1920 growing numbers of commuters launched the suburban era. The Great Depression halted all growth until World War II fueled a regional housing shortage and brought the development of working class–oriented Independence Park, rows of brick duplexes, and even a few apartment houses. By 1945 Munster was an uneasy mixture of small farmers, industrial workers, and well-to-do commuters.

Munster moved further toward suburban status in the 1950s with the construction of 1,500 homes, which doubled the town's population to 10,313. The new residents were young, well educated, upwardly mobile, and family-oriented. They created a prosperous community of comfortable and occasionally grand houses. Modern public services were introduced. An industrial park attracted several large and small tenants. Farm stands were replaced by shops, banks, service stations, garden centers, and a lumberyard. Munster never developed a focused downtown, though a sizable mall was built beside Calumet Avenue.

The booming 1960s and 1970s saw the completion of Munster's transition into a suburban community. Though the town board continued to govern, a town manager was appointed and municipal ordinances multiplied, along with streets and handsome trees, parks, and recreational areas. Long-empty South Munster filled with subdivisions; Don Powers, one businessman among many, had developed almost two thousand home sites by 1990.

Excellent schools absorbed much tax revenue. Munster High School opened in 1966, and curricula were developed to serve a largely college-bound student population. As the century ended, Munster was a mature and prosperous suburban town, home to a well-educated and largely professional population of 21,511. A remarkable hospital complex dominated its skyline. A handsome art center stood beside the ridge. A second business park was attracting a variety of "clean" tenants. The farm village of 1920 had quite disappeared.

Lance Trusty

FURTHER READING: Clipping file. Munster Branch, Lake County Public Library, Munster, IN. ■ Moore, Powell, A. *The Calumet Region: Indiana's Last Frontier.* 1977. ■ Trusty, Lance. *Town on the Ridge: A History of Munster, Indiana.* 1982.

Naperville, IL, DuPage and Will Counties, 28 miles W of the Loop. Joseph Naper is credited with founding Naperville along the DuPage River in 1831. He drew the first plat in 1842 and was elected president of the board when the village of Naperville was incorporated in 1857.

Early families like the Napers, Scotts, Hobsons, and Paines came primarily from the Northeast; by the 1840s they were joined by Pennsylvanians, Germans, English, and Scots. They built at least seven churches, four of which held most services in German.

Naperville became an important stop at the crossroads of two main stage routes that ran from Chicago to Galena and to Ottawa. By 1832 the 180 residents had built sawmills, gristmills, stores, and the Pre-Emption House hotel. The town became the county seat when DuPage County was established in 1839.

Eight Naperville businesses contributed to the development of the Southwest Plank Road, which  was completed in 1851 and connected Chicago, Naperville, and Oswego. These businessmen then opposed granting the Galena & Chicago Union Railroad a Naperville right-of-way when its representatives came prospecting that same year. The Galena line went through WHEATON instead. But the town got a second chance when the Chicago, Burlington & Quincy Railroad ran its line through Naperville in 1864.

Naperville's growth for the next century was tied to this easy rail connection to Chicago. In 1870 North Central College (then North Western College) relocated to Naperville from Plainfield to serve the community and members of the Evangelical Association of North America. Stone quarries flourished, providing building materials for Chicago, especially after its disastrous 1871 fire. The Stenger Brewery shipped beer around the region. The Kroehler Manufacturing Company, which became Naperville's largest employer, shipped furniture by rail into Chicago and its all-important markets.

Naperville organized as a city in 1890 and had a population of 2,629 by 1900. Between 1890 and 1920 residents began receiving city services such

Final assembly of a "pushback" theater chair at the Kroehler plant, Naperville. Photographer: Kroehler Furniture Co. Source: Chicago History Museum.

as water, sewers, electricity, and telephones. Naperville grew to 12,933 by 1960.

While a suburban boom began in the near western suburbs after World War II, Naperville remained out of the range of this growth until 1954, when plans for the East-West Toll Road were announced. The route, which skirted the northern edge of Naperville and included an interchange, linked the city to downtown Chicago via the just completed Eisenhower Expressway. As a result of this new access, residential, retail, industrial, and service industries expanded in and around

A Yankee Recollection

When Judge Henry W. Blodgett arrived in Chicago as a young boy in 1831, his family located on the east branch of the DuPage River in what is now Naperville. Writing over 60 years later, Blodgett remembered that the Potawatomis lived in the country around his family:

> The band of the tribe of which Half-Day or Ap-ta-ke-sic was the chief, had free range for hunting, trapping, and fishing over the territory between the Fox River and Lake Michigan extending north as far as, or further than where Racine is now located, and south nearly, if not quite, to the Kankakee River.

The special hunting grounds of Ap-ta-ke-sic and the members of his family were upon the east branch of the DuPage, although their cornfields were on the Des Plaines River near the mouth of Indian Creek, not far from the site of the present village of Half Day in Lake County.

> It was not long after we got into our log cabin before we had visits from the old chief and members of his family, and my father being a blacksmith, had frequent calls to mend their traps and guns, so that we all became quite intimate with them. . . . At that time, Ap-ta-ke-sic was probably about forty-five or fifty years old. He was a man of fine figure and presence, over six feet in height, straight, well proportioned, with clear bright eyes and a pleasant face and manner.

Letter from Judge Henry W. Blodgett to Hon. A. H. Burley, Waukegan, January 23, 1893. Chicago History Museum.

Naperville. The city grew to 50 square miles in 1993, with a population of 128,358 in 2000. Among municipalities in the metropolitan area only AURORA and Chicago itself were larger.

Many of the new enterprises attracted to the Naperville area were based in research and development. During the late 1950s and 1960s, Argonne National Laboratory, Northern Illinois Gas, Amoco Research Center, AT&T Bell Laboratories, and Fermi National Accelerator Laboratory were established in or near Naperville. Harold Moser led the residential building boom

with his first subdivision in 1956. By 1995 Moser had subdivided 8,000 building lots and had built 3,500 homes in the city.

North Central College, now Methodist-affiliated, continues to serve the Naperville community. The Naper Settlement, established in 1969, has transported historic structures from across the area and serves as a focal point for the Naperville community. Beginning in the early 1980s the Riverwalk revitalized the downtown area and today provides acres of park and paths.

Ann Durkin Keating

FURTHER READING: Ebner, Michael. "Technoburb: The Growth of Naperville, Illinois, from a Small Town to a Midwest Technological Center." *Inland Architect* 37.1 (January 1, 1993). ■ Towsley, Genevieve. *A View of Historic Naperville.* Ed. Peg Sproul. 1979. ■ Wehrli, Jean, and Mary Lou Wehrli. *The Naperville Sesquicentennial Photo Album, 1831–1931.* 1981.

Near North Side, Community Area 8, 1 mile N of the Loop. Lake Michigan and the main stem and North Branch of the Chicago River form three edges of the Near North Side. The different uses that Chicagoans made of these bodies of water divided the Near North into an expensive residential strip in the east and an industrial, low-income area in the west. A residential and commercial corridor grew up around Clark Street, serving as a buffer between the two.

8 Near North Side

When in the 1830s New Yorker William B. Ogden saw the property that his family had bought on the Near North Side of the Chicago River, he was appalled by the swampy condition of the land. Nevertheless, rapidly increasing real-estate values and the possibility of industrial development along the river induced him to buy up large tracts of land there. He gave the Chicago Dock and Canal Company control of the land where in the twentieth century the Chicago North Pier was built. Ogden increased the amount of waterfront by having a canal dug across a bend in the North Branch of the river, thus creating

Medinah Athletic Club swimmers Richard Connell and Elder Halverson at the club's pool, 1929. Photographer: Unknown. Source: Chicago History Museum.

GOOSE ISLAND. Residential patterns followed industrial use. Irish factory workers were settled at the juncture of the river and its North Branch, an area called Kilgubbin or the Patch; Ogden's decision to bring the city's first railroad there in 1848 drove them northward along the river. Communities of German and Swedish farmers and merchants occupied the interior of the Near North Side. Finally, members of the McCormick family established an island of wealth when they built homes in the eastern quarter of the area, near to their Reaper Works located between Pine and Sand Streets, just north of the river.

In the 1850s Chicagoans began to recognize the appeal of lakefront land. The sandy mouth of the river was not yet suitable for permanent building but became the site of an aptly named vice district, the Sands. Ogden and other landowners took exception to its occupation by squatters and in 1857 persuaded Mayor John Wentworth to remove them.

The Chicago Fire of 1871 destroyed most of the structures on the Near North Side but did not alter existing land use. Rather, it was Potter and Bertha Palmer's decision to build their mansion along the future site of Lake Shore Drive that began a century-long process in which the rich took over increasing portions of the Near North Side. Fashionable Chicagoans moved from PRAIRIE AVENUE and built mansions facing the lake, spreading out along Astor Street. The enterprising George Streeter claimed that the sand accumulating around his boat, beached on the shore of Lake Michigan, was outside the legal limits of Illinois, so he could govern it. Although he ultimately lost his case, that section remains STREETERVILLE. The western district, meanwhile, was growing poorer and more disreputable. Increasing industrial pollution earned it the nickname "Smokey Hollow." In the 1880s a colony of Sicilians joined the Irish there. The area had a reputation for crime, and city police so feared "Death Corner" that they refused to investigate numerous murders there.

The 1920 opening of the Michigan Avenue Bridge, inspired by the Burnham Plan of 1909, secured the eastern sector of the Near North Side for the rich. The monumental bridge turned Pine Street into North Michigan Avenue and fostered development of a luxury shopping district. Investors built high-rise apartment buildings and sumptuous hotels. The central portion of the Near North Side became a district of rooming houses, segregating the elite from the concentrated poverty in the west.

Saul Bellow on Chicago

From *The Adventures of Augie March* (1949):

> I am an American, Chicago born—Chicago, that somber city—and go at things as I have taught myself, free-style, and will make the record in my own way: first to knock, first admitted; sometimes an innocent knock, sometimes a not so innocent. But a man's character is his fate, says Heraclitus, and in the end there isn't any way to disguise the nature of the knocks by acoustical work on the door or gloving the knuckles.

From *Humboldt's Gift* (1975), describing the view from the Hancock Building:

> From the skyscraper I could contemplate the air of Chicago on this short December afternoon. A ragged western sun spread orange light over the dark shapes of the town, over the branches of the river and the black trusses of bridges. The lake, gilt silver and amethyst, was ready for its winter cover of ice.

The years after the Great Depression saw shifts in the balance between wealth and poverty on the Near North Side. City officials tried to erode the western slum by replacing part of it with the Frances Cabrini Homes. By 1982 the high-rise Cabrini Extension and William Green Homes constituted a new neighborhood—CABRINI-GREEN. Deterioration spread eastward, however, and the promise of public housing in Chicago was not fulfilled.

In the 1950s the city turned to urban renewal. It cleared and sold the central strip between Clark and LaSalle Streets to developer Arthur Rubloff for SANDBURG VILLAGE. Rubloff also spearheaded the revitalization of North Michigan Avenue under the banner of "the MAGNIFICENT MILE." The success of these developments spurred the erection of more high-rise apartments and new investment in the Near North Side. In the 1980s the River North area became a center for art galleries. The Chicago Dock and Canal Trust, still controlled by William Ogden's descendants, made riverfront property available for new residential and commercial use with the Cityfront Center development. They converted old warehouses into a shopping mall called North Pier and built new skyscrapers. By the mid-1990s, expensive land encircled Cabrini-Green, but its residents were poor people determined to stay in their neighborhood. Mayor Richard M. Daley and other planners called for the demolition of part of the complex and its replacement with mixed-income housing, a process which was largely complete by the end of 2007.

Amanda Seligman

FURTHER READING: Berger, Miles L. *They Built Chicago: Entrepreneurs Who Shaped a Great City's Architecture*. 1992. ■ Stamper, John W. *Chicago's North Michigan Avenue: Planning and Development, 1900–1930*. 1991. ■ Zorbaugh, Harvey Warren. *The Gold Coast and the Slum: A Sociological Study of Chicago's Near North Side*. 1929.

Near South Side, Community Area 33, 2 miles S of the Loop. The Near South Side has probably seen as dramatic change and redevelopment as any Chicago community.

33
Near
South Side

The first settling the removal of the Indians were Germans, Irish, and Scandinavians who worked on the Illinois & Michigan Canal and then found work in the immense lumber district along the South Branch of the Chicago River. In the 1850s railroads entering Chicago established shops and yards nearby and attracted related industries. The city limits were extended south to 31st Street in 1853, and horsecar lines through the area spurred development.

As the business district supplanted the fine houses lining Michigan and Wabash Avenues south of Jackson Boulevard, wealthy families built new mansions on Prairie, Indiana, Calumet, and Michigan Avenues south of 16th Street. By the time of the 1871 Chicago Fire, PRAIRIE AVENUE was the city's most fashionable street. A handful of grand mansions still stand in the 1800 block, including the John J. Glessner House, designed in 1886 by architect H. H. Richardson. Further south, Michigan Avenue and South Parkway (now Dr. Martin Luther King Jr. Drive) were lined with the homes of wealthy businessmen.

The fire spared the area, but displaced businesses found temporary quarters there, and former mansions became boardinghouses. Another large fire in 1874 destroyed Chicago's small original black neighborhood, in the SOUTH LOOP, and it was reestablished west of State Street between 22nd and 31st Streets. Construction of the South Side Elevated Railroad in 1890–1892 brought rapid transit, and hotels and apartment buildings were built for the 1893 World's Columbian Exposition. As the area's character began to change, the wealthiest Chicagoans abandoned Prairie Avenue in the 1890s for the NEAR NORTH SIDE, or moved further south, to KENWOOD.

Wholesale houses, warehouses, and printing firms, displaced from the LOOP, began moving to the area. A particularly dramatic transformation occurred along Michigan Avenue between 14th and 22nd Streets. Grand houses lined the avenue at the turn of the century, but within a few years it had become "Auto Row," lined with elaborate terra cotta and plate-glass showrooms and garages.

Although the infamous Levee vice district around Cermak and State was officially closed in 1912, parts of the Near South Side continued to have an unsavory reputation. When black southerners began moving to Chicago in substantial numbers during and after World War I, many found housing in the low-rent areas west of State Street. As the Great Migration continued, housing discrimination confined blacks to a narrow "Black Belt" and century-old wooden houses became some of the nation's most shameful slums. The worst blocks were cleared in post–World War II urban renewal projects and public housing projects built in their place. At the end of the twentieth century, most of the area's residents lived in two Chicago Housing Authority complexes: the Harold Ickes Homes (1955) and the distinctive round Raymond Hilliard Center (1966).

Meanwhile, significant redevelopment proj-

Illinois Central Railroad station, 1964. Photographer: Unknown. Source: Chicago History Museum.

ects have transformed the district's edges. During the 1920s and 1930s Burnham Park and adjacent Northerly Island were created on landfill in Lake Michigan, and the Field Museum of Natural History, Soldier Field, the Adler Planetarium, and the John G. Shedd Aquarium were completed. The new landfill served as the site of the 1933–1934 Century of Progress Exposition and later the 1948 Railroad Fair. After World War II Northerly Island was offered as a site for the United Nations, then in 1947 became the site of Merrill C. Meigs Field Airport, which closed in 2003.

The Railroad Fair and other trade fairs held on the site renewed interest in a permanent exposition hall, and in 1960 the first McCormick Place building opened on a controversial lakefront site at 23rd Street. When that building was destroyed by fire in 1967, pressure to rebuild quickly led to an even larger building on the same site. The complex was expanded with a second hall west of Lake Shore Drive in 1986, and a third mammoth building south of 23rd Street opened in 1997. Although some exposition-related businesses have located in the neighborhood, hoped-for hotels and retail revitalization had not materialized by the end of the twentieth century.

At the north end of the Near South Side, SOUTH LOOP residential development has expanded into the area. Construction began in 1988 on the second phase of DEARBORN PARK, a neighborhood built on the defunct rail yards between State and Clark Streets south of Roosevelt Road, and a decade later similar projects reached as far south as Archer Avenue. Development began in 1990 on Central Station, a mixed-use development on 72 acres of former rail yards east of Indiana Avenue between Roosevelt Road and 18th Street. Meanwhile, the success of residential loft conversions in

Water Quality in the 1830s

When Caroline Palmer Clarke arrived in Chicago in 1835, she wrote to her sister-in-law describing the city. A few years later, Clarke would settle into her new home, at 16th and Michigan, which remains one of the oldest houses in Chicago, now located in the Prairie Avenue Historic District.

I am thus far much better pleased with Chicago than I expected. . . .
  I had expected to find the water very hard, but am as much disappointed in that as any one thing. The Lake water, which they use for almost every purpose, is as pure and good tasted as any I ever saw in my life. It is soft and washes perfectly well. To be sure they have the trouble of bringing it, but that costs only a *shilling a barrel,* which is nothing you know where they are in such a great way of doing business as they are here at Chicago.

Caroline Palmer Clarke to Mary Clarke Walker,
dated Chicago, November 1, 1835.
Chicago History Museum.

nearby PRINTER'S ROW has spread to buildings on Wabash, Michigan, and Indiana Avenues, making them residential streets again after 100 years.

Dennis McClendon

FURTHER READING: Holt, Glen E., and Dominic A. Pacyga. *Chicago: A Historical Guide to the Neighborhoods: The Loop and South Side.* 1979. ■ Wille, Lois. *At Home in the Loop: How Clout and Community Built Chicago's Dearborn Park.* 1997.

Near West Side, Community Area 28, 2 miles W of the Loop. Between the 1840s and the early 1860s wealthy Chicagoans with interests in the Lake Street business district sought to make the conveniently located Near West Side— bounded by the Chicago & North Western Railway to the north, the Pennsylvania Railroad to the west, the South Branch of the Chicago River to the east, and 16th Street to the south—an elite refuge from the daily commotion of the growing

28
Near
West Side

city, creating Jefferson Park (1850) and Union Park (1854) as small, safe public resorts.

By the 1870s a small middle class had gradually replaced the wealthy families around Union Park. But as early as the city's incorporation in 1837, the area contained the seeds of what would come: residential areas divided along ethnic, economic, and racial lines. The first African American settlement in Chicago emerged around Lake and Kinzie streets in the 1830s. After 1837 Irish immigrants settled in wooden cottages west of the river. The Irish were soon followed by German, Czech, Bohemian, and French immigrants. The section south of Harrison, bounded by Halsted on the west and 12th Street (later Roosevelt Road) on the south, would remain a port of entry for poor European immigrants. After the 1871 fire, over 200,000 people took refuge on the Near West Side, creating overcrowded conditions. Toward the end of the nineteenth century, Jews from Russia and Poland, along with Italians, replaced the Irish and Germans; the Italians settled between Polk and Taylor Streets, the Jews farther south, around 16th Street. The center of the Jewish business community, the MAXWELL STREET Market, or "Jew town," came to life at the intersection of Halsted and Maxwell. A Greek settlement known as the Delta developed between Harrison, Halsted, Polk, and Blue Island.

Wholesale trade businesses and manufacturers located along an east-west axis in the northern portion of the Near West Side in the 1870s and the 1880s. Lined with three- and four-story buildings, many of which housed several business establishments, the area provided a dense center of employment opportunity.

In the middle of this rapidly changing area in 1889, Jane Addams and Ellen Gates Starr opened Hull House, one of the few institutions inclined to combine a policy of Americanization with celebration of the neighborhood's ethnic diversity. African Americans were less welcome, relegated to less comprehensive institutions that catered only to blacks.

Most institution building on the Near West

An 1886 *Harper's Weekly* engraving of Chicago's lumber district viewed from the West Side Water Works (near Ashland and Blue Island). The large factory on the top left is the McCormick Works at Western and Blue Island. Artist: Unknown. Source: Chicago History Museum.

Polk Street before construction of the University of Illinois at Chicago. Photographer: Unknown. Source: University of Illinois at Chicago.

Jane Addams: Halsted Street around 1890

When Jane Addams arrived in Chicago in 1889 with the intention of founding a settlement house in one of Chicago's immigrant neighborhoods, she needed the help of Chicago reporters and businessmen to find a suitable location. Settling on a site somewhere near the junction of Blue Island Avenue, Halsted Street, and Harrison Street, Addams found a "fine old house standing well back from the street, surrounded on three sides by a broad piazza." She and Ellen Gates Starr furnished Hull House "as we would have furnished it were it in another part of the city."

Around Hull House was a neighborhood teeming with immigrants and their own institutions, like the imposing Holy Family Roman Catholic Church just a few blocks away, built by Irish immigrants before the Great Fire of 1871. But this was not a neighborhood of one immigrant group, and Addams understood this diversity just beyond her front porch:

Halsted Street is thirty-two miles long, and one of the great thoroughfares of Chicago. . . . Hull-House once stood in the suburbs, but the city has steadily grown up around it and its site now has corners on three or four foreign colonies. Between Halsted Street and the river live about ten thousand Italians—Neapolitans, Sicilians, and Calabrians, with an occasional Lombard or Venetian. To the south on Twelfth Street are many Germans, and side streets are given over almost entirely to Polish and Russian Jews. Still farther south, these Jewish colonies merge into a huge Bohemian colony, so vast that Chicago ranks as the third Bohemian city in the world. To the northwest are many Canadian-French, clannish in spite of their long residence in America, and to the north are Irish and first-generation Americans. On the streets directly west and farther north are well-to-do English-speaking families, many of whom own their houses and have lived in the neighborhood for years; one man is still living in his old farmhouse.

Addams, Jane. *Twenty Years at Hull-House.* 1910.

Side emerged out of the efforts of individual ethnic groups to reconstruct the cultural worlds they had left behind in Europe. Struggles among ethnic groups over urban space materialized in the construction and relocation of religious and educational institutions, along with the succession of saloons and small businesses. These tensions, sometimes marked by violence, along with economic mobility, led to an ongoing process of neighborhood succession, as older groups were replaced by newcomers. Those who left sold institutional buildings to the groups that stayed behind, or to the newcomers. The home of Sacred Heart Academy (1860), for example, became the site of the Chicago Hebrew Institute (1903).

African Americans and Mexicans moved into the Near West Side in larger numbers during the 1930s and 1940s. Approximately 26,000 African Americans lived there by 1940, with the number increasing to more than 68,000 by 1960, in part due to the Great Migration of black southerners. On the West Side as a whole the African American community grew rapidly during the 1940s and 1950s. Residential opportunities remained largely limited to ghettoes on the South and West Sides, and rivalry between the two districts developed as a significant aspect of local African American neighborhood culture.

The second half of the twentieth century brought major alterations to the Near West Side. The Chicago Circle Expressway interchange wiped out a significant section of GREEKTOWN. The construction of the University of Illinois at Chicago (UIC) resulted in the demolition of most of the Hull House complex, as well as the historic Italian neighborhood. Neither urban renewal nor the construction of public housing, both of which began before 1950 and continued into the 1960s, could alleviate the poverty that had resulted from continued migration in the face of a declining economic base on the West Side. The riots after Martin Luther King Jr.'s assassination in 1968 left a physical devastation on the West Side as a whole that reinforced existing images of the area as crime-ridden and bereft of hope.

University expansion toward the end of twentieth century once again reshaped the Near West Side, almost completely destroying the historical Maxwell Street Market and contributing to gentrification that followed patterns established in other neighborhoods bordering the LOOP. With the increase in real-estate values around UIC and the construction of the new United Center arena, parts of the Near West Side became increasingly attractive to middle-class and upper-middle-class Chicagoans interested in living near the downtown. Public housing in the area has been demolished and replaced by mixed-income projects such as University Village.

Myriam Pauillac

FURTHER READING: Suttles, Gerald D. *The Social Order of the Slum: Ethnicity and Territory in the Inner City.* 1968. ▪ Bryan, Mary Lynn McCree, and Allen F. Davis, eds. *100 Years at Hull-House.* 1990. ▪ Rosen, George. *Decision-Making Chicago-Style: The Genesis of a University of Illinois Campus.* 1980.

New City, Community Area 61, 5 miles SW of the

61
New City

Loop. University of Chicago sociologists who established boundaries for community areas in the 1920s named a large section of land around the Chicago stockyards New City. Yet this area has never represented a single community.

The Union Stock Yard opened for business on December 25, 1865, outside Chicago's city boundaries in Lake Township. In 1889 this area was annexed to Chicago. Throughout its 105-year history, the stockyards represented the key institution for the diverse communities of New City. Although most residents worked for the stockyards or in its auxiliary industries—notably the adjacent meatpacking district—they socialized in different spatial areas. Class and ethnic differences defined this area not as New City but by other separate designations, the most enduring of which are BACK OF THE YARDS and Canaryville.

Inhabited by working-class immigrants, Back of the Yards stretched to the west and south of the stockyards. Irish and German workers moved into this area out of necessity after securing employment nearby; the lack of transportation gave them few alternatives to living within walking distance of the factories. During the 1880s managers imported Polish workers as strikebreakers. The hiring of these workers spurred an influx of Eastern European immigrants that changed the composition of Back of the Yards. The older Irish and German workers left the neighborhood, taking advantage of transportation improvements at the turn of the century. In an attempt to keep themselves ethnically segregated from the newer workers, these older residents moved to EN-GLEWOOD and other neighboring districts. After World War I the neighborhood changed ethnic composition again due to the migration of Mexican American laborers into the neighborhood and African American workers who settled south of 49th Street. While Back of the Yards changed ethnic character over time, its working-class character has remained consistent.

Settlers of Canaryville, to the east of the stockyards, worked as clerks, cattle buyers, and managers. This neighborhood began as a middle-class and largely German-based Protestant community that included the family of Gustavus Swift, one of the founders of the meatpacking empire. Soon after the establishment of Canaryville, lower-middle-class Irish Roman Catholics moved into the neighborhood. While this neighborhood has also become more diverse over time, its residents still earn a higher average income than those in other sections of New City.

The population of New City reached its apex during the 1920s, when the stockyards and other industries employed over 40,000 workers. After World War II, convenient trucking routes replaced centralized train transport, allowing butchers to purchase livestock directly from rural farms. All of the major packinghouses in New City closed between 1952 and 1962. In 1971 the stockyards followed suit. Since this time, new industry has gradually replaced the cattle-based trade. In 1984 Chicago designated these former

Aerial view of the Union Stock Yard, 1936, looking toward the southeast. Photographer: Unknown. Source: Chicago History Museum.

factory sites as an urban enterprise zone. Enticed by the tax breaks this entailed, more than 100 companies moved into the area by 1991, employing over 10,000 workers.

Poor living conditions and a lack of public services made organizing a necessity and way of life for many working-class residents in New City. Despite its burgeoning population in the 1890s, few paved streets or sewers existed. The stockyards and meatpacking plants polluted without consideration of the workers who lived nearby. The tainted water supply of "Bubbly Creek" (a fork of the South Branch of the Chicago River used to dump animal waste) and the stench of garbage heaps adjacent to the factories presented serious sanitation hazards. In response to these conditions, churches organized social services and Mary McDowell founded the University of Chicago Settlement House in 1894. In the 1930s the organizational effort became more effective and less paternalistic with the founding of the Back

of the Yards Neighborhood Council (BYNC). This organization applied community pressure on city officials to obtain school lunch programs, fluoride in its drinking water, and other badly needed services for its members. While the BYNC helped mainly white ethnics and residents of the older Mexican American community area, other organizations coalesced in the 1970s to assist other Latino and African American laborers. The Hispanic United Neighborhood Organization and the African American Organization of New City have assisted residents with securing mortgages and home-improvement loans from banks and provided other basic social services that the older Catholic organizations provided before closing in the 1980s.

Erik Gellman

FURTHER READING: Pacyga, Dominic A. "New City." In *Local Community Fact Book: Chicago Metropolitan Area, 1990*, ed. Chicago Fact Book Consortium. 1995. ■ Slayton, Robert A. *Back of the Yards: The Making of a Local Democracy.* 1986.

New Town, neighborhood in the east LAKE VIEW Community Area that emerged in the early 1970s.

Niles, IL, Cook County, 13 miles NW of Loop. In  the early 1830s German farmers flocked to the area around present-day Waukegan Road and Milwaukee Avenue, which came to be known as Dutchman's Point. John Schadiger and Julius Perren were the first, building an unusual house that had no windows and a single door. In 1837 John Marshall and Benjamin Hall erected the North Branch Hotel, and the following year residents established the area's first schoolhouse.

By 1850 the North West Plank Road, later Milwaukee Avenue, allowed farmers to travel more easily to the markets of downtown Chicago. The Township of Niles formed in 1850; by 1884 the town, centered at Milwaukee, Waukegan, and Touhy Avenues, consisted of several stores, two hotels, three churches, three cemeteries, two schools, and a doctor's office. In 1899, at the time of the village's incorporation, population was 500. The name Niles was probably taken from the nationally distributed *Niles Register* newspaper.

After the turn of the century the Chicago Surface Lines street railway traveled down the middle of Milwaukee Avenue to Niles, bringing immigrants from Chicago. In the 1930s Niles's population of 2,135 included 800 Polish orphans in St. Hedwig's Orphanage.

In 1932 industrialist and inventor Robert Ilg constructed a recreational park for his employees. Although the Ilg Hot Air Electric Ventilating Company, later Ilg Industries, was located in Chicago, Ilg lived in Niles. He installed two swimming pools and a water tower, which he hid behind a half-size replica of Italy's Leaning Tower of Pisa. In 1960 the Ilg family turned over part of the park property to the Leaning Tower YMCA. The tower has since been restored and is a symbol of the community. In 1991 Niles and Pisa became sister cities.

Covering six square miles, Niles has no official downtown area but considers Milwaukee Avenue its commercial center. In the 1950s the village annexed an area at its northwest corner; construction of a commercial complex began soon afterward. The Golf Mill Shopping Center was dedicated in 1959. In 1989 approximately 1,100 businesses were active in the village, generating over $7 million in taxes.

Niles's population totaled 30,068 in 2000; 83 percent were white, 34 percent were foreign-born; 13 percent were Asian. More than a quarter were 64 or older. The only Chicago suburb to offer free bus service to major shopping and recreational facilities, Niles transports more than 350,000 commuters annually. Residents have access to extensive services, ranging from senior citizen centers to park district programs to counseling services.

Marilyn Elizabeth Perry

FURTHER READING: Tyse, Dorothy C. *History of Niles, Illinois.* 1974.

Noble Square, cooperative housing project constructed in the 1970s in the WEST TOWN Community Area.

Normal Park, neighborhood that developed around the teacher's college founded in the ENGLEWOOD Community Area after 1868.

Norridge, IL, 15 miles NW of the Loop. Norridge  shares 70 percent of its border with Chicago but prefers not to be identified with the city that nearly annexed it in 1948. Its name is derived from the names of neighboring areas NORWOOD PARK and PARK RIDGE.

Farmers who bought acreage in the area in the 1830s built their cabins on scattered sites. The area was once called Goat Village because of a woman who raised goats in the eastern portion of town.

Many called it the Swamp because of the muddy conditions and unpaved streets.

During the 1920s development was planned for an 80-acre subdivision from Ozanam to Olcott and Irving Park to Montrose. Residents shopped in neighboring DUNNING until 1932, when a commercial strip was established along Irving Park Road.

In 1948 Norridge was about to be annexed to Chicago when a local improvement association moved to incorporate as a village, stymieing Chicago's efforts. The 1950s ushered in an era of growth and development, encouraged by the construction of a waterworks system, the paving of sidewalks, streets, and curbs, and the installation of storm and sanitary sewers.

In 1954 Norridge annexed land north from Montrose to Lawrence, and farms disappeared quickly. The same year the Norridge Youth Committee was established to promote athletic and social events. The Norridge Community Park District was established after the village purchased 22 acres between Wilson and Lawrence Avenues. The village grew from one-half square mile in 1949 to two square miles in 1958. Many new residents, predominately of Italian and Polish extraction, came from Chicago neighborhoods.

The Harlem-Irving Plaza brought in sales tax revenues that led to decreased property taxes. Begun in 1955 with 45 stores, the center had 140 stores by the 1990s.

Although often compared to Harwood Heights because of their similar histories and their look-alike bungalow and ranch houses, Norridge has more shopping and industry than its eastern neighbor. Residents in the 1990s were still mainly of Polish and Italian heritage. The 2000 census counted 14,582 people, nearly 95 percent white, with small but growing Asian and Hispanic populations.

Marilyn Elizabeth Perry

FURTHER READING: McGowen, Thomas. *Island within a City: A History of the Norridge–Harwood Heights Area.* 1989. ■ Mussen, Craig. "The History and Origin of Norridge, Illinois." Manuscript. 1979. Eisenhower Public Library, Harwood Heights, IL.

North Center, Community Area 5, 5 miles N of the Loop. Bounded on the west by the North Branch of the Chicago River, North Center developed after industrialists' attention turned from the South Branch to the North Branch and working men and women began to settle near North Center's new factories and brickyards.

5
North
Center

In the 1840s John H. Kinzie and William B. Ogden owned most of the property in the North Center area. After trying unsuccessfully to market a few residential subdivisions near the North Western Railway's stops, Ogden sold a large tract to John Turner, who moved out to a large farmhouse there after the 1871 Chicago Fire. Turner rented scattered, smaller tracts to German truck farmers. Most of the North Center area, however, remained uncultivated and undeveloped until the late nineteenth century.

During the last quarter of the nineteenth century, Chicago's industrialists realized the potential of the river's North Branch. In 1880 the Deering Harvester Works opened at Fullerton Avenue and eventually expanded to encompass land in the North Center area. In the wake of the 1871 fire, concern over the flammability of wood intensified the demand for brick buildings in Chicago. As the riverbanks yielded more and more suitable clay, brickyards and clay pits dotted the North Branch, earning the area the nickname "Bricktown." These industries provided work for skilled and unskilled laborers, who moved into the area to avoid the cost of transportation to their jobs. Early in the twentieth century, Ravenswood Avenue, which marks North Center's eastern border, became a light industrial corridor. Working-class immigrants—initially Germans and Swedes, and later Kashubes, Poles, Italians, Hungarians, Slovaks, Serbs, and Croatians—set the unpretentious tone of North Center's residential areas—a striking contrast to the massive church complexes such as St. Benedict's Roman Catholic Church, on Irving Park Road.

Filming a movie set at the Selig Polyscope lot, Western and Irving Park, 1914. Photographer: Unknown. Source: Chicago History Museum.

The last truck farmers did not give up farming until the first decade of the twentieth century, but in the 1890s the tie between work and residence in North Center began to break. New street railway lines and the opening of the Ravenswood "L" prompted a boom in residential development as far as Western Avenue. The lots remained small and the inhabitants working-class, but the combination of transportation and affordable homes enabled people who labored elsewhere in the city to commute to their jobs.

The growing number of residents whose economic subsistence did not depend on local industries increased public objection to the noisome, ugly clay pits along the river. The clay pits did begin to shut down, but unfortunately for the protesting residents, the empty pits became dumping grounds for garbage. Land filled so haphazardly was not suitable for housing. One section of land owned by the Illinois Brick Company was filled in 1923 for the Mid-City Golf Links at Addison and Western Avenues. The Chicago Board of Education acquired this land and in 1934 built Lane Technical High School there. During the Great Depression, one of Chicago's first public housing complexes, the Julia C. Lathrop Homes, was built on the river at Diversey, straddling North Center's boundary with LINCOLN PARK.

In 1879 members of the Krieger Verein, a German social club, acquired the land around Belmont and Western for a family picnic grove. In 1905 owner George Schmidt transformed the grove into Riverview Sharpshooters Park and sought a clientele from around the city. Until

Riverview Park closed unexpectedly after the 1967 season, the amusement park's concessions and rides brought millions of Chicagoans and Midwestern tourists through North Center. In the early 1980s the Riverview Plaza shopping center and a district police office occupied the site of the old park.

Between 1940 and 1990 North Center's population declined from 48,759 to 33,010. Many white Chicagoans moved to suburbs, but people of Hispanic, Korean, and Filipino descent replaced some of them in North Center. Like their predecessors, most of North Center's new inhabitants earned moderate incomes. In the 1990s residents began to worry that they would be displaced by gentrification spilling over from neighboring Lincoln Park and LAKE VIEW. The popularity of newly designated neighborhoods like Roscoe Village provoked fears that longtime residents of North Center would no longer be able to afford their modest homes and small businesses.

Amanda Seligman

FURTHER READING: Drury, John. "Old Chicago Neighborhoods." *Landlord's Guide* (November 1948): 10–11. ■ Griffin, Al. "The Ups and Downs of Riverview Park." *Chicago History* 4.1 (Spring 1975): 14–22. ■ Vivien M. Palmer Papers, Chicago History Museum, Chicago.

North Chicago, IL, Lake County, 32 miles north

of the Loop. Incorporated as a village in 1895, North Chicago was called South Waukegan until 1901. Proximity to Lake Michigan and to Chicago made the area ideal for manufacturing. The fact that it was a temperance town with the motto "No saloons" was also a key selling point. However, workers grew impatient with the restrictions of temperance and demanded a change. By 1912 North Chicago possessed, in addition to its 15 industrial enterprises, no fewer than 26 saloons, all of which generated city revenue in the form of license fees.

Industry expanded rapidly in North Chicago.

In 1892 the Washburn and Moen Manufacturing Company, headquartered in Worcester, Massachusetts, became the first industry to locate in North Chicago. The Illinois division of Washburn and Moen manufactured barbed wire. The Lanyon Zinc Oxide Company and the Morrow Brothers Harness Company, manufacturers of horse-collar pads, were two other major late-nineteenth-century industries to locate in North Chicago. The Chicago Hardware Foundry Company opened in 1900 and the National Envelope Company in 1905. The development of these and other industries sparked a population boom in the area in the first decades of the twentieth century. From merely 20 residents in 1890, North Chicago counted 5,839 in 1920.

Companies like Washburn and Moen helped to stratify North Chicago along ethnic lines. The company transferred workers from its Worcester plant, and then added Swedes, Finns, and other Eastern Europeans. In the far north of North Chicago, Slovaks, who called the area "Kompanija," established Mother of God Roman Catholic Church. More to the south, Polish residents founded Holy Rosary Catholic Church, while German and Irish residents also established schools and churches.

Into the 1950s North Chicago attracted more residents as the industrial base of the community continued to grow; companies with plants in the community included American Motors, Johnson Motors, Goodyear, Abbott Laboratories, and Ocean Spray. Further growth came with the expansion of the Veterans Administration Hospital and the annexation of the Great Lakes Naval Training Station. The population reached 47,275 in 1970, but in the decade that followed many plants shut their doors. Washburn and Moen, one of the city's largest employers in the 1950s, closed in 1979. As jobs dwindled between 1970 and 1980, North Chicago lost 18 percent of its population. The drop in activity at the Naval Training Station after the Vietnam War further contributed to North Chicago's decline in population. By 2000 the population stood at 35,918.

Changes in North Chicago's racial makeup accompanied its decline in population. African Americans, who had lived in North Chicago since its inception, accounted for 34 percent of the city's population by the end of the twentieth century. The city also had become considerably poorer by the 1990s. Of the 261 municipalities in the six counties surrounding Chicago, North Chicago ranked 253rd in per capita income toward the end of the twentieth century. Much of North Chicago is federal land and untaxable, making the tax burden on private residents among the highest in Illinois. Abbott Laboratories remained one of North Chicago's largest taxpayers, but with the decline of other industries and the corresponding drop in commercial development and population, efforts to resuscitate the once-thriving community have met with difficulty.

Wallace Best

FURTHER READING: "North Chicago." In *Local Community Fact Book: Chicago Metropolitan Area, 1990*, ed. Chicago Fact Book Consortium, 1995. ■ Bateman, Newton, and Paul Selby, eds. *Historical Encyclopedia of Illinois and History of Lake County*. 1902. ■ Sayler, Carl E. "City of North Chicago." In *A History of Lake County, Illinois*, ed. John J. Halsey. 1912.

North Lawndale, Community Area 29, 5 miles W of the Loop. Today circumscribed by railroad lines on three sides and extending north to within several blocks of the Eisenhower Expressway, the West Side neighborhood of North Lawndale is home to some of Chicago's poorest black residents. In the past, North Lawndale boomed as a haven for refugees from the Great Fire of 1871 and then bustled as Chicago's Jewish ghetto. The neighborhood's landscape was divided among two-flat apartments, Douglas Park, and massive industrial complexes. North Lawndale's prospects turned on its capacity to balance the needs of its industrial and residential populations.

In the early nineteenth century a portage trail

29
North
Lawndale

extended through the prairie land from Lake Michigan to the Des Plaines River. After 1848 the region's Dutch and English farmers knew the route as Southwest Plank Road (later Ogden Avenue), an improved toll road. The extension of the Chicago, Burlington & Quincy Railroad prompted further settlement in this portion of Cicero Township. After Chicago annexed the eastern part of the township in 1869, the real-estate firm Millard & Decker built a residential suburb. They advertised "Lawndale" as linking "in harmonious union the people of a community." The new western development's fireproof brick buildings attracted people and businesses burned out by the 1871 fire.

In the late nineteenth century, many industrial workers settled in North Lawndale. The McCormick Reaper Works opened a plant in the neighboring LOWER WEST SIDE in 1873. The openings of a Western Electric Plant in nearby CICERO in 1903 and the headquarters of Sears, Roebuck & Co. in 1906 brought North Lawndale's population to 46,225 by 1910.

During the second decade of the twentieth century, Russian Jews became North Lawndale's largest residential group. Eastern European Jews still living in the old NEAR WEST SIDE ghetto mocked those who left for having pretensions of upward mobility; accordingly, they called North Lawndale "Deutschland." Although not reaching the economic heights reached by the city's German Jews in the nineteenth century, North Lawndale's burgeoning population established its own small city of community institutions, including Mt. Sinai Hospital, Herzl Junior College (now Malcolm X College), several bathhouses, and a commercial strip on Roosevelt Road. One study found that in 1946, North Lawndale housed about 65,000 Jews, approximately a quarter of the city's Jewish population.

Fourteen years later 91 percent of the neighborhood's 124,937 residents were black. African Americans began moving into North Lawndale in the early 1950s, some directly from southern states, others displaced from their South Side homes by urban renewal projects. In response, white residents moved out to northern neighborhoods such as ROGERS PARK. Despite severe residential overcrowding, no new private housing was built in North Lawndale. Its physical decline was so severe that late in 1957 the city's Community Conservation Board recognized it as a conservation area.

In contrast to previous residents of North Lawndale, most new black residents could not find work in the neighborhood. North Lawndale's industries now employed people who commuted to the neighborhood only for work. Consequently, the local consumer base became much poorer, and tensions grew between the whites who worked in North Lawndale during the day and the blacks who lived there. In 1966 the neighborhood's poverty prompted Martin Luther King Jr. to pick North Lawndale as the base for the northern civil rights movement. Residents found King's visit highly symbolic: his stay attracted much attention but resulted in little tangible change.

After King's assassination in 1968, however, the neighborhood did change. West Side residents rioted, and although commercial centers run by whites were the targets of physical attack, residential areas burned as well. Most of the large plants and small businesses left because they lost their insurance and feared additional riots. International Harvester closed its factory in 1969, and Sears struck another blow when it moved its international headquarters to the new downtown tower in 1974. The community-based organizations King inspired—the Lawndale People's Planning and Action Council and the Pyramidwest Development Corporation—tried but failed to attract new industries to employ North Lawndale's residents and new housing to revitalize the neighborhood. During the last quarter of the twentieth century, North Lawndale's population dropped precipitously, from its peak in 1960 to 41,768 in 2000. Residents fled its increasing poverty, unemployment, crime, and physical deterioration, but hints of revital-

ization in the late 1990s suggested to some observers that the area was beginning to prosper.

Amanda Seligman

FURTHER READING: Cutler, Irving. *Jews of Chicago: From Shtetl to Suburb.* 1996. ■ Jefferson, Alpine Wade. "Housing Discrimination and Community Response in North Lawndale (Chicago), Illinois, 1948–1978." Ph.D. diss., Duke University. 1979. ■ Ralph, James. *Northern Protest: Martin Luther King, Jr., Chicago, and the Civil Rights Movement.* 1993.

North Park, Community Area 13, 9 miles NW of the Loop. North Park is a stable, quiet, tree-shaded, middle-income community where most homes are owner-occupied. It is located between Cicero Avenue on the west and the North Shore Channel on the east, the city limits and Devon Avenue on the north, and the North Branch of the Chicago River on the south. The presence of the two streams provides a charming and unusual ambience for the area. Chicago's only waterfall (about four feet high) appears where the North Branch of the Chicago River tumbles into the North Shore Channel.

13
North Park

North Park's origins lie in 1855 when a village was platted in the newly organized Jefferson Township. The early residents were German and Swedish farmers who grew vegetables in fields laid out along the south bank of the North Branch of the Chicago River. Czechs moved into the northwestern corner of the area after the Bohemian National Cemetery was opened in 1877. They stayed only a short while, however, and began to move on around 1900.

In 1893 the Swedish University Association of the Swedish Evangelical Mission Covenant purchased a large acreage in the area and donated about 8.5 acres along the river in the southeastern corner of North Park for establishment of a college. Construction at North Park College began in 1894, and the surrounding acreage was subdivided for homes. Within the next few years streets were laid out, sewer lines put in place, and board sidewalks installed. Nonetheless, development proceeded slowly; in 1910 the population numbered only 478. From 1910 to 1930, however, the area burgeoned, especially after the first two-flats and small apartments were built in the 1920s. The population tripled from 1920 to 1930 and the community was rapidly transformed from an area of prairie and woods to a mature residential community of bungalows and two-flats. The 1930s also saw development of a small industrial district in the northwest corner of the area, along Peterson Avenue, which, although declining, remains the only industrial activity in North Park.

Population grew rapidly during World War II and in the postwar period and reached its high point in 1960. Like most city neighborhoods, North Park lost population through the next 20 years, but unlike most others, it grew by over 6 percent from 1980 to 1990. Faculty, staff, and students of local colleges and universities often live in the area, as do employees of nearby Swedish Covenant Hospital. This stabilizes the area, greatly reducing the turnover of homes. Others have also responded to the solid housing stock and the thriving family-oriented character of the neighborhood. In recent years Hispanics and a sizable number of Koreans and Filipinos have joined the Swedes and Germans who long dominated the area.

The neighborhood is strongly supported by the presence of important educational and civic institutions. North Park College has now become North Park University, serving a wider clientele than formerly. In addition, Northeastern Illinois University provides a wide-ranging curriculum and attracts students from throughout Chicago, as does Von Steuben magnet high school. The Municipal Tuberculosis Sanitarium, built just after 1900 at the intersection of Pulaski and Bryn Mawr, was closed in 1974 and converted into senior citizen housing (North Park Village), a school for the mentally handicapped, and the North Park Village Nature Center, the only such facility in the city. A source of pride for area residents, this 46-acre preserve holds wetlands, woods, and sa-

vannas, and features 2.5 miles of hiking trails and a visitor center.

David M. Solzman

FURTHER READING: Chicago Fact Book Consortium, ed. *Local Community Fact Book: Chicago Metropolitan Area, Based on the 1970 and 1980 Censuses.* 1984. ■ Solzman, David M. *The Chicago River: An Illustrated History and Guide to the River and Its Waterways.* 1998, 2006.

North Pullman, neighborhood to the north of the planned town in the PULLMAN Community Area.

North Town, familiar name for the WEST RIDGE Community Area, also known as West Rogers Park.

Norwood Park, Community Area 10, 11 miles NW of the Loop. Prior to Norwood Park's incorporation in 1874, the village had a country setting far away from the bustle of the city. Early developers hoped to create a resort, taking advantage of area woodlands and hills. The subdivision departed from the typical grid pattern and instead, like Frederick Law Olmsted's RIVERSIDE, platted winding roads alternating with rectangular streets. The Circle, a historic street with old Victorian houses, is shaped in an oval.

10
Norwood
Park

In 1833 Mark Noble became one of Chicago's prominent citizens when he purchased substantial acreage in Niles and Jefferson Townships. The frame house built that year by the Noble family, known today as the Noble-Seymour-Crippen house, is the oldest extant house in the city of Chicago.

English farmers settled in the area in the 1830s. Over the years Germans became the major ethnic group, along with substantial numbers of Poles and Scandinavians. In 1853 the Illinois & Wisconsin Railroad (later known as the Chicago & North Western Railway) installed a rail line serving the area. For several months

Swedish Old People's Home, Norwood Park, 1925. Photographer: Unknown. Source: Chicago History Museum.

there was only one passenger, until other residents realized the advantages of railway travel to Chicago.

In 1868 the Norwood Land and Building Association created its curvilinear subdivision. Construction began on the Norwood Park Hotel and an artificial lake in hopes that the area would attract Chicagoans seeking a resort atmosphere. Although the hotel attracted local residents for entertainment purposes, it never drew enough customers to be a success.

Following incorporation in 1874, the village prohibited the sale of liquor. The village's name followed Henry Ward Beecher's novel *Norwood; Or, Village Life in New England*. The word "Park" was added after it was discovered that another post office in the state had the name of Norwood.

In 1893 the village of Norwood Park was annexed to Chicago. Nine trains stopped in the town daily to serve residents commuting to the city.

Although there were houses scattered around the village, most were built close to the railroad.

Improvements to roads such as Milwaukee Avenue, Northwest Highway, Foster, Devon, and Harlem in the 1920s led to easier travel and brought many newcomers to Norwood Park. Despite the hard times of the Great Depression the community continued to add homes and residents during the 1930s. In the 1950s the Kennedy Expressway cut through Norwood Park but was routed around the historic houses on the Circle.

Norwood Park is home to a number of institutions. The Norwegian Old People's Home was built in 1896 on the site of the old hotel; a Passionist monastery (Immaculate Conception) in 1904; the Danish Old People's Home in 1906. The Sisters of Resurrection (Roman Catholic) founded Resurrection High School in 1913, Resurrection Hospital in 1953, and Resurrection Retirement Community in 1977.

The population of 41,827 in 1970 declined to 37,669 by 2000. Housing in Norwood Park ranges from nineteenth-century Victorian houses to post–World War II bungalows, ranches, Georgians, and Cape Cods. Although most housing is single-family, condominiums gained in popularity in the 1990s.

Retail and service businesses line Northwest Highway, and Norwood Park has easy access to O'Hare Airport, trains, and major highways, but the village remains a mostly residential community, with no significant industrial base.

Marilyn Elizabeth Perry

FURTHER READING: Andreas, A. T. *History of Cook County.* 1884. ■ McGowen, Thomas. *Island within a City: A History of the Norridge–Harwood Heights Area.* 1989. ■ Scholl, Edward T. *Seven Miles of Ideal Living.* 1957.

Oak Brook, IL, DuPage County, 17 miles W of the Loop. Oak Brook is located in the lower Salt Creek drainage basin, where Salt Creek turns eastward toward the Des Plaines River. From the late 1600s to the early 1800s, the region was the location of the largest Potawatomi settlement in what is now DuPage County. Oak Brook was then known as Sauganakka.

White settlers began arriving in the 1830s, following major Indian trails that are presently traced by Spring, York, and Butterfield Roads and Ogden Avenue. The Potawatomi, who had sold their land to the federal government, were moving out. Settler Elisha Fish arrived in 1834.

Families from New York, Pennsylvania, Ohio, Indiana, and Kentucky were attracted by the rich soil, clear streams, and abundant woodland. Residents called the area Brush Hill, and later Fullersburg, after Benjamin Fuller. Both names, owing to boundary changes, were shared with what is now HINSDALE.

Before the Civil War, some settlers maintained a way station on the Underground Railroad in the gristmill of Frederick Graue on Salt Creek. Settlement continued after the war. Many of the newcomers were immigrants from Europe, mostly from Germany.

Over the next several decades, the area gradually changed from an agricultural settlement to a cluster of small estates. A significant event in this transformation was the purchase of land along Salt Creek by Frank Osgood Butler of Hinsdale in 1898. It was Butler's son Paul who was largely responsible for the development of Oak Brook as one of the nation's most affluent suburbs in the twentieth century. Butler, a business executive and sportsman, began acquiring neighboring farmland for investment purposes in the 1920s. Small parcels of farmland also were sold to other individuals who built homes on the sites.

In the mid-1930s, home owners and farmers formed the Community Club, which helped unincorporated Oak Brook establish an identity distinct from its neighbors, Hinsdale to the south and ELMHURST to the north.

Butler meanwhile had continued to accumulate land, hoping at some point to build a planned community. On part of his property, he established the multiuse Sports Core, which came to include nationally renowned golf and polo clubs. By 1958, when Oak Brook was incorporated, Butler owned much of the land within its boundaries.

Three factors had forced incorporation—completion of the nearby Tri-State and East-West Tollways, a change in zoning along the tollways to commercial use, and the purchase of land by Marshall Field & Company for a proposed shopping center. The proposed shopping center was also claimed by neighboring Utopia (now Oakbrook Terrace) but was eventually annexed to Oak Brook. The Oakbrook Shopping Center opened

Graue Mill, Oak Brook, 1964. Photographer: Curt Teich & Co. Source: Curt Teich Archives, Lake County Discovery Museum.

in 1962 and became the commercial heart of the village.

Beginning in the 1960s, several luxury subdivisions were built. In the years that followed, many nationally prominent corporations, such as Armour & Company, Eastman Kodak, and McDonald's, opened offices in Oak Brook. Development continued in the 1990s, including a major expansion of the shopping center.

Margaret Franson Pruter

FURTHER READING: Kinnavy, Susan, Audrey Muschler, and Pat Walker. *Oak Brook.* 1990. ■ Thompson, Richard, ed. *DuPage Roots.* 1985.

Oak Lawn, IL, Cook County, 13 miles SW of the Loop. Oak Lawn lies just

beyond the southwestern edge of Chicago and is one of the largest municipalities in Cook County. The intersection of 95th Street (the village's main east-west thoroughfare) and Cicero Avenue is one of the county's busiest. A farming community until the mid-twentieth century, Oak Lawn is now home mainly to commuters.

Settlers established farms in the area in the 1840s and 1850s, attracted by a modest stream called Stony Creek (also spelled Stoney Creek) that meandered through a dense grove of black oak trees. The area was variously known as Black Oaks and Black Oak Grove. By 1860 a schoolhouse and several farmhouses lined Black Oak Grove Road (95th Street). The nearest stores and post office were in BLUE ISLAND, some 10 miles away.

After the Civil War, German immigrants began settling in the area. A new post office opened in neighboring Evergreen Park. In the 1880s the Wabash Railroad connected the area with Chicago, the first subdivision was platted near the train station, and the community was formally called Oak Lawn for the first time. (It had briefly been called Agnes earlier in the decade and was occasionally referred to as Oak

Park.) Residents took the train to ENGLEWOOD to shop, and farm products and milk were sent to markets in Chicago.

A post office was established in 1882, and a portion of Stony Creek was enlarged to form Oak Lawn Lake, a recreational area. By 1909, the year of incorporation, the village's 300 citizens were scattered over 1.5 square miles. Some of these were Dutch truck farmers, who had arrived around the turn of the century. Incorporation meant that gas lines could be installed, unruly visitors picnicking in the wooded areas along the creek and lake could be policed, and the city of Chicago would be less likely to annex the community. In 1911 the village's signature black oaks were replaced by electrical lines and poles.

An innovative plan begun in 1927 concentrated commercial development along major arteries and away from neighborhoods of single-family homes. In 1953 the village changed from a trustee form of government to a managerial form. Oak Lawn's population grew from 8,751 in 1950 to 60,305 in 1970 as white residents moved from Chicago's South Side to the suburbs. Several annexations increased the village's area to more than eight square miles. The village's rapid growth was checked briefly in 1967 by a tornado that killed 37 people and damaged or destroyed 900 buildings. In 1970 Oak Lawn became a home rule unit, allowing the village greater latitude in determining municipal policy.

Commercial and retail businesses occupy about one-third of the village, mainly flanking 95th Street, with some industry in the southern and northwestern areas. The citizenry was 93 percent white in 2000. The community's largest employer is Christ Hospital and Medical Center, but most residents work in Chicago. Oak Lawn Lake is administered by the Oak Lawn Park District, and Stony Creek meanders through the Wolfe Wildlife Refuge on the village's south side.

Betsy Gurlacz

FURTHER READING: *Black Oak and After: A Series on the History of Oak Lawn.* 1991. ■ *Oak Lawn, One Hundred Years: A Century of Growth.* 1982.

Oak Park, IL, Cook County, 8 miles W of the  Loop. Joseph Kettlestrings bought 173 acres of timber and prairie land just east of the Des Plaines River in 1835 and erected a house on the stagecoach route from Galena to Chicago. The area was sparsely populated when the Galena & Chicago Union Railroad laid tracks parallel to the stagecoach route in 1848. Kettlestrings Grove slowly grew into the small village of Oak Ridge, which is now the northwestern portion of Oak Park.

By the end of the Civil War, the village was dotted with a market, a general store, a stationery business, and a small newspaper. The name Oak Ridge, already assigned to another post office in Illinois, was changed to Oak Park in 1872.

Oak Park grew dramatically after the 1871 Chicago Fire. James Scoville bought acreage once owned by Kettlestrings and subdivided the area near the railroad station. The Cicero Water, Gas and Electric Light Company serviced the community, streets were paved, surface transportation lines established, and subdivisions extended beyond the old stagecoach route, later named Lake Street. The village was one of eight communities governed by Cicero Township. In 1902, however, Oak Park seceded from the township and incorporated as a separate municipality.

The extension of the Lake Street "L" to Harlem Avenue at the turn of the twentieth century linked Oak Park more closely to Chicago. It was one of only a few suburban stops in the system. The village's population rose to 10,000 in 1900 and to 40,000 by 1920. By the 1920s the area around the elevated had developed into a regional shopping district that included Marshall Field's, Wieboldt's, and the Fair Store. Many of the older large homes in the central district were replaced by apartments and commercial and office buildings. Builders like Seward Gunderson and Thomas Hulbert developed homes south of Madison Avenue. The prairies north of Lake Street soon vanished, replaced by large homes, including many designed by Frank Lloyd Wright and E. E. Roberts. Wright established his studio in Oak Park in 1898 and designed the nearby Unity Temple, which is on the National Register of Historic Places.

Ernest Hemingway, Doris Humphrey, and Edgar Rice Burroughs are among those associated with Oak Park. Hemingway was born there in 1899, and the Hemingway Foundation has preserved his boyhood home and opened a small museum. Humphrey, who grew up in Oak Park, opened her first dance studio there before joining the Denishawn Company in 1918. The Doris Humphrey Society was established in Oak Park in 1989 to preserve her contributions to modern dance. Burroughs wrote 22 Tarzan books while residing in Oak Park from 1912 to 1919.

After World War II, Oak Park faced dramatic changes. Shopping malls along new expressways drew business away from Oak Park's downtown. Demographic change posed complementary challenges. By 1958 Oak Park's overwhelmingly white, Republican, mainline Protestant population saw rising numbers of Roman Catholics, Jews, and fundamentalist Christians enter the village. This shift did not affect the community's high level of educational or economic attainment, but it sparked fears of a departure from Oak Park's traditional conservative values. By the early 1970s Italians and Irish outnumbered the Germans, English, and Scandinavians who had long predominated, and Catholicism had become a significant presence.

The ability of Oak Parkers to absorb new groups was soon tested again. Oak Park's eastern neighbor, Chicago's AUSTIN neighborhood, had long been characterized by tree-lined streets of gracious homes and small bungalows, with residents who had lived in the community for generations. Both communities, however, had aging housing stock and weak zoning and building codes. Over 50 percent of Oak Park's housing comprised apartment buildings, most concentrated along its eastern border. Oak Parkers watched firsthand in the 1960s as Austin's residents fought desperately to defend their community from a

Unity Church, Oak Park, 1913. Photographer: Percy H. Sloan. Source: The Newberry Library.

destabilizing influx of African American home seekers, with little success—resegregation was rapid and tumultuous.

Oak Park devised a different strategy, which would use planning to ensure that desegregation would not lead to resegregation. The village board created a Community Relations Commission charged with preventing discrimination, forestalling violent neighborhood defense mechanisms, and setting a high standard of behavior as the community prepared for imminent racial change. Village officials, often joined by clergymen, visited blocks to which families of color might move and sought to control the fears and rumors generally associated with neighborhood succession. They identified white families who would welcome the newcomers. They encouraged African American families to disperse throughout the village to counter concerns of clustering and ghetto formation. In 1968, after lengthy and angry debate and the passage of the federal Fair Housing Act, the village board passed an open-housing ordinance allowing officials to control many aspects of racial integration that otherwise were likely to lead to resegregation. Real-estate agents were banned from panic-peddling, block-busting, and the use of For Sale signs (a tool used by blockbusters). A community relations department addressed rumors, monitored the quality of services and amenities throughout the village, and established block clubs to promote resident cohesion and local problem solving. The police force expanded by one-third, with a residency requirement whose impact was magnified because police generally lived in the areas most likely to be threatened by resegregation. An equity assurance program for home owners reassured residents that they were financially protected against a downward spiral of property values. Leaders acted on a vision of Oak Park as a community strong enough both to achieve integration and to challenge the Chicago pattern of block-by-block resegregation with a policy of managed integration through dispersal.

The most controversial policies involved racial steering. A group of residents led by Roberta (Bobbie) Raymond established the Oak Park Housing Center, which retrained real-estate agents to prevent racial steering and encouraged black home seekers to live throughout Oak Park. The center worked with the village to improve areas that white home seekers or residents might find unattractive and steered whites toward these areas to limit the concentration of black residents in a particular neighborhood. A public relations campaign targeted white home seekers across the country to promote an image of Oak Park as a multicultural, cosmopolitan, middle-class community, close to the city, with good transportation and schools.

Despite these programs, during the 1970s the village experienced a net loss of 10,000 white Oak Parkers, coinciding with a net increase of only 5,500 black residents. Urbanologists' predictions that the ghetto would roll over Oak Park, however, proved inaccurate. Oak Park maintained its majority white population through extensive and white-oriented planning, and it has remained an integrated village. Pockets of racial segregation have persisted, but the community has succeeded in maintaining a public culture that takes pride in racial diversity.

Tina Reithmaier
Camille Henderson Zorich

FURTHER READING: Goodwin, Carole. *The Oak Park Strategy.* 1979. ■ Guarino, Jean. *Oak Park: A Pictorial History.* 1988. ■ Halley, William. *Early Days in Oak Park.* 1933.

Oakland, Community Area 36, 4 miles SE of the Loop. Oakland is bounded by 35th and 43rd Streets, Lake Michigan, Cottage Grove, Pershing, and Vincennes Avenues. The entire area of the community is approximately one square mile.

36
Oakland

Oakland originally grew out of the Cleaverville settlement. In 1851 industrialist Charles Cleaver purchased from Samuel Ellis 22 acres of swampy ground near 38th Street and Lake Michigan, and built a soap factory and company town that included a commissary, house of worship, town hall, and homes for workers. Part of the area was annexed to Chicago in 1863, the rest in 1889.

Residents were attracted to the area because of nearby Camp Douglas, the stockyards, and a commercial district that included popular saloons. The addition of a horsecar line in 1867 improved access to the city. In 1871 real-estate developers subdivided the area and renamed it Oakland. In less than five years the community became home to many of Chicago's elite. In 1881 transportation was greatly improved with an Illinois Central Railroad terminal at 39th and Cottage Grove. This area of commercial activity became known as the "Five Crossings." By the end of the century, more affluent residents moved out and were replaced by working-class Irish residents. Numerous single-family houses and apartments were constructed to accommodate the influx of immigrants.

In 1905 the Abraham Lincoln Center was founded by Jenkin Lloyd Jones as a meeting place for people of various races, religions, and nationalities. Located at 700 E. Oakwood Boulevard, this historic landmark designed by Frank Lloyd Wright now serves as the home of Northeastern Illinois University's Center for Inner City Studies.

During the first wave of the Great Migration between 1916 and 1920 many African Americans settled in Oakland. During the 1930s Oakland experienced its greatest diversity, with a mixture of African Americans, Germans, Jews, English, Irish, Canadians, and Japanese. Racial tensions escalated as the African American population increased. Some white residents resorted to violence and restrictive covenants to prevent blacks from moving into Oakland, but such efforts proved unsuccessful, and by 1950 Oakland was 77 percent African American.

In the 1970s Oakland experienced a declining economic base. Public housing projects such as Ida B. Wells, once the pride of the community, became crime-infested. The former Oakland Theatre, located in the heart of Oakland near 39th

Poster for the dedication ceremony for Ida B. Wells Homes, 1940. Designer: Unknown. Source: Library of Congress.

and Cottage Grove, became the headquarters of the notorious El Rukn street gang. The city of Chicago demolished dilapidated buildings, and vacant lots were left scattered throughout the community. Oakland's average income fell below the poverty level as middle-class residents moved further south.

During the 1990s, under the leadership of Robert Lucas, the Kenwood-Oakland Community Organization (KOCO) rehabilitated several buildings in the community and successfully pressured the city to invest in Oakland. Beginning in 1994 the North Kenwood–Oakland Conservation Community Council, led by Shirley Newsome, cosponsored the Kenwood-Oakland Parade of Homes, which promoted development of single-family houses, town houses, and rehabbed buildings.

Claudette Tolson

FURTHER READING: Holt, Glen E., and Dominic A. Pacyga. *Chicago: A Historical Guide to the Neighborhoods: The Loop and South Side.* 1981. ■ Jones, LeAlan, and Lloyd Newman. *Our America: Life and Death on the South Side of Chicago.* 1997. ■ Travis, Dempsey. *An Autobiography of Black Chicago.* 1981.

O'Hare, Community Area 76, 14 miles NW of the  Loop. The land constituting the O'Hare Community Area was only thinly developed before World War II. The 1829 Treaty of Prairie du Chien gave two square miles along the Des Plaines River to Alexander Robinson, a Scottish-Ottawa interpreter who had aided whites escaping the Fort Dearborn Massacre. In the early 1840s a few families settled along what would become Higgins Road, while immigrants from Germany settled in the southwest section of the area, establishing a church and St. Johannes Cemetery in 1849. The northeastern section was an unincorporated area called Orchard Place, named for the depot the Wisconsin Central Railroad opened there in 1887. Despite the railroad, however, few people settled in Orchard Place. A residential subdivision opened in the 1930s, but all traces of it vanished with the developments of World War II.

In 1942 Douglas Aircraft took over Orchard Place for the production of cargo planes. After war production ended, the facility became a commercial airport, and in 1947 the Chicago City Council picked it as the site for the city's new international airport (named for aviator Edward H. "Butch" O'Hare). All local facilities, except for St. Johannes Cemetery, were removed.

In order to consolidate its control over the airport area, Chicago annexed it in March 1956, including the western edge, in DuPage County. Because the law required that annexed areas be contiguous with the existing city, the city council also annexed a narrow stretch of Higgins Road. Concerned that this tie between the airport and the body of the city was too tenuous, Chicago overrode the objections of surrounding suburbs

76
O'Hare

like Schiller Park, annexing the forest preserve areas named for Alexander Robinson and his wife in 1958 and exchanging Higgins Road for a wider stretch along Foster Avenue in 1961. The building of the Kennedy Expressway in the late 1950s further reinforced the link between air travelers and the LOOP. The addition of such a large amount of land necessitated the creation of a new community area on the city's planning map, setting a precedent for the secession of EDGEWATER from UPTOWN.

The rapid success of the airport inspired a tremendous increase in nearby land values. Along the expressway, developers built a gleaming row of office towers occupied by businesses taking advantage of the proximity to other cities provided by the airport. High-rise apartment buildings and a few small tracts of single-family houses and condominiums made the portion of the O'Hare Community Area bisected by NORRIDGE a residential area in the 1960s. Employees of the airport and its airlines occupied many of these homes.

Amanda Seligman

FURTHER READING: Chicago Fact Book Consortium, ed. *Local Community Fact Book: Chicago Metropolitan Area, 1990.* 1995. ▪ Doherty, Richard P. "The Origin and Development of Chicago-O'Hare International Airport." Ph.D. diss., Ball State University. 1970.

Old Town, neighborhood in the LINCOLN PARK Community Area. During World War II, Chicago's Civil Defense Agency designated the triangle bounded by North, Clark, and Ogden Avenues a neighborhood defense unit. The neighbors in this residential section of "North Town" continued their association after the war, sponsoring annual art fairs dubbed the "Old Town Holiday." The name Old Town, evoking a cozy, neighborly spirit, persisted when residents concerned about the area's physical deterioration formed the Old Town Triangle Association in 1948. OTTA's activities inspired urban renewal throughout Lincoln Park.

During the 1960s residents began to worry that OTTA's success undermined the insularity of their neighborhood. The rehabilitation of beautiful nineteenth-century houses and the increasingly popular art fair brought thousands of visitors to the area. Old Towners relished the presence of the Second City theater company and the Old Town School of Folk Music. But when Wells Street, a commercial strip that cut through Old Town, enjoyed a boom, drawing wealthy patrons to fashionable restaurants and stores, residents resented the noise, trash, and crowds. During the late 1960s, as Wells Street became a gathering place for hippies, some of the new shops failed and were replaced by stores marketing junky trinkets and pornography. Wells Street and Old Town resecured their status when Lincoln Park's urban renewal effort brought young professionals with money to the rehabbed cottages and new high-rises.

Amanda Seligman

FURTHER READING: Callaway, John D. "Will Excess Spoil Old Town?" *Chicago Scene* 4.8 (August 1963): 21–23. ▪ Commission on Chicago Historical and Architectural Landmarks. *Old Town: Preliminary Summary of Information.* 1975. ▪ Pacyga, Dominic A., and Ellen Skerrett. *Chicago, City of Neighborhoods: Histories and Tours.* 1986.

Orchard Place, sparsely settled area around a depot of the Wisconsin Central Railroad that became part of the airport in the O'HARE Community Area.

Orland Park, IL, Cook County, 22 miles SW of the Loop. During the past 20 years, Orland Park has been one of the focal points for growth in the metropolitan region southwest of Chicago. Commercial growth has been dramatic, with Orland Square Mall and the surrounding blocks of business, especially along LaGrange Road (Route 45). The area is wholly oriented toward automobiles, and its growth is supported by the continuing outward spread of residential subdivisions.

Although it is a classic example of the American

automobile-based suburb, Orland Park also has a town center next to a railroad commuter station. The center includes many of the early stores, a bank, and Twin Towers, formerly a Methodist church and Orland Park's only structure on the National Register of Historic Places. These are bordered by some of the village's original residential areas.

The beginnings of this community were somewhat to the east, in the area of the current commercial concentration. Known as the English Settlement, the community centered on a grade school and a Methodist church. Settlers include Henry Taylor, who arrived in 1834, and Thomas Hardy, who came in 1836. They were followed by other immigrants from the British Isles—including the family of a 10-year-old named John Humphrey, who arrived from England in 1848.

In the 1840s Luxembourgers and Germans began to arrive. Their presence is commemorated in the original Hostert family log cabins, now situated in a wooded park on the southern edge of the old village area.

The "father" of Orland Park was John Humphrey. When he was 21, he joined a wagon train going to California, later returning to work with his family. When the Wabash, St. Louis & Pacific Railroad completed its rail line through the area in 1879, Humphrey purchased a significant piece of land next to what was platted as the town center for the railroad stop. The Wabash had named its train stop Sedgewick, but the locals, under Humphrey's leadership, changed the name to Orland Park.

Humphrey participated in almost all aspects of the growth of the community. He was elected to the state house of representatives in 1870 and to the state senate in 1886. He was instrumental in the incorporation of the village in 1892 and served as its first president. In 1881 he had built the second house in Orland Park. This house has now passed into the hands of the Orland Historical Society.

Orland Park grew in population from 366 in 1900 to 51,077 in 2000. While retaining its old commercial and residential core, the village has built an innovative municipal facility that sits between the old and new sections.

Larry A. McClellan

FURTHER READING: "Orland Park." In *Local Community Fact Book: Chicago Metropolitan Area, 1990,* ed. Chicago Fact Book Consortium, 1995. ■ *The Orland Story: From Prairie to Pavement.* 1991.

Palatine, IL, Cook County, 26 miles NW of the Loop. In the early nineteenth century, this was a rather swampy area, through which Salt Creek (then as now) passed. To the northwest was Deer Grove, so named for the

numerous deer that it sheltered; English Grove lay due west, and Plum Grove about two miles to the south. Plum Grove was particularly important to the Potawatomi, who continued to visit area burial sites after they were removed to Iowa in the 1830s.

Early settlers tended to choose forested sites. Thus George Ela settled near Deer Grove in 1835, while Ben Lincoln and Ben Porter traveled from Vermont to Plum Grove. In 1853 the Illinois & Wisconsin Railroad was constructed across the township. A town emerged around the railroad depot, built just south of the Salt Creek swamp. Some people wanted to call it Yankton, but the name Palatine was adopted, after a town in New York.

By the time Palatine was incorporated, in 1866, it was already a community of some size with a Methodist church. While the earliest settlers were Yankees, there was an influx of Germans beginning in the 1850s; by 1869 a substantial Lutheran church could be built. These Germans were mostly farmers, who joined the earlier settlers in bringing their produce to the Palatine depot for shipment to Chicago. Some commuters also began to settle in the little town, but it remained very rural down to World War II, in spite of the construction of the Northwest Highway in the 1930s.

All that changed in the 1950s, particularly with the construction of the Northwest Toll Road in 1955, a couple of miles south of Palatine's southern boundary. The whole area was opened up to rapid automobile travel, and residential building accelerated. The streets were generally laid out in irregular patterns, to avoid the excessively rectilinear appearance of many of the suburbs nearer Chicago. By 1970 virtually all the land had been taken up, and the only large open area was the Palatine Hills Golf Course, on the northwest edge of town. Beyond that lay the Deer Grove Forest Preserve, a substantial remnant of the forested area that had drawn Indians and Europeans to these parts in the first place.

David Buisseret

FURTHER READING: Paddock, Stuart R., et al. *Palatine Centennial Book*. 1991.

Palos Heights, IL, Cook County, 17 miles SW of the Loop. Palos Heights is bordered by the Calumet Sag Channel on the north, Cook County Forest Preserves on the south, Palos Park on the west, and Crestwood on the east. Harlem Avenue, the main commercial thoroughfare, bisects the city and is also the dividing line between Palos Township, on the west side, and Worth Township, on the east.

Little is known of the early history of this community; an 1851 map shows no farmhouses. The only road that ran through the area was 127th Street. A swampy area (later the route of the Calumet Sag Channel) stretched across the northern part of the Palos Heights region and may have discouraged development.

By the 1860s the more level parts of the area were farmed by German and Irish families, while the hills were used for pasture. An 1861 map shows that Harlem Avenue ran through the area, which was occupied by several farms. The east side of Harlem was divided into woodlots, used as sources of lumber and fuel by local farmers.

Ridgeland Avenue ran along the east side of the future townsite, according to an 1886 map, and 76th Avenue bordered the west side. The only indication of activity other than farming was a blacksmith shop on 76th Avenue. Near the northwest corner of town, train tracks ran to Chicago and ORLAND PARK, although the nearest train station was in the Palos Park area.

It was not until 1901 that a school district was formed in the Palos Heights area. About this time, Dutch farmers began to settle there.

While the area continued as farmland and pasture in the 1920s, the completion of the Southwest Highway in 1928 improved automobile access and led to development. In 1935 a real-estate developer laid out a grid of streets flanking Harlem Avenue. The Harlem Heights subdivision featured quarter-acre home sites ("farmettes") that included tree saplings, grapevines, and incubators for chicken eggs. Property deeds included racial restrictive covenants. Businesses sprang up along Harlem Avenue.

In 1937 members of the growing community formed the Palos Heights Community Club, which was instrumental in the development of a public school and a fire department. Not until 1939 did Palos Heights acquire its own post office.

The building of subdivisions continued throughout the 1940s and 1950s. In 1959, on the fourth try, Palos Heights was incorporated as a city. That same year, Trinity Christian College was established in the northeast corner of the city.

The last remaining farmland in Palos Heights was sold to subdividers in 1965. The Palos Community Hospital, the city's largest employer, opened its doors in 1972. There is no industry in the community. Palos Heights is governed by a mayor and eight aldermen. The city's first train station opened in 2005.

Betsy Gurlacz

FURTHER READING: Local history files. Palos Heights Public Library, Palos Heights, IL.

Park Forest, IL, Cook County, 28 miles S of the Loop. The future Park Forest's first permanent white resident, Adam Brown, settled at what is now the corner of Sauk Trail and Chicago Road in 1833. John and Sabra McCoy established a farmstead in 1834; like the Batcheldor family, whose property became the largest part of Park Forest, they were Methodist abolitionists who offered their homes as stops for runaway slaves on the Underground Railroad.

In 1852 the Illinois Central Railroad was built along the northwestern border of the future suburb; the Michigan Central Railroad came through in 1853 to intersect with the Illinois Central in neighboring MATTESON.

Chicago's south suburbs experienced extensive residential growth throughout the first half of the twentieth century. In the 1920s developers planned to construct Indian Wood, a complete city centered on a newly built 18-hole golf course, on the as yet undeveloped Batcheldor land, but early speculation failed to attract buyers. Another attempt was made during the 1933 Century of Progress World's Fair, again with little success. A third failed effort involved a housing development marketed to African Americans around the existing golf course.

The successful plan for developing Park Forest came on the heels of World War II. On October 28, 1946, developer Philip M. Klutznick, along with Nathan Manilow and Carroll F. Sweet, held a press conference at the Palmer House in Chicago to announce that American Community Builders (ACB) planned to privately develop a new self-governing community in Chicago's south suburbs. The village would provide a variety of housing options for more than 5,000 families, an extensive park system, one of the first major outdoor shopping centers in the country (based on the Plaza San Marco in Venice), and a town hall supporting all municipal functions with a village manager at its head. This announcement received national attention in the *New York Times* and *Collier's* magazine.

Park Forest was designed by Elbert Peets in the tradition of other planned communities (such as Radburn, New Jersey, and RIVERSIDE, Illinois) to provide housing for veterans returning from the war, earning it the nickname "GI town." ACB placed advertisements in the *Chicago Tribune* to lure prospective residents to Park Forest. New tenants applied to live in the village and ACB screened applicants according to income level, education, status as a veteran, and need. The first residents arrived in August 1948, and on February 1, 1949, Park Forest was incorporated as a village. By 1950 more than 3,000 families had settled in Park Forest. The first black family took up residence in 1959.

Park Forest was honored in 1954 as an "All-America City" for its citizens' help in the creation of Rich Township High School, and again in 1976 for racial integration and open-housing initiatives. The population was 23,462 in 2000, when Park Forest received the Daniel H. Burnham Award for planning to redevelop the outdated shopping center into a traditional downtown. In 2003 meteorites landed in Park Forest and neighboring areas, in the first known meteorite fall in Illinois since 1938.

Todd J. Tubutis

FURTHER READING: *The Oral History of Park Forest: OH! Park Forest.* Park Forest Historical Society. 1982. ■ Randall, Gregory C. *America's Original GI Town: Park Forest, Illinois.* 2000. ■ Whyte, William H. *The Organization Man.* 1956.

Park Manor, neighborhood in the GREATER GRAND CROSSING Community Area.

Park Ridge, IL, Cook County, 18 miles NW of the Loop. Local legend claims that the suburb of Park Ridge contains the highest point in Cook County. While this is not true, the name is appropriate, reflecting the town's parklike setting along a gentle ridge.

The first residents of the area were the Potawatomi. After their removal under terms of the 1833 treaty, Yankee settlers from New England and upstate New York began trickling in and laying out farms. They honored their eastern heritage by calling the district Maine Township. Most prominent among these early people was Mancel Talcott, who built a log cabin and a bridge over the Des Plaines River near the present site of Touhy Avenue and served as postmaster.

Industry came to Maine Township in 1854 with the opening of George Penny's brickworks. When the Chicago, St. Paul & Fond du Lac Railroad (later the Chicago & North Western) began running shortly afterward, Penny arranged to have the trains stop by building his own station. The community that grew up around the station was informally known as Pennyville, until Penny himself suggested the name Brickton.

By 1873 the population of Brickton was 405. The brick pits had been worked out, so when residents voted to incorporate that year, the village was renamed Park Ridge. Over the next decades, as Park Ridge established its identity as a residential community, its leaders sought to develop the look of a traditional New England town, with large homes on wide lots and a profusion of trees. Apartments were banned and industrial development discouraged.

Anticipating annexation pressure from Chicago, the village reorganized as the city of Park Ridge in 1910. The 1910s and 1920s brought a major building boom, as city dwellers discovered the pleasant surroundings and convenient commuter trains. From 2,009 in 1910, the population ballooned to 10,417 in 1930. Maine East High School and the landmark Pickwick Theater date from this era.

The depression of the 1930s halted the boom. During the 1940s, some housing for war-industry workers was built, but significant expansion of Park Ridge did not resume until the 1950s, as part of America's postwar suburbanization. The population rose from 16,602 in 1950 to 42,466 two decades later. Aiding the growth was the opening of nearby O'Hare Airport, as well as the construction of two tollways and the Northwest (now Kennedy) Expressway.

As its population grew, Park Ridge moved to increase its tax base by encouraging office development and allowing a limited number of apartments. Lutheran General Hospital relocated from Chicago, and a second high school (Maine South) opened in 1964. In later years, as the community filled up its vacant land and property values soared, builders began to tear down small, older homes and replace them with huge new dwellings.

Park Ridge entered the twenty-first century as a mature, upper-middle-class residential suburb. The population continues to be largely white Anglo-Saxon Protestant, but now with a significant number of Polish Roman Catholics. Concerns include maintaining the residential strengths of the community and alleviating the noise from O'Hare Airport.

John R. Schmidt

FURTHER READING: Blouin, Nancy. *Park Ridge, Illinois: A Photo History.* 1994. ■ Park Ridge Chamber of Commerce. *Park Ridge, 1873–1973: A Century of Pride.* 1973. ■ Park Ridge Library has various clippings in its Heritage Room, as well as four videotapes of oral history interviews conducted from 1985 to 1987.

Pennytown, an early name for the AVALON PARK Community Area.

Pilsen, neighborhood in the LOWER WEST SIDE Community Area. German and Irish immigrants settled in this neighborhood in the 1840s, encouraged by the construction of the Southwest Plank Road (now Ogden Avenue), the Illinois &

Good Friday parade, Pilsen, 1978. Photographer: Chicago Journal. Source: Chicago History Museum.

Michigan Canal (the South Branch of the Chicago River forms the southern and eastern borders of the neighborhood), and the Burlington Railroad (the western boundary of Pilsen).

After the 1871 fire the McCormick Reaper Company (later International Harvester), lumber mills, garment finishing sweatshops, and railroad yards defined the neighborhood. The creation of thousands of unskilled jobs induced many Bohemian immigrants to settle along Evans Street (18th Street); when one opened a restaurant called At the City of Plzen, honoring the second largest city in West Bohemia (now in the Czech Republic), residents began to refer to the neighborhood as Pilsen. The subsequent naming of the post office as Pilsen Station institutionalized the moniker.

Lumber shover strikes in 1875–1876 inspired the 1877 Railroad Strike (part of a national strike) that spread to all industrial workers in Pilsen. The 22nd U.S. Infantry marched into Pilsen that July to put down the strikers, killing 30 residents and injuring hundreds more. Pilsen workers also were involved in strikes in 1886 that culminated in the Haymarket Riot.

During World War I, labor shortages in area industries induced over two dozen different immigrant groups to settle in Pilsen, including a modest number of Mexicans. Due to liberal immigration law and the forced removal of Mexicans from the NEAR WEST SIDE to expand the University of Illinois at Chicago, Mexican migrants became predominant in the 1950s and 1960s. This ethnic shift spurred cultural changes in Pilsen, as Mexican artists decorated the neighborhood with colorful murals and mosaics.

The turnover from Eastern European to Mexican residents did not diminish Pilsen's tradition of strong working-class organization to control community space. Rubin J. Torres's neighborhood-based newsletter the *Crown* (1938–1998) supported and initiated youth club activities; the Pilsen Neighbors Community Council, in addition to functioning as a benevolent society, applied the community organizing tactics of Saul Alinsky to obtain city and industrial improvements; and community activists like Rudy Lozano, labor organizer and Midwest director of the International Ladies Garment Workers Union, helped propel antimachine politicians like Harold Washington into elected office and keep them there.

At the turn of the twenty-first century, Pilsen's residents have resisted attempts to gentrify their neighborhood and have preserved the community as a gateway for Hispanic immigrants. During the first weekend in August, the Fiesta del Sol festival demonstrates the pride and determination of the residents of Pilsen to continue its rich working-class legacy.

Erik Gellman

FURTHER READING: Baker, Anthony. "The Social Production of Space in Two Chicago Neighborhoods: Pilsen and Lincoln Park." Ph.D. diss., University of Illinois at Chicago. 1995. ■ Bartolozzi, Lorraine. "Community Study of the Lower West Side." 1930s, Lower West Side Community Collection, Box 1, Folder 11. Special Collections, Harold Washington Library, Chicago. ■ Schneirov, Richard. *Labor and Urban Politics: Class Conflict and the Origins of Modern Liberalism in Chicago, 1864–1897.* 1998.

Portage Park, Community Area 15, 9 miles NW of the Loop. Portage Park has long-standing connections to water. During wet weather, early Indian inhabitants could paddle their canoes from the Chicago River to the Des Plaines on a minor portage along present-day Irving Park Road. They were reported to have built a village on the top of an elevation west of Cicero and Irving Park Avenues. Another ridge two miles west near Narragansett formed the natural watershed between the Mississippi and Great Lakes drainage system.

15
Portage Park

Following an 1816 treaty, the Indians relinquished their rights to the land. E. B. Sutherland set up a tavern in 1841 along the North West Plank Road. By 1845 a post office was established, and the following year Chester Dickinson bought the inn and job as postmaster. The inn's central location in Jefferson Township made it a popular stopping-off place for locals, and it served as a temporary town hall. The township became part of the city of Chicago in an 1889 annexation.

Farming in the area proved to be difficult, as the land remained marshy, and ditch digging was the only way to maintain dry property. Residential properties sprang up mostly in the northern and eastern sections. In 1912 neighbors formed the Portage Park District, and the following year the park district board of commissioners condemned 40 acres on the northeast corner of Irving Park Road and Central Avenue for the purpose of developing a park.

Initially the commissioners tried to raise money through a property tax. When residents objected that the tax was inequitable and that it might lead to corruption and graft, the assessment was invalidated in court. It was soon discovered, however, that the tax was an unnecessary measure, since park development was progressing without it. A portion of the park officially opened in midsummer 1916, and the Portage Park Citizen's Celebration Association formed to organize park events.

Visitors to the park that summer enjoyed a cool swim in a small sand-bottomed lagoon. In later years the park became a popular gathering place as other recreational facilities, including tennis courts and baseball fields, were added. In 1922 the field house was completed. To mark the completion of the park, a spectacular Fourth of July festival was held, complete with parade and athletic exhibitions; attendance reached an estimated 40,000 persons, who came from numerous Chicago neighborhoods. In 1934 Portage Park was merged into the Chicago Park District.

With improved transportation and the inducement of the beautiful park, developers began building homes and urban dwellers flocked to the community. By 1940 its population had risen to 66,357.

Poor drainage, which had created problems with flooding over the years, was finally corrected in the 1950s through the construction of an extensive drainage system. In the late 1950s and early 1960s improved public transportation and the Northwest (Kennedy) Expressway connected

The Henry B. Clarke House, one of the oldest buildings in Chicago, was built in 1836 and stood near 16th Street and Michigan Avenue. After the 1871 fire, the structure was moved to 1855 S. Indiana, becoming part of the Prairie Avenue Historic District. Photographer: Chicago Daily News. Source: Chicago History Museum.

residents to downtown Chicago. During the same period residents prevailed in their opposition to a proposed Crosstown Expressway.

Over the years the park remained the center of community activities. A gymnasium was constructed, and in 1959 the old pond was replaced by an Olympic-sized concrete pool. The swimming events of the Pan American Games were held there that year, and the American Olympic team trials in 1972. By 1989 the park had expanded to 36 acres and offered additional tennis courts, an athletic field, and basketball courts.

By 1990 Portage Park's population had decreased to 56,513 and consisted mainly of residents of Polish, Italian, Irish, and German descent. The main shopping center of the area was concentrated around SIX CORNERS (the intersection of Irving Park, Milwaukee, and Cicero). By 2000 population had rebounded to 65,340.

Marilyn Elizabeth Perry

FURTHER READING: Clipping files. Chicago History Museum and Portage-Cragin Branch of the Chicago Public Library, both in Chicago. ■ Derx, Jacob J. G. "Portage Park: Yesterday and Today." *Portage Park Bulletin*, July 4, 1922. ■ Ryan, David Joseph. "The Development of Portage Park from the Earliest Period to the 1920s." Senior History Seminar, Northwestern University. May 24, 1974.

Prairie Avenue. Prairie Avenue was an exclusive address for Chicago's elite in the late nineteenth century. This north-south boulevard, close to the lakefront, begins at 16th Street and continues to the city's southern limits. The sections between 16th and 22nd Streets and between 26th and 30th Streets were well known for grand homes.

The wealthy settled on Prairie Avenue after the Civil War because it was close to the LOOP, and a trip downtown did not require residents to cross the Chicago River. The first large home on the upper portion of Prairie Avenue was built by Daniel Thompson in 1870. Marshall Field followed in 1871 with a grand home designed by Richard Morris Hunt. George Pullman's palace was constructed in 1873, and mansions for other magnates were not far behind. This section of the avenue was dominated by Second Empire homes. The lower section of Prairie Avenue, between 26th and 30th Streets, began to attract wealthy residents in the mid-1880s; this segment was made up of many Queen Anne and Richardson Romanesque houses.

Perhaps the best-known building on Prairie Avenue is H. H. Richardson's Glessner House at 18th Street. This imposing house, in the architect's signature Richardson Romanesque style, was completed in 1887 for John Glessner, a farm equipment manufacturing executive, and his wife Frances. The structure is not set back from the lot line like most homes, and it appears fortresslike in its use of rugged granite for the exterior. Richardson's aim was to provide the family with a truly urban home that embraced a central courtyard while shielding the inhabitants from the city street. As such, it caused a major stir among the Glessners' neighbors. But the design was prescient—Prairie Avenue was becoming a less desirable area in the late 1880s. Soot from the nearby railroad was a major nuisance, and an infamous vice district was encroaching on the neighborhood.

Prairie Avenue became home to light industry and vacant lots in the mid- to late twentieth century. Many mansions were torn down, and others became dilapidated. In 1966 the Glessner House was purchased by a group of architects called the Chicago School of Architecture Foundation. The home is now a museum, and Prairie Avenue, although devoid of most of its mansions, was declared a historic district in 1978.

Heidi Pawlowski Carey

FURTHER READING: Harrington, Elaine, and Kevin Harrington. "H. H. Richardson and the Glessners." *Perspectives on the Professions* 3.4 (December 1983). ■ Hubka, Thomas C. "H. H. Richardson's Glessner House." *Winterthur Portfolio* 24.4 (Winter 1989): 209–229. ■ Molloy, Mary Alice. "Prairie Avenue." In *The Grand American Avenue, 1850–1920*, ed. Jan Cigliano and Sarah Bradford Landau. 1994.

Prairie Shores, neighborhood built on urban renewal lands in the DOUGLAS Community Area and completed in the early 1960s.

Princeton Park, residential neighborhood in the WASHINGTON HEIGHTS Community Area, marketed to African Americans in the 1940s.

Printer's Row. After the completion of Dearborn Street Station in 1885, this area on the NEAR SOUTH SIDE became the printing center of the Midwest. The heart of Printer's Row—a two-block area between Congress Parkway and Polk Street along Dearborn—features examples of the First Chicago School of architecture, including the Duplicator Building (1886) and the Pontiac Building (1891). In the late 1970s developers began to convert printing centers such as the Donohue Building into loft-style apartments, and Dearborn Street Station was converted to retail space.

Erik Gellman

FURTHER READING: Bach, Ira J., and Susan Wolfson. *Chicago on Foot: Walking Tours of Chicago's Architecture*. 1987. ■ *Sweet Home Chicago: The Real City Guide*. 1993.

Pullman, Community Area 50, 14 miles SE of Loop. Once the most famous planned community in America, the oldest part of Pullman is notable for its role in American labor and planning history. The town had its origins in the late 1870s as George M. Pullman looked for solutions to two problems. The first was where to build a new factory for his Pullman Palace Cars, sleeping and parlor cars that were becoming increasingly popular with those traveling on the country's expanding rail system. The second was how to attract and encourage workers who would share his vision of American society. Pullman wanted to avoid the types of workers who participated in the turbulent 1877 Railroad Strike, or those he believed to be discouraged and morally corrupted by urban poverty and social dislocation.

50
Pullman

Although his primary manufacturing plant was located in Detroit, Pullman was a longtime Chicago resident. With the assistance of Colonel James Bowen, the Pullman Land Association quietly purchased 4,000 acres near Lake Calumet in an area both thought had a bright industrial future. Pullman hired architect Solon Beman and landscape architect Nathan Barrett to erect a town that would provide its residents with decent housing in a socially and physically healthy environment—and at the same time generate a 6 percent annual profit for the Pullman Palace Car Company. Even before Pullman's first residents settled there in 1881, visitors came to admire the town's beauty, which stood in stark contrast to other working-class areas in industrial cities, and to marvel at the success of its social planning. Not only did Pullman workers live in brick houses, they and their families had access to schools, parks, a library, a theater, educational programs, and many other activities. When state labor commissioners visited in 1884, they proclaimed it a successful venture, especially for the women and children, who seemed protected from the worst aspects of industrial America.

Not all observers viewed Pullman from the same perspective. In 1885 Richard T. Ely published an exposé in *Harper's Monthly* charging that the town and its design were un-American, a paternalistic system that took away men's rights as citizens, including the right to control their own domestic environment. When Pullman workers went on strike in 1894, protesting cuts in wages while rents and dividends remained unchanged, the strike captured a national audience. Commentators from across the nation debated the proper relationship between employers and employees, as well as the broader question of the political, social, and economic rights of working-class men and women.

By the close of the strike, even such bulwarks of Chicago's business community as the *Chicago Tribune* and Swift & Co. publicly decried the suffering inflicted on law-abiding employees by an inflexible Pullman management. The Illinois State Supreme Court gave legal weight to this sentiment in 1898 when it ordered the company to divest itself of residential property in Pullman. By the end of the first decade of the twentieth century, Pullman had become another Chicago neighborhood, tied closely to the surrounding communities of KENSINGTON and ROSELAND.

In subsequent years, Pullman experienced changes familiar to other neighborhoods in the city: ethnic succession, the aging of housing stock, and changing employment opportunities that drew residents away from the Pullman Car Works and into jobs elsewhere. Residents still perceived Pullman as a good place to live; neighbors maintained strong ties to each other, to their predominantly Italian and Polish ethnic communities, and to the neighborhood itself. Outsiders, however, saw old housing and vacant industrial land. Pullman's reputation fell most dramatically in the late 1920s and 1930s, when unemployment and bootlegging activities made it seem a nascent slum. By then, Chicago sociologists delineating community areas had applied the name Pullman to a broader area that included the largely unsettled area between the historic town and 95th Street.

In 1960 consultants to the South End Chamber of Commerce recommended that Pullman be demolished between 111th and 115th to make way for industrial expansion to benefit the remainder of the Calumet region. Pullman residents fought this destruction. In 1960 they reactivated the Pullman Civic Organization to remove any signs of blight and to lobby to keep their neighborhood. Realizing that the community's own history could provide a valuable wedge in that fight, they founded the Historic Pullman Foundation in 1973. The community was designated a national historic landmark in 1971 and has received similar state and local designations. Pullman retains much of its original architecture and spatial organization and attracts thousands of visitors each year. In 1994 North Pullman residents, largely an African American population, achieved city landmark status for their area of Pullman as well. At the same time, they established a museum honoring

Pullman Labor Day Parade, 111th and Pullman Avenue (later Cottage Grove), 1901. Photographer: Unknown. Source: Chicago Public Library.

Pullman porters. Since then, the city has joined the two separate districts into one Chicago landmark district.

The Pullman Car Works produced its last railroad car in 1981. A decade later the state of Illinois purchased a section of the plant, along with the Hotel Florence, the largest public building in Pullman, with the hope of creating a museum honoring the history of the community and the company. In December 1998 a fire swept through the vacant clock tower and construction shops, putting the museum plans in doubt and creating a new challenge for the community and its residents.

Janice L. Reiff

FURTHER READING: Pullman Archives. Newberry Library, Chicago. ▪ Reiff, Janice L. "Rethinking Pullman: Urban Space and Working-Class Activism." *Social Science History* 24.1 (2001): 7–32. ▪ Smith, Carl. *Urban Disorder and the Shape of Belief: The Great Chicago Fire, the Haymarket Bomb, and the Model Town of Pullman.* 1995.

Ravenswood, neighborhood in the Lincoln Square Community Area. Ravenswood, a residential subdivision in the township of Lake View, was designed to be one of Chicago's first and most exclusive commuter suburbs. In 1868 a group of real-estate speculators formed the Ravenswood Land Company and purchased 194 acres of farm and wooded land eight miles north of Chicago. The company made a deal with the Chicago & North Western Railway guaranteeing it a certain number of passengers if it would open a new stop. Hoping that the fee of $7.20 for a hundred rides would attract only wealthy residents, the company divided the property into large lots. The speculators hedged their real-estate gamble by building the Sunnyside Hotel adjacent to the would-be village, so that potential customers might first come as visitors to a resort. By 1874 the suburb had 75 railroad commuters.

The Ravenswood Land Company did not build houses, sewers, or sidewalks. Longtime Ravenswood residents interviewed in the 1920s recalled open ditches and muddy streets alongside the lovely lawns, houses, and trees. Private subscriptions paid for some local improvements, but neighboring Jefferson Township would not permit Ravenswood's sewers to run through its land into the Chicago River. With the annexation of both Lake View and Jefferson Townships to Chicago in 1889, authority over improvements shifted to the larger municipality and Ravenswood got its sewers. The introduction of electric streetcar lines in the 1890s and the extension of the "L" in 1907 made the area accessible to less affluent residents, whose small houses, two-flats, and apartment buildings filled in the gap between Chicago and its former suburb. The name Ravenswood remained in popular use, even after the area was officially designated part of the Lincoln Square Community Area.

Amanda Seligman

FURTHER READING: Andreas, A. T. *History of Cook County, Illinois, from the Earliest Period to the Present Time.* 1884. ■ Keating, Ann Durkin. *Building Chicago: Suburban Developers and the Creation of a Divided Metropolis.* 1988. ■ Zatterberg, Helen. *An Historical Sketch of Ravenswood and Lake View.* 1941.

Ravenswood Manor and **Ravenswood Gardens,** neighborhoods in the LINCOLN SQUARE Community Area developed in the early twentieth century.

Ridgemoor Estates, neighborhood adjacent to the Ridgemoor Country Club in the DUNNING Community Area.

Ridgeville, early farming settlement at Ridge and Devon in the WEST RIDGE Community Area.

Riverdale, Community Area 54, 16 miles SE of the Loop. Riverdale became a community area by default, an industrial area bound by the Illinois Central Railroad on the west, the city limits on the south, the Bishop Ford Expressway on the east, and 115th Street on the north. Its first nonnative residents settled on the banks of the Little Calumet River in 1836, farming and operating a toll bridge across the river along the Chicago-Thornton Road. A second settlement grew up around the junction of the Illinois Central and Michigan Central Railroads at Kensington in 1852. Between the two at Wildwood, James H. Bowen of the Calumet and Chicago Canal and Dock Company built a summer home where Chicago's elites gathered in the 1870s and 1880s. Until 1945, however, almost all of Riverdale's residents lived in the part of the KENSINGTON settlement south of 115th Street and around the original settlement at its far southwest edge.

54
Riverdale

Most of Riverdale's swampy land was used or zoned for manufacturing and industrial purposes. From the 1850s on, the railroads that cut through the area claimed significant pieces of its land for rights-of-way and yards. The Pullman Land Association controlled significant acreage along Lake Calumet into the second half of the twentieth century; Riverdale was home to the Pullman Farm, fertilized by the sewage from the famous town, and the Pullman brickyards. Its largest industry began as the Calumet Paint Company in an abandoned church near both PULLMAN and the lake. By beginning of the twentieth century, Sherwin-Williams had purchased the plant and turned it into one of America's largest paint manufactories. Jobs there, along with those at Chicago Drop Forge, the Illinois Terra Cotta Works, and the Swift and Knickerbocker Ice plants, made Riverdale a place where far more people worked than lived until the end of World War II.

City, county, metropolitan, state, and federal agencies also controlled a substantial amount of land in Riverdale, and their actions shaped Riverdale's development. The Metropolitan Sanitary District (Metropolitan Water Reclamation District of Greater Chicago) located a sewage treatment plant there in the 1922 to service the growing communities nearby. Riverdale's most eastern region became part of the Beaubien Forest Preserve. Governmental improvements on the Little Calumet and Lake Calumet and the construction of the Cal-Sag Channel shaped industrial development in Riverdale more generally.

Government actions also transformed Riverdale into a residential community when the National Housing Agency, the Federal Public Housing Authority, and the Chicago Housing Authority opened the massive Altgeld Gardens housing project in 1945. In 1954 the CHA built the Phillip Murray Homes nearby. The rapid transformation of Riverdale from an industrial area with 1,500 people in the 1940s into a residential area with 12,000 by the 1960s overtaxed the limited services available in the community. The fact that most of the new residents were African American made sharing services with the nearby white communities problematic. Community leaders in ROSELAND spearheaded a drive against Altgeld Gardens even before it was built. Discriminatory practices in nearby hospitals made it extremely difficult to get emergency health care. In the 1960s schools became a battleground when district boundaries would have sent white students from WEST PULLMAN to Carver High School and black students from Riverdale to grade schools in West Pullman.

Riverdale's population reached a peak of 15,018 in 1970 after the construction in 1968 of Eden Greens, one of the nation's first majority black-owned and -operated town house and apartment developments. Eventually the project, sponsored by the Antioch Missionary Baptist Church and targeted for low- and moderate-income families, included 1,000 units.

Since that time, the area has lost both population and jobs. Industrial waste from the factories that once operated there have polluted large tracts of land. By 1990 only 10,821 people

lived in Riverdale; 63percent of its households lived in poverty, and 35 percent of its workers were unemployed.

Janice L. Reiff

FURTHER READING: Andreas, A. T. *History of Cook County, Illinois.* 1884. ■ *Calumet Index.* Various issues. ■ *South End Reporter.* Various issues.

Riverside, IL, Cook County, 10 miles W of the Loop. Riverside, on the Des Plaines River, was designed in 1868 by Frederick Law Olmsted, the nation's most famous landscape architect. The innovative street plan and the striking open spaces are regarded as landmarks in American residential planning.

In 1863 the Chicago, Burlington & Quincy Railroad was built through the area, and five years later a group of local investors decided to take advantage of both the railroad and the uniquely attractive site where it crossed the Des Plaines River. Forming the Riverside Improvement Company, they purchased a 1,600-acre tract of land along the river and hired Olmsted, a New Yorker, to design an elite suburban community. Olmsted and his partner, Calvert Vaux, were already famous for creating Central Park in New York City. Their reputation, plus the lovely curvilinear streets, open spaces, and attractive village center they designed for Riverside, attracted Chicago's elite. By the fall of 1871 a number of large, expensive houses were occupied or under construction and an elegant hotel had opened.

Unfortunately for the developers, the Chicago Fire of 1871 drained both construction crews and capital from the village. The financial panic of 1873 compounded the company's troubles and it went bankrupt.

The demise of the improvement company brought new construction nearly to a halt for some time. A village government was established in September 1875, and Olmsted's original development plan remained in force. In 1893 several wealthy local residents formed an association and opened the Riverside Golf Club, one of the oldest golf clubs in the Chicago area. Frank Lloyd Wright, Louis Sullivan, William Le Baron Jenney, and several other prominent local architects drew up plans for houses that still stand in the village. A striking Romanesque village hall was built in 1895, and in 1901 the Burlington line constructed a charming stone railroad station.

A major period of residential development came in the 1920s and late 1930s, when many modest houses were constructed on smaller parcels. The population, 7,935 by 1940, comprised primarily small proprietors, managers, and professionals, most of Anglo-American and German American background. The remaining residential areas were developed during the post–World War II boom, and by 1960 no space was left. Population peaked at 10,357 in 1970 and dropped below 8,500 by the mid-1990s.

Riverside remains a beautiful, upscale suburban community, but one with a wider price range of homes than is found in the more uniformly wealthy suburbs along the North Shore. It includes small, well-maintained bungalows, larger comfortable houses from the 1920s and 1950s, and huge Victorian and early-twentieth-century mansions that attract architectural tours. The charming village center is replete with chic restaurants, cappuccino bars, and stores selling antiques and Victorian house fixtures. Riverside was fairly affluent and all white in 1940 and predominantly so at the end of the century. The only recent demographic changes are the growing number of older residents and the influx of younger families of Irish, Polish, Czech, and Scandinavian backgrounds, the wealthy children and grandchildren of Chicago's old ethnic working class. The entire village was designated a national historical landmark in 1970.

Joseph L. Arnold

FURTHER READING: Bassman, Herbert J., ed. *Riverside Then and Now: A History of Riverside, Illinois.* 1936. ■ Frederick Law Olmsted Society of Riverside. *Riverside: A Village in a Park.* 1970. ■ Riverside Historical Commission. *Tell Me a Story: Memories of Riverside.* 1995.

Robbins, IL, Cook County, 17 miles south of the

Loop. Robbins is the oldest majority-black suburb in the Chicago area and one of the oldest incorporated black municipalities in the United States. Robbins is also characteristic of semi-rural black suburbs that developed in the United States during the Great Migration.

Located in the bottomlands southwest of BLUE ISLAND, the area was largely farmland until 1910, when white real-estate agents Henry and Eugene Robbins opened the first of several subdivisions, which they marketed to African Americans. As in many working-class subdivisions, lots in Robbins, cost as little as $90 each, lacked paved streets, sewers, and other modern amenities.

The people who settled in Robbins were predominantly working-class African Americans, immigrants from the South who were willing to sacrifice urban services for home ownership, open space, tightly knit community life, and country atmosphere. At the same time, Robbins's location in the Calumet region offered men access to the factory jobs that many had come north to obtain. Domestic service and seasonal work canning and packing vegetables dominated women's paid labor. As workers near the bottom of the urban economy, some African Americans also valued home ownership in a suburb like Robbins because it allowed them to supplement wages with garden produce and small livestock. Many settlers cut costs even further by building their own houses and living without utilities. The result was a makeshift landscape that outsiders labeled a slum; for many residents, however, the suburb represented a welcome compromise between North and South.

In 1917 residents of Robbins incorporated as a separate municipality, a bold step for a blue-collar community with almost no commercial tax base. Robbins grew from 431 persons in 1920 to 1,300 by 1940. Residents established a newspaper, the *Robbins Herald*, plus many churches and small stores. Bessie Coleman, Cornelius Coffey, and Johnny

Bessie Coleman: Pioneer Chicago Aviator

Bessie Coleman migrated to Chicago from Texas in 1915. Like many other African Americans, she sought better opportunities in the northern cities, but Coleman followed an unusual dream: to become an airplane pilot. Facing prejudice both as a woman and as an African American, Coleman was unable to train in the United States. With the encouragement of Robert Abbott, publisher of the *Chicago Defender*, Coleman learned French and gained entrance into the Caudron School of Aviation in France in 1920.

After earning her international pilot's license, she became a barnstormer, with the Chicago Defender as her sponsor. Coleman toured the United States. On October 15, 1922, more than 2,000 people came to the Checkerboard Field in MAYWOOD (now Miller Meadow Forest Preserve) for Coleman's first exhibition in Chicago. Coleman died in a plane crash in Florida in 1926.

A group of African American pilots organized the Challenger Air Pilot's Association in 1931, inspired by Bessie Coleman. This association founded an airport at ROBBINS in 1933 to accommodate African American pilots who faced discrimination at other Chicago airports.

Ann Durkin Keating

Robinson were among those who created Robbins Airport, a center for black aviation in the North. Robbins also became a popular recreation spot for black Chicagoans, who crowded its picnic grounds and nightclubs on summer weekends.

Robbins was one of the few places in the Chicago suburbs where African Americans could purchase homes without risking violence. Population expanded to 4,766 in 1950 and 9,644 by 1970 (98 percent black), as developers opened new subdivisions and the village annexed territory. In the 1960s black developer Edward Starks opened the Golden Acres subdivision, which brought modern, suburban-style houses to the community.

Although village officials undertook modest improvements, the community's small tax base inhibited efforts to upgrade services. As late as 1950, 22 percent of Robbins homes lacked indoor plumbing, and over 40 percent were considered substandard in 1960. The community did pave streets and install sewers in the 1950s, but these costs, combined with plant layoffs in the 1970s, saddled the suburb with municipal debts. Economic woes notwithstanding, Robbins remained one of the few places in greater Chicago where African Americans with limited resources could afford to buy a home of their own.

Andrew Wiese

FURTHER READING: Chicago Commission on Race Relations. *The Negro in Chicago: A Study of Race Relations and a Race Riot in 1919.* 1968 [1921], 138–139. ■ Rose, Harold M. "The All-Negro Town: Its Evolution and Function." *Geographical Review* 55 (July 1965): 362–381. ■ Wiese, Andrew. "Places of Our Own: Suburban Black Towns before 1960." *Journal of Urban History* 19 (May 1993): 30–54.

Robert Taylor Homes, neighborhood in the GRAND BOULEVARD and WASHINGTON PARK Community Areas. Upon completion in 1962, Chicago's Robert Taylor Homes became the largest public housing project in the United States. Built along two miles of State Street, from 39th to 54th Streets, the project comprised 28 16-story buildings, mostly in U-shaped clusters of three, containing almost 4,300 apartments and 27,000 people.

This massive housing project was, ironically, named after Robert Taylor, an African American activist and Chicago Housing Authority (CHA) board member who resigned in 1950 when the city council refused to endorse potential building locations conducive to racially integrated housing.

Within forty years this neighborhood was being dismantled. Despite the structurally sound exteriors of the buildings and an academic study that found two out of three Taylor residents opposed to the demolition, the CHA demolished the buildings, with plans to replace them with mixed-income developments.

Erik Gellman

FURTHER READING: Lemann, Nicholas. *The Promised Land: The Great Black Migration and How It Changed America.* 1991. ■ Venkatesh, Sudhir Alladi. *American Project: The Rise and Fall of a Modern Ghetto.* 2000.

Rockwell Gardens, neighborhood in the EAST GARFIELD PARK Community Area, built by the Chicago Housing Authority.

Rogers Park, Community Area 1, 9 miles N of

1
Rogers Park

the Loop. Rogers Park ranks among Chicago's most diverse and populous neighborhoods. Between the late 1830s and his death in 1856 Irishman Phillip Rogers purchased approximately 1,600 acres of government land, part of which formed the basis of Rogers Park. In 1872 Rogers's son-in-law, Patrick Touhy, subdivided the land near the present-day intersection of Lunt and Ridge Avenues. By 1878 enough settlers had moved into the area to incorporate the village of Rogers Park. The number of residents increased steadily, and further growth accompanied the village's annexation to Chicago in 1893. The 1915 annexation of the area north of Howard Street, east of the "L" tracks, and south of Calvary Cemetery, variously known as Germania and South EVANSTON, brought Rogers Park and Chicago a new northern boundary.

Rail connections between Rogers Park and Chicago date from the 1860s. Both the Chicago & North Western Railway and the Chicago, Milwaukee & St. Paul Railroad (Chicago, Milwaukee, St. Paul & Pacific Railroad) provided service to downtown Chicago. By the end of the nineteenth century large houses on sizable lots clustered between Greenview and Ridge Avenues and north of Touhy along Sheridan Road.

When the Northwestern Elevated Railroad opened the Howard Station in 1908, population jumped dramatically. The construction of single-family houses slowed as subdividers built multi-unit dwellings and the neighborhood's suburban qualities faded. Construction of large apartment buildings was most intense north of Howard Street and along the "L" tracks in the eastern portion of the community. Rogers Park became and remains primarily a renter community.

The rush of apartment construction consumed almost all available land. Housing shortages during World War II encouraged the subdivision of large apartments into smaller ones, and population density increased, especially in the area north of Howard Street. Deteriorating buildings brought lower rents and a poorer, more transient population. Neighborhood concerns about congestion, poverty, and increased crime led to public-private partnerships to upgrade the housing stock, provide a variety of social services, and stabilize the community. New construction in the neighborhood since the 1960s has consisted of moderately sized apartment buildings, town houses, and nursing homes.

Neighborhood business activities, entertainment spots, and religious institutions are clustered on main streets and at transportation breaks. Commercial districts developed along Clark Street, Devon Avenue, and around the four neighborhood "L" stations. Until the 1980s entertainment venues were an important part of these districts. During the first half of the twentieth century Rogers Park possessed four large, elaborate movie palaces (the Howard, Adelphi, Granada, and Norshore Theaters), which ultimately succumbed to changes in the movie industry and in viewers' tastes. The neighborhood also has been home to a ballpark, a country club, and, most recently, a live-theater community. Finally, religious activity flourished as population grew. Although identified historically as a Roman Catholic and Jewish community, the neighborhood has always supported a variety of religious denominations.

Two institutions of higher education have been located in Rogers Park. The Jesuits purchased property in 1906 to expand the operations of St. Ignatius College, now Loyola University Chicago. Mundelein College, now a part of Loyola, opened in 1930; run by the Sisters of Charity of the Blessed Virgin Mary, Mundelein was Chicago's second Catholic women's college.

Over the years Rogers Park's population has grown older and increasingly diverse. Irish, Germans, and Luxembourgers represented the major

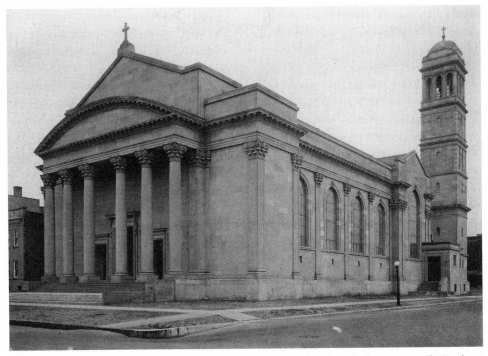

St. Ignatius Church, Greenwood and Loyola Avenues, 1910s. Photographer: Percy H. Sloan. Source: The Newberry Library.

ethnic groups during the early years of community building. By the late 1960s the neighborhood had become home to Russian and Eastern European immigrants. The 1970s saw the arrival of immigrants from Asia and the Americas as well as growth in the African American population. According to the 2000 census, 63,484 people lived in Rogers Park. Of these, 46 percent were white, 30 percent African American, and 6 percent Asian or Pacific Islander. A total of 28 percent were of Latino origin, 79 percent of whom were of Mexican ancestry. Thirty-four percent of those living in Rogers Park were foreign-born.

Patricia Mooney-Melvin

FURTHER READING: Mooney-Melvin, Patricia. *Reading Your Neighborhood: A Brief History of East Rogers Park.* 1993. ■ Palmer, Vivien M., comp. *Documents: History of the Rogers Park Community, Chicago, 1925–1930,* vol. 1. 1966. ■ The Rogers Park/West Ridge Historical Society and Museum, Chicago.

Roscoe Village, recently designated neighborhood in the NORTH CENTER Community Area.

Roseland, Community Area 49, 13 miles S of the Loop. The village of Roseland had its origins in 1849, when a band of recently arrived Dutch families built their homes along the Chicago-Thornton Road. Perched on the ridge west of Lake Calumet between what are now 103rd and 111th Streets, High Prairie, as it was then known, took shape around the Reformed Church, the small truck farms, and the stores located on the road later known as Michigan Avenue. High Prairie prospered, its farms made profitable by Chicago to its north and the stockyards to the west. Its population grew, most often with additional Dutch settlers who, after 1852, arrived from the east at the Michigan Central Railroad station in nearby KENSINGTON.

49
Roseland

In 1873 James H. Bowen, president of the Calumet and Chicago Canal and Dock Company, suggested the name Roseland for the tidy village with its beautiful flowers. Residents agreed. Seven years later, Bowen initiated even more substantial changes when his company sold more than 4,000 acres of land on Roseland's eastern edge to the Pullman Land Association for the Pullman Car Works and the town of PULLMAN. Within a decade, Roseland's and Pullman's fates had been inextricably merged, along with those of the other communities that eventually grew in Pullman's shadow: Kensington, Gano, BURNSIDE, and WEST PULLMAN. Its Michigan Avenue stores served customers from all those communities. Pullman workers bought and rented homes from the Dutch who preceded them. By the 1890s, when all of Roseland was finally annexed to Chicago, it had become an ethnically and religiously diverse retail and residential community surrounded by a growing number of large industries.

The hiring policies of Pullman and other industries shaped Roseland's population and politics. The 1894 Pullman Strike created a larger community that transcended old town boundaries and left it with a legacy of political radicalism. Twice before World War I, this Greater Pullman/Roseland district elected a socialist alderman. Local real-estate agents fought against this radicalism, selling an image of comfortable homes on tree-lined streets easily accessible to downtown Chicago via the Illinois Central and the Chicago & Eastern Illinois. By the 1920s the community that was once a stop on the Underground Railroad added whiteness to its list of advantages. Local real-estate agents urged racially restrictive covenants on new developers and current home owners. The South End Businessmen's Association even lobbied University of Chicago sociologists, unsuccessfully, to draw the Roseland Community Area's boundaries to exclude the small African American community of Lilydale, just north of the original High Prairie settlement on Michigan Avenue.

Strains between Roseland's diverse neighborhoods continued throughout the 1920s and 1930s. Neighborhoods of residents whose religion committed them to temperance stood next to neigh-borhoods that manufactured alcohol for the Capones. The Great Depression and the end of Prohibition shattered the local economy as banks and building associations collapsed, workers lost their jobs, and the return of legal alcohol sales stopped the profits from home brewing. Michigan Avenue became the site of vigorous debate and protest about Roseland's future as organizations from the Unemployed Citizens' Council to the Anti–Property Tax League sought support for their solutions.

World War II returned prosperity to the community, but the debate over the nature of Roseland continued. The successful efforts of local businessman Donald O'Toole to construct housing for African Americans in nearby Princeton Park split Roseland apart. Spurred on by the *Calumet Index,* local leaders launched a 1943 petition drive to fight the construction of Altgeld Gardens in nearby RIVERDALE by the Chicago Housing Authority. More than 11,000 residents signed the unsuccessful petition. In 1947 Roselanders joined in the violence aimed at African American residents living in veterans' housing in Fernwood, one of Greater Roseland's oldest residential neighborhoods.

New housing development on Roseland's vacant edges brought a short-lived growth spurt in the 1950s and early 1960s. Changing industrial patterns, however, led to a decline in the community's economic fortunes. Production at Pullman and other local industries slowed, and workers followed their jobs to the suburbs. Joining them there were residents who feared integration. Despite sporadic efforts to create an integrated community and the commitment of several European ethnic communities to stay in place, the racial composition of the community area changed dramatically between 1965 and 1975. Its economic geography, however, changed more slowly. Greater Roseland continued to be home to the middle-class and elite on its edges, and elsewhere to successful working-class families.

The inflation of the 1970s followed by the collapse of the steel and automotive industries

South Michigan Avenue between 111th and 115th Streets in Roseland drew shoppers from all over Chicago's far South Side and the southern suburbs from the 1860s through the 1960s. This 1915 postcard illustrates why its range of stores attracted so much business in the mass transit era and why, with the wider use of automobiles, areas like this one with limited parking lost many of their customers to shopping malls. Photographer: Curt Teich & Co. Source: Curt Teich Archives, Lake County Discovery Museum.

in the 1980s left many of Roseland's newest families without jobs. The virtually complete turnover of population meant that community institutions that had helped residents in earlier times no longer existed or were not established enough to carry the burden. Ventures like the Peoples Store, which had accepted city scrip during the Depression, had also moved to the suburbs. The Pullman Company, which had loaned money to the local bank and juggled jobs to keep income in the community during the same decade, had closed its doors permanently. The out-of-state lending companies that financed more recent mortgages had little incentive to help individual lenders. By the mid-1980s, Roseland had become known for its high rates of HUD repossessions and was designated an Urban Homestead area.

Roseland has yet to recover from the effects of those decades of economic decline. The evolution and growing influence of community organizations, however, offer the possibility that Roseland might come to share in Chicago's new prosperity.

Janice L. Reiff

FURTHER READING: *Calumet Index.* Various issues. ■ Rowlands, Marie K. *Down an Indian Trail in 1849: The Story of Roseland.* 1987. ■ *South End Reporter.* Various issues.

Sandburg Village, neighborhood in the NEAR NORTH SIDE Community Area. Sandburg Village stands on the former divide between the slums of the Near North Side and the GOLD COAST. In 1961 the city accepted a $6,411,000 bid from a group of investors headed by Arthur Rubloff to erect high-rise rental apartment buildings on cleared urban renewal land located between Division Street and North Avenue along Clark and LaSalle. They named the complex for poet Carl Sandburg and the buildings for other literary luminaries. Although less expensive than those in neighboring Gold Coast, the apartments were far beyond the range of former residents; the new inhabitants were mostly middle-income, young professionals. Subsequent town houses appealed to white families contemplating moving to the suburbs. In 1979 Sandburg Village converted to condominium ownership.

Amanda Seligman

FURTHER READING: Berger, Miles L. *They Built Chicago.* 1992.

Sauganash, neighborhood in the FOREST GLEN Community Area.

Schaumburg, IL, 25 miles NW of the Loop. Schaumburg differs from many other northwestern suburban towns in that it did not start around a railroad depot. The area, which was very marshy, attracted its first settlers from eastern states in the mid-1830s. Trumbull Kent of Oswego County, New York, was the first Yankee arrival. He was soon joined not only by other easterners but also by Germans, many of whom came from Schaumburg-Lippe, between Dortmund and Hannover. They settled along the Chicago–Elgin Road (Irving Park) and other local highways.

These farmers organized a German Lutheran congregation as early as 1840, and in 1847 they built their first church. A few years later there was a controversy over the name for the

Woodfield Mall, Schaumburg, 1973. Photographer: LeRoy L. Mick. Source: Chicago History Museum.

little town that was emerging near the church; some wanted it to be Lutherville, but in the end it became known as Schaumburg Center. It grew very slowly, for the area, though fertile, remained swampy and there was no railroad depot to facilitate commerce with Chicago and stimulate rapid growth.

By the end of the nineteenth century the township boasted three cheese factories but a population of only about 1,000. It continued to grow very slowly during the first half of the twentieth century, as did the little town.

The construction of the Northwest Toll Road in 1956 wrenched Schaumburg from its isolation. Area farmers took an active role in industrial, commercial, and residential development. Soon a large number of streets, often at dizzying angles to avoid quadrilateral monotony, spread out from the old center, until by 1980 the population numbered 53,305 and the land was almost entirely built up.

I-290 came to border Schaumburg to the east, cutting it off from the forests and sloughs of the Ned Brown Forest Preserve. To the north the town extended as far as the old Algonquin Road, once an Indian trail and then the route of the Chicago–Galena stagecoach. Woodfield Mall, one of the region's largest shopping centers, opened in 1971 in the northeastern area. It was not by chance that the mall developed close by both I-290 and the Northwest Tollway. While Schaumburg's dramatic growth came with the automobile, the community now has a rail depot and is a regional public transportation center. Schaumburg today is a mature community, with a small industrial area in its southwestern section and a great variety of churches, schools, and open places. Its German origins are now muted, though they live on in road names like Biesterfield.

While Woodfield defines Schaumburg to outsiders, residents returned to the old crossroads at Plum Grove and Schaumburg Roads to develop a new town center in the 1990s. Local shopping, a public library, public recreational facilities, the government center, and a bandstand now provide residents with a service core.

David Buisseret

FURTHER READING: Gould, Alice. *Schaumburg: A History of the Township.* 1982. ■ Hurban, Renie. *Schaumburg: A Pictorial History.* 1987.

Schorsch Village, neighborhood in the Dunning Community Area.

Sheridan Park, residential subdivision in the Uptown Community Area, dating to 1894.

Six Corners, neighborhood in the Portage Park Community Area. Six Corners is a commercially active area surrounding the three-way intersection of Irving Park Boulevard and Milwaukee and Cicero Avenues. Business interests began in 1841 with Dickinson's Inn, which located one block north of the intersection. The town hall for Jefferson Township was built on the site in 1862, and the area was annexed to the city of Chicago in 1889. As residential subdivisions extended to the area, development as a retail center began with Brenner's grocery, Bauer's bakery, Fabish's restaurant, and in the late 1870s D. D. Mee's general store. A dairy farm and a cherry orchard occupied one corner until the coming of the Irving Park and Milwaukee Avenue street railway lines boosted retail development. A contracting and painting establishment opened in 1907, a dry goods store began operations in 1908, and German immigrant Emil Bengson followed with a coal and feed store, starting out with two horses and two dilapidated wagons. Business expansion included a moving business, which by 1915 employed 20 men with a number of trucks and moving vans. In 1914 Jacob Derx began publishing the *Weekly Bulletin*, a local paper carrying neighborhood news and advertisements of area merchants.

The architecturally elaborate Portage Theater was built in the 1920s. People came in droves to see a feature movie and listen to the theater's organ. In 1938 major retailer Sears, Roebuck & Co. became an anchor. By the 1980s there were 150 stores at Six Corners, a mix of national chains and established and family businesses.

Marilyn Elizabeth Perry

FURTHER READING: Fitzgerald, Michael. "Six Corners, 150 Stores." *Chicago Sun-Times*, "Cityscape" (supplement), August 1988. ■ Howard, T. J. "A Three-dimensional Success: Six Corners' Commerce Is Built on a Strong Residential Foundation." *Chicago Tribune*, March 10, 1983.

Skokie, IL, Cook County, 12 miles NW of the Loop. Called Niles Center until 1940, Skokie emerged in the mid-1850s at the confluence of two Indian trails, one going north to Gross Point (Gross Point Road), and the other veering west toward what is now Morton Grove (Lincoln Avenue). Most of this area was wooded, with a marshy prairie extending down from the north. The Potawatomi maintained several villages along the banks of the North Branch of the Chicago River, which bounds Skokie to the west.

Immigrants from Germany and Luxembourg came in the 1850s, giving the area a strong German flavor, expressed by Lutheran (1867) and Roman Catholic (1868) churches. By the 1870s a little town was emerging, and in 1888 the village of Niles Center was incorporated. Without rail connections to Chicago, farming remained the principal source of income for the area's residents until the 1920s. A flurry of land speculation occurred after 1925 when Samuel Insull built the Skokie Valley line of the North Shore Railroad (which became the Skokie Swift in 1964). Although the Great Depression thwarted the real-estate boom, leaving many lots vacant in Skokie throughout the 1930s, by the late 1940s revitalization and rezoning efforts stimulated renewed commercial and residential growth.

Skokie continued to grow with the completion of the Edens Expressway in 1951, which provided greater access to Chicago. The Old Orchard Shopping Center, opened in 1956, generated further commercial development in the area. During the

Philip Klutznick: Shopping as a Real-Estate Deal

Philip M. Klutznick's work as a real-estate developer in the second half of the twentieth century had a profound effect on the Chicago region. He was instrumental in the development of PARK FOREST, in the late 1940s, as a community planned around a shopping center. His subsequent involvement in the creation of Oak Brook and Old Orchard Shopping Centers related to his understanding of the important role such centers could play in suburban life.

Old Orchard, designed as an outdoor, unenclosed mall with a good mix of high-quality, competitive merchants, was meant to attract the year-round patronage of people who would enjoy walking around the mall as part of the experience of shopping.

Klutznick brought this perspective into Chicago in 1973, when Marshall Field's asked him to help develop a new store on the NEAR NORTH SIDE:

> Several sites considered for the Marshall Field store proved too costly or were unavailable. But one location near the north end of Michigan Avenue seemed to have real possibilities. It was owned by the liquor firm of Joseph Seagram and Company, whose principal stockholder was the Sam Bronfman family. Sam was an old friend whom I used to see in New York when I was working at the United Nations.

Klutznick arranged the purchase of the Seagram property for $10 million, as well as additional property from the John Hancock Life Insurance Company. On the site, Klutznick supervised development of Water Tower Place.

Klutznick, Philip M., and Sidney Hyman. *Angles of Vision: A Memoir of My Lives.* 1991.

1950s and 1960s great numbers of houses were built, often using the streets laid out in the 1920s, and by 1970 the population reached 68,627.

Many of the new inhabitants of Skokie were Jews moving out of Chicago. They built a number of synagogues, which have continued to attract Jewish immigrants, most recently from Russia. In 1978 the American Nazi Party received court permission to march in Skokie. Although they ultimately marched in MARQUETTE PARK instead, the Nazis provoked thousands of counterdemonstrators. To commemorate the Holocaust, of which many of Skokie's Jewish residents were survivors, a memorial sculpture was dedicated in the community's village center in 1987.

Since the early 1970s Skokie has attracted people from many parts of the world. The 2000 census reported that 21 percent of Skokie's population was Asian, with 6 percent Hispanic and 5 percent African American; 37 percent were foreign-born. Although the population of Skokie had been dropping since reaching its peak in 1970, it stood at 63,348 in 2000, up from a decade earlier.

Skokie has also been home for nearly four hundred companies. Rand McNally and G. D. Searle & Company were longtime residents, and Bell & Howell, which has facilities in other Chicago suburbs, is headquartered in Skokie.

David Buisseret

FURTHER READING: Buisseret, David, Rosemary Schmitt, and Richard J. Witry. *St. Peter Catholic Church, Skokie, Illinois: Building God's Community of Faith, 1868–89 to 1993–94.* 1994. ■ Strum, Philippa. *When the Nazis Came to Skokie.* 1999. ■ Whittingham, Richard. *Skokie, 1888–1988: A Centennial History.* 1988.

South Chicago, Community Area 46, 10 miles SE of the Loop. Situated at the mouth of the Calumet River, South Chicago first evolved as a rural settlement for fishermen and farmers. In 1833 speculators began buying up land, projecting that the area would become developed as a shipping center. The town was first named Ainsworth. Settlers included Irish Catholics, who established St. Patrick's parish in 1857. South Chicago's location at the intersection of river and railroad routes fostered early growth.

46
South
Chicago

Following the Great Fire of 1871, industry migrated south from Chicago proper. Swedes, Scots, Welsh, and Germans provided skilled labor for the flourishing steel, grain, railroad, and lumber industries. The Brown Iron and Steel Company opened its doors on the Calumet in 1875, followed by the South Works of the North Chicago Rolling Mill Company in 1880. A commercial area serving the growing number of workers developed around South Works at Commercial Avenue and 92nd Street. South Works provided the steel that fortified many of the city's landmarks, such as the Sears Tower and McCormick Place.

A part of Hyde Park Township, South Chicago was annexed to Chicago in 1889. At the time of annexation, half of the area's residents had been born outside the country.

In 1901 the U.S. Steel Corporation acquired South Works. Poles, Italians, African Americans, and Mexicans entered the area before and after World War I. African Americans tended to work as stevedores and were generally segregated in small residential neighborhoods, including the oldest housing at the mouth of the river. A trend of ethnic succession developed: older, more established groups tended to migrate across the river to the better neighborhoods on the EAST SIDE, while newer groups settled in the original mill neighborhoods. One of these was known as the Bush. Bathed in the soot of the steel furnaces, the neighborhood became notorious throughout Chicago for its poor environmental and economic conditions. Workers in South Chicago established complex social bonds built on ethnic ties and work groups. The Roman Catholic church, the Democratic Party precinct organizations, and later the United Steelworkers union helped bridge the ethnic divisions. In 1919 a major strike against U.S. Steel erupted involving some 365,000 workers nationwide. Though the strike proved unsuccessful, it drew recent, unskilled immigrants into union activities. Mexicans, first hired as strikebreakers in 1919, eventually formed one of the largest, most stable Latino communities in the Midwest.

The Great Depression era witnessed intense battles over worker efforts to unionize. At South Works, union activists led by George Patterson captured the company-sponsored employee rep-

Open-hearth blast furnace, U.S. Steel Company's South Works, ca. 1952. Photographer: Unknown. Source: Chicago History Museum.

resentation plan and in 1937 won company recognition of the Steel Workers Organizing Committee as an independent bargaining representative. SWOC became the United Steelworkers International Union of America (USWA) in 1942. USWA Local 65, with headquarters on South Commercial Ave., emerged as one of the community's key power bases and played a role in larger civic affairs.

After World War II, South Chicago's racial and ethnic composition began to shift as refugees from

Lake steamer and grain elevator, 98th Street at the Calumet River, 1948. Photographer: Otho B. Turbyfill. Source: Chicago History Museum.

Serbia and Croatia arrived and the descendants of earlier European immigrants left for the south suburbs. By the 1980s African Americans constituted almost half of the population, and Latinos, many recent immigrants from Mexico, nearly 40 percent. Concurrently, South Works endured a prolonged shutdown of its facilities. Though the union attempted to restore the mill's economic viability by agreeing to many concessions, USX, successor to U.S. Steel, closed South Works in April 1992, preferring to concentrate production at its larger, nearby Gary Works.

South Works' decline damaged local businesses. The South Chicago community reached out to city leaders to support redevelopment schemes, including a new airport, and new enterprise zones, all without success. In 1998 urban planners began a new study of the area's potential for redevelopment. In 2002 the Solo Cup Company began construction of a new facility on the southern portion of the former South Works plant.

David Bensman

FURTHER READING: Bensman, David, and Roberta Lynch. *Rusted Dreams: Hard Times in a Steel Community.* 1988. ■ Pacyga, Dominic A., and Ellen Skerrett. *Chicago, City of Neighborhoods: Histories and Tours.* 1986. ■ Squires, Gregory D., et al. *Chicago: Race, Class, and the Responses to Urban Decline.* 1987.

South Commons, neighborhood built between 1966 and 1970 on urban renewal land in the Douglas Community Area, on Michigan Avenue south of 26th Street.

South Deering, Community Area 51, 13 miles SE of the Loop. Following improvements by the federal government and the Calumet Canal and Dock Company, the Joseph H. Brown Iron and Steel Company located in the area south of 95th

Street and west of the Calumet River in 1875. The surrounding settlement of steelworkers became known as Irondale. In 1903 community leaders renamed the area South Deering. Irish, Welsh, and English workers arrived first, followed by Swedes and Germans. Irondale was initially Protestant; Irish Roman Catholics worshiped in nearby SOUTH CHICAGO. After 1900 new settlers arrived from Eastern and Southern Europe, and Mexicans came following World War I. Founded by Irish workers at 105th and Torrence, St. Kevin's Roman Catholic Church developed as an ethnically diverse congregation.

International Harvester, an agricultural machinery manufacturer, acquired Brown's mill in  1902 and then announced the construction of a new facility, Wisconsin Steel, to produce steel for its tractors and combines. Gold Medal Flour Company, Illinois Slag and Ballast Company, and the Federal Furnace Company also opened here. As the local economy boomed, a number of improvement campaigns were launched, including the construction of Trumbull Park at 103rd Street and Yates.

51
South Deering

New neighborhoods, including the Trumbull Park Homes and the Manors, were constructed in the 1930s and 1940s. Labor shortages during World War II opened new opportunities for women in the workforce.

In 1953 an African American family moved into the Trumbull Park Homes, sparking a decade-long period of violence and protest by white residents. African Americans had been working in the mill for some time in less desirable jobs, but they did not live in South Deering. Civil rights legislation in the 1960s banning discrimination in hiring and segregation in housing slowly brought African Americans better jobs and access to area housing.

In exchange for the workers' loyalty, Wisconsin Steel provided services such as supplying coal and electricity to local churches. Because most of

Wisconsin Steel's production went to Harvester, rather than to the open market, management did not push production as much as at neighboring mills. When the Steel Workers Organizing Committee began to organize South Chicago mills in 1936, they faced difficulties at the paternalistic Harvester mill. Workers there voted to establish their own independent organization, the Progressive Steelworkers Union (PSWU), rather than affiliate with SWOC. In the 1960s and 1970s the union's leadership enjoyed close relationships with both management and with the leader of the local Democratic organization, Edward Vrdolyak.

Following a series of bad financial decisions, International Harvester stopped investing in Wisconsin Steel in 1969. Because closing the mill would have necessitated payment of large unfunded pension liabilities and shutdown benefits, Harvester sold the mill to EDC Holding Company, an assetless subsidiary of Envirodyne Industries, in 1977. The Progressive Steelworkers Union signed an agreement with Harvester releasing the company from all nonpension contractual benefits. When Envirodyne shut the mill without notice in March 1980, workers lost all benefits that were not covered by the Pension Benefit Guarantee Corporation. It appeared that Harvester had succeeded in avoiding $85 million in liabilities.

The community responded to its economic devastation in a variety of ways. At first they turned to traditional points of leverage in the Southeast Side: churches, local politicians, and union officials. But as the unemployment crisis intensified, people also turned to community organizing. New groups such as the United Neighborhoods Organization and the Save Our Jobs Committee emerged. The SOJC, led by Frank Lumpkin, a former Wisconsin Steel worker, filed a class-action lawsuit against International Harvester (renamed Navistar) to recover the benefits surrendered by the PSWU contract. In 1988 Harvester settled the suit by agreeing to pay $14.8 million. While the settlement brought some satisfaction, it did not reverse South Deering's decline. Hundreds of families left, seeking jobs in Texas, Arizona, and California or retiring to Mexico.

David Bensman

FURTHER READING: Bensman, David, and Roberta Lynch. *Rusted Dreams: Hard Times in a Steel Community.* 1988. ■ Pacyga, Dominic A., and Ellen Skerrett. *Chicago, City of Neighborhoods: Histories and Tours.* 1986. ■ Squires, Gregory D., et al., *Chicago: Race, Class, and the Responses to Urban Decline.* 1987.

The cover of a local history of South Holland, showing the transition from Dutch farmers to suburbanites. Designer: Unknown. Source: The Newberry Library.

South Holland, IL, Cook County, 20 miles S of the Loop. South Holland evolved from a nineteenth-century agricultural community of Dutch immigrants into a twentieth-century commuter suburb.

Founded in 1846 and incorporated as a village in 1894, the community retained much of its ethnic and agricultural heritage for over a hundred years. As farmlands were converted to housing developments and industrial parks, and as the population grew larger and more varied, South Holland assumed a new role as a racially and ethnically diverse residential suburb.

The community began as an enclave of Dutch farmers. Attracted to the flat stretches of prairie in the Calumet region, these settlers at first pursued self-sufficient farming but soon moved into market gardening, supplying the burgeoning city of Chicago with fresh produce. In 1892 Dutch and German farmers began raising onion sets (small bulb onions ready for planting) and came to dominate the commercial production and distribution of this crop. Their efforts earned for South Holland the title "Onion Set Capital of the World." This crop and truck farming provided the economic base for the community through the 1940s. Though diminishing in importance after this point, agriculture continued to provide income for Dutch farmers and Mexican migrant workers into the 1960s.

After World War II, South Holland's role in the metropolitan system began to change. Chicago-

ans hoping to escape the troubles of urban life and developers wanting to satisfy their housing needs found the suburb a desirable location. Once again the open lands proved attractive as farms and farmers gave way to subdivisions and families. Interstate Highways 57 and 94, which offered easy access to downtown, further encouraged the transformation. The final assault on agriculture came as the local government turned to industrial parks as a tax base.

Though developers and former city dwellers altered the rural economy of South Holland, they did little to change the conservative character given to the community by its Dutch founders. Blue laws prohibiting certain businesses from opening on Sundays (first introduced in 1959), a ban on liquor sales, and zoning restrictions that disallow apartment buildings and condominiums have all helped to shape and maintain a religious, family-oriented lifestyle. This conservatism was most notably challenged in 1969 when elementary School District 151, which included South Holland, was ordered by federal authorities to desegregate, the first school district in the North to be ordered to do so. Though the order roused some protest from South Hollanders, the issue passed without violence. The school district integrated later that year.

No longer reliant on agriculture and no longer predominantly Dutch, South Holland nevertheless holds onto its ethnic past. Tulip festivals capitalize on it and Dutch-denominated churches remind us of it.

Jonathan J. Keyes

FURTHER READING: Cook, Richard A. *A History of South Holland, Illinois [1846–1966].* 1966. ■ Hahn, Arvin William. *The South Holland Onion Set Industry.* 1952. ■ *South Holland, Illinois: Seventy-fifth Anniversary, 1894–1969.* 1969.

Two faces of agriculture in South Holland. The Paarlberg house reflects the economic success achieved by many early settlers who owned and worked their own farms. The Mexican migrant worker's home demonstrates the shift to itinerant and seasonal labor recruited from outside the community. Photographers: Unknown. Source: The Newberry Library.

South Lawndale, Community Area 30, 5 miles SW of the Loop. "Bienvenidos a Little Village." Traveling under an arch stretching powerfully over 26th Street, a visitor heading west on Albany Avenue is immediately aware that he or she has entered the Mexican and Mexican American enclave of LITTLE VILLAGE, *La Villita.* Situated between the Stevenson Expressway on the south, Western Avenue on the east, and Cicero Avenue on the west and roughly bounded by Cermak Road on the north, South Lawndale was settled first in the aftermath of the Great Fire of 1871 by Germans and Czechs (Bohemians). Other groups, such as Poles and now Hispanics, have followed to take advantage of employment opportunities in nearby industry.

30
South
Lawndale

This blue-collar community area has experienced major economic dislocations since the late 1960s, with the closure of the huge International Harvester plant in the southeast quadrant and the Western Electric complex along its western boundary. The 1990 census recorded a disastrous unemployment rate of 14 percent. Residents have seen jobs disappear in the high-wage industrial sector, so have sought employment in the service and public sectors. Job training for the economy of the twenty-first century is offered at the West Side Technical Institute, part of the City Colleges of Chicago.

By 2000, 91,071 people made their home in the area; 83 percent were Hispanic, and nearly half were foreign-born. This represented an appreciable increase in South Lawndale's Hispanic population, from 47 percent in 1980 and 4 percent in 1970. As the Hispanic population expanded, ethnic white neighborhoods disappeared as those residents migrated west, out of the city. Over the last several decades, 40 percent of the total

The area historically known as "Mud Lake" as it looked in 1908, seen from the Kedzie Avenue Bridge along the South Branch of the Chicago River. Photographer: Unknown. Source: Chicago History Museum.

population has been under 20 years of age. With this youthful population, the local public schools have been filled to capacity, and overcrowding has been exacerbated by the financial collapse of parochial schools.

The housing stock dates primarily to the period before World War I. Only 5 percent of the 20,000 housing units standing in 1990 were less than 20 years old. However, commercial revitalization has begun to drive property values higher, with more than 1,600 businesses located along 22nd and 26th Streets. The median home value in 2000 was $105,000, compared to slightly less than $50,000 in 1990. Rents that averaged $360 per month in 1990 increased at least 50 percent in the following decade. While not a middle-class community, Little Village has struggled to remain affordable to the working families who attend half a dozen Roman Catholic churches and sustain the variety of restaurants, shops, and banking institutions on 26th Street, or Calle Mexico. The community also struggles to counterbalance the effects of gang activity.

With more than 5,000 inmates, the Cook County Jail and the city of Chicago's House of Corrections add many non-Hispanics to the area's overall demographic profile. The Hispanic community has struggled for community-based political representation at least since the 1970s. By the end of the twentieth century, Latinos represented the community in the Chicago City Council, the Cook County Board, the Illinois General Assembly, and the U.S. Congress.

Christopher R. Reed

FURTHER READING: Chicago Fact Book Consortium, ed. *Local Community Fact Book: Chicago Metropolitan Area.* For the years 1990, 1980, 1960, 1950, and 1938. ■ Little Village Chamber of Commerce. 1999 Business Directory.

South Loop, neighborhood in the LOOP Community Area. The South Loop was one of Chicago's first residential districts, which recent redevelopment has again transformed into a residential neighborhood.

Working-class immigrants, primarily Irish, initially settled south of the young city near the river, while the well-to-do built houses along Michigan and Wabash Avenues. Railroads entering Chicago in the 1850s established passenger stations and freight houses at the southern edge of the business district. The Chicago Fire of 1871 spared the area, but displaced Loop businesses found temporary quarters there. Another fire, in 1874, ended the area's remaining residential character.

By 1900 railroad tracks filled the area from State Street to Clinton Street, serving freight depots and passenger stations—Central, Dearborn, LaSalle Street, and Grand Central—that marked the southern edge of the central business district. An infamous vice district flourished around the stations, including the brothels mapped in *If Christ Came to Chicago* (1894). As Chicago became the nation's printing center, high loft buildings filled the narrow blocks near Dearborn Station, convenient both for printing salesmen and express shipments.

The decline of passenger trains left the rail yards vacant, while changes in the printing industry had emptied out PRINTER'S ROW. The 1973 Chicago 21 Plan reflected business leaders' worries about the derelict South Loop and called for construction of an urban new town there. Downtown businessmen organized a corporation to build such a community, on 51 acres of Dearborn Station rail yards, and residents moved into DEARBORN PARK in 1979. Middle-class residents were attracted to an integrated neighborhood in the heart of the city, and a second phase was built south of Roosevelt Road after 1988.

Pioneering architects and developers had recognized the potential of loft buildings on Printer's Row, and those were converted to apartments as Dearborn Park was being built. Redevelopment spread west to the river when River City opened

in 1985, and then east and south with residential conversions along Wabash and Michigan Avenues. In 1992 construction began on Central Station, a 72-acre redevelopment project on former Illinois Central rail yards east of Michigan Avenue south of Roosevelt Road. Redevelopment work on the Museum Campus, new dormitories and buildings for local universities, and residential growth continued into the new century.

Dennis McClendon

FURTHER READING: Cassidy, Robert. "Laying the Groundwork for Chicago's New-Town-in-Town." *Planning* (August 1977). ■ Wille, Lois. *At Home in the Loop: How Clout and Community Built Chicago's Dearborn Park.* 1997.

South Shore, Community Area 43, 9 miles SE of the Loop. A 1939 description of South Shore, stating that it was "predominately middle class–upper middle class, to be sure, but not social register," offers an apt though antiquated characterization of this South Side community. Though the class gap among its residents has at times run quite wide, for most of its history South Shore has been a solidly middle-class enclave. The area, bounded by 67th and 79th Streets to the north and south and by Stony Island Avenue and Lake Michigan to the east and west, was mostly swampland in the 1850s when Ferdinand Rohn, a German truck farmer, utilized trails along the area's high ground to transport his goods to Chicago.

43
South Shore

Before the community came to be known as South Shore in the 1920s, it was a collection of settlements in southern Hyde Park Township with names like Essex, Bryn Mawr, Parkside, Cheltenham Beach, and Windsor Park. Most of these settlements were already in place when the Illinois Central built the South Kenwood Station in 1881 at what is now 71st and Jeffrey Boulevard.

As with many South Side Chicago communities, the two events that sparked commercial and residential development were annexation to Chicago in 1889 and the World's Columbian Exposi-

Golfers at South Shore Country Club, 1908. Photographer: Unknown. Source: Chicago History Museum.

tion in 1893. The location of the fair in nearby Jackson Park prompted the sale of land and building lots and subsequently a housing explosion. White Protestants fled neighboring WASHINGTON PARK as immigrants and African Americans moved in. In 1905 these former residents of Washington Park built Jackson Park Highlands, an exclusive residential community ensconced within South Shore. In 1906 they established the South Shore Country Club, a posh 67-acre lakeside playground that excluded blacks and Jews.

A housing boom in the 1920s generated not only a substantial increase in the area's population but also greater diversity among its residents and in housing stock. Between 1920 and 1930 the population of South Shore jumped from 31,832 to 78,755. Many of the new residents were Irish, Swedish, German, or Jewish and had followed native white Protestants from Wash-

ington Park to live in South Shore's high-rises, single-family homes, and apartment houses. Institutions built in South Shore during these years reflected the community's growing diversity; by 1940 South Shore contained 15 Protestant churches, 4 Roman Catholic parishes, and 4 Jewish synagogues.

As African American families moved to South Shore in the 1950s, white residents became concerned about the neighborhood's stability. The South Shore Commission initiated a program it called "managed integration," designed to check the physical decline of the community and to achieve racial balance. The initiative was largely unsuccessful on both counts. Although residential and commercial decline did coincide with an increase in the African American population (69 percent by 1970 and 95 percent by 1980), it had more to do with real-estate "redlining" and commercial disinvestment. In the early 1970s a collaboration between the Renewal Effort Service Corporation (RESCORP) and the Illinois Housing Development Authority resulted in two rehabilitation programs called "New Vistas." When in 1973 the South Shore Bank attempted to relocate to the Loop, the federal Comptroller of the Currency denied its petition to move under pressure from local activists, who then assumed management of the bank. The bank's reinvestment in South Shore led to both residential and commercial revitalization.

By the late 1990s South Shore had reemerged as a solidly middle-class African American community. Although the commercial strips on 71st and 75th still struggled, developers built a shopping plaza at 71st and Jeffrey. The cultural life of the area has been enhanced since the Chicago Park District purchased the waning South Shore Country Club in 1972, converting it into a cultural center. The New Regal Theater opened in 1987 on 79th Street and remained open until 2003. Perhaps still not "social register," South Shore remained a choice destination for those desiring a congenial middle-class community on Chicago's South Side.

Wallace Best

FURTHER READING: "The South Shore Commission Plan: A Comprehensive Plan for Present and Future by the Residents of South Shore." Municipal Library of Chicago, 1967. ■ Chicago Fact Book Consortium, ed. *Local Community Fact Book: Chicago Metropolitan Area, 1990. 1995.* ■ Pacyga, Dominic A., and Ellen Skerrett. "South Shore." In *Chicago, City of Neighborhoods: Histories and Tours,* 1986.

St. Charles, IL, DuPage and Kane Counties, 35 miles W of the Loop. The site of St. Charles was well known to the Potawatomi, who established two summer camps near the shallows, where they forded the Fox River and fished. Later settlers were similarly attracted by the varied nature of the country, with prairie to the west and extensive woods on both sides of the river to

the north. They also prized the creeks that ran into the Fox River for mills and used rock outcrops in the area for building stone.

By 1836 a bridge and dam had been built, and a little town was growing up around them on both the east and west banks. It was at first called Charleston, but as there was already a town in Illinois with that name, it was changed to St. Charles. Most of the early settlers came from New England, and the Yankee influence remained strong throughout the nineteenth century.

From 1849 to about 1859 St. Charles was served by the St. Charles Branch Railroad. But regular rail service did not come until 1871 when the Chicago, St. Paul & Kansas City Railroad established a depot, ushering in a period of economic growth. Some new industries, like the cheese factory and the milk condensery, processed local farm produce; but others, like the iron works, paper mill, piano factory, and cutglass factory, took advantage of St. Charles's water power and strategic location. Factory work drew many hundreds of Swedish immigrants, along with substantial numbers of Lithuanians, Belgians, and Danes.

By the end of the nineteenth century the built-up area of the town extended for about half a mile in each direction from the Fox River crossing, and the woodland to the north was being cleared for farms and outlying houses. The coming of the automobile in the 1920s drew St. Charles into the expanding Chicago market. The population grew from 2,675 in 1900 to 6,709 in 1950. But the town did not experience the explosive postwar growth of some of the towns to the east, and as late as 1970 did not extend for more than a mile each way from the historic center. The 1980s and 1990s saw the development of new residential subdivisions on both sides of the river and to the north and south. The population reached 27,896 in 2000.

There have also been major economic changes, as factories have given way to a variety of service-based enterprises. Still, St. Charles retains

St. Charles bridge over Fox River, 1932. Photographer: Unknown. Source: Chicago History Museum.

evidence of its past, not only in the many early buildings at the center of town, but also in names like Ferson's Creek, named for a Yankee settler, and Brewster and Norton Creeks, called after the mills that once lined their banks.

David Buisseret

FURTHER READING: Badger, David Alan. *St. Charles of Illinois.* 1985. ■ Pearson, Ruth. *Reflections of St. Charles: A History of St. Charles, Illinois, 1833–1976.* 1976.

Stateway Gardens. Built in 1958, this 33-acre public housing project, between 35th and 39th Streets along State Street in the DOUGLAS Community Area, replaced the Federal Street slum area. Residents were almost exclusively African American. By the 1970s municipal neglect and budget cuts created opportunities for gangs to gain control over the project's underground economy. In 2001 the Chicago Housing Authority began the process of demolishing the existing 1,644

units and replacing them with new mixed-income low-rise housing.

Erik Gellman

FURTHER READING: Downey, Sarah, and John McCormick. "Razing the Vertical Ghettoes: Mayor Daley Plans to Rescue His City's Squalid Public Housing by Destroying It." *Newsweek,* May 15, 2000. ■ Pacyga, Dominic A., and Ellen Skerrett. *Chicago, City of Neighborhoods: Histories and Tours.* 1986.

Stewart Ridge, neighborhood in the WEST PULLMAN Community Area established in the early twentieth century.

Streeterville, neighborhood in the NEAR NORTH SIDE Community Area. Early maps of Chicago show little but lake immediately north of the Chicago River and east of Pine Street (now Michigan Avenue). But sand and silt accumulated north of a 1,500-foot pier built at the mouth of the river in 1834 and the area was nicknamed "the

Dearborn Street looking north to Stateway Gardens, 1959, showing the kind of buildings razed to make way for high-rise housing. Photographer: Clarence W. Hines. Source: Chicago History Museum.

Sands." The arrival of squatters on the Sands and the emergence a vice district alarmed investors in lakefront property, and in 1857 they persuaded Mayor "Long John" Wentworth to clear out the trespassers.

Confrontations between squatters and lakefront property owners recurred after 1886, when George Wellington Streeter (1837–1921) stranded his boat on the Sands. "Cap'n" Streeter claimed that his grounded ship created this land, which was therefore outside of Illinois' jurisdiction. Streeter's brashness endeared him to local newspapers, which delighted in reporting on his "Deestric of Lake Michigan." A series of eviction attempts escalated into gun battles and eventually landed him in prison. Finally, in 1918 the court ruled Streeter's claims invalid. Some of Chicago's most expensive land and famous buildings, including the John Hancock Center and Water Tower Place, now stand on the formerly contested site.

Amanda Seligman

FURTHER READING: Stamper, John W. "Shaping Chicago's Shoreline." *Chicago History* (Winter–Spring 1985–86). ■ Tessendorf, K. C. "Captain Streeter's District of Lake Michigan." *Chicago History* (Fall 1976).

Summit, IL, Cook County, 12 miles SW of the Loop. Aptly named, Summit sits on the gentle rise separating the Chicago River from the Des Plaines. Various Indian tribes traveled for centuries through a network of trails and portages that crossed the swampy interfluve. A hint of the original landscape can be found in the Chicago Portage National Historic Site, on Harlem Avenue in LYONS, just north of Summit.

Father Jacques Marquette and Louis Jolliet first used that portage during their return from the Mississippi in 1673. In the early 1830s Russell Heacock built an inn and farmed in the area. Summit is located along the Illinois & Michigan Canal, and in 1845 canal commissioners sold area land to defray construction costs. Peter Kern bought much of what would become Summit in 1851. His children sold most of this land to Frederick Petersdorf and John Wentworth.

From the start, Summit was marked by an extremely diverse ethnic mix. Native-born settlers, lured by frontier opportunities, were joined by Irish canal workers by the late 1830s. Germans followed shortly thereafter. From the 1880s to the early 1900s, the flow of immigration became a flood as Poles, Croatians, Slovaks, Russians, Italians, and Dutch all arrived. A few African American and Mexican households were present at the turn of the century, and the first Greek family arrived in 1910. Incorporated in 1890, Summit's population was 547 in 1900; it rose to 4,019 by 1920.

The early settlement was known for the quality of its produce, and large shipments of vegetables were sold in Chicago. In those early days, the village formed around Lawndale and Douglas Streets on the north side. As population increased, the business district grew along Archer.

Since the mid-nineteenth century, Summit has been served by several major railroad lines that run through the valley; its importance as a rail junction increased when the Indiana Harbor Belt Railroad entered from the east along 63rd Street. The I&M Canal was replaced by the larger Sanitary and Ship Canal, completed in 1900.

South of the village, in 1907, the Corn Products Refining Company began building what would become the largest corn-milling plant in the world. Summit annexed this area in 1911. Called Argo after one of the firm's products, this area continues to pull development in its direction.

After World War I, manufacturing and services diversified in Summit. The *Des Plaines Valley News* began in 1913 and in 2000 was one of the last independent suburban newspapers. Between 1916 and 1922 the Elgin Motor Car Company produced over 8,000 automobiles. Food processing companies, functionally related to the Argo plant, were

established. The rail yards transferred meat products from the Chicago stockyards. In the 1950s the canal was filled in at Summit, so the land could be used for the Stevenson Expressway.

Restricted at the start of the century to the home, shops, or—if widowed—to maintaining rooming houses, women now play a leading role not only in Summit's civic affairs, but in business and politics. In 1995 this was exemplified by the election of Summit's first female mayor.

John D. Schroeder

FURTHER READING: Summit Bicentennial Commission, Heritage Committee. *Summit Heritage.* 1990.

Taylorville, early industrial neighborhood in the EAST SIDE Community Area.

Thornton, IL, Cook County, 21 miles S of the Loop. Thornton shares boundaries with SOUTH HOLLAND to the north, Glenwood to the south, and HOMEWOOD and East Hazel Crest to the west. Cook County Forest Preserves are to the east and south. The northern part of Thornton is traversed east to west by the Tri-State Tollway (I-80/I-294). Halsted Street (Route 1) is part of Thornton's western border and has an interchange with I-80. The first railroad (later the Chicago & Eastern Illinois, now the Union Pacific) came to Thornton in 1869. At one time there was a depot in Thornton, but there is no longer passenger service.

Thornton has been shaped by its geologic past. The western part contains 400-foot-deep sedimentary deposits of dolomite and was first quarried by Gurdon Hubbard in the mid-1830s. The

Thornton Quarry is one of the largest commercial stone quarries in the world, operated by Material Service Corporation since 1938.

Ten-mile-long Thorn Creek flows through the village from the south into the Little Calumet River. In the early years, Thorn Creek was about 40 feet wide and 4 to 6 feet deep; noted for its clear spring-fed water, it was navigable to Thornton.

Evidence of Native American occupation of the Thornton area abounds, especially along Thorn Creek. The Hoxie site, to the east of Thornton, dates to around AD 1400.

The village of Thornton is the oldest settlement in Thornton Township, and both are named after William F. Thornton, one of the commissioners of the Illinois & Michigan Canal. The first white settler was William Woodbridge in 1834.

The town was first platted in 1835 by John H. Kinzie. In 1836 Kinzie, Hubbard, and John Blackstone established a sawmill on Thorn Creek, which provided the lumber for the first school in that same year. In 1852 John S. Bielfeldt, a German immigrant, established a brewery that was operated by his family until Prohibition. During Prohibition the brewery continued to produce beer and was sometimes raided by federal agents. The Frederick brothers bought the brewery and operated it in the 1940s. A Lithuanian immigrant, Ildefonsas Sadauskas, owned it in the early 1950s. Later the site housed a restaurant and other small businesses.

The Great Depression had a profound impact on Thornton. The bank closed in 1934 and moved to BLUE ISLAND. In 1939 and 1940 the Works Projects Administration created the public library and constructed sidewalks, curbs, and sewers in the village. In the 1930s the Civilian Conservation Corps operated Camp Thornton in the Sweet Woods Forest Preserve. The camp, which housed German POWs during World War II, was later used by the Girls Scouts until 1988.

Thornton's population has been stable for years at around 3,000, with its housing in great demand. Like much of the surrounding area, Thornton attracted a large number of Germans in its early years. Later, many Eastern Europeans arrived to work in the quarry, living south of the quarry in an area that became known as "Hunkeyville."

Dave Bartlett

FURTHER READING: "History of Thornton, Illinois." In *Where the Trails Cross*, vol. 3, no. 4. South Suburban Genealogical and Historical Society, South Holland, IL. ■ Andreas, A. T. *History of Cook County, Illinois.* 1884. ■ Markman, Charles W. *Chicago Before History: The Prehistoric Archaeology of a Modern Metropolitan Area.* 1991.

Tinley Park, IL, Cook and Will Counties, 23 miles S of the Loop. There is much evidence of Native American residents in the area of Tinley Park, especially at the Oak Forest site east of town. The site, on the Tinley Moraine overlooking a marshy area of glacial lake plain, dates to the 1600s. The 1816 Indian Boundary Line crosses to the southeast of the village.

After the John Fulton family arrived in 1835 from New York, a community developed, with the early names of English Settlement and Yorktown. As large numbers of Germans arrived in the 1840s it became known as New Bremen, after their port of departure. Bremen Township was organized in 1850. The Chicago, Rock Island & Pacific Railroad arrived in 1852 and became an important asset in the area's early growth and economic development. In 1892 the village was incorporated and named Tinley Park, in honor of Samuel Tinley Sr., the longtime Rock Island station master.

Tinley Park developed as an agricultural service center. In 1869 a grain elevator opened, and a Dutch-style windmill was constructed in 1872. In the 1890s a soft-drink bottling plant opened and operated until the 1940s. Telephone service began in 1898, and a municipal water system was built in 1899. In 1905 the Diamond Spiral Washing Machine Company built the first factory in Tinley Park. In 1909 an electric utility was created by local businessmen.

The village had a population of 300 by 1900 and grew very slowly until World War II. After the war young families from Chicago were attracted by the affordable housing. From 1950 the population doubled every decade until 1980, and Tinley Park was one of Cook County's fastest-growing communities; 80 percent of the housing stock has been built since 1970. In recent years larger, more expensive houses have been built and the village continues to annex land. Tinley Park became the home of the World Music Theater and has experienced major commercial growth as industrial and office parks have located along the I-80 corridor. The village is committed to "controlled growth," however, with the goal of maintaining a livable community. Population had grown to 48,401 by 2000.

Tinley Park's residents have included John Rauhoff, who created Ironite, an additive for waterproofing cement that was important in the building of Hoover Dam. John Poorman invented an improved chicken brooder. The Bettenhausen family produced famous race car drivers.

Tinley Park has been working to preserve its history. The area of the 1892 village has been designated a historic district, where property owners are encouraged to restore and preserve their historic buildings and homes. The Carl Vogt Building, listed on the National Register of Historic Places, has been restored and is now used for commercial purposes. The Tinley Park Historical Society has renovated the Old Zion Landmark Church for use as its museum and headquarters.

Dave Bartlett

FURTHER READING: "Featuring Bremen Township." *Where the Trails Cross* 7.1 (Fall 1976): 1–3. ■ Schwertfeger, Krista A., and Gail D. Welter. "Tinley Park." In *Local Community Fact Book: Chicago Metropolitan Area, 1990*, ed. Chicago Fact Book Consortium. 1995. ■ Tinley Park Chamber of Commerce. *Tinley Park, Illinois: A World Class Community*. 1995.

Towertown, neighborhood in the NEAR NORTH SIDE Community Area. Towertown was Chicago's bohemia in the early twentieth century. Lacking precise boundaries, the district took its name from the Water Tower, which stood to its north and east on Michigan Avenue. An art colony took root in Towertown when Anna and Lambert Tree built Tree Studios to tempt artists to stay in Chicago after the 1893 World's Columbian Exposition. The concentration of artists, writers, and poets attracted bookshops and coffeehouses, the most famous of which was the Dill Pickle Club. Soapbox orators gathered in Bughouse Square (Washington Square Park) to debate the issues of the day. Gays, lesbians, and experimenters in free love took refuge among Towertown's radicals. By the mid-1920s, rising property values driven by the luxury shopping district on nearby Michigan Avenue were pricing out many of the artists. Towertown became a tourist attraction, further alienating its bohemian denizens. By the Great Depression, the art colony had dispersed, although Tree Studios remains a going concern.

Amanda Seligman

Trumbull Park Homes, neighborhood built by the Chicago Housing Authority in the 1930s in the SOUTH DEERING Community Area.

Ukrainian Village, neighborhood in the WEST TOWN Community Area. In the aftermath of the Chicago Fire of 1871, German immigrants developed the area bounded by Division, Damen, Chicago, and Western. After the first of wave of Ukrainian and Russian immigration from 1880 to 1910, however, Ukrainians outnumbered other ethnic groups in the neighborhood. By 1930, estimates placed the Chicago Ukrainian population between 25,000 and 30,000, and the majority resided within this small, 160-acre tract.

In contrast to WICKER PARK, Ukrainian Village began as a predominately working-class neighborhood. Many of the area's first residents were craftsmen employed to build the mansions of their wealthy Wicker Park neighbors. Ukrainian Village came to boast many ornate churches, including SS. Volodymyr and Olha, St. Nicholas Ukrainian Catholic Cathedral, and Holy Trinity Orthodox Cathedral, designed by Louis Sullivan.

Although Mayor Jane Byrne designated Ukrainian Village an official neighborhood on January 18, 1983 (the first such designation in the city's history), steady outmigration throughout the latter portion of the twentieth century depleted the Ukrainian population. By 1990 only 2,500 people living in the Ukrainian Village claimed to be of Ukrainian descent, and many of the residents were young white professionals with no Ukrainian heritage. The cultural impact of Ukrainians on this neighborhood, however, was still apparent at the end of the century, evidenced by many institutions, including churches, the Ukrainian Cultural Center, the Ukrainian Institute of Modern Art, and the Ukrainian National Museum.

Wallace Best

FURTHER READING: "Ukrainian Village: Ethnic Enclave 'Discovered' by Well-to-Do Outsiders." *Chicago Sun-Times*, February 12, 1982. ■ Kuropas, Myron. "Ukrainian Chicago." In *Ethnic Chicago*, ed. Melvin G. Holli and Peter d'A. Jones, 1995. ■ Pacyga, Dominic A., and Ellen Skerrett. *Chicago, City of Neighborhoods: Histories and Tours.* 1986.

Union Park, neighborhood in the NEAR WEST SIDE Community Area, first developed in the 1850s.

University Park, IL, Will and Cook Counties, 31 miles S of the Loop. This village, one of the region's few planned communities, was known as Wood Hill, Park Forest South, and finally University Park.

In the late 1950s Woodhill Enterprises purchased land south of PARK FOREST for a large subdivision. Building began in 1961, but by 1967 Wood Hill had only 240 homes. Residents created a home owners association, which fostered a community identity.

In 1966 Nathan Manilow, one of the developers of Park Forest, started to purchase land around Wood Hill. Park Forest had been a model for planning in the 1940s, and Lewis Manilow, son of Nathan, formed New Community Enterprises (NCE) to build "a whole new town." Major partners included Illinois Central Industries and United States Gypsum Company.

NCE supported the incorporation of Park Forest South in 1967 with projections for 100,000 residents. Planning included space for residential, commercial, and industrial development and addressed the needs of education, recreation, and faith communities. Racial integration was a goal from the beginning, and Park Forest South became a leader in support of open housing. Under the federal New Communities Act of 1968, the town was designated as one of 15 "new communities" that would serve as national demonstration projects.

Governors State University opened in 1969, and the Illinois Central Railroad made its first commuter extension in 40 years to Park Forest South. In 1970 the state of Illinois allocated $24 million for the GSU campus. Plans for wooded preserves and recreation areas were addressed, building on recreation area set-asides and major land donations by the Manilow organization.

The creativity and energy of the developers and village leadership led to great hopes for their "whole new town." In 1971 the federal Department of Housing and Urban Development (HUD) guaranteed $30 million in loans to bring the vision to reality. The developers modernized the water and sewage treatment facilities and in 1970 initiated the first elementary school, the first apartment complex, and Governors Gateway Industrial Park.

However, difficulties soon arose. The economy faltered, HUD requirements and lack of resources created challenges, and projections for growth proved unrealistic. Development was suspended in late 1974, and intense activity at public and private levels over the next two-plus years was necessary to untangle many of the problems. The new town, intended for 100,000, adopted a new, slow-growth plan anticipating an eventual population of 20,000 to 25,000 residents. The 2000 population was 6,662, up slightly from the previous decade.

New town planning remains evident. The industrial park next to I-57 is integral to the village, and residential areas continue to offer open space, bikeways, and additional development. The new town heritage includes the Nathan Manilow Sculpture Park, an internationally recognized outdoor sculpture park at GSU developed by Lewis Manilow to honor his father.

Larry A. McClellan

FURTHER READING: McClellan, Larry. *Park Forest South/University Park: A Guide to Its History and Development.* 1986.

University Village, neighborhood built at the turn of the twentieth century in the NEAR WEST SIDE Community Area.

Uptown, Community Area 3, 6 miles N of the

3
Uptown

Loop. Only sparsely settled in the nineteenth century, Uptown has become one of the densest and most ethnically diverse residential areas of Chicago. In 1861 Graceland Cemetery was opened in what is now the southwest quarter of Uptown and soon became a destination for outings. German and Swedish immigrants operated scattered farms. The Cedar Lawn (1869), Buena Park (1860), Sheridan Park (1894), and EDGEWATER (1887) developments in Lake View Township brought middle-income and wealthy residents to the area. Land speculator John Lewis Cochran's (1857–1923) Edgewater set a building pattern for the area that fostered a broad mix of classes. Along the lakefront he favored mansions, but west of Evanston Avenue (Broadway) he encouraged multifamily housing. Cochran convinced the Chicago, Milwaukee & St. Paul Railroad (Chicago, Milwaukee, St. Paul & Pacific Railroad) to stop at Bryn Mawr

Avenue and two decades later was instrumental in the building of the Northwestern Elevated Railroad tracks near his developments. These routes made Uptown one of Chicago's most populous residential centers.

A commercial boom in the first quarter of the twentieth century ushered in days of glamour. To compete with the LOOP and WOODLAWN, the Central Uptown Chicago Association promoted the area's shopping and recreational opportunities with images of New York City; the main thoroughfare was renamed Broadway and the area called Uptown. Loren Miller's department store (later Goldblatt's) anchored the shopping district. Revelers visited the Aragon Ballroom (1926), the Riviera Theater (1919), the Uptown Theater (1925), and the Marine Room of the tony Edgewater Beach Hotel (1916). Thousands of worshipers flocked to the People's Church and tuned their radios to hear the sermons of Unitarian minister Preston Bradley. For a decade (1907–1917), Essanay Studios made Uptown the heart of the American film industry. Luxury apartment buildings and hotels appeared along Winthrop and Kenmore Avenues.

Uptown's fortunes changed during the Great Depression. The extension of Lake Shore Drive to Foster Avenue in 1933 made it possible for shoppers to bypass Uptown for places further north. During the housing crisis of World War II, the large rooms of the luxury apartments along the Winthrop-Kenmore corridor seemed ideal for conversion into more profitable smaller accommodations. Some landlords neglected their property or did not require long-term leases or security deposits, which made Uptown accessible to recent migrants and Chicago's poor. In the 1950s whites from Appalachia, Japanese Americans from California, and Native Americans from Wisconsin, Minnesota, and Oklahoma settled in Uptown's affordable but deteriorating housing. In addition, the state of Illinois channeled released mental health patients to Uptown's small apartments and halfway houses.

The changes in Uptown's economy, popula-

The stage for one of the popular Broncho Billy westerns, Essanay Studios, 1345 W. Argyle, ca. 1910. Photographer: Unknown. Source: Chicago History Museum.

tion, and housing stock drew the attention of residents, business owners, community organizers, and public officials. Longtime residents and commercial institutions created the Uptown Chicago Commission, which successfully sought designation as a conservation area (1966). The federal government also made Uptown a Model Cities area. New residents joined community organizations, including Jobs or Income Now, sponsored by Students for a Democratic Society; Slim Coleman's Heart of Uptown Coalition; and the Uptown Hull House's Organization of the Northeast. Wary of the land clearance that had accompanied urban renewal in HYDE PARK and LINCOLN PARK, they wanted to improve local conditions while keeping Uptown within the means of the poor. They protested the building of Truman College (1976), which displaced several hundred residents.

Dozens of social service organizations opened to serve the needs of Uptown's diverse poor, including the American Indian Center, St. Augustine's Center for American Indians, the Lakefront SRO Corporation, a federal Urban Progress Center, and the Edgewater-Uptown Community Mental Health Center. Uptown continued to attract immigrants from Central America, Asia, Africa, and the Middle East into the twenty-first century.

Residents of the northern half of Uptown, who wished to distance themselves from the neighborhood's image of poverty and blight, rediscovered the name "Edgewater" and in 1980 achieved recognition as a distinct community area, halving Uptown's population. Home owners in Buena Park (the area between Graceland Cemetery and the lake) and Sheridan Park (between Graceland and St. Boniface Cemeteries)

Schloesser & Co. (John W. Schloesser) grocery store at 4633 N. Broadway in Uptown, 1908. Photographer: Unknown. Source: Chicago History Museum.

won recognition as historic landmark districts. The secession of these prosperous neighborhoods reinforced Uptown's reputation as an area of diversity amid faded glamour.

Amanda Seligman

FURTHER READING: Gitlin, Todd, and Nanci Hollander. *Uptown: Poor Whites in Chicago.* 1970. ■ Hansen, Marty. *Behind the Golden Door: Refugees in Uptown.* 1991. ■ Warren, Elizabeth. *Chicago's Uptown: Public Policy, Neighborhood Decay, and Citizen Action in an Urban Community.* 1979.

Villa District, residential area in the IRVING PARK Community Area, bounded by the alley east of Pulaski Road, Avondale Avenue, Hamlin Avenue, and Addison Street. Albert Haentze and Charles M. Wheeler purchased the land in 1907, when restrictive covenants were already in place determining lot lines and spacing. Most of the houses were built between 1907 and 1922. Set in parklike landscapes, they sold for $4,000 to, for a relative mansion, $20,000.

The neighborhood is noted for its bungalows, designed in the "Chicago" and "California" styles with numerous variations. Also present are the simple American Foursquare, a boxlike structure with a broad front porch inspired by Prairie School architecture, and houses with elements of colonial or Tudor design. Exteriors variously combined materials such as clapboard, brick, shingles, and stucco. Bungalow interiors were typically long and narrow. Although Haentze and Wheeler sold most of their vacant Villa property in 1913, subsequent building followed the same patterns.

The Villa Improvement League was begun in 1907 by area builders to foster community participation and preserve the uniqueness of the neighborhood. In 1923 the group enhanced the Villa District by building six-foot-tall rock structures crowned with flower boxes on every street corner.

Between 1986 and 1991 residents planted 120 trees to replace those killed in the 1960s epidemic of Dutch elm disease. In 1992 the Villa's 126 home owners bought their own snow equipment to clear their streets. Named a National Historic District, the picture-perfect, tree-lined streets of the Villa District bring a quiet suburban quality to the heart of the city.

Marilyn Elizabeth Perry

FURTHER READING: Commission on Chicago Historical and Architectural Landmarks. "The Villa District: Preliminary Summary of Information." May 1982. ∎ Prosser, Daniel J. "Chicago and the Bungalow Boom of the 1920s." *Chicago History* (Summer 1981): 86–95. ∎ Roberts, Gary. "Villa Neighbors Find Life Easy." *Portage Park Times*, September 10, 1992.

Washington Heights, Community Area 73, 12 miles S of the Loop. Located on the far South Side of Chicago, Washington Heights, is bounded by 89th and 107th Streets and two railroad lines at roughly Ashland Boulevard to the west and Stewart Avenue to the east. The community area includes the settlements once known as Brainerd and Fernwood. From the 1830s to the 1860s the area was populated mostly by farmers. After the 1860s railroads dominated the economy of the region, beginning in 1864–1865 when railroad workers temporarily settled in the area.

73
Washington
Heights

Subdivision followed the arrival of the railroad. In 1866 Willis M. Hitt and Laurin P. Hill-iard bought the land from 103rd to 107th Streets from farmers and subdivided for development along 103rd street from Loomis to Racine. In 1869 the Blue Island Land and Building Company purchased and subdivided 1,500 acres between 99th and 107th Streets. By 1874 Washington Heights had enough residents to incorporate. In 1883 the Fernwood subdivision was registered between 99th and 103rd Streets. Fernwood lay to the southeast of Washington Heights and had over 185 houses by 1885. The Brainerd subdivision, named after an early farm family, was developed from 87th to 91st Streets, but owing to a lack of transit there were only six houses standing by 1885. In 1890 Washington Heights and Brainerd were annexed to the city of Chicago; in 1891 Fernwood was annexed and designated as part of Washington Heights.

By 1900 the "heights" area of Washington Heights had developed separately as a settlement for upper-income residents and was renamed BEVERLY. The Washington Heights Community Area grew to nearly 18,000 people by 1930. Brick bungalows constructed between 1920 and 1950 defined its residential character. In this period, the community was made up of white ethnics, Germans and Swedes but mainly Irish, many of whom had moved to Washington Heights from South Englewood and GREATER GRAND CROSSING for better housing.

After World War II, Washington Heights experienced racial succession as African Americans began to settle just east of Halsted. By 1960 African Americans constituted 12 percent of a population of 29,793. Real-estate firms practiced blockbusting tactics, scaring whites into selling their homes "before property values went down." White families did move, but property values remained steady. A journalist wrote in 1969: "The economic level of the new residents is no different from that of the old. Neither are the social values. . . . But many whites are running scared." By 1970 the population of Washington Heights peaked at 36,540, 75 percent black. A decade later the community had declined to 29,843 people, 98 percent black.

Throughout the change, Washington Heights has retained its essentially middle-class character; over three-fourths of the population own homes and incomes are well above the city median. Washington Heights also boasts the Woodson Branch of the Chicago Public Library at 95th and Halsted. Its Vivian Harsh Collection is the second-largest collection of African American history and literature in the Midwest.

Clinton E. Stockwell

FURTHER READING: Chicago Fact Book Consortium, ed. *Local Community Fact Book: Chicago Metropolitan Area, 1990.* 1995. ■ *Chicago Historic Resources Survey: An Inventory of Architecturally and Historically Significant Structures.* 1996.

Washington Park, Community Area 40, 7 miles S of the Loop. Washington Park takes its name from the recreational area situated along the eastern border of the community, stretching from 51st to 60th streets along Cottage Grove Avenue. The western edge of Washington Park is the Chicago, Rock Island & Pacific Railroad. Low-lying and swampy prior to being dredged in 1884, the western portion of Washington Park was settled by Irish and German railroad and meatpacking workers in the 1860s and 1870s. By the 1890s German Jews had begun to settle in east Washington Park, a small number of African Americans had moved into the working-class district south of Garfield and west of State Street, and affluent American-born whites settled on the wide avenues that ran northward from the area into Chicago. This amalgam of ethnicities and classes made Washington Park an early example of neighborhood diversity and suburban development.

40
Washington
Park

Transportation routes stimulated rapid growth during the latter part of the nineteenth century. By 1887 cable cars reached 63rd on State Street, and 67th on Cottage Grove. The "L" train reached beyond 55th Street by 1892, and in 1907 extended the length of Washington Park into the WOOD-LAWN area. Washington Park's wide boulevards

were part of this transportation network, which provided easy access to Chicago's central business district, but they also contributed to growth by attracting wealthy Chicagoans, who built mansions and elegant apartments on Grand Boulevard (now Dr. Martin Luther King Jr. Drive) and Calumet, Indiana, and Michigan Avenues.

A boom in the construction of apartments around the turn of the century played a role in the racial transition of Washington Park. As Chicago's African American ghetto expanded southward during the Great Migration, blacks gained entrance to the large number of apartments in Washington Park, many of which had been converted into kitchenettes. Native whites, German Jews, and members of other ethnic groups moved to points south and north in Chicago, and Washington Park was transformed into a largely black neighborhood (92 percent) as early as 1930. The area's racial transition was rapid and punctuated with violence. A stark example of conflicts to follow, Washington Park, along with the GRAND BOULEVARD community, became a hotbed of racial tension during the race riot of 1919.

Cultural and religious institutions of Washington Park have reflected the area's racial transition and its predominately black population. St. Anselm Church, built in 1909 by Irish Catholics and celebrated in the James T. Farrell trilogy *Studs Lonigan*, became a black parish in the early 1930s. Greek Orthodox residents built SS. Constantine and Helen, also in 1909, at 61st and Michigan; in 1948 the building was taken over by the Church of St. Edmund, an Episcopal congregation formed in Washington Park in 1905 that was entirely African American by 1928. B'nai Sholom Temple Israel at 5301 S. Michigan was sold to black Baptists and became Bethesda Baptist Church in 1925. St. Mary's African Methodist Episcopal Church at 52nd and Dearborn was established in 1897 and is the oldest black congregation in the area. The DuSable Museum of African American History (1961) is a Washington Park landmark, having moved to the area in

1973. This nonprofit institution devoted to the collection and preservation of African American history and culture is one of the largest African American museums in the country.

In more recent years Washington Park has been associated with poverty, urban blight, and public housing. The presence of industry in Washington Park has been negligible, nor is there any significant commercial center. Since 1950, due in part to the initiatives of the Chicago Land Clearance Commission, the population of the community has declined, down from nearly 57,000 in 1950 to 14,146 in 2000. As the twentieth century drew to a close, nearly half of Washington Park residents lived below the poverty level. The area contained one of the highest concentrations of public housing in the United States, including roughly a third of the ROBERT TAYLOR HOMES (1962), the largest housing complex in the world, as well as the Washington Park Homes (1962). Mixed-income residential development is set to replace the now demolished Taylor Homes.

Wallace Best

FURTHER READING: Chicago Fact Book Consortium, ed. *Local Community Fact Book: Chicago Metropolitan Area, 1990.* 1995. ■ Cutler, Irving. *Chicago: Metropolis of the Mid-Continent.* 3rd ed. 1982. ■ Pacyga, Dominic A., and Ellen Skerrett. *Chicago, City of Neighborhoods: Histories and Tours.* 1986.

Washington Park Subdivision, neighborhood in the WOODLAWN Community Area. If the WASHINGTON PARK neighborhood had rectangular rather than ragged edges, it would include the Washington Park Subdivision. Just south of the eponymous park, the Washington Park Subdivision is instead a three-by-eight-block portion of northwestern Woodlawn.

The prestigious Washington Park racetrack occupied the southern two-thirds of the subdivision from 1884 to 1905, when the city outlawed betting. By 1912 developers had built new housing in the subdivision, but several prominent commercial recreation facilities continued to attract visitors to Woodlawn until the Great Depression. Revelers could visit the White City Amusement Park, watch movies at the Tivoli Theater and the Woodlawn Theater, or dance at the Trianon Ballroom. The Sans Souci Amusement Park, a beer garden with a band shell, was remodeled into the tony Midway Gardens by architect Frank Lloyd Wright in 1914; World War I and Prohibition dampened the establishment's potential, however, and after a stint under the ownership of the Edelweiss Brewing Company, the site became a garage and car wash before being demolished in 1929.

Between 1928 and 1940 the newly residential subdivision was the center of a legal battle over the expansion of the Black Belt. Alarmed by the prospect of poor blacks moving into Woodlawn through the corridor between Washington Park and middle-class black West Woodlawn, the Woodlawn Businessmen's Association and the University of Chicago cajoled landlords in Washington Park Subdivision into signing restrictive covenants; property owners thereby agreed that if enough other owners complied, none of them would rent or sell homes to nonwhites. With the onset of the Great Depression, however, landlords found fewer whites who would pay the rents they wanted and instead began subdividing their apartments and renting to blacks. The covenant's organizers sued to prevent the Carl Hansberry family from occupying 6140 S. Rhodes. Despite the legal action, African Americans continued to seek housing in the western half of the subdivision. In 1940 the U.S. Supreme Court held, in *Hansberry v. Lee,* that the areawide covenant was unenforceable. Blacks quickly moved into the Washington Park Subdivision and the rest of Woodlawn, while most of the white population moved out. In 1950 over 99 percent of the subdivision's population was black.

Amanda Seligman

FURTHER READING: Holt, Glen E., and Dominic A. Pacyga. *Chicago: A Historical Guide to the Neighborhoods: The Loop and South Side.* 1979. ■ Plotkin, Wendy. "Deeds of Mistrust: Race, Housing, and Restrictive Covenants in Chicago, 1900–1948." Ph.D. diss., University of Illinois at Chicago. 1999.

Waukegan, IL, Lake County, 36 miles N of the

Loop. French traders were familiar with the Waukegan area as early as 1650, and explorers Louis Jolliet and Jacques Marquette encamped there in 1673 on their journey to find the Mississippi River. By 1725 traders established the Little Fort trading post, which existed until 1760. Thomas Jenkins of Chicago constructed a two-story frame structure on Lake Michigan in 1835 (on the site of the old trading post), and by 1841 Little Fort was established as the county seat of Lake County. In March 1849 residents approved the name Waukegan, the Potawatomi equivalent to Little Fort.

The phenomenal growth of Waukegan, located 36 miles north of Chicago and 60 miles south of Milwaukee, can be attributed to industry, Lake Michigan, and the railroads. Toward the middle of the nineteenth century, Waukegan became a thriving center of industry with enterprises that included ship and wagon building, flour milling, sheep raising, pork packing, and dairying. The most successful of these early industries was the brewing of malt liquors. By the late 1860s William Begley's Waukegan Brewing Company sold throughout America and beyond. It was also in the 1860s that a substantial German population developed in the area. In the mid-nineteenth century, Waukegan harbor was one of the busiest on the Great Lakes, with nearly a thousand ships sailing per year. Growth was further stimulated by the construction, by 1855, of the Chicago & Milwaukee Railroad (Chicago & North Western Railway), which was followed by the Elgin, Joliet & Eastern Railway. These railroads became indispensable to the larger industries that appeared in Waukegan in the later part of the century: U.S. Sugar Refinery, Washburn and Moen Wire Mill (U.S. Steel Corporation), U.S. Starch Works, and Thomas Brass and Iron Works.

Trolley service reached Waukegan by 1896 and the first electric train service by way of the Chicago & Milwaukee Electric Interurbans by 1899. Further infrastructural improvements occurred between 1900 and 1910, spurring middle-class residential development. Jack Benny, Ray Bradbury, and Otto Graham are among the community's most famous former residents. Waukegan is home to Roman Catholic, Congregationalist, and Baptist churches and to Shimer College (1853).

Though largely a residential community throughout the twentieth century, Waukegan remained an industrial center with companies such as Abbott Laboratories, Fansteel, Anchor Glass, Baxter International, and National Gypsum. In the latter twentieth century, shopping districts and financial, governmental, and legal services have added to that industrial core. The near north historic district, which includes houses in the Victorian, Prairie School, Greek revival, and Italianate styles, was placed on the National Register of Historic Places in 1978. The population of Waukegan was 67,653 in 1980 and 87,901 in 2000, by which time a small African American community that had existed since the 1870s had grown to nearly 20 percent of the total population.

Wallace Best

FURTHER READING: Bateman, Newton, and Paul Selby, eds. *Historical Encyclopedia of Illinois and History of Lake County.* 1902. ■ Dorsey, Curtis L. "Black Migration to Waukegan and the Conditions Encountered up to 1933." M.A. thesis, Northeastern Illinois University. 1974. ■ Osling, Louise, and Julia. *Historical Highlights of the Waukegan Area.* 1976.

West Chicago, IL, DuPage County, 30 miles W

of the Loop. Although travelers arrived in West Chicago as early as the 1830s, Alonzo Harvey is credited as the community's first settler in 1842. The site developed a reputation as the first Illinois community created as the result of the railroads.

Chicago's first railroad, the Galena & Chicago Union, arrived in 1849 with plans to extend toward ELGIN. Immediately, the surrounding towns of St. Charles, Batavia, and Aurora added branches (the latter becoming the Burlington railroad), intersecting in what is now West Chicago. Water and fuel facilities for the locomotives and an eating house and hotel for travelers were built. In 1853 a three-stall roundhouse and a mill for repairing rails were added.

In 1855 John B. Turner, president of the G&CU, platted his acreage and donated land for a Congregational church, naming the town Junction. Two years later, Joseph McConnell and his wife, Mary, platted a second area, just north of Turner's plat. Grateful for Turner's donation of land to the Congregational church, they recorded their plat as the town of Turner in his honor.

Many of the first residents of Turner were New Englanders of English or Irish heritage who migrated west as railroad workers. German immigrants predominantly sought farmlands. In 1873 Turner Public School opened. It was renamed Northside School in 1887 when a second school (Southside) was built.

During the 1880s factory sites were offered free of charge to attract businesses to "Chicago's Coming Great Manufacturing Suburb." In 1894 the Bolles' Opera House Block was built for traveling shows and other community events. Turner was renamed West Chicago in 1896 to help prospective industrialists visualize the town's location and to sound more industrial and metropolitan; it was reincorporated as a city in 1906.

Numerous businesses, including Belding Engineering Company (1878), Turner Brick Company (1892), Borden's milk condensing plant (1906), and three woodworking plants, established there. From 1918 to 1964 the stockyards in West Chicago provided a stopover point for livestock being shipped east from western grazing lands. In 1928 Route 64 and a private airport (paved and used in World War II by the federal government; later known as DuPage Airport) were built.

Christ the King Seminary, a Spanish-style structure at Routes 59 and 64, housed the Franciscan brothers until converted to a convalescent center in the mid-1970s. Originally opened as Illinois Institute in 1853, Wheaton Academy moved to West Chicago in 1944, where it remains the oldest high school in continuous operation in the county.

As railroad transportation declined, the town changed. In the 1970s the city government acquired the 1912 Chicago & North Western Railway depot to develop for community purposes. In the 1980s West Chicago became known as the fastest-growing industrial and manufacturing center in the county. With the tracks removed and land sold for commercial use, there are few hints of what was once a prominent and prosperous railroad community.

Jane S. Teague

FURTHER READING: Scobey, Frank F. *A Random Review of West Chicago History.* 1976. ■ Thompson, Richard, ed. *DuPage Roots.* 1985.

West Elsdon, Community Area 62, 8 miles SW of the Loop. Before the early twentieth century, the area now designated West Elsdon was a marshy remnant of an ancient lake. The Grand Trunk Railroad (Grand Trunk Western Railroad) tracks defined the eastern boundary of the area in 1880. Among the early settlers were German farmers and Irish railroad workers.

62
West Elsdon

The area became part of Chicago with the annexation of the town of Lake in 1889. A small hamlet of railroad workers called Elsdon grew up around car shops built by the Grand Trunk Railroad near 51st Street and Central Park, in what is now neighboring Gage Park. The railroad eventually opened passenger stations at 51st, 55th, and 59th Streets, but most residential development remained east of the tracks, as the land in West Elsdon was swampier and unimproved.

By the 1920s people were settling in the area in greater numbers. Population grew from 855 in 1920 to 2,861 in 1930. The development of the nearby Kenwood and Clearing Industrial Districts and the opening of Chicago Municipal Airport (Midway Airport) in 1927, just to the west, made the area an attractive place to settle. The new residents were primarily Polish and Czech, with smaller numbers of Italian, Yugoslavian, and Lithuanian immigrants. The Roman Catholic Archdiocese of Chicago established St. Turibius parish in 1927 to serve the growing Catholic population. An elementary school was established with the church, and Lourdes High School was built in 1936.

During the 1920s Crawford Avenue (Pulaski), 55th Street, and other streets were paved, sewers were installed, and two public schools were built. Though some street improvements were made in the section west of Pulaski during the 1930s, the Great Depression economy suspended growth for a time. The area remained rural, and as late as 1938 cows and goats still grazed along 55th Street.

During World War II growth resumed, and the West Elsdon Civic Association organized itself to lobby for street improvements and other community goals. West Elsdon grew from a population of 3,255 in 1940 to its peak of 14,215 in 1960. Almost all of the new building consisted of detached single-family brick houses, and West Elsdon became an extension of the bungalow belt.

Many new residents were second-generation or established first-generation immigrants, some drawn from BACK OF THE YARDS or other Southwest Side neighborhoods by the prospect of owning a house in a quiet residential area. Predominately Polish, many were part of the white flight from neighborhoods to the east.

West Elsdon residents played a central role in the history of racial segregation in Chicago during the Airport Homes race riots in 1946, the first of a series of public housing riots in Chicago. "Airport Homes" was the name of the site in nearby WEST LAWN established by the Chicago Housing Authority to provide temporary housing to returning veterans and their families during the postwar housing shortage. Residents of West Lawn and West Elsdon rioted and succeeded in intimidating a few black war veterans and their families from joining white veterans in the homes.

The West Elsdon Civic Association became one of the first vocal political enemies of the CHA and its first executive secretary, Elizabeth Wood, and for many years opposition to public housing remained strong in the area. In the early 1970s the West Elsdon Civic Association was an active participant in the citywide "No-CHA" coalition that opposed scattered-site public housing in predominantly middle-class white neighborhoods.

In the half century following World War II, West Elsdon remained a quiet, blue-collar white community with a high rate of home ownership. Several processes brought changes in the 1990s. As the older white ethnic generation aged, new families with young children moved to the area. Mexican residents increasingly settled in the eastern part of West Elsdon. As the number of children classified as Hispanic increased in the public elementary schools in the early 1990s, the number of black children admitted from other communities under a school desegregation consent decree rapidly declined.

In 1993 the Chicago Transit Authority began rapid transit service to the LOOP on its Orange Line, with a station at Pulaski on the northern edge of the community. This brought suburban-style retail development on Pulaski and raised property values nearby.

Douglas Knox

West Englewood, Community Area 67, 8 miles SW of the Loop. West Englewood was swamp and oak savanna when white homesteaders, predominately German and Swedish farmers, first came to the area in the late 1840s. Development followed as railroads began crisscrossing the area. In February 1852 the Michigan Southern & Northern Indiana Railroad (New York Central) began rail service to the region. The Rock Island Railroad (Chicago, Rock Island & Pacific Railroad) and the Wabash Railroad also laid track in the area by the close of the 1850s. The rail stop and the adjacent area of switch tracks, junctions, and scattered

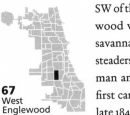

67
West
Englewood

farms became known as Chicago Junction, and later Junction Grove. New residents arrived following job opportunities with the railroads and the Chicago stockyards just to the north of the district. These workers, mostly Irish and German immigrants, lived in the area of Junction Avenue (now 63rd Street) between Indiana Avenue and Halsted Street. Farther west, a small African American community was located at 63rd Street and Loomis Boulevard.

In 1865 Junction Grove became part of the incorporated town of Lake. In 1868 Henry B. Lewis, a wool merchant on South Water Street, and a member of both the Cook County and town of Lake boards of education, suggested the name of Englewood (after Englewood, New Jersey), since the area was heavily wooded. Displaced survivors of the Chicago Fire of 1871 and others seeking to escape urban congestion prompted some development in an area that became known as West Englewood in the early 1870s. Chicago annexed the area in 1889, and by 1896 streetcars connected the community to downtown Chicago. During this time sidewalks were built, single-family frame houses were constructed, and in 1907 the Englewood branch of the "L" was extended into West Englewood to Loomis Boulevard.

The aftermath of World War I saw an influx of Italian immigrants. The railroads and stockyards continued to be important employers, and the employment opportunities of the entire city were only a local train ride away. A transit bus barn at the corner of 74th and Ashland became a leading employer in the area. The community's commercial and retail strip ran along Ashland Avenue between 63rd and 75th Streets.

By 1920 the population of West Englewood totaled 53,276; Germans, Irish, and Italians were most numerous among the foreign-born. In the 1930s the population continued to grow as more African Americans moved into the area, an influx that accelerated in the 1940s and 1950s with migrants from the rural South. The greatest demographic shift occurred between 1970 and 1980,

when the African American population increased from 48 to 98 percent.

The 1970s saw the decline of West Englewood's economic prosperity. The closing of the Chicago Transit Authority bus barn and the loss of stockyard and railroad jobs hit the community hard. For the first time since its founding, West Englewood's population declined, after peaking at 62,069 in 1980. Many residents followed jobs to the suburbs. In 1990 the population was 52,772, and 98 percent African American. Behind the outward bleakness of closed retail shops and gang graffiti, only 14 percent of residents had incomes of $50,000 or more, and little more than a quarter had high-school educations.

Under Mayor Harold Washington's administration, many abandoned homes and vacant buildings were demolished, and repairs were made on sewage lines and major streets. The West Englewood United Organization was organized by three area churches to provide financial and advisory assistance to home owners in the community and to provide summer programs for neighborhood children. In addition, Neighborhood Housing Services, a national network of neighborhood improvement programs, began to address some of the problems of the community.

West Englewood is home to the highly rated Lindblom Technical High School, known for its massive neoclassical facade.

Franklin Forts

West Garfield Park, Community Area 26, 5 miles W of the Loop. Before 1873 most people who saw the farms scattered on the square mile west of the future Garfield Park were on their way somewhere else. Barry Point Road (Fifth Avenue) headed southwest to LYONS. Truck farmers going to Chicago and stagecoaches traveling west to Moreland and OAK PARK took Elgin Road (Lake Street).

26
West Garfield Park

In 1870 the West Chicago Park Commission established three West Side parks, naming the one in the middle Central Park. In 1873 the North Western Railway built its shops north of Kinzie, initiating the area's urbanization. Several thousand employees and their families, mostly Scandinavians and Irish, built the village of Central Park south of Kinzie. The local school was named after G. W. Tilton, superintendent of the railroad shops. Residents from as far south as Harrison Street bought their groceries on Lake Street.

Although the village was primarily residential, it also offered recreation. Central Park, renamed for the assassinated President Garfield in 1881, featured an administrative building with a gilded dome, exhibit houses for exotic plants, picnic groves, and a bicycle track. Horse racing fans went to the Garfield Park Race Track, founded as a gentlemen's club in 1878 and converted for gambling 10 years later. Taverns catering to spectators lined Madison Street. The Garfield Park track, however, could not compete with the prestigious Washington Park course or the Hawthorne track. In 1892 the Chicago police raided the Garfield Park track three times. During the last raid, a horseman shot two police officers and was himself killed, sealing racing's fate there. Various spectator shows, including Buffalo Bill's Wild West Show, appeared in the arena before it was demolished in the early twentieth century.

The demise of the seedy racetrack opened space for both housing and commerce. A policemen's syndicate sold its members homes on Wilcox Street, nicknamed "Uniform Row." The establishment of the Sears plant in neighboring NORTH LAWNDALE drew new residents to the southeast quarter of the area. Lake Street, shadowed by the "L" built in 1893, went into decline, and Madison Street took its place as the district's commercial heart. Entrepreneurs opened department stores, movie palaces, and hotels in the newly advertised Madison-Crawford district after 1914. Merchants so valued this identification that they led a 19-year fight against the renaming of Crawford Avenue (named for Peter Crawford's farm in what is now SOUTH LAWNDALE) as Pulaski Road. West Garfield Park's rise was tempered by bank closures,

deprivation, and neglect during the Great Depression and World War II, but residents and businesspeople emerged into the postwar years ready to restore its standing.

During the 1950s, however, changes in the West Side prompted some residents to reevaluate that commitment. The new Congress (Eisenhower) Expressway displaced residents from the neighborhood's southern sector. Others home owners feared that West Garfield Park would experience the rapid racial change already under way in EAST GARFIELD PARK and North Lawndale. When a black family bought a house on the 4300 block of Jackson in 1959, white home owners formed the United Property Group, which opposed further sales to African Americans. The Garfield Park Good Neighbors Council, by contrast, gave a friendly welcome to black home buyers. These groups unsuccessfully petitioned the state to build the new University of Illinois campus in Garfield Park, hoping to prevent further population change, create a racial buffer zone, and stimulate the local economy.

Middle-class black families did move into the area. Like the whites who were abandoning their homes, they built small organizations and block clubs intended to maintain their new neighborhood. They could not, however, prevent the increasing rolls of absentee landlords from neglecting and overcrowding their apartment buildings. During the early 1960s West Garfield Park was increasingly stigmatized as a poor, disorganized community by observers who did not see its block-by-block variations or its struggling, unpublicized organizations. Rioting that centered on the intersection of Madison and Pulaski in 1965 and 1968 hastened the departure of the remaining white businesspeople from West Garfield Park and further damaged its image.

In the 1970s open-housing laws provided Chicago's black middle class with an avenue of escape from the city's increasing poverty and physical decline. In their absence, the area's economic base eroded further, leaving the West Side vulnerable to illegal drug traffic and accompanying crime.

Nevertheless, a few organizations dedicated themselves to turning around West Garfield Park. Most notable among these was Bethel New Life, which hoped to enshrine the West Side's past with an oral history project and ensure its future with new and rehabilitated housing.

Amanda Seligman

FURTHER READING: Hawkins, Michael Ryan. "The West Side History Project: Tours #1–4, 1928." 1993. Special Collections, Harold Washington Library, Chicago. ▪ *Local Community Fact Book* series. ▪ Seligman, Amanda. "Block by Block: Racing Decay on Chicago's West Side, 1948–1968." Ph.D. diss., Northwestern University. 1999.

West Lawn, Community Area 65, 9 miles SW of the Loop. West Lawn is west of CHICAGO LAWN, from which it is divided by the Grand Trunk Western Railroad tracks. Developers subdivided the land northeast of 67th Street and Pulaski as part of a more extensive promotion of Chicago Lawn in the 1870s. The rail station at 63rd and Central Park attracted settlement primarily to the east of the tracks, while the marshy land of West Lawn remained unsettled.

65
West Lawn

A brickyard and an artesian well were briefly active on land northwest of 67th and Central Park in the late nineteenth century, but both projects were soon abandoned, leaving a cold, dangerous pond that served as a swimming hole and ice-skating rink before it was filled in during the early twentieth century.

With the growth of the industrial district in CLEARING to the west and the extension of a horse-drawn street railway on 63rd Street through West Lawn to Clearing, the population grew to 2,544 by 1920. The area east of Pulaski and north of 63rd was settled with single-family houses by 1930, when the census reported 8,919 people in West Lawn, primarily German, Irish, Czech, Polish, and Italian, with a small Lithuanian immigrant population. Residents included factory, clerical, and professional workers.

Institutional development followed the growth in population. The Roman Catholic parish of St. Nicholas of Tolentine began as a mission in 1909, with a small church and school building. Four Protestant churches were established between 1923 and 1931.

In anticipation of rising real-estate values, streets were paved and other improvements made on the vacant land west of Pulaski during the 1930s. The Great Depression, however, suspended growth, and special assessments and delinquent property taxes discouraged building. In the early 1940s an observer standing on Pulaski near 67th Street saw paved but vacant streets to the west contrasting with unpaved streets lined with new houses to the east.

Growth resumed with World War II. Nearby Chicago Municipal Airport (Midway) expanded. Industrial development in the southwestern corner of West Lawn and in neighboring Clearing attracted new residents. A factory at Cicero Avenue and 77th Street produced bomber engines during the war and afterward was adapted for automobile manufacturing by Tucker and later Ford.

In 1946 the Chicago Housing Authority constructed housing in West Lawn for returning veterans. Residents of West Lawn and WEST ELSDON, to the north rioted that year to prevent racial integration of the Airport Homes at 60th Street and Karlov.

Population grew rapidly in the decades after World War II, from 14,460 in 1950 to 27,644 in 1970. This growth resulted in part from a white ethnic migration out of neighborhoods undergoing racial change. With a growing Catholic population, the parishes of St. Mary Star of the Sea (1948) and Queen of the Universe (1955) were formed from parts of the St. Nicholas of Tolentine parish. Parish schools grew rapidly, with enrollments peaking in the early 1960s.

The Ford City Shopping Center opened in 1965 on the site of the then-abandoned Ford auto factory on Cicero Avenue. Manufacturers such as Tootsie Roll and Sweetheart Cup built near Ford City to take advantage of rail access. Richard J. Daley College, a regional Federal Records Center, and an army reserve base also located west of Pulaski and south of 72nd.

Pulaski and 63rd Street continued to develop as a local retail center and public space. In 1986 the West Lawn branch of the Chicago Public Library opened near the corner, becoming one of the system's busiest branches. Also in 1986 the Balzekas Museum of Lithuanian Culture moved into the defunct Von Solbrig Hospital building at 65th and Pulaski.

While political, community area, and neighborhood boundaries often crosscut each other, West Lawn became the heart of the Thirteenth Ward, a conservative, white Democratic stronghold. No ward in the city gave a smaller percentage of votes to Harold Washington in the 1983 and 1987 mayoral elections.

Since the 1970s younger Mexican families have been attracted to the area, and some Arab families and businesses have followed the 63rd Street retail corridor west from Chicago Lawn. The revival of activity at Midway Airport and the opening of the CTA Orange Line in neighboring areas have raised residential property values and brought renewed attention to the area from other parts of the city.

Douglas Knox

FURTHER READING: Fremon, David. *Chicago Politics Ward by Ward*. 1987. ■ Hirsch, Arnold. *Making the Second Ghetto: Race and Housing in Chicago, 1940–1960*. 1983.

West Pullman, Community Area 53, 14 miles S of the Loop. When University of Chicago sociologists created the West Pullman Community Area in the 1920s, they merged several existing communities. The first was KENSINGTON, a

53
West Pullman

town established at the junction of the Illinois Central and Michigan Central Railroads in the 1850s that grew rapidly in the 1880s along with the adjoining town of PULLMAN. The second was the former village of Gano, first offered by Cincinnati developers in the 1880s and populated by

Pullman workers anxious to own their own homes and escape from the corporate control of the company town. West Pullman, launched as an industrial and residential subdivision in 1891 by the West Pullman Land Association (WPLA), was the largest of the identifiable communities and home to working-class families whose livelihood depended on the factories the WPLA had recruited to its industrial district. Stewart Ridge emerged at the turn of the century when the WPLA put size and building restrictions on its most desirable property to attract a wealthier class of resident. The new community area of West Pullman also incorporated large adjacent tracts of vacant land.

By the 1920s the area of West Pullman had developed into a residential community of over 20,000, with a large industrial base, several retail areas, schools, parks, and a variety of other institutions. Mechanics, laborers, and their families lived in the neighborhoods closest to Pullman and surrounding the West Pullman industrial area, where they worked at International Harvester, tool maker Whitman & Barnes, Carter White Lead Paint, and the other factories that had located there. Ethnic pockets flourished. Joining Gano's Germans and Scandinavians were Italians, Poles, Hungarians, Lithuanians, and later Armenians, all of whom built their own churches and other ethnic institutions. Different neighborhoods also reflected the great economic diversity that marked West Pullman. Corporate officers lived in large homes in Stewart Ridge, while the area's poorest lived in small homes that were already a quarter of a century old and boasted no modern conveniences. And there were a growing number of families who could afford the newer homes being built on the edges of the older neighborhoods.

The developers who built many of those homes put a new kind of restriction on their property, one that prohibited African Americans from living anywhere in their subdivisions. In doing so, they contributed to a growing effort to keep West Pullman white, at least outside of Kensington, which had some 170 African American residents in

Funeral of Silvio Tosi, St. Anthony Catholic Church, West Pullman, 1929. Photographer: Unknown. Source: University of Illinois at Chicago.

1930. Employers helped. International Harvester, for example, did not hire African Americans at its West Pullman works until mandated to do so during World War II. After an African American woman bought a two-flat near 120th and Stewart in 1933, irate neighbors exploded a black powder bomb at the house, reflecting what the *South End Reporter* described as high "public indignation." A decade later, West Pullmanites joined in the battle against the Chicago Housing Authority's Altgeld Gardens in nearby RIVERDALE and against smaller projects in Greater ROSELAND.

West Pullman's population fell during the Great Depression, but it boomed in the years following World War II. Land originally offered by the WPLA and reoffered in the 1920s finally found purchasers anxious for new homes with the conveniences offered by the increasingly middle-class community area and its excellent transpor-

tation links to the LOOP, the industrial Calumet region, and the far south suburbs. By 1960 over 35,000 people called West Pullman home, all of them white.

Beginning in the 1960s, some of the vacant land on West Pullman's western edges finally opened to African Americans. Built on formerly restricted land, Maple Park offered comfortable new homes to black Chicagoans anxious to find the same amenities European Americans had found in West Pullman earlier. Gradually, African Americans began moving into other West Pullman neighborhoods as well. By 1980, 90 percent of West Pullman's 45,000 residents were black.

Like other racially changing neighborhoods, West Pullman was victimized by predatory lenders in the 1970s. In the 1980s its residents lost both industrial and professional jobs, making unemployment the community's single biggest problem. Additionally, the numerous factories that had closed in West Pullman left a toxic legacy behind. Lead from the paint factories and contaminants from other factories created health problems for residents and led to the designation of part of the industrial district as an EPA brownfield.

The city, the federal government, and private investors, spurred on by the efforts of neighborhood and community organizations, have finally begun to correct some of the intentional and accidental harm done to the community, with measures that include cleaning up toxic wastes and recruiting new industries and businesses.

Janice L. Reiff

FURTHER READING: Chicago Plan Commission. *Housing in Chicago Communities: Community Area Number 53.* 1940. ■ Melaniphy and Associates, Inc. *Chicago Comprehensive Neighborhood Needs Analysis, West Pullman Community Area.* 1982. ■ West Pullman Land Association. *West Pullman and Stewart Ridge, Chicago, Illinois, 1892–1900.* 1900.

West Ridge, Community Area 2, 9 miles N of the Loop. West Ridge, also called West Rogers Park or North Town, lies nestled between Ridge Avenue and the North Shore Channel. Potawatomi established villages in this area in the seventeenth century but were forced to abandon their claims in a series of treaties between 1816 and 1829. Indian Boundary Park (1922) is situated along the northern boundary of the 1816 Indian cession. During the 1830s and 1840s German and Luxembourger farmers settled in the area, and a small community known as Ridgeville grew up around the intersection of Ridge and Devon Avenues.

2
West Ridge

During most of the nineteenth century West Ridge remained relatively rural. St. Henry's Roman Catholic Church served as both the religious and social center of the community. West Ridge was home to two cemeteries, Rosehill and St. Henry's, and Angel Guardian Orphanage. Much of the remaining land was occupied by truck farms, greenhouses, and open prairie. Disagreements with ROGERS PARK about taxes for local improve-

ments led to incorporation as a village in 1890; on 1893, despite local controversy, West Ridge was annexed to Chicago. Unlike in Rogers Park, annexation did not bring immediate growth. The number of residents remained under 500 until after 1900. No prominent business districts existed, as community members relied on either Rogers Park or EVANSTON for goods and services.

The pace of growth quickened after 1900. Brickyards formerly located along the North Branch of the Chicago River moved into the area of present-day Kedzie Avenue to take advantage of the sand and natural clay deposits. (Construction of the North Shore Channel of the Sanitary District of Chicago in 1909 increased the amount of clay available.) Scandinavian and German workers moved from other parts of Chicago to find jobs in the expanding brickyard operations, and workers' cottages appeared in the western part of the community. Real-estate interests began to market West Ridge both locally and nationally.

The end of World War I triggered a real-estate boom. Brick bungalows and two-flats became the dominant residential structures in the neighborhood. Apartment buildings also appeared, but relatively poor transportation facilities in the area before 1930 limited demand for large multiunit buildings. By the end of the 1920s Park Gables and a number of Tudor revival apartment buildings clustered around Indian Boundary Park. A tennis club built in the Tudor revival style opened at 1925 W. Thome. A business district along Devon Avenue also developed during this period as the area's population swelled from about 7,500 in 1920 to almost 40,000 by 1930 and local residents looked to their own community for goods and services.

Unlike many Chicago communities, West Ridge grew steadily during the 1930s. Population growth and economic development, however, did not alter the overwhelming residential character of the community. The area possesses no manufacturing establishments and its economic base remains primarily commercial. Population growth necessitated more housing units. One of the largest residential construction projects in Chicago dur-

Interior view of the Nortown Theater, 6326 N. Western Avenue, 1960. Built in 1931 as part of the Balaban & Katz chain, the Nortown could seat over 2,000 patrons. Photographer: Unknown. Source: Chicago History Museum.

ing the 1930s, the Granville Garden Apartments in the 6200 block of Hoyne Avenue, was built in 1938 to help meet the need for housing.

The end of World War II sparked a final surge of growth which began to level off by the end of the 1960s. A large number of Jews moved to West Ridge from other parts of Chicago and were joined by a steady stream of Jewish immigrants from the Soviet Union and Poland. Although the pace of growth has slowed since the 1960s, West Ridge has been a popular destination for many ethnic groups; its commercial centers cater to Jews, Middle Easterners, Indians, Pakistanis, and Koreans. As of the 2000 census, 73,199 people resided in West Ridge, of whom approximately 46 percent were foreign-born.

Patricia Mooney-Melvin

FURTHER READING: Chicago Fact Book Consortium, ed. *Local Community Fact Book: Chicago Metropolitan Area,* 1990. 1995. ■ Palmer, Vivien M., comp. *Documents: History of the West Rogers Park Community, Chicago, 1925–1930,* vol. 2. 1966. ■ The Rogers Park/West Ridge Historical Society and Museum. Chicago.

West Town, Community Area 24, 3 miles NW of the Loop. The West Town Community Area, located on Chicago's near northwest side, is perhaps best understood as an amalgam of several distinct neighborhoods. Its official boundaries roughly correspond to Bloomingdale on the north, Kinzie on the south, and the Chicago River's North Branch to the east, with a shifting western boundary that goes as far as Kedzie.

24
West Town

Most of the area east of Wood Street was within the original 1837 city limits. Workers came to the

St. Stanislaus Church, 1300 N. Noble, 1910s. Photographer: Percy H. Sloan. Source: The Newberry Library.

area in the late 1840s to build railroad lines. Other settlers were attracted to factories near the river. By the turn of the twentieth century, Germans and Scandinavians tended to live in the north and northwestern sections, particularly near WICKER PARK, while Polish immigrants settled around Division and Ashland Streets, an area that became known as "Polish Downtown." Russian Jews tended to live near HUMBOLDT PARK to the west, while Italians concentrated on the southeastern portions, particularly along Grand Avenue. The Ukrainian community settled in the section be-

Holy Trinity Russian Orthodox Church, 1121 N. Leavitt Street, 1958. Photographer: Unknown. Source: Chicago History Museum.

tween Chicago and Division, Damen and Western—popularly known as UKRAINIAN VILLAGE—and their presence there is still marked by such institutions as the Ukrainian Institute of Modern Art and a number of architecturally imposing churches, including St. Nicholas Ukrainian Catho-

lic Cathedral and Holy Trinity Orthodox Cathedral, the latter designed by Louis Sullivan.

In the second half of the twentieth century, West Town became a port of entry primarily for Latinos. First Puerto Ricans moved westward from Lincoln Park toward Humboldt Park, then

Mexicans concentrated in areas east of the Ukrainian Village. By 1990 Mexicans formed the dominant Latino group. Their presence is reflected in the shopping district along Chicago Avenue, particularly east of Damen. African Americans have settled in the area since the 1930s but became particularly numerous in the 1970s with the construction of the Noble Square Cooperative and other subsidized housing projects in the vicinity. In the late twentieth century, black artists and other more affluent blacks moved in as part of the overall evolution of Wicker Park as a hip, "alternative" area catering to musicians and artists. The African American percentage of the community area population stood at a solid 10 percent during the last two decades of the twentieth century.

At the turn of the twenty-first century, West Town was changing again. The influx of artists, students, and other younger "bohemian" populations drew more affluent residents, particularly in the BUCKTOWN section north of North Avenue. This gentrification subsequently spread to the southeast areas along Milwaukee Avenue and Halsted, with restaurants, nightclubs, and shops opening near the cultural landmarks and institutions created and sustained by earlier residents. The various Latino groups remained a clear majority into the early 1990s but fell to 47 percent by 2000. Lower-income residents of West Town have moved to areas further north and west to escape the area's rising real-estate values.

Steven Essig

FURTHER READING: Pacyga, Dominic A., and Ellen Skerrett. *Chicago, City of Neighborhoods: Histories and Tours.* 1986.

Wheaton, IL, DuPage County, 25 miles W of the Loop. Erastus Gary arrived in 1831 to develop a farm and mill on the west branch of the DuPage River in Warrenville, several miles west of present-day Wheaton. Gary's neighbors from

Connecticut, brothers Jesse and Warren Wheaton, claimed nearly a thousand acres of nearby land in 1838–1839. Other settlers from New England soon followed. The settlement was formally incorporated in 1859, and by 1880 the population approached 1,000. The community became the county seat in 1867 following a decade-long contest with NAPERVILLE that culminated in a successful midnight raid on the Naperville courthouse for the county records. In 1887 Wheaton began a long-term prohibition of the sale of alcohol.

A Wesleyan Methodist congregation organized in 1843 was the first formal church in the community. The Wesleyans opened Illinois Institute in 1853, which became Wheaton College in 1860. Methodists formed their own congregation in 1853, and Jonathan Blanchard organized a Congregational church (temporarily subsuming the Wesleyans) in 1860. Baptists, Roman Catholics, Lutherans, Episcopalians, and others followed shortly thereafter. In the decades following World War II, many new congregations were formed as the population of the community increased rapidly from its 1940 level of 7,400.

In 1874 local residents built one of the first public schools in the county that included grades 1–12. Additional grammar schools were built as the population increased: Holmes, Whittier, and Lowell, each in a different quarter of the town. A new high school was added in 1925, Wheaton North in 1964, and Wheaton South (later Wheaton-Warrenville) in 1973.

Wheaton was becoming a suburban community. The Galena & Chicago Union Railroad arrived in 1849, on land donated by Warren Wheaton, whose name identified the local station. Commuter service became a regular feature of the community. The establishment of the banking house of Gary and Wheaton, a new courthouse, and the Adams Memorial Library, along with construction of residences and places of business, gave evidence of a growing, prospering community at the end of the nineteenth century. In 1902 a second railroad, the Chicago, Aurora & Elgin

Horse-drawn buggy wrecked in collision with Chicago, Aurora & Elgin interurban train, Wheaton, 1909. Photographer: Unknown. Source: DuPage County Historical Museum.

electric line, connected Wheaton to the Fox River Valley until 1957.

Wheaton was the site of summer residences for some wealthy Chicagoans, offering a course for horse racing and the Chicago Golf Club (the first 18-hole golf course in the United States). The community was also home to several persons of national note: Judge Elbert Gary (founder of U.S. Steel and the city of GARY, Indiana), U.S. senator C. Wayland Brooks, John Quincy Adams (financier and philanthropist), Edwin Hubble and Grote Reber (astronomers), Red Grange and Vic Gustafson (football players), and Margaret Mortenson Landon (author of *Anna and the King of Siam*). Wheaton College, the Billy Graham Center, the Theosophical Society in America, and World Evangelical Fellowship help make Wheaton a metropolitan religious center.

Thomas O. Kay

FURTHER READING: Burnham, Graham. *Wheaton and Its Homes*. 1892. ■ Moore, Jean. *From Tower to Tower: A History of Wheaton, Illinois*. 1974. ■ Moore, Jean. *Wheaton, Illinois: A Pictorial History*. 1994.

Whiskey Point, early settlement centered on the intersection of Grand and Armitage Avenues, now in the BELMONT CRAGIN Community Area.

Whiting, IN, Lake County, 16 miles SE of the Loop. In 1889 the Standard Oil Company decided that it needed a refinery west of Cleveland to serve its growing kerosene and lubricant trade in the interior of the country. Company officials selected a site south of downtown Chicago on Lake Michigan filled with large sand ridges and populated by some 50 German families who hunted, fished, and supplied lodging and meals to the many sportsmen who used the area. The settlement of Whiting itself dates to 1871 when a post office was established at the place where "Old Pap Whiting," a conductor on the Lake Shore Railroad, had wrecked his train.

The refinery altered the remote outpost forever as it brought construction teams, saloons, stores, workers, and immigrant families to the town. Shortly after construction commenced, boardinghouses sprouted at both entrances to the refinery. In a short while 119th Street became the chief center of commerce and trade. At the corner of 119th and Front Streets Henry Schrage sold food and clothing and distributed the mail. The first stage of the refinery was completed on September 2, 1890, and the facility was altered and expanded many times after that.

Refinery jobs proved especially attractive to immigrants and led to the creation of an ethnically diverse community. The workforce soon included Americans, Croatians, Finns, Germans, Hungarians, Irish, Poles, Russians, and Slovaks, who were probably the largest ethnic group to settle in the town. As in most industrial plants of the time, native-born skilled workers held the best jobs, and unskilled toilers, like Croatians and Slovaks, did the hot, dirty task of cleaning the refinery stills.

Standard Oil of Indiana dominated the life of the town throughout the twentieth century. Its Industrial Relations Plan, created in 1919, gave workers stock-purchase plans, health insurance, retirement programs, and a community center complete with gymnasium and pool that still serves the community. Families who benefited from these plans valued them greatly, and even in the 1990s many households continued to receive Standard Oil pensions. During the Great Depression the company attempted to employ as many workers as possible, even if for only a few days a week.

A turning point in the life of Whiting came in 1955 when an explosion at the plant started a fire so massive that it could be seen from downtown Chicago. The damage caused the company to modernize the facility in a way that reduced the demand for employees and led to layoffs in the early 1960s. Families accustomed to good benefits and stable employment were now angered enough to support, for the first time, a union outside the control of the company: the Oil, Chemical and Atomic Workers. Nevertheless, jobs continued to disappear. The population fell from 10,880 in 1930 to 5,137 by 2000, with most of the loss coming after 1950. As the children of the first immigrant wave left to find work elsewhere, Mexican Americans moved in to take what positions were available.

John Bodnar

FURTHER READING: Federal Writers' Project, Indiana. *The Calumet Region Historical Guide*. 1939.

Wicker Park, neighborhood in the WEST TOWN Community Area. Bounded by Ashland and Western Avenues to the east and west, Bloomingdale and Division Streets to the north and south, Wicker Park became, in the aftermath of the Chicago Fire of 1871, the abode of Chicago's wealthy Germans and Scandinavians. Uninhabited and on the western edge of the city, the area provided an alternative to a population who had already been spurned by the Anglo-Protestant establishment residing on Chicago's lakefront.

The 1871 fire also influenced the architecture of Wicker Park. Having witnessed the vulnerability of wood construction, many Wicker Park residents built mansions made almost entirely of brick and stone. By the 1890s the area was an architectural showplace, possessing houses in a variety of styles, including Victorian Gothic and Italianate. Many of these houses circled the four-acre park after which the community was named.

Not everyone who settled in Wicker Park, however, was wealthy and lived in a large house. By the late nineteenth century, working-class African Americans and Eastern Europeans lived in small cottages dotting Bell Avenue. Labor activists also resided in that section of Wicker Park, including the martyrs of the Haymarket Affair.

By 1930 Wicker Park began to undergo a dramatic racial and class transition. The wealthy Germans and Scandinavians abandoned their mansions, while the number of poor and working-class residents grew. Poles drew the area into the "Old Polonia" of surrounding West Town. Further changes came in the 1950s when a large Spanish-speaking population began to emerge. This transition coincided with a post–World War II housing shortage, and many of the mansions were divided into multifamily rentals and rooming houses. By the 1960s and 1970s Wicker Park was a predominately poor and working-class neighborhood with a large Hispanic population.

Efforts to revitalize Wicker Park in the early 1980s initiated another wave of changes. Young white professionals bought many of the old houses and restored them as single-family residences. Gentrification stirred racial and class tensions, as it displaced much of the area's poor and mostly Hispanic population. By the 1990s, however, Wicker Park had achieved a level of cultural and racial heterogeneity. And with commercial development along Division and North Avenues, the neighborhood had become again one of the most desirable in Chicago.

Wallace Best

FURTHER READING: "Wicker Park Restored to Its Former Elegance." *Chicago Tribune*, July 13, 1986. ■ Pacyga, Dominic A., and Ellen Skerrett. *Chicago, City of Neighborhoods: Histories and Tours*. 1986. ■ Sommers, Nicholas. *The Historic Homes of Old Wicker Park*. 1979.

Wildwood, neighborhood in the FOREST GLEN Community Area.

Wilmette, IL, Cook County, 14 miles N of the Loop. The village of Wilmette is named for Antoine Ouilmette, a French-Canadian fur trader who settled in 1790 on the north bank of the Chicago River. Ouilmette and his part-Potawatomi wife, Archange Chevallier, moved up the Lake Michigan shore to what is now Wilmette around 1826. Ouilmette was instrumental in convincing local Indians to sign the 1829 Treaty of Prairie du Chien, which gave the federal government title to much of northern Illinois. In appreciation, the government deeded 1,280 acres, en-

compassing much of present-day Wilmette and part of EVANSTON, to Archange and her children.

By 1848 the Ouilmette family had sold off the entire parcel of land to farmers and developers such as John G. Westerfield, who in 1857 built pickle and vinegar factories, marking the beginning of commercial development in the area. Other early industries included a cooperage, a tavern, a brick kiln, and an icehouse. In 1854 the Chicago & North Western Railway extended its tracks to WAUKEGAN through Wilmette. Residents, however, were unable to pool the funds needed to build a station along the line until 1869. Wilmette incorporated as a village in 1872, an event commemorated yearly on Charter Day, September 19.

In 1880 Wilmette had 419 residents. Thereafter, the village experienced tremendous population growth, encouraged by increasing train service. By 1900 the population had reached 2,300. The influx strained public services, and Wilmette residents considered annexation to neighboring Evanston. The proposal, however, was defeated in 1894 by a referendum vote of 168 to 165. Annexation of land to Wilmette began in 1912 and continued throughout the first half of the century. The neighboring village of Gross Point was annexed in two parcels, in 1924 and in 1926, as a result of its bankruptcy.

The most controversial annexation came in 1942, when Wilmette laid claim to an unincorporated strip located on the northern border of the village. The absence of zoning restrictions had encouraged the development of entertainment establishments that were open on Sunday, but a 1932 fire had destroyed them, as neighboring fire departments refused to assist the unincorporated area. The area did not regain commercial success until it opened in 1968 as the Plaza del Lago shopping center. Wilmette has opened several additional shopping centers, including Edens Plaza (1956), which encouraged westward residential settlement. The village is also home to the Baha'i House of Wor-

ship (1953), the first such temple to be built in North America.

Wilmette's population, which peaked in 1970 at 32,134, has consistently been over 90 percent white. The late 1990s, however, saw an increase in the number of Asians in the village. The economic status of the residents has remained among the highest in the Chicago area throughout the twentieth century. In 1980 the median household income was $41,640, the fifth highest in the country, and by 2000 the figure had increased to $106,773.

Adam H. Stewart

FURTHER READING: Ebner, Michael. *Creating Chicago's North Shore.* 1988. ■ Holley, Horace. *Wilmette Story.* 1951.

Windsor Park, early settlement in the SOUTH SHORE Community Area.

Winnetka, IL, Cook County, 16 miles N of the Loop. In 1836 Erastus and Zeruah Patterson established the Patterson Tavern along the Green Bay Trail, which connected Chicago to Fort Howard in Green Bay, Wisconsin. Eighteen years later Charles E. Peck and Walter S. Gurnee, president of the newly formed Chicago & North Western Railway, platted 300 acres in New Trier Township along the western shores of Lake Michigan. The town was named Winnetka, a Native American word thought to mean "beautiful place." That year, the Chicago & North Western began servicing Winnetka and other shoreline communities north of the city. In 1869 Winnetka was incorporated as a village, and Charles Peck donated land now known as the Village Green east of Winnetka's main business district.

The village began making municipal improvements in the 1870s. A 119-foot-tall brick water tower constructed near the lake served as a local landmark until 1972. In 1900 the Municipal Electric Utility Plant began operating. Profits from this village-owned utility funded the complete

Crow Island classroom, Winnetka, 1940. Throughout the 1920s and 1930s, the "Winnetka Plan" served as a model of progressive education. It emphasized group and creative activities as well as individualized instruction designed to allow children to learn at their own pace. In this classroom, decorated with pictures and information about American Indians, students sit in a tepee while wearing costumes and weaving, activities designed to teach them about Native American culture. Photographer: Unknown. Source: Chicago History Museum.

construction of Winnetka's village hall and also helped pay the salaries of local teachers during the Great Depression.

In 1890 social activist and Winnetka resident Henry Demarest Lloyd helped found the Winnetka Town Meeting, providing a forum for residents to hear such speakers as Jane Addams and Clarence Darrow. In 1915 the village formed the Winnetka Caucus to maintain citizen control over Winnetka's future. Winnetka continues to operate under this system.

The arrival in 1899 of the Chicago & Milwaukee Electric Railroad (later the Chicago, North Shore & Milwaukee) provided an additional link between suburb and city. Chicagoans looking to escape the crowded city were attracted to Winnetka's lakefront location and commuter services. Between 1880 and 1920 Winnetka's population grew tenfold. Intent on maintaining its suburban repose, Winnetka elected to become dry in 1912. In 1917 the village council appointed a commission to formulate a comprehensive plan for village development. In 1921 the commission published the Winnetka Plan, which emphasized the goal of maintaining Winnetka's quiet character.

The plan also stressed the need for grade separation of the railroad tracks. By 1937, 31 people had been killed at railroad crossings in Winnetka. Concerned that elevating the tracks would divide the community, Winnetka opted to have them lowered instead. Between 1938 and 1943, workers under the Public Works Administration excavated the roadbed and lowered the North Western and North Shore lines' rights-of-way. Winnetka's track depression is unique among North Shore suburbs.

Winnetka native Harold Ickes, who served as secretary of the interior under Franklin Roosevelt, proposed draining the adjacent Skokie wetlands as a New Deal project. Civilian Conservation Corps workers spent 10 years on the massive land-reclamation project that created the Skokie lagoons.

In 1955 the North Shore Interurban line abandoned its passenger service to the communities along the lakeshore. Since the 1960s Winnetka's population has remained below 13,000. At the close of the twentieth century, Winnetka was an affluent, predominantly white (97 percent) community whose members work primarily in professional or managerial occupations.

Elizabeth S. Fraterrigo

FURTHER READING: Dickinson, Lora Townsend. *The Story of Winnetka*. 1956. ▪ Ebner, Michael H. *Creating Chicago's North Shore*. 1988. ▪ Harnsberger, Caroline Thomas. *Winnetka: The Biography of a Village*. 1977.

Woodlawn, Community Area 42, 7 miles SE of the Loop. Surrounded by Oakwoods Cemetery (1853), Jackson Park (1869), the Washington Park Race Track (1884), and the Midway Plaisance, the residential neighborhood of Woodlawn prospered when it could attract commercial enterprises within its limits.

42
Woodlawn

Woodlawn Park's first residents were Dutch farmers who arrived in the 1850s. The population hovered between 500 and 1,000 until 1890. Woodlawn's farmers sent their produce to merchants in nearby Chicago on the Illinois Central Railroad, which opened a station on Junction Avenue (63rd Street) in 1862. By 1889, when Chicago annexed Woodlawn along with the rest of Hyde Park Township, residents had created several active civic organizations, including a Citizen's

Improvement Club and the Woodlawn Businessmen's Association.

The decision that Jackson Park would host the World's Columbian Exposition of 1893 brought 20,000 new residents and entrepreneurs to Woodlawn. In the resulting building boom, developers landscaped Jackson Park, created the Midway, extended the elevated east along 63rd Street, and constructed large apartments and tourist hotels.

When the fair's closing dispersed the tourists, economic depression threatened Woodlawn's future. Local boosters promoted two commercial centers: the WASHINGTON PARK SUBDIVISION, with its amusement parks, racetrack, and beer gardens; and 63rd Street, where dozens of specialty shops attracted "L"-riding Chicagoans throughout the 1920s. The rest of Woodlawn was residential. University of Chicago faculty found the neighborhood congenial. When betting was outlawed in 1905, apartment houses replaced the racetrack in WASHINGTON PARK. West Woodlawn, a trapezoidal subdivision in the southwest part of the neighborhood, attracted middle-class African Americans with the means to buy homes outside the nearby Black Belt.

The combination of racial succession and economic decline distressed local businessmen and officials of the University of Chicago, who organized to preempt the movement of poorer blacks east through the Washington Park Subdivision. In 1928 local landlords agreed to joint restrictive covenants to keep nonwhites out of the subdivision. But the Great Depression made the higher rents blacks were willing to pay for illegally subdivided apartments a temptation to landlords. A lawsuit decided in the U.S. Supreme Court in 1940 found the covenant invalid, ratifying a demographic transformation that was already under way. In addition, 63rd Street's businesses began to fail, and taverns replaced furriers. In 1946 the Chicago Plan Commission deemed that Woodlawn was eligible to become a conservation area, but no plan was

The Sans Souci Amusement Park, at Cottage Grove and East 60th Street, was one of Chicago's most popular attractions when this photo was taken in 1908. It was also a stop on that year's *Daily News* trolley trip, which introduced riders to Chicagoland landmarks and activities within reach of public transportation. Photographer: Unknown. Source: Chicago History Museum.

implemented. By 1960 Woodlawn had deteriorating, crowded housing and few commercial attractions to support a population that was 89 percent African American.

In contrast to West Woodlawn's middle-class home owners, Woodlawn's new residents were recent southern migrants and refugees from redevelopment elsewhere in Chicago. They brought with them anger at being displaced and channeled their energy in two directions. Many young men joined two new street gangs, the Blackstone Rangers and the East Side Disciples. In 1959 other residents, in a coalition of churches, block clubs, and business owners, invited Saul Alinsky's Industrial Areas Foundation into Woodlawn to organize the community against external control. Led by Rev. Arthur Brazier and then Leon Finney, the Temporary Woodlawn Organization (later renamed The Woodlawn Organization, or TWO) initiated a series of well-publicized protests against overcrowding in public schools, slum landlords, exploitative local merchants, and a University of Chicago plan to expand south into land occupied by recent arrivals. In the late 1960s TWO gained national notoriety for participating in the Model Cities program and using a War on Poverty grant to train gang members for jobs.

Despite TWO's organizational capacity and persistent proposals for economic renewal programs, Woodlawn's economy did not recover. Most white business owners, fearing repeats of the riots that devastated the West Side, left the neighborhood after the assassination of Martin Luther King Jr. A rash of arsons destroyed a reported 362 abandoned buildings between 1968 and 1971. Unemployment, poverty, and crime climbed. Those who could afford to, moved out: Woodlawn's population declined from a high of 81,279 in 1960 to 27,086 in 2000. But the neighborhood's tradition of sophisticated civic action continued. In the early 1990s community leaders began to bring private development, commercial enterprises, and a bank back to Woodlawn.

Amanda Seligman

FURTHER READING: Fish, John Hall. *Black Power/White Control: The Struggle of the Woodlawn Organization in Chicago.* 1973. ■ Schietinger, Egbert Frederick. "Racial Succession and Changing Property Values in Residential Chicago." Ph.D. diss., University of Chicago. 1953. ■ Spray, John C. *The Book of Woodlawn.* 1920.

Woodstock, IL, McHenry County, 51 miles NW of the Loop. Woodstock was originally called Centerville in an attempt to attract the seat of McHenry County government in 1842. The Centerville site was chosen over CRYSTAL LAKE and MCHENRY when Alvin Judd donated a two-acre public square for county offices. The square became the hub of a village plat recorded in 1844 by George Dean. In 1845 Woodstock adopted its current name after the Vermont birthplace of early settler Joel Johnson. Woodstock incorporated as a village in 1852 with Alvin Judd as president. The Greek revival courthouse that stands next to the square was built in 1857; it is now privately owned.

In 1855 the Chicago & North Western Railway passed through Woodstock, allowing farmers to send their dairy production quickly to Chicago. The Borden Company opened a dairy processing plant, one of the world's largest. The building later became the home of the Claussen Pickle Company.

Because of increasing population following the Civil War, residents voted to give Woodstock city status in 1873, with John S. Wheat becoming mayor.

In January 1895 a federal court in Chicago sentenced Eugene V. Debs, president of the American Railway Union, to jail in Woodstock for his activity in the 1894 Pullman Strike. The square was filled with over 10,000 onlookers when he was released in November of the same year.

Woodstock's economic strength grew in 1896 when city officials donated empty factory buildings to Thomas Oliver for the manufacture of the noted Oliver Typewriter. In 1910 the Emerson Typewriter Company moved to Woodstock and began producing Woodstock typewriters. By 1922 about half the world's typewriters were made in Woodstock.

Besides the jail, built in 1887, a combined city hall, library, firehouse, and theater was built on the square in 1890. Jane Addams and Leo Tolstoy spoke in the building, known as the Woodstock Opera House, on different occasions. The theater was also used by students from the private Todd School for Boys in Woodstock, including Orson Welles, who was a student between 1926 and 1931. Wells hinted at his experiences at the school and opera house in his 1946 movie *The Stranger.*

As the city vacated the opera house, the building became home to the Woodstock Players, a group that provided young graduates of Chicago's Goodman Theatre School with valuable professional experience in the late 1940s and early 1950s. Shelly Berman, Tom Bosley, Paul Newman, Geraldine Page, and Lois Nettleton performed regularly at the opera house, which is still in use after a major restoration in 1977.

Industrial activity generally declined in Woodstock after World War II. Yet, with reliable rail commuter transportation, the area became a destination for new residents fleeing Chicago's congestion. Residential construction boomed after the 1960s, bringing with it both economic prosperity and the lamented loss of a rural atmosphere. The revitalization of Woodstock's square, prominent in the 1993 movie *Groundhog Day,* displayed this growing prosperity. Population grew from 14,353 in 1990 to 20,151 a decade later.

Craig L. Pfannkuche

FURTHER READING: *History of McHenry County, Illinois.* 1885. ■ *McHenry County in the Twentieth Century: 1968–1994.* McHenry County Historical Society. 1994. ■ Nye, Lowell A., ed. *McHenry County, Illinois, 1832–1968.* 1968.

Wrigleyville, neighborhood around Wrigley Field (Clark and Addison) in the LAKE VIEW Community Area.

Zion, IL, Lake County, 41 miles N of the Loop.

On New Year's Day 1900, John Alexander Dowie announced to the church he had established in 1896, the Christian Catholic Apostolic Church, that he planned to build a utopian city on a tract of land at the extreme northeastern edge of Illinois. When Zion was incorporated in 1902, 5,000 inhabitants joined the Christian utopia. Named after the mountain upon which Jerusalem was built, Zion was to be communitarian and theocratic, a place of Christian cooperation, racial harmony, and strict fundamentalist morals.

Born in Scotland in 1847, Dowie came to the United States from Australia in 1888 and settled in Chicago in 1893 near the site of the World's Columbian Exposition. In accord with reform efforts that swept through many American cities in the late nineteenth century, Dowie desired that Zion be free of crime and vice. He instituted the "Zion City Lease," which forbade gambling, theaters, and circuses, as well as the manufacture and sale of alcohol and tobacco. In addition, the lease banned pork, dancing, swearing, spitting, politicians, doctors, oysters, and tan shoes. Whistling on Sunday was punishable by jail time. Dowie especially opposed alcohol, having signed the temperance pledge at age six, and into the late twentieth century Zion remained dry. The ban against medical doctors reflected Dowie's belief in "divine healing." Many of the original settlers in Zion, primarily of Dutch, German, and Irish origin, had been attracted to the community because of Dowie's reputation as a "faith healer."

Initially, some 25 businesses and commercial interests jump-started Zion's economy, providing work for the people who moved there from around the world. The Zion Department Store and the factory of Zion Lace Industries together employed as many as 3,000 workers. But by 1905 the local economy was in shambles. Despite new leadership after Dowie's death in 1907, industry never flourished in Zion. Commonwealth Edison, which constructed two nuclear plants in Zion in 1973 and 1974, closed both plants by 1998, after a history of safety and maintenance problems.

Despite the lack of industry and low level of employment in Zion, the population increased steadily throughout the century. Zion grew from 17,268 in 1970 to 22,866 in 2000. Although there had been only a small African American population in Zion through much of the twentieth century, by the late 1990s blacks made up nearly 30 percent of the population.

In 1987 the Illinois chapter of American Atheists filed suit against Zion, claiming that its city seal, which contained a cross, a dove, and the phrase "God Reigns," was unconstitutional. In 1992 the U.S. Supreme Court upheld a lower court decision that the city seal violated the principle of separation of church and state and that the Christian symbolism must be removed. City officials were able to incorporate the words "In God We Trust" into the new city seal, because the phrase was deemed acceptable religious language in the public arena.

Wallace Best

FURTHER READING: Bateman, Newton, and Paul Selby, eds. *Historical Encyclopedia of Illinois and History of Lake County.* 1902. ■ Cook, Philip L. *Zion City, Illinois: Twentieth Century Utopia.* 1996. ■ Halsey, John J., ed. *A History of Lake County Illinois.* 1912.

ILLUSTRATION CREDITS

Abbreviations used:

CHM = Chicago History Museum

CPL = Chicago Public Library

NL = Newberry Library

UIC = University of Illinois at Chicago

p. 2   bird's-eye view. NL, *Land Owner*, February 1874, cover.

p. 31   Cabrini Extension. CHM, ICHi-23200. © CHM.

p. 36   Buffalo Grove. CHM, HB-31832-PPN. © CHM.

p. 48   Maxwell St. Library of Congress, Prints & Photographs Division, FSA/OWI Collection, LC-USF33-012984-M1.

p. 56   color line cartoon. *Chicago Tribune*, July 28, 1919.

p. 58   Illinois-Wisconsin boundary. NL, Charles O. Paullin, *Atlas of the Historical Geography of the U.S.* (1932), plate 99C. © Carnegie Institution of Washington.

p. 62   combine harvester. *Chicago Tribune*, Oct. 13, 2000. © Chicago Tribune.

p. 66   grain elevators and ships. CHM, ICHi-17111.

p. 68   Union Stock Yard. NL, J. W. Sheahan, *Chicago Illustrated, 1830–1860*, 1866.

p. 71   Midwest Stock Exchange. CHM, ICHi-29229.

p. 72   Chicago's Place. CHM, Chicago Plan Commission, Chicago Industrial Study Summary Report, 1952, Fig. 1. © Chicago Plan Commission.

p. 92   traffic jam. Lakes Region Historical Society.

p. 98   Pullman car. NL, Pullman Archives, 13/01/03.

p. 100 trolley bus. CPL, ACC 2.169.

p. 102 Riverview Park. CHM, ICHi-23578.

p. 103 public bath. CHM, ICHi-21723. © CHM.

p. 111 Blue Island Opera House. Lake County (IL) Discovery Museum, Curt Teich Postcard Archives, 9388.

p. 114 Great Chicago Sewer. NL, *Land Owner*, Aug. 1871, after p. 248.

p. 121 Cabrini Homes. UIC, Italian American Collection, IAC neg. 91.152.

p. 127 parade. CHM, Chicago Daily News Collection, DN-0086651. © CHM.

p. 128 Hawthorne Race Track. CHM, Chicago Daily News Collection, SDN-064900. © CHM.

p. 133 Plantation Café. CHM, ICHi-14428.

p. 136 Elm Tree Grove. Lake County (IL) Discovery Museum, Curt Teich Postcard Archives, 7280.

p. 141 Edgewater ad. CHM.

p. 142   Danger!! CHM, Chicago Daily News Collection, DN-0069264.

p. 144   Holiday Inn. Lake County (IL) Discovery Museum, Curt Teich Postcard Archives, 8DK705.

p. 145   Old Main. Lake County (IL) Discovery Museum, Curt Teich Postcard Archives, 3BH1613.

p. 146   Swenson's Greenhouse. DuPage County Historical Museum, 85.16.2.1.

p. 147   band. CHM, ICHi-27382.

p. 160   Lake Shore Drive. NL, *Stanolind Record* 10:11, Sept. 1929, p. 2.

p. 162   Michigan Boulevard Garden Apartments. CHM, ICHi-09273. © CHM.

p. 163   49th and Champlain. CHM, from John Taitt, comp., *The Souvenir of Negro Progress, Chicago 1779-1925*, 1925(?).

p. 171   ravine. Lake County (IL) Discovery Museum, Curt Teich Postcard Archives.

p. 172   Hinsdale ad. NL, *Land Owner*, July 1873, p. 112.

p. 176   Grand Basin. CHM, ICHi-02524.

p. 188   fairgoers. CHM, Chicago Daily News Collection, DN-0066676.

p. 190   Lake View town hall. CHM.

p. 192   Argonne. CHM, HB-19294-C. © CHM.

p. 194   playground race. CPL, Municipal Reference Collection, Special Park Commission, *Annual Report*, 1907, p. 34.

p. 203   Clark and Jackson. NL, *Stanolind Record* 10:11, Sept. 1929, p. 12.

p. 207   boulevard drawing. CHM, Charles Moore, *Daniel H. Burnham: Architect, Planner of Cities*, 1921.

p. 222, furniture factory. CHM.

p. 224, Connell and Halverson. CHM, Chicago Daily News Collection, SDN-069501. © CHM.

p. 227   IC Railroad station. CHM, ICHi-23805.

p. 229   lumber. CHM.

p. 229   Polk St. UIC, Italian American Collection, IAC neg. 140.4.

p. 232   above stockyards. CHM, ICHi-14486.

p. 235   Selig Polyscope. CHM, Chicago Daily News Collection, DN-0062406.

p. 240   reading newspapers. CHM, Chicago Daily News Collection, DN-0078707. © CHM.

p. 242   Graue Mill. Lake County (IL) Discovery Museum, Curt Teich Postcard Archives, 4DK1934.

p. 245   Unity Temple exterior. NL, Case folio oF 548.7 .S56, Vol. II.

p. 247   Wells Homes poster. Library of Congress, Prints & Photographs Division, WPA Poster Collection, LC-USZC2-5196.

p. 253   Good Friday parade. CHM, ICHi-26666. © CHM.

p. 255   Clarke House. CHM, Chicago Daily News Collection, DN-A-4601. © CHM.

p. 258   Labor Day parade. CPL, HPC 1.62.

p. 264   St. Ignatius. NL, Case folio oF 548.7 .S56, Vol. 1.

p. 266   S. Michigan Ave. Lake County (IL) Discovery Museum, Curt Teich Postcard Archives, A54790.

p. 267   Woodfield Mall. CHM. © CHM.

p. 271   blast furnace. CHM.

p. 272   grain elevator. CHM, ICHi-24684. © Joan M. Colby.

p. 274   *South Holland: A History*. NL, Richard A. Cook, *South Holland, Illinois: A History, 1846–1966*, 1966. © South Holland Trust and Savings Bank.

INDEX

Page numbers in italics indicate maps or other illustrations.